THE TRAGEDY OF

HAMLET

PRINCE of DENMARK

BY WILLIAM SHAKESPEARE

Edited by

GEORGE LYMAN KITTREDGE

GINN AND COMPANY

BOSTON · NEW YORK · CHICAGO
LONDON · ATLANTA · DALLAS · COLUMBUS · SAN FRANCISCO

The Athenæum Press

GINN AND COMPANY · PRO-
PRIETORS · BOSTON · U.S.A.

PREFACE

THE text is complete and agrees with that in Kittredge's edition of Shakespeare's *Works*. The numbering of the lines accords with that commonly used in citing the plays. This method is preferred to a new counting in order to facilitate reference to such standard works as Bartlett's *Concordance* and Schmidt's *Shakespeare-Lexicon*. In prose passages there results some slight irregularity in computation, but this does not indicate any omission in the text.

G. L. K.

CONTENTS

CONTENTS

INTRODUCTION

On July 26, 1602, 'The Revenge of Hamlett Prince Denmarke as yt was latelie Acted by the Lord Chamberlyne his servantes' (Shakespeare's company) was entered in the Stationers' Register by James Roberts; but Roberts did not bring the book out until 1604. His edition, the Second Quarto,[1] appears to have been printed from Shakespeare's autograph manuscript, and must be accepted as the main authority for the text, though it swarms with misprints. Meantime, in 1603, a pirated version appeared: 'The Tragicall Historie of Hamlet *Prince* of *Denmarke*. By William Shake-speare. As it hath beene diuerse times acted by his Highnesse seruants in the Cittie of London: as also in the two Vniuersities of Cambridge and Oxford, and else-where. At London printed for N[icholas]. L[ing]. and Iohn Trundell. 1603.' This is the First Quarto. It presents the play in a strangely garbled form which will occupy us presently. Bad as it is, it is often helpful in settling some detail of the text.

The First Folio (1623) omits more than two hundred lines that are undoubtedly Shakespeare's;[2] but it supplies (besides a line or two here and there) five genuine passages which the Second Quarto omits,[3] and it often corrects a manifest error or affords a superior reading. The printers of the First Folio certainly used as copy a different manuscript from that used by the printers of the Second Quarto. Wilson thinks that it was a careless transcript made for them in 1622 or 1623 from the manuscript prompt-book of the Globe Theatre, and that this prompt-book, though taken direct from Shakespeare's autograph manuscript, had been edited in many matters of

---

[1] Six copies of the Second Quarto are known. Three of them bear the date 1604 and three the date 1605 in the title page. A few variant readings in the 1605 copies represent changes made in the course of printing. See Wilson, *The Manuscript of Shakespeare's Hamlet*, 1934, pp. 123, 124. The Third Quarto (1611), the Fourth (undated), and the Fifth (1637) are of little or no textual consequence.

[2] See Textual Notes, pp. 299 ff.

[3] ii, 2, 243–276 ('Let . . . attended'), 352–377; iv, 5, 161–163; v, 1, 38–41 ('Why . . . without arms'); v, 2, 68–80.

detail by the Globe book-holder.[1] However this may be—and nothing short of revelation can ever solve such problems beyond dispute—nobody can deny that the Folio (besides supplying several omissions) preserves the correct reading again and again where the Second Quarto goes astray. An editor must use his best judgment, and the authority of the Quarto does not warrant an inferior reading where the Folio furnishes one that is manifestly better.[2] Otherwise we are forced to infer that prompters and proofreaders can (or could) improve Shakespeare.

External evidence for the date of HAMLET is scanty. Meres, writing in 1598, does not mention it. 'The ḥumorous man shall end his part in peace' (ii, 2, 334, 335) may or may not allude to Jonson's *Every Man Out of his Humour*, which seems to have been acted late in 1599. Gabriel Harvey's manuscript note in his copy of Speght's 1598 edition of Chaucer is indecisive: 'The younger sort takes much delight in Shakespeare's Venus, & Adonis: but his Lucrece, & his tragedie of Hamlet, Prince of Denmarke, haue it in them, to please the wiser sort.' It has been argued that the note must have been written before the death of the second Earl of Essex (February 25, 1601) because Harvey remarks, 'The Earle of Essex much commendes Albions England'; but that is forcing the present tense rather hard. However, 1600 or 1601 is a reasonable date for the play.

For the plot Shakespeare went to Volume V of Belleforest's *Histoires Tragiques* (1576). Belleforest worked up his *histoire* from the *Historia Danica* of Saxo Grammaticus (*ca.* 1200; first printed in 1514), expanding and moralizing *more suo*. An English translation of his tale was printed in 1608.

In Belleforest there is no mystery about the King's death. His brother kills him at a banquet and justifies the act by alleging that it was done to rescue the Queen from a murder-

---

[1] Wilson, *The Manuscript*, pp. 64–67; *Hamlet*, p. xxvii. Parrott and Craig maintain that the copy used for the Folio was a transcript, not of the prompt-book but of 'the manuscript on which the final prompt-book prepared for the licenser, from which the actors' parts would be transcribed, was based' (*The Tragedy of Hamlet*, 1938, p. 50).

[2] Wilson's own text (1934) is evidence in this regard, and the same is true of Parrott and Craig's (1938).

ous attack by her husband. Hamlet is a mere stripling, absolutely in his uncle's power. He feigns madness to protect himself until there shall come an opportunity for revenge. The ancient idea that madmen are sacred[1] is implied, though not expressed. His uncle is suspicious, and resolves to put him to death at once if he can satisfy himself that the boy is not mad indeed. He attempts to entrap him by means of a young woman, and also by the agency of a spy who hides in the Queen's chamber; but in vain. The repentant Queen becomes her son's confidante in his plan of revenge. After a riotous feast, Hamlet sets fire to the hall and burns the drunken courtiers to death. His uncle, who has retired to his chamber, he decapitates. Then he delivers an oration to the people, explaining all the facts, and is crowned as king. His further history does not concern us. He is finally killed in a battle with another uncle.

Between Belleforest's story and Shakespeare's HAMLET an old play on the subject intervenes. Henslowe records a performance of it on June 11, 1594, and Thomas Lodge quotes it in his *Wits Miserie, and the Worlds Madnesse* (1596): 'As pale as the Visard of ye ghost which cried so miserally at ye Theator, like an oister wife, *Hamlet, reuenge*' (p. 56). Nashe alludes to it in his Epistle prefixed to Greene's *Menaphon* (1589): 'English *Seneca* read by Candle light yeelds many good sentences . . .; and if you intreate him faire in a frostie morning, hee will afford you whole *Hamlets*, I should say handfuls of Tragicall speeches.' The author is unknown. Nashe seems to glance at Thomas Kyd in the context of the passage just quoted, but his language does not even hint at Kyd's authorship of the old *Hamlet*.[2] The play was evidently of the Senecan sort, like *The Spanish Tragedy*, and one of the characters was a pale-faced ghost (presumably of the murdered King) who cried

---

[1] Thus David protects himself by assuming madness at the court of Achish (*1 Samuel*, xxi, 10–15). The same idea of the sacredness of madmen underlies the legend of Lucius Junius Brutus, whose strategic pretence of idiocy ('his folly's show') is mentioned in *Lucrece*, ll. 1807–1820. See Livy, i, 56; Ovid, *Fasti*, ii, 717, 718. Both David and Brutus are cited by Belleforest in his *histoire* of Hamlet. See Buckle, *Miscellaneous and Posthumous Works*, 1872, III, 357.

[2] See McKerrow's note in his edition of Nashe, IV, 449–452.

'Hamlet, revenge!' Further than this, we have no knowledge
of its contents. The First Quarto seems to be merely a bad
copy of an abridged version of Shakespeare's HAMLET—probably of a version cobbled up by some literary hack for provincial
acting. Some passages are clearly the work of this dramatic
journeyman, and others may possibly be remnants of the old
play. Thus the Queen's vow to assist Hamlet (sig. G 3)[1] agrees
with Belleforest in a point in which Shakespeare differs. That
she keeps her word appears from her conversation with Horatio
(sig. H 2). Here Horatio informs her of Hamlet's return in
secret from the English voyage and of the change made by
Hamlet in 'the Packet sent to the king of England, Wherein
he saw himselfe betray'd to death.' She charges Horatio to

> bid him a while
> Be wary of his presence, lest that he
> Faile in that he goes about.

Der Bestrafte Brudermord,[2] a wild German form of Hamlet
drama, has often been used—with varying degrees of ingenuity—in attempts to reconstruct the old play.[3] This eccentric
offshoot of the Hamlet tradition was first printed in 1781 from
a manuscript dated 1710, which has disappeared. That some
Hamlet or other was acted at Dresden in 1626 is an established
fact; but the relation of this to *Der Bestrafte Brudermord* is a
matter of conjecture. The Prologue of *Der Brudermord* may
be a fragment of the Prologue of the *Ur-Hamlet,* and here and
there one notes a detail that may have come from the lost play.
The utterly comic fashion in which Hamlet disposes of the rep-
resentatives of Rosencrantz and Guildenstern has some resemblance to an incident in Marlowe's *Jew of Malta,* and also to an
incident in the *Alphonsus* eccentrically ascribed to Chapman;[4]

[1] See the passage quoted in the note to iii, 4, 28 (p. 239, below).
[2] Cohn, *Shakespeare in Germany,* 1865; Creizenach, *Die Schauspiele der Englischen Komödianten,* 1889. There is an English translation in Furness's *Variorum.*
[3] For the whole matter (with all necessary references) see Parrott and Craig, pp. 10–15.
[4] See Bowers, *Modern Language Notes,* XLVIII (1933), 105–107.

but one can only hope that the author of the *Ur-Hamlet* is not chargeable with this device. Hamlet's guards land with him on an island and undertake to shoot him. Stationed between them, he throws himself down at the critical moment, and they shoot each other. 'O just heaven!' he exclaims, 'thanks be to thee for this angelic idea!'

Both in Shakespeare and in Belleforest we have a story of necessarily deferred revenge, but the situation at the outset is not the same, and the ground of the necessity differs accordingly. In the old tale the murder is no secret; but the avenger is helpless, a mere boy in his uncle's power. In the drama, on the other hand, the murder is suspected by no one until the Ghost reveals it. But this is 'spectral evidence.' Hamlet believes that the apparition is indeed the ghost of his father and that it has told the truth. Yet it may be a demon in his father's shape, tempting him to kill an innocent man. This doubt as to the ambiguous apparition accords with ancient doctrine and was perfectly intelligible to any Elizabethan audience.[1] Disregard of Hamlet's dilemma has led to misinterpretation of his character, as if he were a procrastinator, a vain dreamer, an impulsive creature of feeble will. But Shakespeare has done his best to enforce the imperative scruple as to the apparition. It inspires and dictates Horatio's challenge (i, 1, 46 ff.); it is implicit in Bernardo's assent (l. 109); it is manifest in Hamlet's declared resolution (i, 2, 244–246), and it finds solemn utterance when he adjures the Ghost to speak (i, 4, 40 ff.). Nothing could be clearer, in this regard, than Horatio's warning (i, 4, 69 ff.):

> What if it tempt you toward the flood, my lord,
> Or to the dreadful summit of the cliff
> That beetles o'er his base into the sea,
> And there assume some other, horrible form
> Which might deprive your sovereignty of reason
> And draw you into madness?[2]

[1] This doctrine is concisely expressed by Increase Mather: 'As the evil Spirit will speak good Words, so doth he sometimes appear in the likeness of good Men, to the end that he may the more effectually deceive and delude all such as shall be so unhappy as to entertain converses with him' (*An Essay for the Recording of Illustrious Providences*, 1684, p. 210).
[2] Cf. *King Lear*, iv, 6, 67 ff.

All this leads up to Hamlet's soliloquy at the end of Act II:

> The spirit that I have seen
> May be a devil; and the devil hath power
> T' assume a pleasing shape; yea, and perhaps
> Out of my weakness and my melancholy,
> As he is very potent with such spirits,
> Abuses me to damn me. I'll have grounds
> More relative than this.

And the substance of this soliloquy is repeated and enforced when Hamlet explains to Horatio the purpose of the play within the play (iii, 2, 80–92):

> There is a play to-night before the King.
> One scene of it comes near the circumstance,
> Which I have told thee, of my father's death.
> I prithee, when thou seest that act afoot,
> Even with the very comment of thy soul
> Observe my uncle. If his occulted guilt
> Do not itself unkennel in one speech,
> It is a damned ghost that we have seen,
> And my imaginations are as foul
> As Vulcan's stithy. Give him heedful note;
> For I mine eyes will rivet to his face,
> And after we will both our judgments join
> In censure of his seeming.

Hamlet cannot act upon mere spectral evidence. The testimony of the Ghost must somehow be corroborated. The murderer must be forced to testify against himself. Then, and not till then, will action be possible for a reasonable man. 'The play's the thing!' Significant, too, is the fact that the calm and philosophic Horatio—Hamlet's sole confidant as to the Ghost's revelation—accepts the crucial experiment as necessary, and agrees with Hamlet that its success is conclusive (iii, 2, 92–94, 297–301).

The necessity for some device like the play within the play is due to the failure of Hamlet's assumed madness to achieve its purpose. In the old saga and in Belleforest, Hamlet feigns madness for self-protection. It is made perfectly clear that the King can kill him at any moment, and that he refrains only because he cannot satisfy himself that the boy is in his right mind. He tries to entrap him into some act that will prove his sanity, but in vain. Hamlet is too shrewd for him and carries through his pretence of insanity until at last he finds the moment for a terrible revenge. Thus his pretended madness, like the deferred vengeance, was an essential element in the saga and the old play. How the old play accounted for it, it is idle to conjecture. In Shakespeare's drama, however, Hamlet's motive for acting the madman is obvious. We speak unguardedly in the presence of children and madmen, for we take it for granted that they will not listen or will not understand ; and so the King or the Queen (for Hamlet does not know that his mother is ignorant of her husband's crime) may say something that will afford the evidence needed to confirm the testimony of the Ghost. The device is adopted on the spur of the moment (i, 5, 169 ff.), and, once adopted, it must be maintained. But it is unsuccessful. The King is always on his guard, and the Queen is not an accomplice.[1]

The earliest moment at which Hamlet is justified in striking the blow does not come until the end of the third scene of the third act—or, in other words, until Shakespeare's play is more than half finished. It is the moment when Hamlet finds his uncle at prayer (iii, 3, 73):

> Now might I do it pat, now he is praying;
> And now I'll do 't.

Now, for the first time, Claudius is off his guard, and his attitude of prayer confirms the evidence—already strong enough —that he is guilty.

Obviously, up to this point, we must acquit Hamlet of procrastination. He had adopted the device of madness on the instant, immediately after the Ghost's revelation; and, when this failed as a detective agency, he had utilized the first opportunity for a further test—the play within the play. Note the promptitude of his action in this regard. No sooner had he heard the players' declamation and observed its emotional effect than his plan was formed. When the players appear at Elsinore

---

[1] So Hamlet learns at last in iii, 4, 28–30 (see the note).

he is at his wit's end for evidence. Partly from love of the drama (for the actors are old favourites), partly to distract his mind from a hideous and hitherto insoluble problem, he calls for a 'taste of their quality.' The emotional effect of the Pyrrhus declamation—both upon the player and upon himself—suggests a device which he instantly puts into action. The interval between the appearance of the Ghost and the arrival of the players, is hardly more than a couple of months.[1]

The sight of the King on his knees gives the finishing touch to the testimony of 'The Mousetrap.' Now, then, at this the first usable opportunity, is Hamlet, if ever, in the mood to kill the King. Yet this is the one moment when it is impossible for anyone but an assassin to strike. This would be true if Shakespeare had merely introduced the King in the attitude of prayer. How much stronger is the case when our very souls have been shaken by the terrific mental and spiritual struggle through which Claudius has just passed—when (for the first time) our sympathies (if we are human) have gone out to the man whom we have hitherto regarded with abhorrence. The strenuous avenger Laertes would not have hesitated to plunge his sword into the King's back as heartily and instinctively as a bulldog bites.[2] But such an act is not in accord with Hamlet's nature and education. This does not mean that he is a born weakling or that he has learned inertia at the university. For we must accept the valedictory tribute of young Fortinbras— the pattern of vigorous soldiership—when he declares that Hamlet 'was likely, had he been put on, to have prov'd most royally' (v, 2, 408, 409). Hamlet cannot butcher a defenceless man. Nor would such an act accord with the emotional mood of the audience at this juncture. It is a dramatic, a moral, almost a physical impossibility.[3]

---

[1] The marriage of Claudius and Gertrude took place about a month after the murder (i, 2, 138–151). The arrival of the players was 'twice two months' after the King's death (iii, 2, 136). Some time had intervened between the marriage and the Ghost's revelation.

[2] Cf. iv, 7, 125–127; iv, 5, 131–136.

[3] Incidentally, one should remember that the Hamlet story has many incidents that are still to come. The play cannot end here with a triumphant revenge.

and everywhere a model of royal dignity. His courage is mani-
fested, under the most terrifying circumstances, when the mob
breaks into the palace. His self-control when the dumb show
enacts his secret crime before his eyes is nothing less than marvellous.[1] It was no accident that Shakespeare gave him that
phrase which has become the ultimate pronouncement of the
divine right of monarchy: 'Such divinity doth hedge a king.'

Intellectually, then, we must admit Claudius to as high a rank
as Hamlet himself.[2] What are we to say of him morally? On
this point there is danger of misinterpretation. Claudius is often
regarded as a moral monster—selfish, calculating, passionless
—subtle and cold as a serpent. From such an error we are
rescued by one of the supreme passages in all Shakespeare—the
King's soliloquy after 'The Mousetrap' has caught his conscience (iii, 3, 36 ff.):

> O, my offence is rank, it smells to heaven;
> It hath the primal eldest curse upon't,
> A brother's murther!

In this soliloquy Claudius unlocks his soul. It reveals him
not only as passionately remorseful—with a heart in no wise
cauterized by crime[3]—but as so clear-sighted, so pitiless in the
analysis of his own offences and of the motives that actuated
them, that he cannot juggle with his conscience.

> What form of prayer
> Can serve my turn? 'Forgive me my foul murther'?
> That cannot be; since I am still possess'd
> Of those effects for which I did the murther—
> My crown, mine own ambition, and my queen.

[1] For the object of the dumb show see the note on iii, 2, 145. Cf. W. W.
Lawrence, *Journal of English and Germanic Philology*, XVIII (1919),
7 ff.; Pearn, *Review of English Studies*, XI (1935), 403; Granville-Barker,
Prefaces to Hamlet, 3d Series, 1937, pp. 89 ff. For Wilson's theory, which
differs *toto caelo*, see his *What Happens in Hamlet*, 2d ed., 1937, pp. 144 ff.

[2] The testimony of the Ghost is well deserved: 'with witchcraft of his
wit' (i, 5, 43). 'Thou know'st,' says Iago, 'we work by wit, and not by
witchcraft'; but Claudius's wit *is* witchcraft. He has bewitched both
Queen and state.

[3] Compare the King's 'aside' in iii, 1, 49–54, which prepares us for
the soliloquy.

His crime was a crime of passion. 'My queen' is the acme of the climax. So she was in the Ghost's revelation to Hamlet (i, 5, 74, 75):

> Thus was I, sleeping, by a brother's hand
> Of life, of crown, of queen, at once dispatch'd.

To neglect or undervalue Claudius destroys the balance of the tragedy. On the stage, for generations, his lines were cut unmercifully, and his rôle was assigned to an inferior actor, so that he became the typical melodramatic villain, who frowns and mouths and struts and beats the air. And Hamlet has suffered accordingly, and has too often been conceived as a pathetic creature of high imagination but feeble will. Otherwise, why did he not abolish this ineffectual obstacle with a sweep of the arm? Of late, however, managers and actors have done better in this regard, but the prejudice lingers. Of Shakespeare's intent there can be no doubt. The play is a contest between two great opponents. This Hamlet understands; and he expresses the truth in his words to Horatio (v, 2, 61, 62), which might well be a summarizing motto for the play:

> The pass and fell incensed points
> Of mighty opposites.

THE TRAGEDY OF
HAMLET, PRINCE OF DENMARK

[Dramatis Personæ.

Claudius, King of Denmark.
Hamlet, son to the former, and nephew to the present King.
Polonius, Lord Chamberlain.
Horatio, friend to *Hamlet*.
Laertes, son to *Polonius*.
Voltemand,
Cornelius,
Rosencrantz,
Guildenstern, } courtiers.
Osric,
A Gentleman,
A Priest.
Marcellus,
Bernardo, } officers.
Francisco, a soldier.
Reynaldo, servant to *Polonius*.
Players.
Two Clowns, gravediggers.
Fortinbras, Prince of Norway.
A Norwegian Captain.
English Ambassadors.

Gertrude, Queen of Denmark, mother to *Hamlet*.
Ophelia, daughter to *Polonius*.

Ghost of *Hamlet's* Father.

Lords, Ladies, Officers, Soldiers, Sailors, Messengers, Attendants.

SCENE.—*Elsinore*.]

THE TRAGEDY OF
HAMLET, PRINCE OF DENMARK

ACT I. Scene I. [*Elsinore. A platform before the Castle.*]

Enter two *Sentinels*—[first,] *Francisco*, [who paces up and down at his post; then] *Bernardo*, [who approaches him].

Ber. Who's there?

Fran. Nay, answer me. Stand and unfold yourself.

Ber. Long live the King!

Fran. Bernardo?

Ber. He.   5

Fran. You come most carefully upon your hour.

Ber. 'Tis now struck twelve. Get thee to bed, Francisco.

Fran. For this relief much thanks. 'Tis bitter cold,
And I am sick at heart.

Ber. Have you had quiet guard?

Fran.   Not a mouse stirring.   10

Ber. Well, good night.
If you do meet Horatio and Marcellus,
The rivals of my watch, bid them make haste.

Enter *Horatio* and *Marcellus*.

Fran. I think I hear them. Stand, ho! Who is there?

Hor. Friends to this ground.

Mar.   And liegemen to the Dane.   15

Fran. Give you good night.

Mar.   O, farewell, honest soldier.
Who hath reliev'd you?

Fran.   Bernardo hath my place.
Give you good night.   *Exit.*

Mar.   Holla, Bernardo!

Ber.   Say—
What, is Horatio there?

Hor.   A piece of him.

3

Ber. Welcome, Horatio. Welcome, good Marcellus.   20
Mar. What, has this thing appear'd again to-night?
Ber. I have seen nothing.
Mar. Horatio says 'tis but our fantasy,
And will not let belief take hold of him
Touching this dreaded sight, twice seen of us.   25
Therefore I have entreated him along,
With us to watch the minutes of this night,
That, if again this apparition come,
He may approve our eyes and speak to it.
Hor. Tush, tush, 'twill not appear.
Ber.   Sit down awhile,   30
And let us once again assail your ears,
That are so fortified against our story,
What we two nights have seen.
Hor.   Well, sit we down,
And let us hear Bernardo speak of this.
Ber. Last night of all,   35
When yond same star that's westward from the pole
Had made his course t' illume that part of heaven
Where now it burns, Marcellus and myself,
The bell then beating one—

Enter *Ghost*.

Mar. Peace! break thee off! Look where it comes again!
Ber. In the same figure, like the King that's dead.   41
Mar. Thou art a scholar; speak to it, Horatio.
Ber. Looks it not like the King? Mark it, Horatio.
Hor. Most like. It harrows me with fear and wonder.
Ber. It would be spoke to.
Mar.   Question it, Horatio.   45
Hor. What art thou that usurp'st this time of night

Together with that fair and warlike form
In which the majesty of buried Denmark
Did sometimes march? By heaven I charge thee speak!

   Mar. It is offended.

   Ber.   See, it stalks away!   50

   Hor. Stay! Speak, speak! I charge thee speak!

                                    Exit Ghost.

   Mar. 'Tis gone and will not answer.

   Ber. How now, Horatio? You tremble and look pale.
Is not this something more than fantasy?
What think you on't?   55

   Hor. Before my God, I might not this believe
Without the sensible and true avouch
Of mine own eyes.

   Mar.   Is it not like the King?

   Hor. As thou art to thyself.
Such was the very armour he had on   60
When he th' ambitious Norway combated.
So frown'd he once when, in an angry parle,
He smote the sledded Polacks on the ice.
'Tis strange.

   Mar. Thus twice before, and jump at this dead hour,   65
With martial stalk hath he gone by our watch.

   Hor. In what particular thought to work I know not;
But, in the gross and scope of my opinion,
This bodes some strange eruption to our state.

   Mar. Good now, sit down, and tell me he that knows,   70
Why this same strict and most observant watch
So nightly toils the subject of the land,
And why such daily cast of brazen cannon
And foreign mart for implements of war;
Why such impress of shipwrights, whose sore task   75
Does not divide the Sunday from the week.

What might be toward, that this sweaty haste
Doth make the night joint-labourer with the day?
Who is't that can inform me?

Hor.   That can I.
At least, the whisper goes so. Our last king,   80
Whose image even but now appear'd to us,
Was, as you know, by Fortinbras of Norway,
Thereto prick'd on by a most emulate pride,
Dar'd to the combat; in which our valiant Hamlet
(For so this side of our known world esteem'd him)   85
Did slay this Fortinbras; who, by a seal'd compact,
Well ratified by law and heraldry,
Did forfeit, with his life, all those his lands
Which he stood seiz'd of, to the conqueror;
Against the which a moiety competent   90
Was gaged by our king; which had return'd
To the inheritance of Fortinbras,
Had he been vanquisher, as, by the same comart
And carriage of the article design'd,
His fell to Hamlet. Now, sir, young Fortinbras,   95
Of unimproved mettle hot and full,
Hath in the skirts of Norway, here and there,
Shark'd up a list of lawless resolutes,
For food and diet, to some enterprise
That hath a stomach in't; which is no other,   100
As it doth well appear unto our state,
But to recover of us, by strong hand
And terms compulsatory, those foresaid lands
So by his father lost; and this, I take it,
Is the main motive of our preparations,   105
The source of this our watch, and the chief head
Of this post-haste and romage in the land.

Ber. I think it be no other but e'en so.
Well may it sort that this portentous figure

Comes armed through our watch, so like the King   110
That was and is the question of these wars.
  Hor. A mote it is to trouble the mind's eye.
In the most high and palmy state of Rome,
A little ere the mightiest Julius fell,
The graves stood tenantless, and the sheeted dead   115
Did squeak and gibber in the Roman streets;
As stars with trains of fire, and dews of blood,
Disasters in the sun; and the moist star
Upon whose influence Neptune's empire stands
Was sick almost to doomsday with eclipse.   120
And even the like precurse of fierce events,
As harbingers preceding still the fates
And prologue to the omen coming on,
Have heaven and earth together demonstrated
Unto our climature and countrymen.   125

Enter Ghost again.

But soft! behold! Lo, where it comes again!
I'll cross it, though it blast me.—Stay, illusion!
Spreads his arms.

If thou hast any sound, or use of voice,
Speak to me.
If there be any good thing to be done,   130
That may to thee do ease, and grace to me,
Speak to me.
If thou art privy to thy country's fate,
Which happily foreknowing may avoid,
O, speak!   135
Or if thou hast uphoarded in thy life
Extorted treasure in the womb of earth
(For which, they say, you spirits oft walk in death),
The cock crows.

Speak of it! Stay, and speak!—Stop it, Marcellus!

Mar. Shall I strike at it with my partisan?   140
Hor. Do, if it will not stand.
Ber.   'Tis here!
Hor.   'Tis here!
Mar. 'Tis gone!

                                              Exit Ghost.
We do it wrong, being so majestical,
To offer it the show of violence;
For it is as the air, invulnerable,   145
And our vain blows malicious mockery.
    Ber. It was about to speak, when the cock crew.
    Hor. And then it started, like a guilty thing
Upon a fearful summons. I have heard
The cock, that is the trumpet to the morn,   150
Doth with his lofty and shrill-sounding throat
Awake the god of day; and at his warning,
Whether in sea or fire, in earth or air,
Th' extravagant and erring spirit hies
To his confine; and of the truth herein   155
This present object made probation.
    Mar. It faded on the crowing of the cock.
Some say that ever, 'gainst that season comes
Wherein our Saviour's birth is celebrated,
The bird of dawning singeth all night long;   160
And then, they say, no spirit dare stir abroad,
The nights are wholesome, then no planets strike,
No fairy takes, nor witch hath power to charm,
So hallow'd and so gracious is the time.
    Hor. So have I heard and do in part believe it.   165
But look, the morn, in russet mantle clad,
Walks o'er the dew of yon high eastward hill.
Break we our watch up; and by my advice
Let us impart what we have seen to-night
Unto young Hamlet; for, upon my life,   170

This spirit, dumb to us, will speak to him.
Do you consent we shall acquaint him with it,
As needful in our loves, fitting our duty?

Mar. Let's do't, I pray; and I this morning know   174
Where we shall find him most conveniently.   *Exeunt.*

Scene II. [*Elsinore. A room of state in the Castle.*]

Flourish. Enter *Claudius, King of Denmark, Gertrude the Queen, Hamlet, Polonius, Laertes* and his sister *Ophelia,* [*Voltemand, Cornelius,*] *Lords Attendant.*

King. Though yet of Hamlet our dear brother's death
The memory be green, and that it us befitted
To bear our hearts in grief, and our whole kingdom
To be contracted in one brow of woe,
Yet so far hath discretion fought with nature   5
That we with wisest sorrow think on him
Together with remembrance of ourselves.
Therefore our sometime sister, now our queen,
Th' imperial jointress to this warlike state,
Have we, as 'twere with a defeated joy,   10
With an auspicious, and a dropping eye,
With mirth in funeral, and with dirge in marriage,
In equal scale weighing delight and dole,
Taken to wife; nor have we herein barr'd
Your better wisdoms, which have freely gone   15
With this affair along. For all, our thanks.
Now follows, that you know, young Fortinbras,
Holding a weak supposal of our worth,
Or thinking by our late dear brother's death
Our state to be disjoint and out of frame,   20
Colleagued with this dream of his advantage,
He hath not fail'd to pester us with message

Importing the surrender of those lands
Lost by his father, with all bands of law,
To our most valiant brother. So much for him. 25
Now for ourself and for this time of meeting.
Thus much the business is: we have here writ
To Norway, uncle of young Fortinbras,
Who, impotent and bedrid, scarcely hears
Of this his nephew's purpose, to suppress 30
His further gait herein, in that the levies,
The lists, and full proportions are all made
Out of his subject; and we here dispatch
You, good Cornelius, and you, Voltemand,
For bearers of this greeting to old Norway, 35
Giving to you no further personal power
To business with the King, more than the scope
Of these dilated articles allow. [*Gives a paper.*]
Farewell, and let your haste commend your duty.
    Cor., Volt. In that, and all things, will we show our duty.
    King. We doubt it nothing. Heartily farewell. 41
                              Exeunt Voltemand and Cornelius.
And now, Laertes, what's the news with you?
You told us of some suit. What is't, Laertes?
You cannot speak of reason to the Dane
And lose your voice. What wouldst thou beg, Laertes, 45
That shall not be my offer, not thy asking?
The head is not more native to the heart,
The hand more instrumental to the mouth,
Than is the throne of Denmark to thy father.
What wouldst thou have, Laertes?
    Laer.   My dread lord, 50
Your leave and favour to return to France;
From whence though willingly I came to Denmark
To show my duty in your coronation,
Yet now I must confess, that duty done,

My thoughts and wishes bend again toward France   55
And bow them to your gracious leave and pardon.

   King. Have you your father's leave? What says Polonius?

   Pol. He hath, my lord, wrung from me my slow leave
By laboursome petition, and at last
Upon his will I seal'd my hard consent.   60
I do beseech you give him leave to go.

   King. Take thy fair hour, Laertes. Time be thine,
And thy best graces spend it at thy will!
But now, my cousin Hamlet, and my son—

   Ham. [*aside*] A little more than kin, and less than kind!

   King. How is it that the clouds still hang on you?   66

   Ham. Not so, my lord. I am too much i' th' sun.

   Queen. Good Hamlet, cast thy nighted colour off,
And let thine eye look like a friend on Denmark.
Do not for ever with thy vailed lids   70
Seek for thy noble father in the dust.
Thou know'st 'tis common. All that lives must die,
Passing through nature to eternity.

   Ham. Ay, madam, it is common.

   Queen.   If it be,
Why seems it so particular with thee?   75

   Ham. Seems, madam? Nay, it is. I know not 'seems.'
'Tis not alone my inky cloak, good mother,
Nor customary suits of solemn black,
Nor windy suspiration of forc'd breath,
No, nor the fruitful river in the eye,   80
Nor the dejected haviour of the visage,
Together with all forms, moods, shapes of grief,
That can denote me truly. These indeed seem,
For they are actions that a man might play;
But I have that within which passeth show—   85
These but the trappings and the suits of woe.

   King. 'Tis sweet and commendable in your nature, Hamlet,

To give these mourning duties to your father;
But you must know, your father lost a father;
That father lost, lost his, and the survivor bound   90
In filial obligation for some term
To do obsequious sorrow. But to persever
In obstinate condolement is a course
Of impious stubbornness. 'Tis unmanly grief;
It shows a will most incorrect to heaven,   95
A heart unfortified, a mind impatient,
An understanding simple and unschool'd;
For what we know must be, and is as common
As any the most vulgar thing to sense,
Why should we in our peevish opposition   100
Take it to heart? Fie! 'tis a fault to heaven,
A fault against the dead, a fault to nature,
To reason most absurd, whose common theme
Is death of fathers, and who still hath cried,
From the first corse till he that died to-day,   105
'This must be so.' We pray you throw to earth
This unprevailing woe, and think of us
As of a father; for let the world take note
You are the most immediate to our throne,
And with no less nobility of love   110
Than that which dearest father bears his son
Do I impart toward you. For your intent
In going back to school in Wittenberg,
It is most retrograde to our desire;
And we beseech you, bend you to remain   115
Here in the cheer and comfort of our eye,
Our chiefest courtier, cousin, and our son.
      Queen. Let not thy mother lose her prayers, Hamlet.
I pray thee stay with us, go not to Wittenberg.
      Ham. I shall in all my best obey you, madam.   120
      King. Why, 'tis a loving and a fair reply.

Be as ourself in Denmark. Madam, come.
This gentle and unforc'd accord of Hamlet
Sits smiling to my heart; in grace whereof,
No jocund health that Denmark drinks to-day   125
But the great cannon to the clouds shall tell,
And the King's rouse the heaven shall bruit again,
Respeaking earthly thunder. Come away.

> *Flourish. Exeunt all but Hamlet.*

Ham. O that this too too solid flesh would melt,
Thaw, and resolve itself into a dew!   130
Or that the Everlasting had not fix'd
His canon 'gainst self-slaughter! O God! God!
How weary, stale, flat, and unprofitable
Seem to me all the uses of this world!
Fie on't! ah, fie! 'Tis an unweeded garden   135
That grows to seed; things rank and gross in nature
Possess it merely. That it should come to this!
But two months dead! Nay, not so much, not two.
So excellent a king, that was to this
Hyperion to a satyr; so loving to my mother   140
That he might not beteem the winds of heaven
Visit her face too roughly. Heaven and earth!
Must I remember? Why, she would hang on him
As if increase of appetite had grown
By what it fed on; and yet, within a month—   145
Let me not think on't! Frailty, thy name is woman!—
A little month, or ere those shoes were old
With which she followed my poor father's body
Like Niobe, all tears—why she, even she
(O God! a beast that wants discourse of reason   150
Would have mourn'd longer) married with my uncle;
My father's brother, but no more like my father
Than I to Hercules. Within a month,
Ere yet the salt of most unrighteous tears

Had left the flushing in her galled eyes,   155
She married. O, most wicked speed, to post
With such dexterity to incestuous sheets!
It is not, nor it cannot come to good.
But break my heart, for I must hold my tongue!

Enter Horatio, Marcellus, and Bernardo.

Hor. Hail to your lordship!
Ham.   I am glad to see you well.   160
Horatio!—or I do forget myself.
Hor. The same, my lord, and your poor servant ever.
Ham. Sir, my good friend—I'll change that name with you.
And what make you from Wittenberg, Horatio?
Marcellus?   165
Mar. My good lord!
Ham. I am very glad to see you.—[*To Bernardo*] Good
        even, sir.—
But what, in faith, make you from Wittenberg?
Hor. A truant disposition, good my lord.
Ham. I would not hear your enemy say so,   170
Nor shall you do my ear that violence
To make it truster of your own report
Against yourself. I know you are no truant.
But what is your affair in Elsinore?
We'll teach you to drink deep ere you depart.   175
Hor. My lord, I came to see your father's funeral.
Ham. I prithee do not mock me, fellow student.
I think it was to see my mother's wedding.
Hor. Indeed, my lord, it followed hard upon.
Ham. Thrift, thrift, Horatio! The funeral bak'd meats 180
Did coldly furnish forth the marriage tables.
Would I had met my dearest foe in heaven
Or ever I had seen that day, Horatio!
My father—methinks I see my father.

Hor. O, where, my lord?

Ham.   In my mind's eye, Horatio.   185

Hor. I saw him once. He was a goodly king.

Ham. He was a man, take him for all in all.
I shall not look upon his like again.

Hor. My lord, I think I saw him yesternight.

Ham. Saw? who?   190

Hor. My lord, the King your father.

Ham.   The King my father?

Hor. Season your admiration for a while
With an attent ear, till I may deliver,
Upon the witness of these gentlemen,
This marvel to you.

Ham.   For God's love let me hear!   195

Hor. Two nights together had these gentlemen
(Marcellus and Bernardo) on their watch
In the dead vast and middle of the night
Been thus encount'red. A figure like your father,
Armed at point exactly, cap-a-pe,   200
Appears before them and with solemn march
Goes slow and stately by them. Thrice he walk'd
By their oppress'd and fear-surprised eyes,
Within his truncheon's length; whilst they distill'd
Almost to jelly with the act of fear,   205
Stand dumb and speak not to him. This to me
In dreadful secrecy impart they did,
And I with them the third night kept the watch;
Where, as they had deliver'd, both in time,
Form of the thing, each word made true and good,   210
The apparition comes. I knew your father.
These hands are not more like.

Ham.   But where was this?

Mar. My lord, upon the platform where we watch'd.

Ham. Did you not speak to it?

Hor.   My lord, I did;
But answer made it none. Yet once methought   215
It lifted up it head and did address
Itself to motion, like as it would speak;
But even then the morning cock crew loud,
And at the sound it shrunk in haste away
And vanish'd from our sight.

Ham.   'Tis very strange.   220

Hor. As I do live, my honour'd lord, 'tis true;
And we did think it writ down in our duty
To let you know of it.

Ham. Indeed, indeed, sirs. But this troubles me.
Hold you the watch to-night?

Both [*Mar. and Ber.*]   We do, my lord.   225

Ham. Arm'd, say you?

Both. Arm'd, my lord.

Ham. From top to toe?

Both.   My lord, from head to foot.

Ham. Then saw you not his face?

Hor. O, yes, my lord! He wore his beaver up.   230

Ham. What, look'd he frowningly?

Hor. A countenance more in sorrow than in anger.

Ham. Pale or red?

Hor. Nay, very pale.

Ham.   And fix'd his eyes upon you?

Hor. Most constantly.

Ham.   I would I had been there.   235

Hor. It would have much amaz'd you.

Ham. Very like, very like. Stay'd it long?

Hor. While one with moderate haste might tell a hundred.

Both. Longer, longer.

Hor. Not when I saw't.

Ham.   His beard was grizzled—no?   240

Hor. It was, as I have seen it in his life,
A sable silver'd.
Ham.   I will watch to-night.
Perchance 'twill walk again.
Hor.   I warr'nt it will.
Ham. If it assume my noble father's person,
I'll speak to it, though hell itself should gape   245
And bid me hold my peace. I pray you all,
If you have hitherto conceal'd this sight,
Let it be tenable in your silence still;
And whatsoever else shall hap to-night,
Give it an understanding but no tongue.   250
I will requite your loves. So, fare you well.
Upon the platform, 'twixt eleven and twelve,
I'll visit you.
All.   Our duty to your honour.
Ham. Your loves, as mine to you. Farewell.
                              Exeunt [all but Hamlet].
My father's spirit—in arms? All is not well.   255
I doubt some foul play. Would the night were come!
Till then sit still, my soul. Foul deeds will rise,
Though all the earth o'erwhelm them, to men's eyes.   *Exit.*

Scene III. [*Elsinore. A room in the house of* Polonius.]

Enter *Laertes* and *Ophelia.*
Laer. My necessaries are embark'd. Farewell.
And, sister, as the winds give benefit
And convoy is assistant, do not sleep,
But let me hear from you.
Oph.   Do you doubt that?
Laer. For Hamlet, and the trifling of his favour,   5
Hold it a fashion, and a toy in blood;
A violet in the youth of primy nature,

Forward, not permanent—sweet, not lasting;
The perfume and suppliance of a minute;
No more.

   Oph. No more but so?

   Laer.   Think it no more.   10
For nature crescent does not grow alone
In thews and bulk; but as this temple waxes,
The inward service of the mind and soul
Grows wide withal. Perhaps he loves you now,
And now no soil nor cautel doth besmirch   15
The virtue of his will; but you must fear,
His greatness weigh'd, his will is not his own;
For he himself is subject to his birth.
He may not, as unvalued persons do,
Carve for himself, for on his choice depends   20   *[choose]*
The safety and health of this whole state,
And therefore must his choice be circumscrib'd
Unto the voice and yielding of that body
Whereof he is the head. Then if he says he loves you,
It fits your wisdom so far to believe it   25
As he in his particular act and place
May give his saying deed; which is no further
Than the main voice of Denmark goes withal.
Then weigh what loss your honour may sustain
If with too credent ear you list his songs,   30   *[believe]*
Or lose your heart, or your chaste treasure open   *[unmarried]*
To his unmast'red importunity.
Fear it, Ophelia, fear it, my dear sister,
And keep you in the rear of your affection,
Out of the shot and danger of desire.   35
The chariest maid is prodigal enough   *[wastful]*
If she unmask her beauty to the moon.
Virtue itself scapes not calumnious strokes.   *[false]*
The canker galls the infants of the spring   *[eating]*

Too oft before their buttons be disclos'd,   40
And in the morn and liquid dew of youth
Contagious blastments are most imminent.   *close*
Be wary then; best safety lies in fear.
Youth to itself rebels, though none else near.

   Oph. I shall th' effect of this good lesson keep   45
As watchman to my heart. But, good my brother,
Do not as some ungracious pastors do,
Show me the steep and thorny way to heaven,
Whiles, like a puff'd and reckless libertine,
Himself the primrose path of dalliance treads   50
And recks not his own rede.

   Laer.   O, fear me not!

Enter *Polonius.*

I stay too long. But here my father comes.
A double blessing is a double grace;
Occasion smiles upon a second leave.

   Pol. Yet here, Laertes? Aboard, aboard, for shame!   55
The wind sits in the shoulder of your sail,
And you are stay'd for. There—my blessing with thee!
And these few precepts in thy memory   *directions*
Look thou character. Give thy thoughts no tongue,
Nor any unproportion'd thought his act.   60
Be thou familiar, but by no means vulgar:
Those friends thou hast, and their adoption tried,
Grapple them unto thy soul with hoops of steel;   *grasp*
But do not dull thy palm with entertainment
Of each new-hatch'd, unfledg'd comrade. Beware   65
Of entrance to a quarrel; but being in,
Bear't that th' opposed may beware of thee.
Give every man thine ear, but few thy voice;
Take each man's censure, but reserve thy judgment.   *blame*
Costly thy habit as thy purse can buy,   70

But not express'd in fancy; rich, not gaudy;
For the apparel oft proclaims the man,
And they in France of the best rank and station
Are most select and generous, chief in that.
Neither a borrower nor a lender be;   75
For loan oft loses both itself and friend,
And borrowing dulls the edge of husbandry.
This above all—to thine own self be true,
And it must follow, as the night the day,
Thou canst not then be false to any man.   80
Farewell. My blessing season this in thee!
   Laer. Most humbly do I take my leave, my lord.
   Pol. The time invites you. Go, your servants tend.
   Laer. Farewell, Ophelia, and remember well
What I have said to you.
   Oph.   'Tis in my memory lock'd,   85
And you yourself shall keep the key of it.
   Laer. Farewell.   *Exit.*
   Pol. What is't, Ophelia, he hath said to you?
   Oph. So please you, something touching the Lord Hamlet.
   Pol. Marry, well bethought!   90
'Tis told me he hath very oft of late
Given private time to you, and you yourself
Have of your audience been most free and bounteous.
If it be so—as so 'tis put on me,
And that in way of caution—I must tell you   95
You do not understand yourself so clearly
As it behooves my daughter and your honour.
What is between you? Give me up the truth.
   Oph. He hath, my lord, of late made many tenders
Of his affection to me.   100
   Pol. Affection? Pooh! You speak like a green girl,
Unsifted in such perilous circumstance.
Do you believe his tenders, as you call them?

Oph. I do not know, my lord, what I should think.

Pol. Marry, I will teach you! Think yourself a baby   105
That you have ta'en these tenders for true pay,
Which are not sterling. Tender yourself more dearly,
Or (not to crack the wind of the poor phrase,
Running it thus) you'll tender me a fool.

Oph. My lord, he hath importun'd me with love   110
In honourable fashion.

Pol. Ay, fashion you may call it. Go to, go to!

Oph. And hath given countenance to his speech, my lord,
With almost all the holy vows of heaven.

Pol. Ay, springes to catch woodcocks! I do know,   115
When the blood burns, how prodigal the soul   *wastful*
Lends the tongue vows. These blazes, daughter,
Giving more light than heat, extinct in both
Even in their promise, as it is a-making,
You must not take for fire. From this time   120
Be something scanter of your maiden presence.
Set your entreatments at a higher rate
Than a command to parley. For Lord Hamlet,   *To hold conference with enemy.*
Believe so much in him, that he is young,
And with a larger tether may he walk   *rope for fastening an animal*   125
Than may be given you. In few, Ophelia,
Do not believe his vows; for they are brokers,
Not of that dye which their investments show,
But mere implorators of unholy suits,
Breathing like sanctified and pious bawds,   *religious*   130
The better to beguile. This is for all: *cheat*
I would not, in plain terms, from this time forth
Have you so slander any moment leisure
As to give words or talk with the Lord Hamlet.
Look to't, I charge you. Come your ways.   135

Oph. I shall obey, my lord.

Exeunt.

[Scene IV. *Elsinore. The platform before the Castle.*]

Enter *Hamlet, Horatio,* and *Marcellus.*

Ham. The air bites shrewdly; it is very cold.

Hor. It is a nipping and an eager air.

Ham. What hour now?

Hor.　　　　　　I think it lacks of twelve.

Mar. No, it is struck.

Hor. Indeed? I heard it not. It then draws near the season
Wherein the spirit held his wont to walk.　　　　　　6

　　　　　　A flourish of trumpets, and two pieces go off.
What does this mean, my lord?

Ham. The King doth wake to-night and takes his rouse,
Keeps wassail, and the swagg'ring upspring reels,
And, as he drains his draughts of Rhenish down,　　10
The kettledrum and trumpet thus bray out
The triumph of his pledge.

Hor.　　　　　　Is it a custom?

Ham. Ay, marry, is't;
But to my mind, though I am native here
And to the manner born, it is a custom　　　　　　15
More honour'd in the breach than the observance.
This heavy-headed revel east and west
Makes us traduc'd and tax'd of other nations;
They clip us drunkards and with swinish phrase
Soil our addition; and indeed it takes　　　　　　20
From our achievements, though perform'd at height,
The pith and marrow of our attribute.
So oft it chances in particular men
That, for some vicious mole of nature in them,
As in their birth,—wherein they are not guilty,　　25
Since nature cannot choose his origin,—
By the o'ergrowth of some complexion,

Oft breaking down the pales and forts of reason,
Or by some habit that too much o'erleavens
The form of plausive manners, that these men   *applauding*   30
Carrying, I say, the stamp of one defect,
Being nature's livery, or fortune's star,
Their virtues else—be they as pure as grace,
As infinite as man may undergo—
Shall in the general censure take corruption   *blame*   35
From that particular fault. The dram of e'il
Doth all the noble substance often dout
To his own scandal.

              Enter *Ghost*.

  Hor.   Look, my lord, it comes!
  Ham. Angels and ministers of grace defend us!
Be thou a spirit of health or goblin damn'd,   40
Bring with thee airs from heaven or blasts from hell,
Be thy intents wicked or charitable,
Thou com'st in such a questionable shape
That I will speak to thee. I'll call thee Hamlet,
King, father, royal Dane. O, answer me!   45
Let me not burst in ignorance, but tell
Why thy canoniz'd bones, hearsed in death,
Have burst their cerements; why the sepulchre
Wherein we saw thee quietly inurn'd,
Hath op'd his ponderous and marble jaws   50
To cast thee up again. What may this mean
That thou, dead corse, again in complete steel,
Revisits thus the glimpses of the moon,
Making night hideous, and we fools of nature
So horridly to shake our disposition   55
With thoughts beyond the reaches of our souls?
Say, why is this? wherefore? What should we do?
                                    Ghost beckons Hamlet.

Hor. It beckons you to go away with it,
As if it some impartment did desire
To you alone.

 Mar.   Look with what courteous action 60
It waves you to a more removed ground.
But do not go with it!

 Hor.   No, by no means!

 Ham. It will not speak. Then will I follow it.

 Hor. Do not, my lord!

 Ham.   Why, what should be the fear?
I do not set my life at a pin's fee; 65
And for my soul, what can it do to that,
Being a thing immortal as itself?
It waves me forth again. I'll follow it.

 Hor. What if it tempt you toward the flood, my lord,
Or to the dreadful summit of the cliff 70
That beetles o'er his base into the sea,
And there assume some other, horrible form
Which might deprive your sovereignty of reason
And draw you into madness? Think of it.
The very place puts toys of desperation, 75
Without more motive, into every brain
That looks so many fadoms to the sea
And hears it roar beneath.

 Ham.   It waves me still.
Go on. I'll follow thee.

 Mar. You shall not go, my lord.

 Ham.   Hold off your hands! 80

 Hor. Be rul'd. You shall not go.

 Ham.   My fate cries out
And makes each petty artire in this body
As hardy as the Nemean lion's nerve.

          [Ghost beckons.]

Still am I call'd. Unhand me, gentlemen.

By heaven, I'll make a ghost of him that lets me!—   85
I say, away!—Go on. I'll follow thee.

Exeunt Ghost and Hamlet.

Hor. He waxes desperate with imagination.

Mar. Let's follow. 'Tis not fit thus to obey him.

Hor. Have after. To what issue will this come?

Mar. Something is rotten in the state of Denmark.   90

Hor. Heaven will direct it.

Mar.   Nay, let's follow him.

Exeunt.

[Scene V. *Elsinore. The Castle. Another part of the*
fortifications.]

Enter *Ghost* and *Hamlet.*

Ham. Whither wilt thou lead me? Speak! I'll go no
further.

Ghost. Mark me.

Ham.   I will.

Ghost.   My hour is almost come,
When I to sulph'rous and tormenting flames
Must render up myself.

Ham.   Alas, poor ghost!

Ghost. Pity me not, but lend thy serious hearing   5
To what I shall unfold.

Ham.   Speak. I am bound to hear.

Ghost. So art thou to revenge, when thou shalt hear.

Ham. What?

Ghost.   I am thy father's spirit,
Doom'd for a certain term to walk the night,   10
And for the day confin'd to fast in fires,
Till the foul crimes done in my days of nature
Are burnt and purg'd away. But that I am forbid

To tell the secrets of my prison house,
I could a tale unfold whose lightest word   15
Would harrow up thy soul, freeze thy young blood,
Make thy two eyes, like stars, start from their spheres,
Thy knotted and combined locks to part,
And each particular hair to stand an end
Like quills upon the fretful porpentine.   20
But this eternal blazon must not be
To ears of flesh and blood. List, list, O, list!
If thou didst ever thy dear father love—

    Ham. O God!

    Ghost. Revenge his foul and most unnatural murther.   25

    Ham. Murther?

    Ghost. Murther most foul, as in the best it is;
But this most foul, strange, and unnatural.

    Ham. Haste me to know't, that I, with wings as swift
As meditation or the thoughts of love,   30
May sweep to my revenge.

    Ghost.   I find thee apt;
And duller shouldst thou be than the fat weed
That rots itself in ease on Lethe wharf,
Wouldst thou not stir in this. Now, Hamlet, hear.
'Tis given out that, sleeping in my orchard,   35
A serpent stung me. So the whole ear of Denmark
Is by a forged process of my death
Rankly abus'd. But know, thou noble youth,
The serpent that did sting thy father's life
Now wears his crown.

    Ham.   O my prophetic soul!   40
My uncle?

    Ghost. Ay, that incestuous, that adulterate beast,
With witchcraft of his wit, with traitorous gifts—
O wicked wit and gifts, that have the power
So to seduce!—won to his shameful lust   45

The will of my most seeming-virtuous queen.
O Hamlet, what a falling-off was there,
From me, whose love was of that dignity
That it went hand in hand even with the vow
I made to her in marriage, and to decline   50
Upon a wretch whose natural gifts were poor
To those of mine!
But virtue, as it never will be mov'd,
Though lewdness court it in a shape of heaven,
So lust, though to a radiant angel link'd,   55
Will sate itself in a celestial bed
And prey on garbage.
But soft! methinks I scent the morning air.
Brief let me be. Sleeping within my orchard,
My custom always of the afternoon,   60
Upon my secure hour thy uncle stole,
With juice of cursed hebona in a vial,
And in the porches of my ears did pour
The leperous distilment; whose effect
Holds such an enmity with blood of man   65
That swift as quicksilver it courses through
The natural gates and alleys of the body,
And with a sudden vigour it doth posset
And curd, like eager droppings into milk,
The thin and wholesome blood. So did it mine;   70
And a most instant tetter bark'd about,
Most lazar-like, with vile and loathsome crust
All my smooth body.
Thus was I, sleeping, by a brother's hand
Of life, of crown, of queen, at once dispatch'd;   75
Cut off even in the blossoms of my sin,
Unhous'led, disappointed, unanel'd,
No reck'ning made, but sent to my account
With all my imperfections on my head.

Ham. O, horrible! O, horrible! most horrible!   80
    Ghost. If thou hast nature in thee, bear it not.
Let not the royal bed of Denmark be
A couch for luxury and damned incest.
But, howsoever thou pursuest this act,
Taint not thy mind, nor let thy soul contrive   85
Against thy mother aught. Leave her to heaven,
And to those thorns that in her bosom lodge
To prick and sting her. Fare thee well at once.
The glowworm shows the matin to be near
And gins to pale his uneffectual fire.   90
Adieu, adieu, adieu! Remember me.   *Exit.*
    Ham. O all you host of heaven! O earth! What else?
And shall I couple hell? Hold, hold, my heart!
And you, my sinews, grow not instant old,
But bear me stiffly up. Remember thee?   95
Ay, thou poor ghost, while memory holds a seat
In this distracted globe. Remember thee?
Yea, from the table of my memory
I'll wipe away all trivial fond records,
All saws of books, all forms, all pressures past   100
That youth and observation copied there,
And thy commandment all alone shall live
Within the book and volume of my brain,
Unmix'd with baser matter. Yes, by heaven!
O most pernicious woman!   105
O villain, villain, smiling, damned villain!
My tables! Meet it is I set it down
That one may smile, and smile, and be a villain;
At least I am sure it may be so in Denmark.   [*Writes.*]
So, uncle, there you are. Now to my word: 110
It is 'Adieu, adieu! Remember me.'
I have sworn't.
    Hor. (*within*) My lord, my lord!

Enter *Horatio* and *Marcellus*.

Mar.   Lord Hamlet!

Hor.   Heaven secure him!

Ham. So be it!

Mar. Illo, ho, ho, my lord!   115

Ham. Hillo, ho, ho, boy! Come, bird, come.

Mar. How is't, my noble lord?

Hor.   What news, my lord?

Ham. O, wonderful!

Hor. Good my lord, tell it.

Ham.   No, you will reveal it.

Hor. Not I, my lord, by heaven!

Mar.   Nor I, my lord.   120

Ham. How say you then? Would heart of man once
   think it?
But you'll be secret?

Both.   Ay, by heaven, my lord.

Ham. There's ne'er a villain dwelling in all Denmark
But he's an arrant knave.

Hor. There needs no ghost, my lord, come from the grave
To tell us this.

Ham.   Why, right! You are in the right!   126
And so, without more circumstance at all,
I hold it fit that we shake hands and part;
You, as your business and desires shall point you,
For every man hath business and desire,   130
Such as it is; and for my own poor part,
Look you, I'll go pray.

Hor. These are but wild and whirling words, my lord.

Ham. I am sorry they offend you, heartily;
Yes, faith, heartily.

Hor.   There's no offence, my lord.   135

Ham. Yes, by Saint Patrick, but there is, Horatio,

And much offence too. Touching this vision here,
It is an honest ghost, that let me tell you.
For your desire to know what is between us,
O'ermaster't as you may. And now, good friends, 140
As you are friends, scholars, and soldiers,
Give me one poor request.

Hor. What is't, my lord? We will.

Ham. Never make known what you have seen to-night.

Both. My lord, we will not.

Ham.   Nay, but swear't.

Hor.   In faith, 145
My lord, not I.

Mar.   Nor I, my lord—in faith.

Ham. Upon my sword.

Mar.   We have sworn, my lord, already.

Ham. Indeed, upon my sword, indeed.

Ghost cries under the stage.

Ghost. Swear.

Ham. Aha boy, say'st thou so? Art thou there, truepenny?
Come on! You hear this fellow in the cellarage. 151
Consent to swear.

Hor.   Propose the oath, my lord.

Ham. Never to speak of this that you have seen.
Swear by my sword.

Ghost. [*beneath*] Swear. 155

Ham. Hic et ubique? Then we'll shift our ground.
Come hither, gentlemen,
And lay your hands again upon my sword.
Never to speak of this that you have heard:
Swear by my sword. 160

Ghost. [*beneath*] Swear by his sword.

Ham. Well said, old mole! Canst work i' th' earth so fast?
A worthy pioner! Once more remove, good friends.

Hor. O day and night, but this is wondrous strange!

Ham. And therefore as a stranger give it welcome.   165
There are more things in heaven and earth, Horatio,
Than are dreamt of in your philosophy.
But come!
Here, as before, never, so help you mercy,
How strange or odd soe'er I bear myself   170
(As I perchance hereafter shall think meet
To put an antic disposition on),
That you, at such times seeing me, never shall,
With arms encumb'red thus, or this head-shake,
Or by pronouncing of some doubtful phrase,   175
As 'Well, well, we know,' or 'We could, an if we would,'
Or 'If we list to speak,' or 'There be, an if they might,'
Or such ambiguous giving out, to note
That you know aught of me—this not to do,
So grace and mercy at your most need help you,   180
Swear.

Ghost. [*beneath*] Swear.

                                            [*They swear.*]

Ham. Rest, rest, perturbed spirit! So, gentlemen,
With all my love I do commend me to you;
And what so poor a man as Hamlet is   185
May do t' express his love and friending to you,
God willing, shall not lack. Let us go in together;
And still your fingers on your lips, I pray.
The time is out of joint. O cursed spite
That ever I was born to set it right!   190
Nay, come, let's go together.

                                            Exeunt.

Enter *Polonius* and *Reynaldo.*

Pol. Give him this money and these notes, Reynaldo.

Rey. I will, my lord.

Pol. You shall do marvell's wisely, good Reynaldo,
Before you visit him, to make inquire
Of his behaviour.

Rey.   My lord, I did intend it.   5

Pol. Marry, well said, very well said. Look you, sir,
Enquire me first what Danskers are in Paris;
And how, and who, what means, and where they keep,
What company, at what expense; and finding
By this encompassment and drift of question   10
That they do know my son, come you more nearer
Than your particular demands will touch it.
Take you, as 'twere, some distant knowledge of him;
As thus, 'I know his father and his friends,
And in part him.' Do you mark this, Reynaldo?   15

Rey. Ay, very well, my lord.

Pol. 'And in part him, but,' you may say, 'not well.
But if't be he I mean, he's very wild
Addicted so and so'; and there put on him
What forgeries you please; marry, none so rank   20
As may dishonour him—take heed of that;
But, sir, such wanton, wild, and usual slips
As are companions noted and most known
To youth and liberty.

Rey.   As gaming, my lord.

Pol. Ay, or drinking, fencing, swearing, quarrelling,   25
Drabbing. You may go so far.

Rey. My lord, that would dishonour him.

Pol. Faith, no, as you may season it in the charge.
You must not put another scandal on him,

32

That he is open to incontinency.   30
That's not my meaning. But breathe his faults so quaintly
That they may seem the taints of liberty,
The flash and outbreak of a fiery mind,
A savageness in unreclaimed blood,
Of general assault.
    Rey.   But, my good lord—   35
    Pol. Wherefore should you do this?
    Rey.   Ay, my lord,
I would know that.
    Pol.   Marry, sir, here's my drift,
And I believe it is a fetch of warrant.
You laying these slight sullies on my son
As 'twere a thing a little soil'd i' th' working,   40
Mark you,
Your party in converse, him you would sound,
Having ever seen in the prenominate crimes
The youth you breathe of guilty, be assur'd
He closes with you in this consequence: 45
'Good sir,' or so, or 'friend,' or 'gentleman'—
According to the phrase or the addition
Of man and country—
    Rey.   Very good, my lord.
    Pol. And then, sir, does 'a this—'a does—What was I about
to say? By the mass, I was about to say something! Where
did I leave?   51
    Rey. At 'closes in the consequence,' at 'friend or so,' and
'gentleman.'
    Pol. At 'closes in the consequence'—Ay, marry!
He closes thus: 'I know the gentleman.   55
I saw him yesterday, or t'other day,
Or then, or then, with such or such; and, as you say,
There was 'a gaming; there o'ertook in's rouse;
There falling out at tennis'; or perchance,

'I saw him enter such a house of sale,'   60
Videlicet, a brothel, or so forth.
See you now—
Your bait of falsehood takes this carp of truth;
And thus do we of wisdom and of reach,
With windlasses and with assays of bias,   65
By indirections find directions out.
So, by my former lecture and advice,
Shall you my son. You have me, have you not?
 Rey. My lord, I have.
 Pol.   God b' wi' ye, fare ye well!
 Rey. Good my lord!   [*Going.*]   70
 Pol. Observe his inclination in yourself.
 Rey. I shall, my lord.
 Pol. And let him ply his music.
 Rey.   Well, my lord.
 Pol. Farewell!

          Exit Reynaldo.

     Enter *Ophelia.*

    How now, Ophelia? What's the matter?
 Oph. O my lord, my lord, I have been so affrighted!   75
 Pol. With what, i' th' name of God?
 Oph. My lord, as I was sewing in my closet,
Lord Hamlet, with his doublet all unbrac'd,
No hat upon his head, his stockings foul'd,
Ungart'red, and down-gyved to his ankle;   80
Pale as his shirt, his knees knocking each other,
And with a look so piteous in purport
As if he had been loosed out of hell
To speak of horrors—he comes before me.
 Pol. Mad for thy love?
 Oph.   My lord, I do not know,   85
But truly I do fear it.

Pol.   What said he?

Oph. He took me by the wrist and held me hard;
Then goes he to the length of all his arm,
And, with his other hand thus o'er his brow,
He falls to such perusal of my face   90
As he would draw it. Long stay'd he so.
At last, a little shaking of mine arm,
And thrice his head thus waving up and down,
He rais'd a sigh so piteous and profound
As it did seem to shatter all his bulk   95
And end his being. That done, he lets me go,
And with his head over his shoulder turn'd
He seem'd to find his way without his eyes,
For out o' doors he went without their help
And to the last bended their light on me.   100

  Pol. Come, go with me. I will go seek the King.
This is the very ecstasy of love,
Whose violent property fordoes itself
And leads the will to desperate undertakings
As oft as any passion under heaven   105
That does afflict our natures. I am sorry.
What, have you given him any hard words of late?

  Oph. No, my good lord; but, as you did command,
I did repel his letters and denied
His access to me.

  Pol.   That hath made him mad.   110
I am sorry that with better heed and judgment
I had not quoted him. I fear'd he did but trifle
And meant to wrack thee; but beshrew my jealousy!
By heaven, it is as proper to our age
To cast beyond ourselves in our opinions   115
As it is common for the younger sort
To lack discretion. Come, go we to the King.
This must be known; which, being kept close, might move

More grief to hide than hate to utter love.   119
Come.

Exeunt.

Scene II. [*Elsinore. A room in the Castle.*]

Flourish. Enter *King* and *Queen*, *Rosencrantz*, and *Guildenstern*, cum aliis.

 King. Welcome, dear Rosencrantz and Guildenstern.
Moreover that we much did long to see you,
The need we have to use you did provoke
Our hasty sending. Something have you heard
Of Hamlet's transformation. So I call it,   5
Sith nor th' exterior nor the inward man
Resembles that it was. What it should be,
More than his father's death, that thus hath put him
So much from th' understanding of himself,
I cannot dream of. I entreat you both   10
That, being of so young days brought up with him,
And since so neighbour'd to his youth and haviour,
That you vouchsafe your rest here in our court
Some little time; so by your companies
To draw him on to pleasures, and to gather   15
So much as from occasion you may glean,
Whether aught to us unknown afflicts him thus
That, open'd, lies within our remedy.
 Queen. Good gentlemen, he hath much talk'd of you,
And sure I am two men there are not living   20
To whom he more adheres. If it will please you
To show us so much gentry and good will
As to expend your time with us awhile
For the supply and profit of our hope,
Your visitation shall receive such thanks   25
As fits a king's remembrance.

Ros.   Both your Majesties
Might, by the sovereign power you have of us,
Put your dread pleasures more into command
Than to entreaty.
    Guil.   But we both obey,
And here give up ourselves, in the full bent,   30
To lay our service freely at your feet,
To be commanded.
    King. Thanks, Rosencrantz and gentle Guildenstern.
    Queen. Thanks, Guildenstern and gentle Rosencrantz.
And I beseech you instantly to visit   35
My too much changed son.—Go, some of you,
And bring these gentlemen where Hamlet is.
    Guil. Heavens make our presence and our practices
Pleasant and helpful to him!
    Queen.   Ay, amen!
    Exeunt Rosencrantz and Guildenstern, [with some At-
                                tendants].
                    Enter *Polonius.*

    Pol. Th' ambassadors from Norway, my good lord,   40
Are joyfully return'd.
    King. Thou still hast been the father of good news.
    Pol. Have I, my lord? Assure you, my good liege,
I hold my duty as I hold my soul,
Both to my God and to my gracious king;   45
And I do think—or else this brain of mine
Hunts not the trail of policy so sure
As it hath us'd to do—that I have found
The very cause of Hamlet's lunacy.
    King. O, speak of that! That do I long to hear.   50
    Pol. Give first admittance to th' ambassadors.
My news shall be the fruit to that great feast.
    King. Thyself do grace to them, and bring them in.
                                  [Exit Polonius.]

He tells me, my dear Gertrude, he hath found
The head and source of all your son's distemper. 55

Queen. I doubt it is no other but the main,
His father's death and our o'erhasty marriage.

King. Well, we shall sift him.

Enter *Polonius, Voltemand*, and *Cornelius*.

                        Welcome, my good friends.
Say, Voltemand, what from our brother Norway?

Volt. Most fair return of greetings and desires. 60
Upon our first, he sent out to suppress
His nephew's levies; which to him appear'd
To be a preparation 'gainst the Polack,
But better look'd into, he truly found
It was against your Highness; whereat griev'd, 65
That so his sickness, age, and impotence
Was falsely borne in hand, sends out arrests
On Fortinbras; which he, in brief, obeys,
Receives rebuke from Norway, and, in fine,
Makes vow before his uncle never more 70
To give th' assay of arms against your Majesty.
Whereon old Norway, overcome with joy,
Gives him three thousand crowns in annual fee
And his commission to employ those soldiers,
So levied as before, against the Polack; 75
With an entreaty, herein further shown,

                                   [Gives a paper.]

That it might please you to give quiet pass
Through your dominions for this enterprise,
On such regards of safety and allowance
As therein are set down.

King.   It likes us well; 80
And at our more consider'd time we'll read,
Answer, and think upon this business.

Meantime we thank you for your well-took labour.
Go to your rest; at night we'll feast together.
Most welcome home!   *Exeunt Ambassadors.*
    Pol.   This business is well ended.   85
My liege, and madam, to expostulate
What majesty should be, what duty is,
Why day is day, night night, and time is time,
Were nothing but to waste night, day, and time.
Therefore, since brevity is the soul of wit,   90
And tediousness the limbs and outward flourishes,
I will be brief. Your noble son is mad.
Mad call I it; for, to define true madness,
What is't but to be nothing else but mad?
But let that go.
    Queen.   More matter, with less art.   95
    Pol. Madam, I swear I use no art at all.
That he is mad, 'tis true: 'tis true 'tis pity;
And pity 'tis 'tis true. A foolish figure!
But farewell it, for I will use no art.
Mad let us grant him then. And now remains   100
That we find out the cause of this effect—
Or rather say, the cause of this defect,
For this effect defective comes by cause.
Thus it remains, and the remainder thus.
Perpend.   105
I have a daughter (have while she is mine),
Who in her duty and obedience, mark,
Hath given me this. Now gather, and surmise.
                    [*Reads*] *the letter.*

'To the celestial, and my soul's idol, the most beautified Ophelia,'—

That's an ill phrase, a vile phrase; 'beautified' is a vile phrase.
But you shall hear. Thus: [*Reads.*]

'In her excellent white bosom, these, &c.'

Queen. Came this from Hamlet to her?
Pol. Good madam, stay awhile. I will be faithful. [*Reads.*]

> 'Doubt thou the stars are fire;   116
>   Doubt that the sun doth move;
>   Doubt truth to be a liar;
>   But never doubt I love.

'O dear Ophelia, I am ill at these numbers; I have not art to
reckon my groans; but that I love thee best, O most best, believe
it. Adieu.

> 'Thine evermore, most dear lady, whilst this machine is to
>   him, HAMLET.'

This, in obedience, hath my daughter shown me;   125
And more above, hath his solicitings,
As they fell out by time, by means, and place,
All given to mine ear.
    King.   But how hath she
Receiv'd his love?
    Pol.   What do you think of me?
    King. As of a man faithful and honourable.   130
    Pol. I would fain prove so. But what might you think,
When I had seen this hot love on the wing
(As I perceiv'd it, I must tell you that,
Before my daughter told me), what might you,
Or my dear Majesty your queen here, think,   135
If I had play'd the desk or table book,
Or given my heart a winking, mute and dumb,
Or look'd upon this love with idle sight?
What might you think? No, I went round to work
And my young mistress thus I did bespeak: 140
'Lord Hamlet is a prince, out of thy star.
This must not be.' And then I prescripts gave her,
That she should lock herself from his resort,
Admit no messengers, receive no tokens.
Which done, she took the fruits of my advice,   145

And he, repulsed, a short tale to make,
Fell into a sadness, then into a fast,
Thence to a watch, thence into a weakness,
Thence to a lightness, and, by this declension,
Into the madness wherein now he raves,　　　150
And all we mourn for.

   King.　　　　　　Do you think 'tis this?

   Queen. It may be, very like.

   Pol. Hath there been such a time—I would fain know
     that—
That I have positively said ' 'Tis so,'
When it prov'd otherwise?

   King.　　　　　Not that I know.　　155

   Pol. [*points to his head and shoulder*] Take this from this,
     if this be otherwise.
If circumstances lead me, I will find
Where truth is hid, though it were hid indeed
Within the centre.

   King.　　　　　How may we try it further?　　159

   Pol. You know sometimes he walks four hours together
Here in the lobby.

   Queen.　　　So he does indeed.

   Pol. At such a time I'll loose my daughter to him.
Be you and I behind an arras then.
Mark the encounter. If he love her not,
And be not from his reason fall'n thereon,　　　165
Let me be no assistant for a state,
But keep a farm and carters.

   King.　　　　　　We will try it.

Enter *Hamlet*, reading on a book.

   Queen. But look where sadly the poor wretch comes read-
     ing.

   Pol. Away, I do beseech you, both away!

I 'll board him presently. O, give me leave.   170

      Exeunt King and Queen, [with Attendants].

How does my good Lord Hamlet?

Ham. Well, God-a-mercy.

Pol. Do you know me, my lord?

Ham. Excellent well. You are a fishmonger.

Pol. Not I, my lord.   175

Ham. Then I would you were so honest a man.

Pol. Honest, my lord?

Ham. Ay, sir. To be honest, as this world goes, is to be one man pick'd out of ten thousand.

Pol. That's very true, my lord.   180

Ham. For if the sun breed maggots in a dead dog, being a god kissing carrion—Have you a daughter?

Pol. I have, my lord.   184

Ham. Let her not walk i' th' sun. Conception is a blessing, but not as your daughter may conceive. Friend, look to 't.

Pol. [*aside*] How say you by that? Still harping on my daughter. Yet he knew me not at first. He said I was a fishmonger. He is far gone, far gone! And truly in my youth I suff'red much extremity for love—very near this. I 'll speak to him again.—What do you read, my lord?

Ham. Words, words, words.

Pol. What is the matter, my lord?   195

Ham. Between who?

Pol. I mean, the matter that you read, my lord.

Ham. Slanders, sir; for the satirical rogue says here that old men have grey beards; that their faces are wrinkled; their eyes purging thick amber and plum-tree gum; and that they have a plentiful lack of wit, together with most weak hams. All which, sir, though I most powerfully and potently believe, yet I hold it not honesty to have it thus set down; for you yourself, sir, should be old as I am if, like a crab, you could go backward.

Pol. [*aside*] Though this be madness, yet there is method in't.—Will you walk out of the air, my lord?

Ham. Into my grave?   210

Pol. Indeed, that is out o' th' air. [*Aside*] How pregnant sometimes his replies are! a happiness that often madness hits on, which reason and sanity could not so prosperously be delivered of. I will leave him and suddenly contrive the means of meeting between him and my daughter.—My honourable lord, I will most humbly take my leave of you.   218

Ham. You cannot, sir, take from me anything that I will more willingly part withal—except my life, except my life, except my life.

Enter *Rosencrantz* and *Guildenstern*.

Pol. Fare you well, my lord.

Ham. These tedious old fools!

Pol. You go to seek the Lord Hamlet. There he is.

Ros. [*to Polonius*] God save you, sir!   225

Exit [*Polonius*].

Guil. My honour'd lord!

Ros. My most dear lord!

Ham. My excellent good friends! How dost thou, Guildenstern? Ah, Rosencrantz! Good lads, how do ye both? 230

Ros. As the indifferent children of the earth.

Guil. Happy in that we are not over-happy.
On Fortune's cap we are not the very button.

Ham. Nor the soles of her shoe?

Ros. Neither, my lord.   235

Ham. Then you live about her waist, or in the middle of her favours?

Guil. Faith, her privates we.

Ham. In the secret parts of Fortune? O, most true! she is a strumpet. What news?   240

Ros. None, my lord, but that the world's grown honest.

Ham. Then is doomsday near! But your news is not true. Let me question more in particular. What have you, my good friends, deserved at the hands of Fortune that she sends you to prison hither?

Guil. Prison, my lord?

Ham. Denmark's a prison.

Ros. Then is the world one. 250

Ham. A goodly one; in which there are many confines, wards, and dungeons, Denmark being one o' th' worst.

Ros. We think not so, my lord. 254

Ham. Why, then 'tis none to you; for there is nothing either good or bad but thinking makes it so. To me it is a prison.

Ros. Why, then your ambition makes it one. 'Tis too narrow for your mind. 259

Ham. O God, I could be bounded in a nutshell and count myself a king of infinite space, were it not that I have bad dreams.

Guil. Which dreams indeed are ambition; for the very substance of the ambitious is merely the shadow of a dream. 265

Ham. A dream itself is but a shadow.

Ros. Truly, and I hold ambition of so airy and light a quality that it is but a shadow's shadow.

Ham. Then are our beggars bodies, and our monarchs and outstretch'd heroes the beggars' shadows. Shall we to th' court? for, by my fay, I cannot reason. 272

Both. We'll wait upon you.

Ham. No such matter! I will not sort you with the rest of my servants; for, to speak to you like an honest man, I am most dreadfully attended. But in the beaten way of friendship, what make you at Elsinore?

Ros. To visit you, my lord; no other occasion. 279

Ham. Beggar that I am, I am even poor in thanks; but I thank you; and sure, dear friends, my thanks are too dear a

halfpenny. Were you not sent for? Is it your own inclining?
Is it a free visitation? Come, deal justly with me. Come,
come! Nay, speak.   285

Guil. What should we say, my lord?

Ham. Why, anything—but to th' purpose. You were sent
for; and there is a kind of confession in your looks, which
your modesties have not craft enough to colour. I know the
good King and Queen have sent for you.   291

Ros. To what end, my lord?

Ham. That you must teach me. But let me conjure you by
the rights of our fellowship, by the consonancy of our youth,
by the obligation of our ever-preserved love, and by what more
dear a better proposer could charge you withal, be even and
direct with me, whether you were sent for or no.   299

Ros. [*aside to Guildenstern*] What say you?

Ham. [*aside*] Nay then, I have an eye of you.—If you love
me, hold not off.

Guil. My lord, we were sent for.   303

Ham. I will tell you why. So shall my anticipation prevent
your discovery, and your secrecy to the King and Queen moult
no feather. I have of late—but wherefore I know not—lost
all my mirth, forgone all custom of exercises; and indeed, it
goes so heavily with my disposition that this goodly frame, the
earth, seems to me a sterile promontory; this most excellent
canopy, the air, look you, this brave o'erhanging firmament,
this majestical roof fretted with golden fire—why, it appeareth
no other thing to me than a foul and pestilent congregation of
vapours. What a piece of work is a man! how noble in reason!
how infinite in faculties! in form and moving how express and
admirable! in action how like an angel! in apprehension how
like a god! the beauty of the world, the paragon of animals!
And yet to me what is this quintessence of dust? Man delights
not me—no, nor woman neither, though by your smiling you
seem to say so.

Ros. My lord, there was no such stuff in my thoughts. 325

Ham. Why did you laugh then, when I said 'Man delights not me'?

Ros. To think, my lord, if you delight not in man, what lenten entertainment the players shall receive from you. We coted them on the way, and hither are they coming to offer you service. 331

Ham. He that plays the king shall be welcome—his Majesty shall have tribute of me; the adventurous knight shall use his foil and target; the lover shall not sigh gratis; the humorous man shall end his part in peace; the clown shall make those laugh whose lungs are tickle o' th' sere; and the lady shall say her mind freely, or the blank verse shall halt for't. What players are they? 340

Ros. Even those you were wont to take such delight in, the tragedians of the city.

Ham. How chances it they travel? Their residence, both in reputation and profit, was better both ways. 345

Ros. I think their inhibition comes by the means of the late innovation.

Ham. Do they hold the same estimation they did when I was in the city? Are they so follow'd? 350

Ros. No indeed are they not.

Ham. How comes it? Do they grow rusty?

Ros. Nay, their endeavour keeps in the wonted pace; but there is, sir, an eyrie of children, little eyases, that cry out on the top of question and are most tyrannically clapp'd for't. These are now the fashion, and so berattle the common stages (so they call them) that many wearing rapiers are afraid of goosequills and dare scarce come thither. 360

Ham. What, are they children? Who maintains 'em? How are they escoted? Will they pursue the quality no longer than they can sing? Will they not say afterwards, if they should grow themselves to common players (as it is most like, if their

means are no better), their writers do them wrong to make
them exclaim against their own succession.   368

Ros. Faith, there has been much to do on both sides; and
the nation holds it no sin to tarre them to controversy. There
was, for a while, no money bid for argument unless the poet
and the player went to cuffs in the question.

Ham. Is't possible?   374

Guil. O, there has been much throwing about of brains.

Ham. Do the boys carry it away?

Ros. Ay, that they do, my lord—Hercules and his load too.

Ham. It is not very strange; for my uncle is King of Denmark, and those that would make mows at him while my
father lived give twenty, forty, fifty, a hundred ducats apiece
for his picture in little. 'Sblood, there is something in this more
than natural, if philosophy could find it out.   385

Flourish for the Players.

Guil. There are the players.

Ham. Gentlemen, you are welcome to Elsinore. Your
hands, come! Th' appurtenance of welcome is fashion and
ceremony. Let me comply with you in this garb, lest my extent to the players (which I tell you must show fairly out-
wards) should more appear like entertainment than yours.
You are welcome. But my uncle-father and aunt-mother are
deceiv'd.

Guil. In what, my dear lord?   395

Ham. I am but mad north-north-west. When the wind is
southerly I know a hawk from a handsaw.

Enter Polonius.

Pol. Well be with you, gentlemen!

Ham. Hark you, Guildenstern—and you too—at each ear
a hearer! That great baby you see there is not yet out of his
swaddling clouts.   401

Ros. Happily he's the second time come to them; for they say an old man is twice a child.

Ham. I will prophesy he comes to tell me of the players. Mark it.—You say right, sir; a Monday morning; 'twas so indeed.

Pol. My lord, I have news to tell you.

Ham. My lord, I have news to tell you. When Roscius was an actor in Rome— 410

Pol. The actors are come hither, my lord.

Ham. Buzz, buzz!

Pol. Upon my honour—

Ham. Then came each actor on his ass—

Pol. The best actors in the world, either for tragedy, comedy, history, pastoral, pastoral-comical, historical-pastoral, tragical-historical, tragical-comical-historical-pastoral; scene individable, or poem unlimited. Seneca cannot be too heavy, nor Plautus too light. For the law of writ and the liberty, these are the only men.

Ham. O Jephthah, judge of Israel, what a treasure hadst thou!

Pol. What treasure had he, my lord?

Ham. Why, 425

'One fair daughter, and no more,
The which he loved passing well.'

Pol. [*aside*] Still on my daughter.

Ham. Am I not i' th' right, old Jephthah?

Pol. If you call me Jephthah, my lord, I have a daughter that I love passing well. 431

Ham. Nay, that follows not.

Pol. What follows then, my lord?

Ham. Why,

'As by lot, God wot,' 435

and then, you know,

> 'It came to pass, as most like it was.'

The first row of the pious chanson will show you more; for
look where my abridgment comes.   439

Enter four or five Players.

You are welcome, masters; welcome, all.—I am glad to see
thee well.—Welcome, good friends.—O, my old friend?
Why, thy face is valanc'd since I saw thee last. Com'st thou
to beard me in Denmark?—What, my young lady and
mistress? By'r Lady, your ladyship is nearer to heaven than
when I saw you last by the altitude of a chopine. Pray God
your voice, like a piece of uncurrent gold, be not crack'd within
the ring.—Masters, you are all welcome. We'll e'en to't like
French falconers, fly at anything we see. We'll have a speech
straight. Come, give us a taste of your quality. Come, a
passionate speech.   452

1. Play. What speech, my good lord?

Ham. I heard thee speak me a speech once, but it was never
acted; or if it was, not above once; for the play, I remember,
pleas'd not the million, 'twas caviary to the general; but it
was (as I receiv'd it, and others, whose judgments in such
matters cried in the top of mine) an excellent play, well di-
gested in the scenes, set down with as much modesty as cunning. I remember one said there were no sallets in the lines
to make the matter savoury, nor no matter in the phrase that
might indict the author of affectation; but call'd it an honest
method, as wholesome as sweet, and by very much more handsome than fine. One speech in't I chiefly lov'd. 'Twas Æneas'
tale to Dido, and thereabout of it especially where he speaks of
Priam's slaughter. If it live in your memory, begin at this
line—let me see, let me see: 471

> 'The rugged Pyrrhus, like th' Hyrcanian beast—'

'Tis not so; it begins with Pyrrhus:

'The rugged Pyrrhus, he whose sable arms,
Black as his purpose, did the night resemble   475
When he lay couched in the ominous horse,
Hath now this dread and black complexion smear'd
With heraldry more dismal. Head to foot
Now is he total gules, horridly trick'd
With blood of fathers, mothers, daughters, sons,   480
Bak'd and impasted with the parching streets,
That lend a tyrannous and a damned light
To their lord's murther. Roasted in wrath and fire,
And thus o'ersized with coagulate gore,
With eyes like carbuncles, the hellish Pyrrhus   485
Old grandsire Priam seeks.'

So, proceed you.

Pol. Fore God, my lord, well spoken, with good accent and good discretion.

1. Play.   'Anon he finds him,   490
Striking too short at Greeks. His antique sword,
Rebellious to his arm, lies where it falls,
Repugnant to command. Unequal match'd,
Pyrrhus at Priam drives, in rage strikes wide;
But with the whiff and wind of his fell sword   495
Th' unnerved father falls. Then senseless Ilium,
Seeming to feel this blow, with flaming top
Stoops to his base, and with a hideous crash
Takes prisoner Pyrrhus' ear. For lo! his sword,
Which was declining on the milky head   500
Of reverend Priam, seem'd i' th' air to stick.
So, as a painted tyrant, Pyrrhus stood,
And, like a neutral to his will and matter,
Did nothing.
But, as we often see, against some storm,   505
A silence in the heavens, the rack stand still,
The bold winds speechless, and the orb below
As hush as death—anon the dreadful thunder

Doth rend the region; so, after Pyrrhus' pause,
Aroused vengeance sets him new awork;   510
And never did the Cyclops' hammers fall
On Mars's armour, forg'd for proof eterne,
With less remorse than Pyrrhus' bleeding sword
Now falls on Priam.
Out, out, thou strumpet Fortune! All you gods,   515
In general synod take away her power;
Break all the spokes and fellies from her wheel,
And bowl the round nave down the hill of heaven,
As low as to the fiends!'

Pol. This is too long.   520
Ham. It shall to the barber's, with your beard.—Prithee
say on. He's for a jig or a tale of bawdry, or he sleeps. Say on;
come to Hecuba.

  1. Play. 'But who, O who, had seen the mobled queen—'

Ham. 'The mobled queen'?   526
Pol. That's good! 'Mobled queen' is good.

  1. Play. 'Run barefoot up and down, threat'ning the flames
With bisson rheum; a clout upon that head
Where late the diadem stood, and for a robe,   530
About her lank and all o'erteemed loins,
A blanket, in the alarm of fear caught up—
Who this had seen, with tongue in venom steep'd
'Gainst Fortune's state would treason have pronounc'd.
But if the gods themselves did see her then,   535
When she saw Pyrrhus make malicious sport
In mincing with his sword her husband's limbs,
The instant burst of clamour that she made
(Unless things mortal move them not at all)
Would have made milch the burning eyes of heaven   540
And passion in the gods.'

Pol. Look, whe'r he has not turn'd his colour, and has tears
in's eyes. Prithee no more!

Ham. 'Tis well. I'll have thee speak out the rest of this
soon.—Good my lord, will you see the players well bestow'd?
Do you hear? Let them be well us'd; for they are the abstract
and brief chronicles of the time. After your death you were
better have a bad epitaph than their ill report while you
live.   551

Pol. My lord, I will use them according to their desert.

Ham. God's bodykins, man, much better! Use every man
after his desert, and who should scape whipping? Use them
after your own honour and dignity. The less they deserve, the
more merit is in your bounty. Take them in.

Pol. Come, sirs.   559

Ham. Follow him, friends. We'll hear a play to-morrow.
            Exeunt Polonius and Players [except the First].
Dost thou hear me, old friend? Can you play 'The Murther
of Gonzago'?

1. Play. Ay, my lord.   564

Ham. We'll ha't to-morrow night. You could, for a need,
study a speech of some dozen or sixteen lines which I would
set down and insert in't, could you not?

1. Play. Ay, my lord.   569

Ham. Very well. Follow that lord—and look you mock
him not. [*Exit First Player*.] My good friends, I'll leave you
till night. You are welcome to Elsinore.

Ros. Good my lord!

Ham. Ay, so, God b' wi' ye!
            Exeunt [Rosencrantz and Guildenstern].
                Now I am alone.   575
O, what a rogue and peasant slave am I!
Is it not monstrous that this player here,
But in a fiction, in a dream of passion,
Could force his soul so to his own conceit
That, from her working, all his visage wann'd,   580
Tears in his eyes, distraction in's aspect.

A broken voice, and his whole function suiting
With forms to his conceit? And all for nothing!
For Hecuba!
What's Hecuba to him, or he to Hecuba,   585
That he should weep for her? What would he do,
Had he the motive and the cue for passion
That I have? He would drown the stage with tears
And cleave the general ear with horrid speech;
Make mad the guilty and appal the free,   590
Confound the ignorant, and amaze indeed
The very faculties of eyes and ears.
Yet I,
A dull and muddy-mettled rascal, peak
Like John-a-dreams, unpregnant of my cause,   595
And can say nothing! No, not for a king,
Upon whose property and most dear life
A damn'd defeat was made. Am I a coward?
Who calls me villain? breaks my pate across?
Plucks off my beard and blows it in my face?   600
Tweaks me by th' nose? gives me the lie i' th' throat
As deep as to the lungs? Who does me this, ha?
'Swounds, I should take it! for it cannot be
But I am pigeon-liver'd and lack gall
To make oppression bitter, or ere this   605
I should have fatted all the region kites
With this slave's offal. Bloody, bawdy villain!
Remorseless, treacherous, lecherous, kindless villain!
O, vengeance!
Why, what an ass am I! This is most brave,   610
That I, the son of a dear father murther'd,
Prompted to my revenge by heaven and hell,
Must (like a whore) unpack my heart with words
And fall a-cursing like a very drab,
A scullion!   615

Fie upon't! foh! About, my brain! Hum, I have heard
That guilty creatures, sitting at a play,
Have by the very cunning of the scene
Been struck so to the soul that presently
They have proclaim'd their malefactions;   620
For murther, though it have no tongue, will speak
With most miraculous organ. I'll have these players
Play something like the murther of my father
Before mine uncle. I'll observe his looks;
I'll tent him to the quick. If he but blench,   625
I know my course. The spirit that I have seen
May be a devil; and the devil hath power
T' assume a pleasing shape; yea, and perhaps
Out of my weakness and my melancholy,
As he is very potent with such spirits,   630
Abuses me to damn me. I'll have grounds
More relative than this. The play's the thing
Wherein I'll catch the conscience of the King.   *Exit.*

Enter *King, Queen, Polonius, Ophelia, Rosencrantz, Guilden-*
stern, and *Lords.*

   King. And can you by no drift of circumstance
Get from him why he puts on this confusion,
Grating so harshly all his days of quiet
With turbulent and dangerous lunacy?
   Ros. He does confess he feels himself distracted,   5
But from what cause he will by no means speak.
   Guil. Nor do we find him forward to be sounded,
But with a crafty madness keeps aloof
When we would bring him on to some confession
Of his true state.
   Queen.   Did he receive you well?   10
   Ros. Most like a gentleman.
   Guil. But with much forcing of his disposition.
   Ros. Niggard of question, but of our demands
Most free in his reply.
   Queen.   Did you assay him
To any pastime?   15
   Ros. Madam, it so fell out that certain players
We o'erraught on the way. Of these we told him,
And there did seem in him a kind of joy
To hear of it. They are here about the court,
And, as I think, they have already order   20
This night to play before him.
   Pol.   'Tis most true;
And he beseech'd me to entreat your Majesties
To hear and see the matter.
   King. With all my heart, and it doth much content me
To hear him so inclin'd.   25
Good gentlemen, give him a further edge
And drive his purpose on to these delights.

Ros. We shall, my lord.

       Exeunt Rosencrantz and Guildenstern.

 King.   Sweet Gertrude, leave us too;
For we have closely sent for Hamlet hither,
That he, as 'twere by accident, may here   30
Affront Ophelia.
Her father and myself (lawful espials)
Will so bestow ourselves that, seeing unseen,
We may of their encounter frankly judge
And gather by him, as he is behav'd,   35
If't be th' affliction of his love, or no,
That thus he suffers for.
 Queen.   I shall obey you;
And for your part, Ophelia, I do wish
That your good beauties be the happy cause
Of Hamlet's wildness. So shall I hope your virtues 40
Will bring him to his wonted way again,
To both your honours.
 Oph.   Madam, I wish it may.

            [Exit Queen.]

 Pol. Ophelia, walk you here.—Gracious, so please you,
We will bestow ourselves.—[*To Ophelia*] Read on this
 book,
That show of such an exercise may colour   45
Your loneliness.—We are oft to blame in this,
'Tis too much prov'd, that with devotion's visage
And pious action we do sugar o'er
The devil himself.
 King. [*aside*] O, 'tis too true!
How smart a lash that speech doth give my conscience! 50
The harlot's cheek, beautied with plast'ring art,
Is not more ugly to the thing that helps it
Than is my deed to my most painted word.
O heavy burthen!

Pol. I hear him coming. Let's withdraw, my lord.   55

Exeunt [*King and Polonius*].

Enter *Hamlet*.

Ham. To be, or not to be—that is the question:
Whether 'tis nobler in the mind to suffer
The slings and arrows of outrageous fortune
Or to take arms against a sea of troubles,
And by opposing end them. To die—to sleep—   60
No more; and by a sleep to say we end
The heartache, and the thousand natural shocks
That flesh is heir to. 'Tis a consummation
Devoutly to be wish'd. To die—to sleep.
To sleep—perchance to dream: ay, there's the rub!   65
For in that sleep of death what dreams may come
When we have shuffled off this mortal coil,
Must give us pause. There's the respect
That makes calamity of so long life.
For who would bear the whips and scorns of time,   70
Th' oppressor's wrong, the proud man's contumely,
The pangs of despis'd love, the law's delay,
The insolence of office, and the spurns
That patient merit of th' unworthy takes,
When he himself might his quietus make   75
With a bare bodkin? Who would these fardels bear,
To grunt and sweat under a weary life,
But that the dread of something after death—
The undiscover'd country, from whose bourn
No traveller returns—puzzles the will,   80
And makes us rather bear those ills we have
Than fly to others that we know not of?
Thus conscience does make cowards of us all,
And thus the native hue of resolution
Is sicklied o'er with the pale cast of thought,   85

And enterprises of great pith and moment
With this regard their currents turn awry
And lose the name of action.—Soft you now!
The fair Ophelia!—Nymph, in thy orisons
Be all my sins rememb'red.

Oph. Good my lord, 90
How does your honour for this many a day?

Ham. I humbly thank you; well, well, well.

Oph. My lord, I have remembrances of yours
That I have longed long to re-deliver.
I pray you, now receive them.

Ham. No, not I! 95
I never gave you aught.

Oph. My honour'd lord, you know right well you did,
And with them words of so sweet breath compos'd
As made the things more rich. Their perfume lost,
Take these again; for to the noble mind 100
Rich gifts wax poor when givers prove unkind.
There, my lord.

Ham. Ha, ha! Are you honest?

Oph. My lord?

Ham. Are you fair? 105

Oph. What means your lordship?

Ham. That if you be honest and fair, your honesty should
admit no discourse to your beauty.

Oph. Could beauty, my lord, have better commerce than
with honesty? 110

Ham. Ay, truly; for the power of beauty will sooner transform honesty from what it is to a bawd than the force of
honesty can translate beauty into his likeness. This was sometime a paradox, but now the time gives it proof. I did love
you once. 116

Oph. Indeed, my lord, you made me believe so.

Ham. You should not have believ'd me; for virtue cannot

so inoculate our old stock but we shall relish of it. I loved
you not.   120

Oph. I was the more deceived.

Ham. Get thee to a nunnery! Why wouldst thou be a
breeder of sinners? I am myself indifferent honest, but yet I
could accuse me of such things that it were better my mother
had not borne me. I am very proud, revengeful, ambitious;
with more offences at my beck than I have thoughts to put
them in, imagination to give them shape, or time to act them in.
What should such fellows as I do, crawling between earth and
heaven? We are arrant knaves all; believe none of us. Go
thy ways to a nunnery. Where's your father?   134

Oph. At home, my lord.

Ham. Let the doors be shut upon him, that he may play the
fool nowhere but in's own house. Farewell.

Oph. O, help him, you sweet heavens!   138

Ham. If thou dost marry, I'll give thee this plague for thy
dowry: be thou as chaste as ice, as pure as snow, thou shalt
not escape calumny. Get thee to a nunnery. Go, farewell. Or
if thou wilt needs marry, marry a fool; for wise men know
well enough what monsters you make of them. To a nunnery,
go; and quickly too. Farewell.   146

Oph. O heavenly powers, restore him!

Ham. I have heard of your paintings too, well enough. God
hath given you one face, and you make yourselves another.
You jig, you amble, and you lisp; you nickname God's creatures and make your wantonness your ignorance. Go to, I'll
no more on't! it hath made me mad. I say, we will have no
moe marriages. Those that are married already—all but one
—shall live; the rest shall keep as they are. To a nunnery, go.
                                                              Exit.

Oph. O, what a noble mind is here o'erthrown!
The courtier's, scholar's, soldier's, eye, tongue, sword,
Th' expectancy and rose of the fair state,   160

The glass of fashion and the mould of form,
Th' observ'd of all observers—quite, quite down!
And I, of ladies most deject and wretched,
That suck'd the honey of his music vows,
Now see that noble and most sovereign reason,   165
Like sweet bells jangled, out of tune and harsh;
That unmatch'd form and feature of blown youth
Blasted with ecstasy. O, woe is me
T' have seen what I have seen, see what I see!

Enter King and Polonius.

King. Love? his affections do not that way tend;   170
Nor what he spake, though it lack'd form a little,
Was not like madness. There's something in his soul
O'er which his melancholy sits on brood;
And I do doubt the hatch and the disclose
Will be some danger; which for to prevent,   175
I have in quick determination
Thus set it down: he shall with speed to England
For the demand of our neglected tribute.
Haply the seas, and countries different,
With variable objects, shall expel   180
This something-settled matter in his heart,
Whereon his brains still beating puts him thus
From fashion of himself. What think you on't?
Pol. It shall do well. But yet do I believe
The origin and commencement of his grief   185
Sprung from neglected love.—How now, Ophelia?
You need not tell us what Lord Hamlet said.
We heard it all.—My lord, do as you please;
But if you hold it fit, after the play
Let his queen mother all alone entreat him   190
To show his grief. Let her be round with him;

And I'll be plac'd, so please you, in the ear
Of all their conference. If she find him not,
To England send him; or confine him where
Your wisdom best shall think.

    King.   It shall be so.   195
Madness in great ones must not unwatch'd go.   *Exeunt*.

[Scene II. *Elsinore. A hall in the Castle*.]

Enter *Hamlet* and three of the *Players*.

Ham. Speak the speech, I pray you, as I pronounc'd it to
you, trippingly on the tongue. But if you mouth it, as many
of our players do, I had as live the town crier spoke my lines.
Nor do not saw the air too much with your hand, thus, but
use all gently; for in the very torrent, tempest, and (as I may
say) whirlwind of your passion, you must acquire and beget
a temperance that may give it smoothness. O, it offends me
to the soul to hear a robustious periwig-pated fellow tear a
passion to tatters, to very rags, to split the ears of the groundlings, who (for the most part) are capable of nothing but inexplicable dumb shows and noise. I would have such a fellow
whipp'd for o'erdoing Termagant. It out-herods Herod. Pray
you avoid it.   16

Player. I warrant your honour.

Ham. Be not too tame neither; but let your own discretion
be your tutor. Suit the action to the word, the word to the
action; with this special observance, that you o'erstep not the
modesty of nature: for anything so overdone is from the purpose of playing, whose end, both at the first and now, was and
is, to hold, as 'twere, the mirror up to nature; to show virtue
her own feature, scorn her own image, and the very age and
body of the time his form and pressure. Now this overdone,

or come tardy off, though it make the unskilful laugh, cannot but make the judicious grieve; the censure of the which one must in your allowance o'erweigh a whole theatre of others. O, there be players that I have seen play, and heard others praise, and that highly (not to speak it profanely), that, neither having the accent of Christians, nor the gait of Christian, pagan, nor man, have so strutted and bellowed that I have thought some of Nature's journeymen had made men, and not made them well, they imitated humanity so abominably.

Player. I hope we have reform'd that indifferently with us, sir.   41

Ham. O, reform it altogether! And let those that play your clowns speak no more than is set down for them. For there be of them that will themselves laugh, to set on some quantity of barren spectators to laugh too, though in the mean time some necessary question of the play be then to be considered. That's villanous and shows a most pitiful ambition in the fool that uses it. Go make you ready.   50

Exeunt Players.

Enter *Polonius, Rosencrantz,* and *Guildenstern.*

How now, my lord? Will the King hear this piece of work?

Pol. And the Queen too, and that presently.

Ham. Bid the players make haste. (*Exit Polonius.*) Will you two help to hasten them?

Both. We will, my lord.   *Exeunt they two.*

Ham. What, ho, Horatio!

Enter *Horatio.*

Hor. Here, sweet lord, at your service.

Ham. Horatio, thou art e'en as just a man
As e'er my conversation cop'd withal.   60

Hor. O, my dear lord!

Ham.   Nay, do not think I flatter;

For what advancement may I hope from thee,
That no revenue hast but thy good spirits
To feed and clothe thee? Why should the poor be flatter'd?
No, let the candied tongue lick absurd pomp,   65
And crook the pregnant hinges of the knee
Where thrift may follow fawning. Dost thou hear?
Since my dear soul was mistress of her choice
And could of men distinguish, her election
Hath seal'd thee for herself. For thou hast been   70
As one, in suff'ring all, that suffers nothing;
A man that Fortune's buffets and rewards
Hast ta'en with equal thanks; and blest are those
Whose blood and judgment are so well commingled
That they are not a pipe for Fortune's finger   75
To sound what stop she please. Give me that man
That is not passion's slave, and I will wear him
In my heart's core, ay, in my heart of heart,
As I do thee. Something too much of this!
There is a play to-night before the King.   80
One scene of it comes near the circumstance,
Which I have told thee, of my father's death.
I prithee, when thou seest that act afoot,
Even with the very comment of thy soul
Observe my uncle. If his occulted guilt   85
Do not itself unkennel in one speech,
It is a damned ghost that we have seen,
And my imaginations are as foul
As Vulcan's stithy. Give him heedful note;
For I mine eyes will rivet to his face,   90
And after we will both our judgments join
In censure of his seeming.
   Hor.   Well, my lord.
If he steal aught the whilst this play is playing,
And scape detecting, I will pay the theft.

Sound a flourish. Enter *Trumpets* and *Kettledrums*. Danish march. Enter *King, Queen, Polonius, Ophelia, Rosencrantz, Guildenstern*, and other *Lords* attendant, with the *Guard* carrying torches.

Ham. They are coming to the play. I must be idle. 95
Get you a place.

King. How fares our cousin Hamlet?

Ham. Excellent, i' faith; of the chameleon's dish. I eat the air, promise-cramm'd. You cannot feed capons so. 100

King. I have nothing with this answer, Hamlet. These words are not mine.

Ham. No, nor mine now. [*To Polonius*] My lord, you play'd once i' th' university, you say?

Pol. That did I, my lord, and was accounted a good actor. 106

Ham. What did you enact?

Pol. I did enact Julius Cæsar; I was kill'd i' th' Capitol; Brutus kill'd me.

Ham. It was a brute part of him to kill so capital a calf there. Be the players ready?

Ros. Ay, my lord. They stay upon your patience.

Queen. Come hither, my dear Hamlet, sit by me. 115

Ham. No, good mother. Here's metal more attractive.

Pol. [*to the King*] O, ho! do you mark that?

Ham. Lady, shall I lie in your lap?

[*Sits down at Ophelia's feet.*]

Oph. No, my lord. 120

Ham. I mean, my head upon your lap?

Oph. Ay, my lord.

Ham. Do you think I meant country matters?

Oph. I think nothing, my lord.

Ham. That's a fair thought to lie between maids' legs. 126

Oph. What is, my lord?

Ham. Nothing.

Oph. You are merry, my lord.

Ham. Who, I?   130

Oph. Ay, my lord.

Ham. O God, your only jig-maker! What should a man do but be merry? For look you how cheerfully my mother looks, and my father died within 's two hours.   135

Oph. Nay, 'tis twice two months, my lord.

Ham. So long? Nay then, let the devil wear black, for I'll have a suit of sables. O heavens! die two months ago, and not forgotten yet? Then there's hope a great man's memory may outlive his life half a year. But, by'r Lady, he must build churches then; or else shall he suffer not thinking on, with the hobby-horse, whose epitaph is 'For O, for O, the hobby-horse is forgot!'   145

Hautboys play. The dumb show enters.

Enter a *King* and a *Queen* very lovingly; the *Queen* embracing him, and he her. She kneels, and makes show of protestation unto him. He takes her up, and declines his head upon her neck. He lays him down upon a bank of flowers. She, seeing him asleep, leaves him. Anon comes in a fellow, takes off his crown, kisses it, pours poison in the sleeper's ears, and leaves him. The *Queen* returns, finds the *King* dead, and makes passionate action. The *Poisoner* with some three or four *Mutes*, come in again, seem to condole with her. The dead body is carried away. The *Poisoner* wooes the *Queen* with gifts; she seems harsh and unwilling awhile, but in the end accepts his love.

Exeunt.

Oph. What means this, my lord?

Ham. Marry, this is miching malhecho; it means mischief.

Oph. Belike this show imports the argument of the play.

Enter *Prologue*.

Ham. We shall know by this fellow. The players cannot
keep counsel; they'll tell all.   152

Oph. Will he tell us what this show meant?

Ham. Ay, or any show that you'll show him. Be not you
asham'd to show, he'll not shame to tell you what it means.

Oph. You are naught, you are naught! I'll mark the play.

Pro. For us, and for our tragedy,
　　Here stooping to your clemency,   160
　　We beg your hearing patiently.   [*Exit.*]

Ham. Is this a prologue, or the posy of a ring?
Oph. 'Tis brief, my lord.
Ham. As woman's love.

Enter [two *Players* as] *King* and *Queen*.

King. Full thirty times hath Phœbus' cart gone round   165
Neptune's salt wash and Tellus' orbed ground,
And thirty dozen moons with borrowed sheen
About the world have times twelve thirties been,
Since love our hearts, and Hymen did our hands,
Unite comutual in most sacred bands.   170
Queen. So many journeys may the sun and moon
Make us again count o'er ere love be done!
But woe is me! you are so sick of late,
So far from cheer and from your former state,
That I distrust you. Yet, though I distrust,   175
Discomfort you, my lord, it nothing must;
For women's fear and love holds quantity,
In neither aught, or in extremity.
Now what my love is, proof hath made you know;
And as my love is siz'd, my fear is so.   180
Where love is great, the littlest doubts are fear;
Where little fears grow great, great love grows there.
King. Faith, I must leave thee, love, and shortly too;
My operant powers their functions leave to do.

And thou shalt live in this fair world behind,   185
Honour'd, belov'd, and haply one as kind
For husband shalt thou—
    Queen.   O, confound the rest!
Such love must needs be treason in my breast.
In second husband let me be accurst!
None wed the second but who killed the first.   190

    Ham. [*aside*] Wormwood, wormwood!

    Queen. The instances that second marriage move
Are base respects of thrift, but none of love.
A second time I kill my husband dead
When second husband kisses me in bed.   195
    King. I do believe you think what now you speak;
But what we do determine oft we break.
Purpose is but the slave to memory,
Of violent birth, but poor validity;
Which now, like fruit unripe, sticks on the tree,   200
But fall unshaken when they mellow be.
Most necessary 'tis that we forget
To pay ourselves what to ourselves is debt.
What to ourselves in passion we propose,
The passion ending, doth the purpose lose.   205
The violence of either grief or joy
Their own enactures with themselves destroy.
Where joy most revels, grief doth most lament;
Grief joys, joy grieves, on slender accident.
This world is not for aye, nor 'tis not strange   210
That even our loves should with our fortunes change;
For 'tis a question left us yet to prove,
Whether love lead fortune, or else fortune love.
The great man down, you mark his favourite flies,
The poor advanc'd makes friends of enemies;   215
And hitherto doth love on fortune tend,
For who not needs shall never lack a friend,
And who in want a hollow friend doth try,
Directly seasons him his enemy.

But, orderly to end where I begun,   220
Our wills and fates do so contrary run
That our devices still are overthrown;
Our thoughts are ours, their ends none of our own.
So think thou wilt no second husband wed;
But die thy thoughts when thy first lord is dead.   225

    Queen. Nor earth to me give food, nor heaven light,
Sport and repose lock from me day and night,
To desperation turn my trust and hope,
An anchor's cheer in prison be my scope,
Each opposite that blanks the face of joy   230
Meet what I would have well, and it destroy,
Both here and hence pursue me lasting strife,
If, once a widow, ever I be wife!

    Ham. If she should break it now!

    King. 'Tis deeply sworn. Sweet, leave me here awhile.   235
My spirits grow dull, and fain I would beguile
The tedious day with sleep.
    Queen.   Sleep rock thy brain,

[He] sleeps.

And never come mischance between us twain!

Exit.

    Ham. Madam, how like you this play?
    Queen. The lady doth protest too much, methinks.   240
    Ham. O, but she'll keep her word.
    King. Have you heard the argument? Is there no offence in't?
    Ham. No, no! They do but jest, poison in jest; no offence i' th' world.   245
    King. What do you call the play?
    Ham. 'The Mousetrap.' Marry, how? Tropically. This play is the image of a murther done in Vienna. Gonzago is the duke's name; his wife, Baptista. You shall see anon. 'Tis a knavish piece of work; but what o' that? Your Majesty,

and we that have free souls, it touches us not. Let the gall'd
jade winch; our withers are unwrung.

Enter Lucianus.

This is one Lucianus, nephew to the King.

Oph. You are as good as a chorus, my lord.   255

Ham. I could interpret between you and your love, if I
could see the puppets dallying.

Oph. You are keen, my lord, you are keen.

Ham. It would cost you a groaning to take off my edge.

Oph. Still better, and worse.   261

Ham. So you must take your husbands.—Begin, murtherer.
Pox, leave thy damnable faces, and begin! Come, the croaking
raven doth bellow for revenge.   265

Luc. Thoughts black, hands apt, drugs fit, and time agreeing;
Confederate season, else no creature seeing;
Thou mixture rank, of midnight weeds collected,
With Hecate's ban thrice blasted, thrice infected,
Thy natural magic and dire property   270
On wholesome life usurp immediately.

Pours the poison in his ears.

Ham. He poisons him i' th' garden for's estate. His name's
Gonzago. The story is extant, and written in very choice
Italian. You shall see anon how the murtherer gets the love
of Gonzago's wife.   275

Oph. The King rises.

Ham. What, frighted with false fire?

Queen. How fares my lord?

Pol. Give o'er the play.

King. Give me some light! Away!   280

All. Lights, lights, lights!

Exeunt all but Hamlet and Horatio.

Ham. Why, let the strucken deer go weep,
    The hart ungalled play;

For some must watch, while some must sleep:
    Thus runs the world away. 285
Would not this, sir, and a forest of feathers—if the rest of my
fortunes turn Turk with me—with two Provincial roses on
my raz'd shoes, get me a fellowship in a cry of players, sir?

Hor. Half a share. 290

Ham. A whole one I!
    For thou dost know, O Damon dear,
      This realm dismantled was
    Of Jove himself; and now reigns here
      A very, very—pajock. 295

Hor. You might have rhym'd.

Ham. O good Horatio, I'll take the ghost's word for a
thousand pound! Didst perceive?

Hor. Very well, my lord.

Ham. Upon the talk of the poisoning? 300

Hor. I did very well note him.

Ham. Aha! Come, some music! Come, the recorders!
    For if the King like not the comedy,
      Why then, belike he likes it not, perdy.
Come, some music! 306

          Enter *Rosencrantz* and *Guildenstern.*

Guil. Good my lord, vouchsafe me a word with you.

Ham. Sir, a whole history.

Guil. The King, sir— 310

Ham. Ay, sir, what of him?

Guil. Is in his retirement, marvellous distemper'd.

Ham. With drink, sir?

Guil. No, my lord; rather with choler. 315

Ham. Your wisdom should show itself more richer to signify this to the doctor; for for me to put him to his purgation
would perhaps plunge him into far more choler. 319

Guil. Good my lord, put your discourse into some frame, and start not so wildly from my affair.

Ham. I am tame, sir; pronounce.

Guil. The Queen, your mother, in most great affliction of spirit hath sent me to you.

Ham. You are welcome.   325

Guil. Nay, good my lord, this courtesy is not of the right breed. If it shall please you to make me a wholesome answer, I will do your mother's commandment; if not, your pardon and my return shall be the end of my business.

Ham. Sir, I cannot.   331

Guil. What, my lord?

Ham. Make you a wholesome answer; my wit's diseas'd. But, sir, such answer as I can make, you shall command; or rather, as you say, my mother. Therefore no more, but to the matter! My mother, you say—   337

Ros. Then thus she says: your behaviour hath struck her into amazement and admiration.

Ham. O wonderful son, that can so stonish a mother! But is there no sequel at the heels of this mother's admiration? Impart.

Ros. She desires to speak with you in her closet ere you go to bed.   344

Ham. We shall obey, were she ten times our mother. Have you any further trade with us?

Ros. My lord, you once did love me.

Ham. And do still, by these pickers and stealers!   349

Ros. Good my lord, what is your cause of distemper? You do surely bar the door upon your own liberty, if you deny your griefs to your friend.

Ham. Sir, I lack advancement.   354

Ros. How can that be, when you have the voice of the King himself for your succession in Denmark?

Ham. Ay, sir, but 'while the grass grows'—the proverb is something musty.   359

Enter the Players with recorders.

O, the recorders! Let me see one. To withdraw with you—
why do you go about to recover the wind of me, as if you
would drive me into a toil?

Guil. O my lord, if my duty be too bold, my love is too
unmannerly.

Ham. I do not well understand that. Will you play upon
this pipe?   366

Guil. My lord, I cannot.

Ham. I pray you.

Guil. Believe me, I cannot.

Ham. I do beseech you.   370

Guil. I know no touch of it, my lord.

Ham. It is as easy as lying. Govern these ventages with
your fingers and thumbs, give it breath with your mouth, and
it will discourse most eloquent music. Look you, these are the
stops.   376

Guil. But these cannot I command to any utt'rance of harmony. I have not the skill.

Ham. Why, look you now, how unworthy a thing you make
of me! You would play upon me; you would seem to know
my stops; you would pluck out the heart of my mystery; you
would sound me from my lowest note to the top of my compass; and there is much music, excellent voice, in this little
organ, yet cannot you make it speak. 'Sblood, do you think
I am easier to be play'd on than a pipe? Call me what instrument you will, though you can fret me, you cannot play
upon me.

Enter Polonius.

God bless you, sir!   390

Pol. My lord, the Queen would speak with you, and presently.

Ham. Do you see yonder cloud that's almost in shape of a camel?

Pol. By th' mass, and 'tis like a camel indeed.   395

Ham. Methinks it is like a weasel.

Pol. It is back'd like a weasel.

Ham. Or like a whale.

Pol. Very like a whale.   399

Ham. Then will I come to my mother by-and-by.—They fool me to the top of my bent.—I will come by-and-by.

Pol. I will say so.   *Exit.*

Ham. 'By-and-by' is easily said.—Leave me, friends.   405
                                   [*Exeunt all but Hamlet.*]

'Tis now the very witching time of night,
When churchyards yawn, and hell itself breathes out
Contagion to this world. Now could I drink hot blood
And do such bitter business as the day
Would quake to look on. Soft! now to my mother!   410
O heart, lose not thy nature; let not ever
The soul of Nero enter this firm bosom.
Let me be cruel, not unnatural;
I will speak daggers to her, but use none.
My tongue and soul in this be hypocrites—   415
How in my words somever she be shent,
To give them seals never, my soul, consent!   *Exit.*

[Scene III. *A room in the Castle.*]

Enter *King, Rosencrantz*, and *Guildenstern.*

King. I like him not, nor stands it safe with us
To let his madness range. Therefore prepare you;
I your commission will forthwith dispatch,
And he to England shall along with you.
The terms of our estate may not endure   5

Hazard so near us as doth hourly grow
Out of his lunacies.

   Guil.   We will ourselves provide.
Most holy and religious fear it is
To keep those many many bodies safe
That live and feed upon your Majesty.   **10**

   Ros. The single and peculiar life is bound
With all the strength and armour of the mind
To keep itself from noyance; but much more
That spirit upon whose weal depends and rests
The lives of many. The cesse of majesty   **15**
Dies not alone, but like a gulf doth draw
What's near it with it. It is a massy wheel,
Fix'd on the summit of the highest mount,
To whose huge spokes ten thousand lesser things
Are mortis'd and adjoin'd; which when it falls,   **20**
Each small annexment, petty consequence,
Attends the boist'rous ruin. Never alone
Did the king sigh, but with a general groan.

   King. Arm you, I pray you, to this speedy voyage;
For we will fetters put upon this fear,   **25**
Which now goes too free-footed.

   Both.   We will haste us.

                         Exeunt Gentlemen.

Enter *Polonius.*

   Pol. My lord, he's going to his mother's closet.
Behind the arras I'll convey myself
To hear the process. I'll warrant she'll tax him home;
And, as you said, and wisely was it said,   **30**
'Tis meet that some more audience than a mother,
Since nature makes them partial, should o'erhear
The speech, of vantage. Fare you well, my liege.

I'll call upon you ere you go to bed
And tell you what I know.

   King.   Thanks, dear my lord.   35

                                   Exit [Polonius].

O, my offence is rank, it smells to heaven;
It hath the primal eldest curse upon't,
A brother's murther! Pray can I not,
Though inclination be as sharp as will.
My stronger guilt defeats my strong intent,   40
And, like a man to double business bound,
I stand in pause where I shall first begin,
And both neglect. What if this cursed hand
Were thicker than itself with brother's blood,
Is there not rain enough in the sweet heavens   45
To wash it white as snow? Whereto serves mercy
But to confront the visage of offence?
And what's in prayer but this twofold force,
To be forestalled ere we come to fall,
Or pardon'd being down? Then I'll look up;   50
My fault is past. But, O, what form of prayer
Can serve my turn? 'Forgive me my foul murther'?
That cannot be; since I am still possess'd
Of those effects for which I did the murther—
My crown, mine own ambition, and my queen.   55
May one be pardon'd and retain th' offence?
In the corrupted currents of this world
Offence's gilded hand may shove by justice,
And oft 'tis seen the wicked prize itself
Buys out the law; but 'tis not so above.   60
There is no shuffling; there the action lies
In his true nature, and we ourselves compell'd,
Even to the teeth and forehead of our faults,
To give in evidence. What then? What rests?
Try what repentance can. What can it not?   65

Yet what can it when one cannot repent?
O wretched state! O bosom black as death!
O limed soul, that, struggling to be free,
Art more engag'd! Help, angels! Make assay.
Bow, stubborn knees; and heart with strings of steel,   70
Be soft as sinews of the new-born babe!
All may be well.   *He kneels.*

Enter Hamlet.

  Ham. Now might I do it pat, now he is praying;
And now I'll do't. And so he goes to heaven,
And so am I reveng'd. That would be scann'd.   75
A villain kills my father; and for that,
I, his sole son, do this same villain send
To heaven.
Why, this is hire and salary, not revenge!
He took my father grossly, full of bread,   80
With all his crimes broad blown, as flush as May;
And how his audit stands, who knows save heaven?
But in our circumstance and course of thought,
'Tis heavy with him; and am I then reveng'd,
To take him in the purging of his soul,   85
When he is fit and seasoned for his passage?
No.
Up, sword, and know thou a more horrid hent.
When he is drunk asleep; or in his rage;
Or in th' incestuous pleasure of his bed;   90
At gaming, swearing, or about some act
That has no relish of salvation in't—
Then trip him, that his heels may kick at heaven,
And that his soul may be as damn'd and black
As hell, whereto it goes. My mother stays.   95
This physic but prolongs thy sickly days.   *Exit.*

  King. [*rises*] My words fly up, my thoughts remain below.
Words without thoughts never to heaven go.   *Exit.*

[Scene IV. *The* Queen's *closet*.]

Enter *Queen* and *Polonius*.

Pol. He will come straight. Look you lay home to him.
Tell him his pranks have been too broad to bear with,
And that your Grace hath screen'd and stood between
Much heat and him. I'll silence me even here.
Pray you be round with him.   5

Ham. (*within*) Mother, mother, mother!

Queen. I'll warrant you; fear me not. Withdraw; I hear
him coming.

[*Polonius hides behind the arras.*]

Enter *Hamlet.*

Ham. Now, mother, what's the matter?

Queen. Hamlet, thou hast thy father much offended.

Ham. Mother, you have my father much offended.   10

Queen. Come, come, you answer with an idle tongue.

Ham. Go, go, you question with a wicked tongue.

Queen. Why, how now, Hamlet?

Ham.   What's the matter now?

Queen. Have you forgot me?

Ham.   No, by the rood, not so!

You are the Queen, your husband's brother's wife,   15
And (would it were not so!) you are my mother.

Queen. Nay, then I'll set those to you that can speak.

Ham. Come, come, and sit you down. You shall not budge!
You go not till I set you up a glass
Where you may see the inmost part of you.   20

Queen. What wilt thou do? Thou wilt not murther me?
Help, help, ho!

Pol. [*behind*] What, ho! help, help, help!

Ham. [*draws*] How now? a rat? Dead for a ducat, dead!

[*Makes a pass through the arras and*] *kills Polonius.*

Pol. [*behind*] O, I am slain!

Queen.   O me, what hast thou done?

Ham. Nay, I know not. Is it the King?   25

Queen. O, what a rash and bloody deed is this!

Ham. A bloody deed—almost as bad, good mother,
As kill a king, and marry with his brother.

Queen. As kill a king?

Ham.   Ay, lady, it was my word.   30

[*Lifts up the arras and sees Polonius.*]

Thou wretched, rash, intruding fool, farewell!
I took thee for thy better. Take thy fortune.
Thou find'st to be too busy is some danger.
Leave wringing of your hands. Peace! sit you down
And let me wring your heart; for so I shall   35
If it be made of penetrable stuff;
If damned custom have not braz'd it so
That it is proof and bulwark against sense.

Queen. What have I done that thou dar'st wag thy
    tongue
In noise so rude against me?

Ham.   Such an act   40
That blurs the grace and blush of modesty;
Calls virtue hypocrite; takes off the rose
From the fair forehead of an innocent love,
And sets a blister there; makes marriage vows
As false as dicers' oaths. O, such a deed   45
As from the body of contraction plucks
The very soul, and sweet religion makes
A rhapsody of words! Heaven's face doth glow;
Yea, this solidity and compound mass,
With tristful visage, as against the doom,   50
Is thought-sick at the act.

Queen.   Ay me, what act,
That roars so loud and thunders in the index?

Ham. Look here upon this picture, and on this,
The counterfeit presentment of two brothers.
See what a grace was seated on this brow;   55
Hyperion's curls; the front of Jove himself;
An eye like Mars, to threaten and command;
A station like the herald Mercury
New lighted on a heaven-kissing hill:
A combination and a form indeed   60
Where every god did seem to set his seal
To give the world assurance of a man.
This was your husband. Look you now what follows.
Here is your husband, like a mildew'd ear
Blasting his wholesome brother. Have you eyes?   63
Could you on this fair mountain leave to feed,
And batten on this moor? Ha! have you eyes?
You cannot call it love; for at your age
The heyday in the blood is tame, it's humble,
And waits upon the judgment; and what judgment   70
Would step from this to this? Sense sure you have,
Else could you not have motion; but sure that sense
Is apoplex'd; for madness would not err,
Nor sense to ecstacy was ne'er so thrall'd
But it reserv'd some quantity of choice   75
To serve in such a difference. What devil was't
That thus hath cozen'd you at hoodman-blind?
Eyes without feeling, feeling without sight,
Ears without hands or eyes, smelling sans all,
Or but a sickly part of one true sense   80
Could not so mope.
O shame! where is thy blush? Rebellious hell,
If thou canst mutine in a matron's bones,
To flaming youth let virtue be as wax
And melt in her own fire. Proclaim no shame   85
When the compulsive ardour gives the charge,

Since frost itself as actively doth burn,
And reason panders will.

Queen.   O Hamlet, speak no more!
Thou turn'st mine eyes into my very soul,
And there I see such black and grained spots   90
As will not leave their tinct.

Ham.   Nay, but to live
In the rank sweat of an enseamed bed,
Stew'd in corruption, honeying and making love
Over the nasty sty!

Queen.   O, speak to me no more!
These words like daggers enter in mine ears.   95
No more, sweet Hamlet!

Ham.   A murtherer and a villain!
A slave that is not twentieth part the tithe
Of your precedent lord; a vice of kings;
A cutpurse of the empire and the rule,
That from a shelf the precious diadem stole   100
And put it in his pocket!

Queen.   No more!

Enter the *Ghost* in his nightgown.

Ham. A king of shreds and patches!—
Save me and hover o'er me with your wings,
You heavenly guards! What would your gracious figure?

Queen. Alas, he's mad!   105

Ham. Do you not come your tardy son to chide,
That, laps'd in time and passion, lets go by
Th' important acting of your dread command?
O, say!

Ghost. Do not forget. This visitation   110
Is but to whet thy almost blunted purpose.
But look, amazement on thy mother sits.
O, step between her and her fighting soul!

Conceit in weakest bodies strongest works.
Speak to her, Hamlet.

   Ham.   How is it with you, lady?   115
   Queen. Alas, how is't with you,
That you do bend your eye on vacancy,
And with th' incorporal air do hold discourse?
Forth at your eyes your spirits wildly peep;
And, as the sleeping soldiers in th' alarm,   120
Your bedded hairs, like life in excrements,
Start up and stand an end. O gentle son,
Upon the heat and flame of thy distemper
Sprinkle cool patience! Whereon do you look?
   Ham. On him, on him! Look you how pale he glares!   125
His form and cause conjoin'd, preaching to stones,
Would make them capable.—Do not look upon me,
Lest with this piteous action you convert
My stern effects. Then what I have to do
Will want true colour—tears perchance for blood.   130
   Queen. To whom do you speak this?
   Ham.   Do you see nothing there?
   Queen. Nothing at all; yet all that is I see.
   Ham. Nor did you nothing hear?
   Queen.   No, nothing but ourselves.
   Ham. Why, look you there! Look how it steals away!
My father, in his habit as he liv'd!   135
Look where he goes even now out at the portal!

                              Exit Ghost.

   Queen. This is the very coinage of your brain.
This bodiless creation ecstasy
Is very cunning in.
   Ham.   Ecstasy?
My pulse as yours doth temperately keep time   140
And makes as healthful music. It is not madness
That I have utt'red. Bring me to the test,

And I the matter will reword; which madness
Would gambol from. Mother, for love of grace,
Lay not that flattering unction to your soul,   145
That not your trespass but my madness speaks.
It will but skin and film the ulcerous place,
Whiles rank corruption, mining all within,
Infects unseen. Confess yourself to heaven;
Repent what's past; avoid what is to come;   150
And do not spread the compost on the weeds
To make them ranker. Forgive me this my virtue;
For in the fatness of these pursy times
Virtue itself of vice must pardon beg—
Yea, curb and woo for leave to do him good.   155
    Queen. O Hamlet, thou hast cleft my heart in twain.
    Ham. O, throw away the worser part of it,
And live the purer with the other half.
Good night—but go not to my uncle's bed.
Assume a virtue, if you have it not.   160
That monster, custom, who all sense doth eat
Of habits evil, is angel yet in this,
That to the use of actions fair and good
He likewise gives a frock or livery,
That aptly is put on. Refrain to-night,   165
And that shall lend a kind of easiness
To the next abstinence; the next more easy;
For use almost can change the stamp of nature,
And either [master] the devil, or throw him out
With wondrous potency. Once more, good night;   170
And when you are desirous to be blest,
I'll blessing beg of you.—For this same lord,
I do repent; but heaven hath pleas'd it so,
To punish me with this, and this with me,
That I must be their scourge and minister.   175
I will bestow him, and will answer well

The death I gave him. So again, good night.
I must be cruel, only to be kind;
Thus bad begins, and worse remains behind.
One word more, good lady.
    Queen.   What shall I do?   180
    Ham. Not this, by no means, that I bid you do:
Let the bloat King tempt you again to bed;
Pinch wanton on your cheek; call you his mouse;
And let him, for a pair of reechy kisses,
Or paddling in your neck with his damn'd fingers,   185
Make you to ravel all this matter out,
That I essentially am not in madness,
But mad in craft. 'Twere good you let him know;
For who that's but a queen, fair, sober, wise,
Would from a paddock, from a bat, a gib,   190
Such dear concernings hide? Who would do so?
No, in despite of sense and secrecy,
Unpeg the basket on the house's top,
Let the birds fly, and like the famous ape,
To try conclusions, in the basket creep   195
And break your own neck down.
    Queen. Be thou assur'd, if words be made of breath,
And breath of life, I have no life to breathe
What thou hast said to me.
    Ham. I must to England; you know that?
    Queen.   Alack,   200
I had forgot! 'Tis so concluded on.
    Ham. There's letters seal'd; and my two schoolfellows,
Whom I will trust as I will adders fang'd,
They bear the mandate; they must sweep my way
And marshal me to knavery. Let it work;   205
For 'tis the sport to have the enginer
Hoist with his own petar; and 't shall go hard
But I will delve one yard below their mines

And blow them at the moon. O, 'tis most sweet
When in one line two crafts directly meet.   210
This man shall set me packing.
I'll lug the guts into the neighbour room.—
Mother, good night.—Indeed, this counsellor
Is now most still, most secret, and most grave,
Who was in life a foolish prating knave.   215
Come, sir, to draw toward an end with you.
Good night, mother.

> [*Exit the Queen. Then*] *exit Hamlet, tugging in*
>   *Polonius.*

[ACT IV. Scene I. *Elsinore. A room in the Castle.*]

Enter *King* and *Queen*, with *Rosencrantz* and *Guildenstern*.

King. There's matter in these sighs. These profound heaves
You must translate; 'tis fit we understand them.
Where is your son?

Queen. Bestow this place on us a little while.

                          [Exeunt Rosencrantz and Guildenstern.]

Ah, mine own lord, what have I seen to-night!   5

King. What, Gertrude? How does Hamlet?

Queen. Mad as the sea and wind when both contend
Which is the mightier. In his lawless fit,
Behind the arras hearing something stir,
Whips out his rapier, cries 'A rat, a rat!'   10
And in this brainish apprehension kills
The unseen good old man.

King.   O heavy deed!
It had been so with us, had we been there.
His liberty is full of threats to all—
To you yourself, to us, to every one.   15
Alas, how shall this bloody deed be answer'd?
It will be laid to us, whose providence
Should have kept short, restrain'd, and out of haunt
This mad young man. But so much was our love
We would not understand what was most fit,   20
But, like the owner of a foul disease,
To keep it from divulging, let it feed
Even on the pith of life. Where is he gone?

Queen. To draw apart the body he hath kill'd;
O'er whom his very madness, like some ore   25
Among a mineral of metals base,
Shows itself pure. He weeps for what is done.

King. O Gertrude, come away!
The sun no sooner shall the mountains touch

But we will ship him hence; and this vile deed   30
We must with all our majesty and skill
Both countenance and excuse. Ho, Guildenstern!

Enter Rosencrantz and Guildenstern.

Friends both, go join you with some further aid.
Hamlet in madness hath Polonius slain,
And from his mother's closet hath he dragg'd him.   35
Go seek him out; speak fair, and bring the body
Into the chapel. I pray you haste in this.

                    Exeunt [Rosencrantz and Guildenstern].

Come, Gertrude, we'll call up our wisest friends
And let them know both what we mean to do
And what's untimely done. [So haply slander—]   40
Whose whisper o'er the world's diameter,
As level as the cannon to his blank,
Transports his pois'ned shot—may miss our name
And hit the woundless air.—O, come away!
My soul is full of discord and dismay.   45

                    Exeunt.

[Scene II. *Elsinore. A passage in the Castle.*]

Enter Hamlet.

Ham. Safely stow'd.

Gentlemen. (*within*) Hamlet! Lord Hamlet!

Ham. But soft! What noise? Who calls on Hamlet? O,
here they come.

Enter Rosencrantz and Guildenstern.

Ros. What have you done, my lord, with the dead body?

Ham. Compounded it with dust, whereto 'tis kin.   6

Ros. Tell us where 'tis, that we may take it thence
And bear it to the chapel.

Ham. Do not believe it.

Ros. Believe what?   10

Ham. That I can keep your counsel, and not mine own. Besides, to be demanded of a sponge, what replication should be made by the son of a king?

Ros. Take you me for a sponge, my lord?   15

Ham. Ay, sir; that soaks up the King's countenance, his rewards, his authorities. But such officers do the King best service in the end. He keeps them, like an ape, in the corner of his jaw; first mouth'd, to be last swallowed. When he needs what you have glean'd, it is but squeezing you and, sponge, you shall be dry again.

Ros. I understand you not, my lord.

Ham. I am glad of it. A knavish speech sleeps in a foolish ear.   25

Ros. My lord, you must tell us where the body is and go with us to the King.

Ham. The body is with the King, but the King is not with the body. The King is a thing—

Guil. A thing, my lord?

Ham. Of nothing. Bring me to him. Hide fox, and all after.

Exeunt.

[Scene III. *Elsinore. A room in the Castle.*]

Enter *King.*

King. I have sent to seek him and to find the body.
How dangerous is it that this man goes loose!
Yet must not we put the strong law on him.
He's lov'd of the distracted multitude,
Who like not in their judgment, but their eyes;   5
And where 'tis so, th' offender's scourge is weigh'd,
But never the offence. To bear all smooth and even,

This sudden sending him away must seem
Deliberate pause. Diseases desperate grown
By desperate appliance are reliev'd,   10
Or not at all.

Enter Rosencrantz.

        How now? What hath befall'n?
  Ros. Where the dead body is bestow'd, my lord,
We cannot get from him.
  King.   But where is he?
  Ros. Without, my lord; guarded, to know your pleasure.
  King. Bring him before us.   15
  Ros. Ho, Guildenstern! Bring in my lord.

Enter Hamlet and Guildenstern [with Attendants].

  King. Now, Hamlet, where's Polonius?
  Ham. At supper.
  King. At supper? Where?   19
  Ham. Not where he eats, but where he is eaten. A certain
convocation of politic worms are e'en at him. Your worm is
your only emperor for diet. We fat all creatures else to fat us,
and we fat ourselves for maggots. Your fat king and your lean
beggar is but variable service—two dishes, but to one table.
That's the end.
  King. Alas, alas!
  Ham. A man may fish with the worm that hath eat of a
king, and eat of the fish that hath fed of that worm.   30
  King. What dost thou mean by this?
  Ham. Nothing but to show you how a king may go a
progress through the guts of a beggar.
  King. Where is Polonius?   34
  Ham. In heaven. Send thither to see. If your messenger
find him not there, seek him i' th' other place yourself. But

indeed, if you find him not within this month, you shall nose
him as you go up the stairs into the lobby.

King. Go seek him there. [*To Attendants.*]

Ham. He will stay till you come.   41

[*Exeunt Attendants.*]

King. Hamlet, this deed, for thine especial safety,—
Which we do tender as we dearly grieve
For that which thou hast done,—must send thee hence
With fiery quickness. Therefore prepare thyself.   45
The bark is ready and the wind at help,
Th' associates tend, and everything is bent
For England.

Ham.   For England?

King.   Ay, Hamlet.

Ham.   Good.

King. So is it, if thou knew'st our purposes.

Ham. I see a cherub that sees them. But come, for England!
Farewell, dear mother.   51

King. Thy loving father, Hamlet.

Ham. My mother! Father and mother is man and wife;
man and wife is one flesh; and so, my mother. Come, for
England!   *Exit.*

King. Follow him at foot; tempt him with speed aboard.
Delay it not; I'll have him hence to-night.
Away! for everything is seal'd and done
That else leans on th' affair. Pray you make haste.

[*Exeunt Rosencrantz and Guildenstern.*]

And, England, if my love thou hold'st at aught,—   60
As my great power thereof may give thee sense,
Since yet thy cicatrice looks raw and red
After the Danish sword, and thy free awe
Pays homage to us,—thou mayst not coldly set
Our sovereign process, which imports at full,   65
By letters congruing to that effect,

The present death of Hamlet. Do it, England;
For like the hectic in my blood he rages,
And thou must cure me. Till I know 'tis done,
Howe'er my haps, my joys were ne'er begun.　　*Exit.*

[Scene IV. *Near Elsinore.*]

Enter *Fortinbras* with his *Army* over the stage.

For. Go, Captain, from me greet the Danish king.
Tell him that by his license Fortinbras
Craves the conveyance of a promis'd march
Over his kingdom. You know the rendezvous.
If that his Majesty would aught with us,　　5
We shall express our duty in his eye;
And let him know so.
　　Capt.　　　　　I will do't, my lord.
For. Go softly on.

　　　　　　　　　Exeunt [all but the Captain].

Enter *Hamlet, Rosencrantz, [Guildenstern,]* and others.

Ham. Good sir, whose powers are these?
Capt. They are of Norway, sir.　　10
Ham. How purpos'd, sir, I pray you?
Capt. Against some part of Poland.
Ham. Who commands them, sir?
Capt. The nephew to old Norway, Fortinbras.
Ham. Goes it against the main of Poland, sir,　　15
Or for some frontier?
Capt. Truly to speak, and with no addition,
We go to gain a little patch of ground
That hath in it no profit but the name.
To pay five ducats, five, I would not farm it;　　20
Nor will it yield to Norway or the Pole
A ranker rate, should it be sold in fee.

Ham. Why, then the Polack never will defend it.

Capt. Yes, it is already garrison'd.

Ham. Two thousand souls and twenty thousand ducats   25
Will not debate the question of this straw.
This is th' imposthume of much wealth and peace,
That inward breaks, and shows no cause without
Why the man dies.—I humbly thank you, sir.

Capt. God b' wi' you, sir.   [*Exit.*]

Ros.   Will 't please you go, my lord?

Ham. I'll be with you straight. Go a little before.   31
                                    [*Exeunt all but Hamlet.*]
How all occasions do inform against me
And spur my dull revenge! What is a man,
If his chief good and market of his time
Be but to sleep and feed? A beast, no more.   35
Sure he that made us with such large discourse,
Looking before and after, gave us not
That capability and godlike reason
To fust in us unus'd. Now, whether it be
Bestial oblivion, or some craven scruple   40
Of thinking too precisely on th' event,—
A thought which, quarter'd, hath but one part wisdom
And ever three parts coward,—I do not know
Why yet I live to say 'This thing's to do,'
Sith I have cause, and will, and strength, and means   45
To do't. Examples gross as earth exhort me.
Witness this army of such mass and charge,
Led by a delicate and tender prince,
Whose spirit, with divine ambition puff'd,
Makes mouths at the invisible event,   50
Exposing what is mortal and unsure
To all that fortune, death, and danger dare,
Even for an eggshell. Rightly to be great
Is not to stir without great argument,

But greatly to find quarrel in a straw   55
When honour's at the stake. How stand I then,
That have a father kill'd, a mother stain'd,
Excitements of my reason and my blood,
And let all sleep, while to my shame I see
The imminent death of twenty thousand men   60
That for a fantasy and trick of fame
Go to their graves like beds, fight for a plot
Whereon the numbers cannot try the cause,
Which is not tomb enough and continent
To hide the slain? O, from this time forth,   65
My thoughts be bloody, or be nothing worth!   *Exit.*

[Scene V. *Elsinore. A room in the Castle.*]

Enter *Horatio, Queen,* and a *Gentleman.*

Queen. I will not speak with her.
Gent. She is importunate, indeed distract.
Her mood will needs be pitied.
Queen.   What would she have?
Gent. She speaks much of her father; says she hears
There's tricks i' th' world, and hems, and beats her heart;   5
Spurns enviously at straws; speaks things in doubt,
That carry but half sense. Her speech is nothing,
Yet the unshaped use of it doth move
The hearers to collection; they aim at it,
And botch the words up fit to their own thoughts;   10
Which, as her winks and nods and gestures yield them,
Indeed would make one think there might be thought,
Though nothing sure, yet much unhappily.
Hor. 'Twere good she were spoken with; for she may strew
Dangerous conjectures in ill-breeding minds.   15

Queen. Let her come in.

[*Exit Gentleman.*]

[*Aside*] To my sick soul (as sin's true nature is)
Each toy seems prologue to some great amiss.
So full of artless jealousy is guilt
It spills itself in fearing to be spilt.   20

Enter *Ophelia* distracted.

Oph. Where is the beauteous Majesty of Denmark?
Queen. How now, Ophelia?

Oph. (*sings*)
            How should I your true-love know
                From another one?
            By his cockle hat and staff   25
                And his sandal shoon.

Queen. Alas, sweet lady, what imports this song?
Oph. Say you? Nay, pray you mark.

(*Sings*) He is dead and gone, lady,
                He is dead and gone;   30
            At his head a grass-green turf,
                At his heels a stone.

O, ho!
Queen. Nay, but Ophelia—
Oph. Pray you mark.

(*Sings*) White his shroud as the mountain snow—   35

Enter *King.*

Queen. Alas, look here, my lord!

Oph. (*sings*)
            Larded all with sweet flowers;
            Which bewept to the grave did not go
                With true-love showers.

King. How do you, pretty lady?   40

Oph. Well, God dild you! They say the owl was a baker's daughter. Lord, we know what we are, but know not what we may be. God be at your table!

King. Conceit upon her father.   45

Oph. Pray let's have no words of this; but when they ask you what it means, say you this:

(*Sings*) To-morrow is Saint Valentine's day,
　　　All in the morning betime,
　　And I a maid at your window,   50
　　　To be your Valentine.

Then up he rose and donn'd his clo'es
　　And dupp'd the chamber door,
Let in the maid, that out a maid
　　Never departed more.   55

King. Pretty Ophelia!

Oph. Indeed, la, without an oath, I'll make an end on't!

[*Sings*] By Gis and by Saint Charity,
　　　Alack, and fie for shame!
　　Young men will do't if they come to't.   60
　　　By Cock, they are to blame.

Quoth she, 'Before you tumbled me,
　　You promis'd me to wed.'

He answers:

'So would I 'a' done, by yonder sun,
　　An thou hadst not come to my bed.'

King. How long hath she been thus?   67

Oph. I hope all will be well. We must be patient; but I cannot choose but weep to think they would lay him i' th' cold ground. My brother shall know of it; and so I thank you for your good counsel. Come, my coach! Good night, ladies. Good night, sweet ladies. Good night, good night.   *Exit*

    King. Follow her close; give her good watch, I pray you.
                                           [*Exit Horatio.*]
O, this is the poison of deep grief; it springs   76
All from her father's death. O Gertrude, Gertrude,
When sorrows come, they come not single spies.
But in battalions! First, her father slain;
Next, your son gone, and he most violent author   80
Of his own just remove; the people muddied,
Thick and unwholesome in their thoughts and whispers
For good Polonius' death, and we have done but greenly
In hugger-mugger to inter him; poor Ophelia
Divided from herself and her fair judgment,   85
Without the which we are pictures or mere beasts;
Last, and as much containing as all these,
Her brother is in secret come from France;
Feeds on his wonder, keeps himself in clouds,
And wants not buzzers to infect his ear   90
With pestilent speeches of his father's death,
Wherein necessity, of matter beggar'd,
Will nothing stick our person to arraign
In ear and ear. O my dear Gertrude, this,
Like to a murd'ring piece, in many places   95
Gives me superfluous death.   *A noise within.*
    Queen.   Alack, what noise is this?
    King. Where are my Switzers? Let them guard the door.

Enter a *Messenger.*

What is the matter?
    Mess.   Save yourself, my lord:
The ocean, overpeering of his list,
Eats not the flats with more impetuous haste   100
Than young Laertes, in a riotous head,
O'erbears your officers. The rabble call him lord;
And, as the world were now but to begin,

Antiquity forgot, custom not known,
The ratifiers and props of every word,   105
They cry 'Choose we! Laertes shall be king!'
Caps, hands, and tongues applaud it to the clouds,
'Laertes shall be king! Laertes king!'

                                                    A noise within.
  Queen. How cheerfully on the false trail they cry!
O, this is counter, you false Danish dogs!   110
  King. The doors are broke.

     Enter *Laertes* with others.

  Laer. Where is this king?—Sirs, stand you all without.
  All. No, let's come in!
  Laer.   I pray you give me leave.
  All. We will, we will!
  Laer. I thank you. Keep the door. [*Exeunt his Followers.*]
   O thou vile king,   115
Give me my father!
  Queen.   Calmly, good Laertes.
  Laer. That drop of blood that's calm proclaims me bastard;
Cries cuckold to my father; brands the harlot
Even here between the chaste unsmirched brows
Of my true mother.
  King.   What is the cause, Laertes,   120
That thy rebellion looks so giantlike?
Let him go, Gertrude. Do not fear our person.
There's such divinity doth hedge a king
That treason can but peep to what it would,
Acts little of his will. Tell me, Laertes,   125
Why thou art thus incens'd. Let him go, Gertrude.
Speak, man.
  Laer. Where is my father?
  King.   Dead.
  Queen.   But not by him!

   King. Let him demand his fill.

   Laer. How came he dead? I'll not be juggled with: 130
To hell, allegiance! vows, to the blackest devil!
Conscience and grace, to the profoundest pit!
I dare damnation. To this point I stand,
That both the worlds I give to negligence,
Let come what comes; only I'll be reveng'd 135
Most throughly for my father.

   King.   Who shall stay you?

   Laer. My will, not all the world!
And for my means, I'll husband them so well
They shall go far with little.

   King.   Good Laertes,
If you desire to know the certainty 140
Of your dear father's death, is't writ in your revenge
That swoopstake you will draw both friend and foe,
Winner and loser?

   Laer. None but his enemies.

   King.   Will you know them then?

   Laer. To his good friends thus wide I'll ope my arms 145
And, like the kind life-rend'ring pelican,
Repast them with my blood.

   King.   Why, now you speak
Like a good child and a true gentleman.
That I am guiltless of your father's death,
And am most sensibly in grief for it, 150
It shall as level to your judgment pierce
As day does to your eye.

                A noise within: 'Let her come in.'

   Laer. How now? What noise is that?

Enter *Ophelia.*

O heat, dry up my brains! Tears seven times salt
Burn out the sense and virtue of mine eye! 155

By heaven, thy madness shall be paid by weight
Till our scale turn the beam. O rose of May!
Dear maid, kind sister, sweet Ophelia!
O heavens! is't possible a young maid's wits
Should be as mortal as an old man's life?   16C
Nature is fine in love, and where 'tis fine,
It sends some precious instance of itself
After the thing it loves.

    Oph. (*sings*)
           They bore him barefac'd on the bier
             (Hey non nony, nony, hey nony)   16$
           And in his grave rain'd many a tear.

Fare you well, my dove!

    Laer. Hadst thou thy wits, and didst persuade revenge,
It could not move thus.   169

    Oph. You must sing 'A-down a-down, and you call him
a-down-a.' O, how the wheel becomes it! It is the false steward,
that stole his master's daughter.

    Laer. This nothing's more than matter.   174

    Oph. There's rosemary, that's for remembrance. Pray you,
love, remember. And there is pansies, that's for thoughts.

    Laer. A document in madness! Thoughts and remembrance
fitted.   179

    Oph. There's fennel for you, and columbines. There's
rue for you, and here's some for me. We may call it herb
of grace o' Sundays. O, you must wear your rue with a difference! There's a daisy. I would give you some violets, but
they wither'd all when my father died. They say he made a
good end.   186

    [*Sings*] For bonny sweet Robin is all my joy.

    Laer. Thought and affliction, passion, hell itself,
She turns to favour and to prettiness.

Oph. (sings)

And will he not come again?   190
And will he not come again?
  No, no, he is dead;
  Go to thy deathbed;
He never will come again.

His beard was as white as snow,   195
All flaxen was his poll.
  He is gone, he is gone,
  And we cast away moan.
God 'a' mercy on his soul!

And of all Christian souls, I pray God. God b' wi' you.   *Exit.*

  Laer. Do you see this, O God?   201

  King. Laertes, I must commune with your grief,
Or you deny me right. Go but apart,
Make choice of whom your wisest friends you will,
And they shall hear and judge 'twixt you and me.   205
If by direct or by collateral hand
They find us touch'd, we will our kingdom give,
Our crown, our life, and all that we call ours,
To you in satisfaction; but if not,
Be you content to lend your patience to us,   210
And we shall jointly labour with your soul
To give it due content.

  Laer.   Let this be so.
His means of death, his obscure funeral—
No trophy, sword, nor hatchment o'er his bones,
No noble rite nor formal ostentation,—   215
Cry to be heard, as 'twere from heaven to earth,
That I must call't in question.

  King.   So you shall;
And where th' offence is let the great axe fall.
I pray you go with me.

Exeunt

[Scene VI. *Elsinore. Another room in the Castle.*]

Enter Horatio *with an* Attendant.

Hor. What are they that would speak with me?

Servant. Seafaring men, sir. They say they have letters for you.

Hor. Let them come in.

[*Exit Attendant.*]

I do not know from what part of the world
I should be greeted, if not from Lord Hamlet.   5

Enter Sailors.

Sailor. God bless you, sir.

Hor. Let him bless thee too.

Sailor. 'A shall, sir, an't please him. There's a letter for you, sir,—it comes from th' ambassador that was bound for England—if your name be Horatio, as I am let to know it is.   11

Hor. (*reads the letter*) 'Horatio, when thou shalt have overlook'd this, give these fellows some means to the King. They have letters for him. Ere we were two days old at sea, a pirate of very warlike appointment gave us chase. Finding ourselves too slow of sail, we put on a compelled valour, and in the grapple I boarded them. On the instant they got clear of our ship; so I alone became their prisoner. They have dealt with me like thieves of mercy; but they knew what they did: I am to do a good turn for them. Let the King have the letters I have sent, and repair thou to me with as much speed as thou wouldst fly death. I have words to speak in thine ear will make thee dumb; yet are they much too light for the bore of the matter. These good fellows will bring thee where I am. Rosencrantz and Guildenstern hold their course for England. Of them I have much to tell thee. Farewell.   30

'He that thou knowest thine, HAMLET.'

Come, I will give you way for these your letters,
And do't the speedier that you may direct me
To him from whom you brought them.   *Exeunt.*

[Scene VII. *Elsinore. Another room in the Castle.*]

Enter *King* and *Laertes*.

King. Now must your conscience my acquittance seal,
And you must put me in your heart for friend,
Sith you have heard, and with a knowing ear,
That he which hath your noble father slain
Pursued my life.

Laer.   It well appears. But tell me   5
Why you proceeded not against these feats
So crimeful and so capital in nature,
As by your safety, wisdom, all things else,
You mainly were stirr'd up.

King.   O, for two special reasons,
Which may to you, perhaps, seem much unsinew'd,   10
But yet to me they are strong. The Queen his mother
Lives almost by his looks; and for myself,—
My virtue or my plague, be it either which,—
She's so conjunctive to my life and soul
That, as the star moves not but in his sphere,   15
I could not but by her. The other motive
Why to a public count I might not go
Is the great love the general gender bear him,
Who, dipping all his faults in their affection,
Would, like the spring that turneth wood to stone,   20
Convert his gyves to graces; so that my arrows,
Too slightly timber'd for so loud a wind,
Would have reverted to my bow again,
And not where I had aim'd them.

Laer. And so have I a noble father lost;   25
A sister driven into desp'rate terms,
Whose worth, if praises may go back again,
Stood challenger on mount of all the age
For her perfections. But my revenge will come.

King. Break not your sleeps for that. You must not think   30
That we are made of stuff so flat and dull
That we can let our beard be shook with danger,
And think it pastime. You shortly shall hear more.
I lov'd your father, and we love ourself,
And that, I hope, will teach you to imagine—   35

Enter a *Messenger* with letters.

How now? What news?
   Mess.   Letters, my lord, from Hamlet:
This to your Majesty; this to the Queen.
   King. From Hamlet? Who brought them?
   Mess. Sailors, my lord, they say; I saw them not.
They were given me by Claudio; he receiv'd them   40
Of him that brought them.
   King.   Laertes, you shall hear them.
Leave us.

Exit Messenger.

[*Reads*]'High and Mighty,—You shall know I am set naked
on your kingdom. To-morrow shall I beg leave to see your kingly
eyes; when I shall (first asking your pardon thereunto) recount
the occasion of my sudden and more strange return.

'HAMLET.'

What should this mean? Are all the rest come back?   50
Or is it some abuse, and no such thing?
   Laer. Know you the hand?
   King.   'Tis Hamlet's character. 'Naked!'
And in a postscript here, he says 'alone.'
Can you advise me?
   Laer. I am lost in it, my lord. But let him come!   55
It warms the very sickness in my heart
That I shall live and tell him to his teeth,
'Thus didest thou.'
   King.   If it be so, Laertes

(As how should it be so? how otherwise?),
Will you be rul'd by me?

    Laer.   Ay, my lord,   60
So you will not o'errule me to a peace.

    King. To thine own peace. If he be now return'd,
As checking at his voyage, and that he means
No more to undertake it, I will work him
To an exploit now ripe in my device,   65
Under the which he shall not choose but fall;
And for his death no wind of blame shall breathe,
But even his mother shall uncharge the practice
And call it accident.

    Laer.   My lord, I will be rul'd;
The rather, if you could devise it so   70
That I might be the organ.

    King.   It falls right.
You have been talk'd of since your travel much,
And that in Hamlet's hearing, for a quality
Wherein they say you shine. Your sum of parts
Did not together pluck such envy from him   75
As did that one; and that, in my regard,
Of the unworthiest siege.

    Laer.   What part is that, my lord?

    King. A very riband in the cap of youth—
Yet needful too; for youth no less becomes
The light and careless livery that it wears   80
Than settled age his sables and his weeds,
Importing health and graveness. Two months since
Here was a gentleman of Normandy.
I have seen myself, and serv'd against, the French,
And they can well on horseback; but this gallant   85
Had witchcraft in't. He grew unto his seat,
And to such wondrous doing brought his horse
As had he been incorps'd and demi-natur'd

With the brave beast. So far he topp'd my thought
That I, in forgery of shapes and tricks,   90
Come short of what he did.

    Laer.   A Norman was't?

    King. A Norman.

    Laer. Upon my life, Lamound.

    King.   The very same.

    Laer. I know him well. He is the brooch indeed
And gem of all the nation.   95

    King. He made confession of you;
And gave you such a masterly report
For art and exercise in your defence,
And for your rapier most especially,
That he cried out 'twould be a sight indeed   100
If one could match you. The scrimers of their nation
He swore had neither motion, guard, nor eye,
If you oppos'd them. Sir, this report of his
Did Hamlet so envenom with his envy
That he could nothing do but wish and beg   105
Your sudden coming o'er to play with you.
Now, out of this—

    Laer.   What out of this, my lord?

    King. Laertes, was your father dear to you?
Or are you like the painting of a sorrow,
A face without a heart?

    Laer.   Why ask you this?   110

    King. Not that I think you did not love your father;
But that I know love is begun by time,
And that I see, in passages of proof,
Time qualifies the spark and fire of it.
There lives within the very flame of love   115
A kind of wick or snuff that will abate it;
And nothing is at a like goodness still;
For goodness, growing to a plurisy,

Dies in his own too-much. That we would do,
We should do when we would; for this 'would' changes, 120
And hath abatements and delays as many
As there are tongues, are hands, are accidents;
And then this 'should' is like a spendthrift sigh,
That hurts by easing. But to the quick o' th' ulcer!
Hamlet comes back. What would you undertake 125
To show yourself your father's son in deed
More than in words?

Laer.   To cut his throat i' th' church!

King. No place indeed should murther sanctuarize;
Revenge should have no bounds. But, good Laertes,
Will you do this? Keep close within your chamber. 130
Hamlet return'd shall know you are come home.
We'll put on those shall praise your excellence
And set a double varnish on the fame
The Frenchman gave you; bring you in fine together
And wager on your heads. He, being remiss, 135
Most generous, and free from all contriving,
Will not peruse the foils; so that with ease,
Or with a little shuffling, you may choose
A sword unbated, and, in a pass of practice,
Requite him for your father.

Laer.   I will do't! 140
And for that purpose I'll anoint my sword.
I bought an unction of a mountebank,
So mortal that, but dip a knife in it,
Where it draws blood no cataplasm so rare,
Collected from all simples that have virtue 145
Under the moon, can save the thing from death
This is but scratch'd withal. I'll touch my point
With this contagion, that, if I gall him slightly,
It may be death.

King.   Let's further think of this,

Weigh what convenience both of time and means   150
May fit us to our shape. If this should fail,
And that our drift look through our bad performance,
'Twere better not assay'd. Therefore this project
Should have a back or second, that might hold
If this did blast in proof. Soft! let me see.   155
We'll make a solemn wager on your cunnings—
I ha't!
When in your motion you are hot and dry—
As make your bouts more violent to that end—
And that he calls for drink, I'll have prepar'd him   160
A chalice for the nonce; whereon but sipping,
If he by chance escape your venom'd stuck,
Our purpose may hold there.—But stay, what noise?

Enter *Queen*.

How now, sweet queen?
   Queen. One woe doth tread upon another's heel,   165
So fast they follow. Your sister's drown'd, Laertes.
   Laer. Drown'd! O, where?
   Queen. There is a willow grows aslant a brook,
That shows his hoar leaves in the glassy stream.
There with fantastic garlands did she come   170
Of crowflowers, nettles, daisies, and long purples,
That liberal shepherds give a grosser name,
But our cold maids do dead men's fingers call them.
There on the pendent boughs her coronet weeds
Clamb'ring to hang, an envious sliver broke,   175
When down her weedy trophies and herself
Fell in the weeping brook. Her clothes spread wide
And, mermaid-like, awhile they bore her up;
Which time she chaunted snatches of old tunes,
As one incapable of her own distress,   180
Or like a creature native and indued

Unto that element; but long it could not be
Till that her garments, heavy with their drink,
Pull'd the poor wretch from her melodious lay
To muddy death.

    Laer.   Alas, then she is drown'd? 185
    Queen. Drown'd, drown'd.
    Laer. Too much of water hast thou, poor Ophelia,
And therefore I forbid my tears; but yet
It is our trick; nature her custom holds,
Let shame say what it will. When these are gone, 190
The woman will be out. Adieu, my lord.
I have a speech of fire, that fain would blaze
But that this folly douts it.   *Exit.*
    King.   Let's follow, Gertrude.
How much I had to do to calm his rage!
Now fear I this will give it start again; 195
Therefore let's follow.

                                    Exeunt.

Enter two *Clowns*, [with spades and pickaxes].

Clown. Is she to be buried in Christian burial when she wilfully seeks her own salvation?

Other. I tell thee she is; therefore make her grave straight. The crowner hath sate on her, and finds it Christian burial. 5

Clown. How can that be, unless she drown'd herself in her own defence?

Other. Why, 'tis found so.

Clown. It must be *se offendendo*; it cannot be else. For here lies the point: if I drown myself wittingly, it argues an act; and an act hath three branches—it is to act, to do, and to perform; argal, she drown'd herself wittingly. 13

Other. Nay, but hear you, Goodman Delver!

Clown. Give me leave. Here lies the water; good. Here stands the man; good. If the man go to this water and drown himself, it is, will he nill he, he goes—mark you that. But if the water come to him and drown him, he drowns not himself. Argal, he that is not guilty of his own death shortens not his own life.

Other. But is this law?

Clown. Ay, marry, is't—crowner's quest law. 25

Other. Will you ha' the truth an't? If this had not been a gentlewoman, she should have been buried out o' Christian burial.

Clown. Why, there thou say'st! And the more pity that great folk should have count'nance in this world to drown or hang themselves more than their even-Christen. Come, my spade! There is no ancient gentlemen but gard'ners, ditchers, and grave-makers. They hold up Adam's profession. 35

Other. Was he a gentleman?

Clown. 'A was the first that ever bore arms.

Other. Why, he had none.

Clown. What, art a heathen? How dost thou understand the Scripture? The Scripture says Adam digg'd. Could he dig without arms? I'll put another question to thee. If thou answerest me not to the purpose, confess thyself—

Other. Go to! 45

Clown. What is he that builds stronger than either the mason, the shipwright, or the carpenter?

Other. The gallows-maker; for that frame outlives a thousand tenants. 50

Clown. I like thy wit well, in good faith. The gallows does well. But how does it well? It does well to those that do ill. Now, thou dost ill to say the gallows is built stronger than the church. Argal, the gallows may do well to thee. To't again, come! 56

Other. Who builds stronger than a mason, a shipwright, or a carpenter?

Clown. Ay, tell me that, and unyoke.

Other. Marry, now I can tell! 60

Clown. To't.

Other. Mass, I cannot tell.

Enter Hamlet and Horatio afar off.

Clown. Cudgel thy brains no more about it, for your dull ass will not mend his pace with beating; and when you are ask'd this question next, say 'a grave-maker.' The houses he makes lasts till doomsday. Go, get thee to Yaughan; fetch me a stoup of liquor.

[*Exit Second Clown.*]

[*Clown digs and*] *sings.*

In youth when I did love, did love,
    Methought it was very sweet; 70
To contract—O—the time for—a—my behove,
    O, methought there—a—was nothing—a—meet.

Ham. Has this fellow no feeling of his business, that he sings at grave-making?

Hor. Custom hath made it in him a property of easiness. 76

Ham. 'Tis e'en so. The hand of little employment hath the daintier sense.

Clown. (*sings*)

> But age with his stealing steps
> Hath clawed me in his clutch,
> And hath shipped me intil the land,   80
> As if I had never been such.

[*Throws up a skull.*]

Ham. That skull had a tongue in it, and could sing once. How the knave jowls it to the ground, as if 'twere Cain's jawbone, that did the first murther! This might be the pate of a politician, which this ass now o'erreaches; one that would circumvent God, might it not?

Hor. It might, my lord.   89

Ham. Or of a courtier, which could say 'Good morrow, sweet lord! How dost thou, good lord?' This might be my Lord Such-a-one, that prais'd my Lord Such-a-one's horse when he meant to beg it—might it not?

Hor. Ay, my lord.   95

Ham. Why, e'en so! and now my Lady Worm's, chapless, and knock'd about the mazzard with a sexton's spade. Here's fine revolution, an we had the trick to see't. Did these bones cost no more the breeding but to play at loggets with 'em? Mine ache to think on't.   101

Clown. (*sings*)

> A pickaxe and a spade, a spade,
> For and a shrouding sheet;
> O, a pit of clay for to be made
> For such a guest is meet.   105

Throws up [*another skull*].

Ham. There's another. Why may not that be the skull of a lawyer? Where be his quiddits now, his quillets, his cases, his tenures, and his tricks? Why does he suffer this rude knave now to knock him about the sconce with a dirty shovel, and will not tell him of his action of battery? Hum! This fellow might be in's time a great buyer of land, with his statutes, his recognizances, his fines, his double vouchers, his recoveries. Is this the fine of his fines, and the recovery of his recoveries, to have his fine pate full of fine dirt? Will his vouchers vouch him no more of his purchases, and double ones too, than the length and breadth of a pair of indentures? The very conveyances of his lands will scarcely lie in this box; and must th' inheritor himself have no more, ha?

Hor. Not a jot more, my lord.   122

Ham. Is not parchment made of sheepskins?

Hor. Ay, my lord, and of calveskins too.

Ham. They are sheep and calves which seek out assurance in that. I will speak to this fellow. Whose grave's this, sirrah?

Clown. Mine, sir.

> [*Sings*] O, a pit of clay for to be made
> For such a guest is meet.   130

Ham. I think it be thine indeed, for thou liest in't.

Clown. You lie out on't, sir, and therefore 'tis not yours. For my part, I do not lie in't, yet it is mine.   135

Ham. Thou dost lie in't, to be in't and say it is thine. 'Tis for the dead, not for the quick; therefore thou liest.

Clown. 'Tis a quick lie, sir; 'twill away again from me to you.   140

Ham. What man dost thou dig it for?

Clown. For no man, sir.

Ham. What woman then?

Clown. For none neither.

Ham. Who is to be buried in't?   145

Clown. One that was a woman, sir; but, rest her soul, she's dead.

Ham. How absolute the knave is! We must speak by the card, or equivocation will undo us. By the Lord, Horatio, this three years I have taken note of it, the age is grown so picked that the toe of the peasant comes so near the heel of the courtier he galls his kibe.—How long hast thou been a grave-maker?

Clown. Of all the days i' th' year, I came to't that day that our last king Hamlet overcame Fortinbras.   157

Ham. How long is that since?

Clown. Cannot you tell that? Every fool can tell that. It was the very day that young Hamlet was born—he that is mad, and sent into England.   162

Ham. Ay, marry, why was he sent into England?

Clown. Why, because 'a was mad. 'A shall recover his wits there; or, if 'a do not, 'tis no great matter there.

Ham. Why?

Clown. 'Twill not be seen in him there. There the men are as mad as he.   170

Ham. How came he mad?

Clown. Very strangely, they say.

Ham. How strangely?

Clown. Faith, e'en with losing his wits.

Ham. Upon what ground?   175

Clown. Why, here in Denmark. I have been sexton here, man and boy, thirty years.

Ham. How long will a man lie i' th' earth ere he rot?   179

Clown. Faith, if 'a be not rotten before 'a die (as we have many pocky corses now-a-days that will scarce hold the laying in), 'a will last you some eight year or nine year. A tanner will last you nine year.

Ham. Why he more than another?   185

Clown. Why, sir, his hide is so tann'd with his trade that 'a will keep out water a great while; and your water is a sore de-

cayer of your whoreson dead body. Here's a skull now. This
skull hath lien you i' th' earth three-and-twenty years.   191

   Ham. Whose was it?

   Clown. A whoreson mad fellow's it was. Whose do you
think it was?

   Ham. Nay, I know not.   195

   Clown. A pestilence on him for a mad rogue! 'A pour'd a
flagon of Rhenish on my head once. This same skull, sir, was
Yorick's skull, the King's jester.

   Ham. This?   200

   Clown. E'en that.

   Ham. Let me see. [*Takes the skull.*] Alas, poor Yorick!
I knew him, Horatio. A fellow of infinite jest, of most excellent
fancy. He hath borne me on his back a thousand times. And
now how abhorred in my imagination it is! My gorge rises
at it. Here hung those lips that I have kiss'd I know not how
oft. Where be your gibes now? your gambols? your songs?
your flashes of merriment that were wont to set the table on a
roar? Not one now, to mock your own grinning? Quite chapfall'n? Now get you to my lady's chamber, and tell her, let
her paint an inch thick, to this favour she must come. Make
her laugh at that. Prithee, Horatio, tell me one thing.   216

   Hor. What's that, my lord?

   Ham. Dost thou think Alexander look'd o' this fashion i' th'
earth?

   Hor. E'en so.   220

   Ham. And smelt so? Pah!

                                        [*Puts down the skull.*]

   Hor. E'en so, my lord.

   Ham. To what base uses we may return, Horatio! Why
may not imagination trace the noble dust of Alexander till he
find it stopping a bunghole?   226

   Hor. 'Twere to consider too curiously, to consider so.

   Ham. No, faith, not a jot; but to follow him thither with

modesty enough, and likelihood to lead it; as thus: Alexander died, Alexander was buried, Alexander returneth into dust; the dust is earth; of earth we make loam; and why of that loam (whereto he was converted) might they not stop a beer barrel? 235

Imperious Cæsar, dead and turn'd to clay,
Might stop a hole to keep the wind away.
O, that that earth which kept the world in awe
Should patch a wall t' expel the winter's flaw!
But soft! but soft! aside! Here comes the King— 240

Enter [*Priests* with] a coffin [in funeral procession], *King,*
Queen, Laertes, with *Lords* attendant.

The Queen, the courtiers. Who is this they follow?
And with such maimed rites? This doth betoken
The corse they follow did with desp'rate hand
Fordo it own life. 'Twas of some estate.
Couch we awhile, and mark. 245
                                        [*Retires with Horatio.*]

 Laer. What ceremony else?
 Ham.   That is Laertes,
A very noble youth. Mark.
 Laer. What ceremony else?
 Priest. Her obsequies have been as far enlarg'd
As we have warranty. Her death was doubtful; 250
And, but that great command o'ersways the order,
She should in ground unsanctified have lodg'd
Till the last trumpet. For charitable prayers,
Shards, flints, and pebbles should be thrown on her.
Yet here she is allow'd her virgin crants, 255
Her maiden strewments, and the bringing home
Of bell and burial.
 Laer. Must there no more be done?

Priest.   No more be done.
We should profane the service of the dead
To sing a requiem and such rest to her   260
As to peace-parted souls.
    Laer.   Lay her i' th' earth;
And from her fair and unpolluted flesh
May violets spring! I tell thee, churlish priest,
A minist'ring angel shall my sister be
When thou liest howling.
    Ham.   What, the fair Ophelia?   265
    Queen. Sweets to the sweet! Farewell.
                              [*Scatters flowers.*]
I hop'd thou shouldst have been my Hamlet's wife;
I thought thy bride-bed to have deck'd, sweet maid,
And not have strew'd thy grave.
    Laer.   O, treble woe
Fall ten times treble on that cursed head   270
Whose wicked deed thy most ingenious sense
Depriv'd thee of! Hold off the earth awhile,
Till I have caught her once more in mine arms.
                              Leaps in the grave.
Now pile your dust upon the quick and dead
Till of this flat a mountain you have made   275
T' o'ertop old Pelion or the skyish head
Of blue Olympus.
    Ham. [*comes forward*] What is he whose grief
Bears such an emphasis? whose phrase of sorrow
Conjures the wand'ring stars, and makes them stand
Like wonder-wounded hearers? This is I,   280
Hamlet the Dane.   *Leaps in after Laertes.*
    Laer.   The devil take thy soul!
                              [*Grapples with him.*]
    Ham. Thou pray'st not well.
I prithee take thy fingers from my throat;

For, though I am not splenitive and rash,
Yet have I in me something dangerous,   285
Which let thy wisdom fear. Hold off thy hand!
   King. Pluck them asunder.
   Queen.   Hamlet, Hamlet!
   All. Gentlemen!
   Hor.   Good my lord, be quiet.
      [*The Attendants part them, and they come out of the
                               grave.*]

   Ham. Why, I will fight with him upon this theme
Until my eyelids will no longer wag.   290
   Queen. O my son, what theme?
   Ham. I lov'd Ophelia. Forty thousand brothers
Could not (with all their quantity of love)
Make up my sum. What wilt thou do for her?
   King. O, he is mad, Laertes.   295
   Queen. For love of God, forbear him!
   Ham. 'Swounds, show me what thou't do.
Woo't weep? woo't fight? woo't fast? woo't tear thyself?
Woo't drink up esill? eat a crocodile?
I'll do't. Dost thou come here to whine?   300
To outface me with leaping in her grave?
Be buried quick with her, and so will I.
And if thou prate of mountains, let them throw
Millions of acres on us, till our ground,
Singeing his pate against the burning zone,   305
Make Ossa like a wart! Nay, an thou'lt mouth,
I'll rant as well as thou.
   Queen.   This is mere madness;
And thus a while the fit will work on him.
Anon, as patient as the female dove
When that her golden couplets are disclos'd,   310
His silence will sit drooping.
   Ham.   Hear you, sir!

What is the reason that you use me thus?
I lov'd you ever. But it is no matter.
Let Hercules himself do what he may,
The cat will mew, and dog will have his day.   315
                                                   Exit.

  King. I pray thee, good Horatio, wait upon him.
                                              Exit Horatio.
[*To Laertes*] Strengthen your patience in our last night's
    speech.—
We'll put the matter to the present push.—
Good Gertrude, set some watch over your son.—
This grave shall have a living monument.   320
An hour of quiet shortly shall we see;
Till then in patience our proceeding be.

                                                Exeunt.

[Scene II. *Elsinore. A hall in the Castle.*]

Enter *Hamlet* and *Horatio.*

  Ham. So much for this, sir; now shall you see the other.
You do remember all the circumstance?
  Hor. Remember it, my lord!
  Ham. Sir, in my heart there was a kind of fighting
That would not let me sleep. Methought I lay   5
Worse than the mutines in the bilboes. Rashly—
And prais'd be rashness for it; let us know,
Our indiscretion sometime serves us well
When our deep plots do pall; and that should learn us
There's a divinity that shapes our ends,   10
Rough-hew them how we will—
  Hor.   That is most certain.
  Ham. Up from my cabin,
My sea-gown scarf'd about me, in the dark

Grop'd I to find out them; had my desire,
Finger'd their packet, and in fine withdrew   15
To mine own room again; making so bold
(My fears forgetting manners) to unseal
Their grand commission; where I found, Horatio
(O royal knavery!), an exact command,
Larded with many several sorts of reasons,   20
Importing Denmark's health, and England's too,
With, hoo! such bugs and goblins in my life—
That, on the supervise, no leisure bated,
No, not to stay the grinding of the axe,
My head should be struck off.

    Hor.   Is't possible?   25
    Ham. Here's the commission; read it at more leisure.
But wilt thou hear me how I did proceed?

    Hor. I beseech you.

    Ham. Being thus benetted round with villanies,
Or I could make a prologue to my brains,   30
They had begun the play. I sat me down;
Devis'd a new commission; wrote it fair.
I once did hold it, as our statists do,
A baseness to write fair, and labour'd much
How to forget that learning; but, sir, now   35
It did me yeoman's service. Wilt thou know
Th' effect of what I wrote?

    Hor.   Ay, good my lord.
    Ham. An earnest conjuration from the King,
As England was his faithful tributary,
As love between them like the palm might flourish,   40
As peace should still her wheaten garland wear
And stand a comma 'tween their amities,
And many such-like as's of great charge,
That, on the view and knowing of these contents,
Without debatement further, more or less,   45

He should the bearers put to sudden death,
Not shriving time allow'd.
   Hor.   How was this seal'd?
   Ham. Why, even in that was heaven ordinant.
I had my father's signet in my purse,
Which was the model of that Danish seal;   50
Folded the writ up in the form of th' other,
Subscrib'd it, gave't th' impression, plac'd it safely,
The changeling never known. Now, the next day
Was our sea-fight; and what to this was sequent
Thou know'st already.   55
   Hor. So Guildenstern and Rosencrantz go to't.
   Ham. Why, man, they did make love to this employment!
They are not near my conscience; their defeat
Does by their own insinuation grow.
'Tis dangerous when the baser nature comes   60
Between the pass and fell incensed points
Of mighty opposites.
   Hor.   Why, what a king is this!
   Ham. Does it not, thinks't thee, stand me now upon—
He that hath kill'd my king, and whor'd my mother;
Popp'd in between th' election and my hopes;   65
Thrown out his angle for my proper life,
And with such coz'nage—is't not perfect conscience
To quit him with this arm? And is't not to be damn'd
To let this canker of our nature come
In further evil?   70
   Hor. It must be shortly known to him from England
What is the issue of the business there.
   Ham. It will be short; the interim is mine,
And a man's life's no more than to say 'one.'
But I am very sorry, good Horatio,   75
That to Laertes I forgot myself;
For by the image of my cause I see

The portraiture of his. I'll court his favours.
But sure the bravery of his grief did put me
Into a tow'ring passion.
   Hor.   Peace! Who comes here?   80

           Enter young *Osric*, a courtier.

   Osr. Your lordship is right welcome back to Denmark.

   Ham. I humbly thank you, sir. [*Aside to Horatio*] Dost
know this waterfly?

   Hor. [*aside to Hamlet*] No, my good lord.   85

   Ham. [*aside to Horatio*] Thy state is the more gracious; for
'tis a vice to know him. He hath much land, and fertile. Let
a beast be lord of beasts, and his crib shall stand at the king's
mess. 'Tis a chough; but, as I say, spacious in the possession
of dirt.   90

   Osr. Sweet lord, if your lordship were at leisure, I should
impart a thing to you from his Majesty.

   Ham. I will receive it, sir, with all diligence of spirit. Put
your bonnet to his right use. 'Tis for the head.   96

   Osr. I thank your lordship, it is very hot.

   Ham. No, believe me, 'tis very cold; the wind is northerly.

   Osr. It is indifferent cold, my lord, indeed.   100

   Ham. But yet methinks it is very sultry and hot for my
complexion.

   Osr. Exceedingly, my lord; it is very sultry, as 'twere—I
cannot tell how. But, my lord, his Majesty bade me signify to
you that he has laid a great wager on your head. Sir, this is
the matter—

   Ham. I beseech you remember.   108
           [*Hamlet moves him to put on his hat.*]
   Osr. Nay, good my lord; for mine ease, in good faith. Sir,
here is newly come to court Laertes; believe me, an absolute
gentleman, full of most excellent differences, of very soft society and great showing. Indeed, to speak feelingly of him, he

is the card or calendar of gentry; for you shall find in him the continent of what part a gentleman would see. 116

Ham. Sir, his definement suffers no perdition in you; though, I know, to divide him inventorially would dozy th' arithmetic of memory, and yet but yaw neither in respect of his quick sail. But, in the verity of extolment, I take him to be a soul of great article, and his infusion of such dearth and rareness as, to make true diction of him, his semblable is his mirror, and who else would trace him, his umbrage, nothing more. 125

Osr. Your lordship speaks most infallibly of him.

Ham. The concernancy, sir? Why do we wrap the gentleman in our more rawer breath?

Osr. Sir? 130

Hor. [aside to Hamlet] Is't not possible to understand in another tongue? You will do't, sir, really.

Ham. What imports the nomination of this gentleman?

Osr. Of Laertes? 135

Hor. [aside] His purse is empty already. All's golden words are spent.

Ham. Of him, sir.

Osr. I know you are not ignorant—

Ham. I would you did, sir; yet, in faith, if you did, it would not much approve me. Well, sir? 142

Osr. You are not ignorant of what excellence Laertes is—

Ham. I dare not confess that, lest I should compare with him in excellence; but to know a man well were to know himself.

Osr. I mean, sir, for his weapon; but in the imputation laid on him by them, in his meed he's unfellowed. 150

Ham. What's his weapon?

Osr. Rapier and dagger.

Ham. That's two of his weapons—but well.

Osr. The King, sir, hath wager'd with him six Barbary

horses; against the which he has impon'd, as I take it, six French
rapiers and poniards, with their assigns, as girdle, hangers, and
so. Three of the carriages, in faith, are very dear to fancy, very
responsive to the hilts, most delicate carriages, and of very
liberal conceit.

Ham. What call you the carriages? 161

Hor. [*aside to Hamlet*] I knew you must be edified by the
margent ere you had done.

Osr. The carriages, sir, are the hangers. 164

Ham. The phrase would be more germane to the matter if
we could carry cannon by our sides. I would it might be
hangers till then. But on! Six Barbary horses against six
French swords, their assigns, and three liberal-conceited carriages: that's the French bet against the Danish. Why is this
all impon'd, as you call it?

Osr. The King, sir, hath laid that, in a dozen passes between
yourself and him, he shall not exceed you three hits; he hath
laid on twelve for nine, and it would come to immediate trial
if your lordship would vouchsafe the answer. 176

Ham. How if I answer no?

Osr. I mean, my lord, the opposition of your person in trial.

Ham. Sir, I will walk here in the hall. If it please his
Majesty, it is the breathing time of day with me. Let the foils
be brought, the gentleman willing, and the King hold his purpose, I will win for him if I can; if not, I will gain nothing
but my shame and the odd hits. 185

Osr. Shall I redeliver you e'en so?

Ham. To this effect, sir, after what flourish your nature will.

Osr. I commend my duty to your lordship.

Ham. Yours, yours. [*Exit Osric.*] He does well to commend
it himself; there are no tongues else for's turn. 192

Hor. This lapwing runs away with the shell on his head.

Ham. He did comply with his dug before he suck'd it. Thus
has he, and many more of the same bevy that I know the drossy

age dotes on, only got the tune of the time and outward habit
of encounter—a kind of yesty collection, which carries them
through and through the most fann'd and winnowed opinions;
and do but blow them to their trial—the bubbles are out.   202

Enter a Lord.

Lord. My lord, his Majesty commended him to you by young
Osric, who brings back to him, that you attend him in the hall.
He sends to know if your pleasure hold to play with Laertes,
or that you will take longer time.

Ham. I am constant to my purposes; they follow the King's
pleasure. If his fitness speaks, mine is ready; now or when-
soever, provided I be so able as now.   211

Lord. The King and Queen and all are coming down.

Ham. In happy time.

Lord. The Queen desires you to use some gentle entertainment to Laertes before you fall to play.

Ham. She well instructs me.   218

[Exit Lord.]

Hor. You will lose this wager, my lord.

Ham. I do not think so. Since he went into France I have
been in continual practice. I shall win at the odds. But thou
wouldst not think how ill all's here about my heart. But it is
no matter.

Hor. Nay, good my lord—   224

Ham. It is but foolery; but it is such a kind of gaingiving
as would perhaps trouble a woman.

Hor. If your mind dislike anything, obey it. I will forestall
their repair hither and say you are not fit.   229

Ham. Not a whit, we defy augury; there's a special providence in the fall of a sparrow. If it be now, 'tis not to come;
if it be not to come, it will be now; if it be not now, yet it will
come: the readiness is all. Since no man knows aught of what
he leaves, what is't to leave betimes? Let be.   235

Enter *King, Queen, Laertes*, [*Osric*], and *Lords*, with other
Attendants with foils and gauntlets. A table and flagons of
wine on it.

 King. Come, Hamlet, come, and take this hand from me.
     [*The King puts Laertes' hand into Hamlet's.*]
 Ham. Give me your pardon, sir. I have done you wrong;
But pardon't, as you are a gentleman.
This presence knows,
And you must needs have heard, how I am punish'd 240
With sore distraction. What I have done
That might your nature, honour, and exception
Roughly awake, I here proclaim was madness.
Was't Hamlet wrong'd Laertes? Never Hamlet.
If Hamlet from himself be ta'en away,   245
And when he's not himself does wrong Laertes,
Then Hamlet does it not, Hamlet denies it.
Who does it, then? His madness. If't be so,
Hamlet is of the faction that is wrong'd;
His madness is poor Hamlet's enemy.   250
Sir, in this audience,
Let my disclaiming from a purpos'd evil
Free me so far in your most generous thoughts
That I have shot my arrow o'er the house
And hurt my brother.
 Laer.   I am satisfied in nature, 255
Whose motive in this case should stir me most
To my revenge. But in my terms of honour
I stand aloof, and will no reconcilement
Till by some elder masters of known honour
I have a voice and precedent of peace   260
To keep my name ungor'd. But till that time
I do receive your offer'd love like love,
And will not wrong it.

Ham.   I embrace it freely,
And will this brother's wager frankly play.
Give us the foils. Come on.

   Laer.   Come, one for me.   265

   Ham. I'll be your foil, Laertes. In mine ignorance
Your skill shall, like a star i' th' darkest night,
Stick fiery off indeed.

   Laer.   You mock me, sir.

   Ham. No, by this hand.

   King. Give them the foils, young Osric. Cousin Hamlet,
You know the wager?

   Ham.   Very well, my lord.   271
Your Grace has laid the odds o' th' weaker side.

   King. I do not fear it, I have seen you both;
But since he is better'd, we have therefore odds.

   Laer. This is too heavy; let me see another.   275

   Ham. This likes me well. These foils have all a length?

                               Prepare to play.

   Osr. Ay, my good lord.

   King. Set me the stoups of wine upon that table.
If Hamlet give the first or second hit,
Or quit in answer of the third exchange,   280
Let all the battlements their ordnance fire;
The King shall drink to Hamlet's better breath,
And in the cup an union shall he throw
Richer than that which four successive kings
In Denmark's crown have worn. Give me the cups;   285
And let the kettle to the trumpet speak,
The trumpet to the cannoneer without,
The cannons to the heavens, the heaven to earth,
'Now the King drinks to Hamlet.' Come, begin.
And you the judges, bear a wary eye.   290

   Ham. Come on, sir.

   Laer.   Come, my lord.   *They play.*

Ham.   One.

Laer.   No.

Ham.   Judgment!

Osr. A hit, a very palpable hit.

Laer.   Well, again!

King. Stay, give me drink. Hamlet, this pearl is thine;
Here's to thy health.

                    Drum; trumpets sound; a piece goes off [*within*].
                    Give him the cup.

Ham. I'll play this bout first; set it by awhile.   295
Come. (*They play.*) Another hit. What say you?

  Laer. A touch, a touch; I do confess't.

  King. Our son shall win.

  Queen.   He's fat, and scant of breath.
Here, Hamlet, take my napkin, rub thy brows.
The Queen carouses to thy fortune, Hamlet.   300

  Ham. Good madam!

  King.   Gertrude, do not drink.

  Queen. I will, my lord; I pray you pardon me.   *Drinks.*

  King. [*aside*] It is the poison'd cup; it is too late.

  Ham. I dare not drink yet, madam; by-and-by.

  Queen. Come, let me wipe thy face.   305

  Laer. My lord, I'll hit him now.

  King.   I do not think't.

  Laer. [*aside*] And yet it is almost against my conscience.

  Ham. Come for the third, Laertes! You but dally.
I pray you pass with your best violence;
I am afeard you make a wanton of me.   310

  Laer. Say you so? Come on.   *Play.*

  Osr. Nothing neither way.

  Laer. Have at you now!

    [*Laertes wounds Hamlet; then,*] *in scuffling, they*
       change rapiers, [*and Hamlet wounds Laertes*].

  King.   Part them! They are incens'd.

Ham. Nay come! again!   *The Queen falls.*

Osr.   Look to the Queen there, ho!

Hor. They bleed on both sides. How is it, my lord?   315

Osr. How is't, Laertes?

Laer. Why, as a woodcock to mine own springe, Osric.
I am justly kill'd with mine own treachery.

Ham. How does the Queen?

King.   She sounds to see them bleed.

Queen. No, no! the drink, the drink! O my dear Hamlet!
The drink, the drink! I am poison'd.   [*Dies.*]

Ham. O villany! Ho! let the door be lock'd.   322
Treachery! Seek it out.

[*Laertes falls.*]

Laer. It is here, Hamlet. Hamlet, thou art slain;
No med'cine in the world can do thee good.   325
In thee there is not half an hour of life.
The treacherous instrument is in thy hand,
Unbated and envenom'd. The foul practice
Hath turn'd itself on me. Lo, here I lie,
Never to rise again. Thy mother's poison'd.   330
I can no more. The King, the King's to blame.

Ham. The point envenom'd too?
Then, venom, to thy work.   *Hurts the King.*

All. Treason! treason!

King. O, yet defend me, friends! I am but hurt.   335

Ham. Here, thou incestuous, murd'rous, damned Dane,
Drink off this potion! Is thy union here?
Follow my mother.   *King dies.*

Laer.   He is justly serv'd.
It is a poison temper'd by himself.
Exchange forgiveness with me, noble Hamlet.   340
Mine and my father's death come not upon thee,
Nor thine on me!   *Dies.*

Ham. Heaven make thee free of it! I follow thee.

I am dead, Horatio. Wretched queen, adieu!
You that look pale and tremble at this chance,   345
That are but mutes or audience to this act,
Had I but time (as this fell sergeant, Death,
Is strict in his arrest) O, I could tell you—
But let it be. Horatio, I am dead;
Thou liv'st; report me and my cause aright   350
To the unsatisfied.

    Hor.   Never believe it.
I am more an antique Roman than a Dane.
Here's yet some liquor left.

    Ham.   As th'art a man,
Give me the cup. Let go! By heaven, I'll ha't.
O good Horatio, what a wounded name   355
(Things standing thus unknown) shall live behind me!
If thou didst ever hold me in thy heart,
Absent thee from felicity awhile,
And in this harsh world draw thy breath in pain,
To tell my story.   *March afar off, and shot within.*
                What warlike noise is this?   360

    Osr. Young Fortinbras, with conquest come from Poland,
To the ambassadors of England gives
This warlike volley.

    Ham.   O, I die, Horatio!
The potent poison quite o'ercrows my spirit.
I cannot live to hear the news from England,   365
But I do prophesy th' election lights
On Fortinbras. He has my dying voice.
So tell him, with th' occurrents, more and less,
Which have solicited—the rest is silence.   *Dies.*

    Hor. Now cracks a noble heart. Good night, sweet prince,
And flights of angels sing thee to thy rest!   371
                          [March within.]

Why does the drum come hither?

Enter *Fortinbras* and *English Ambassadors*, with *Drum*,
             Colours, and *Attendants*.

Fort. Where is this sight?
Hor.   What is it you would see?
If aught of woe or wonder, cease your search.
Fort. This quarry cries on havoc. O proud Death,   375
What feast is toward in thine eternal cell
That thou so many princes at a shot
So bloodily hast struck?
   Ambassador.   The sight is dismal;
And our affairs from England come too late.
The ears are senseless that should give us hearing   380
To tell him his commandment is fulfill'd,
That Rosencrantz and Guildenstern are dead.
Where should we have our thanks?
Hor.   Not from his mouth,
Had it th' ability of life to thank you.
He never gave commandment for their death.   385
But since, so jump upon this bloody question,
You from the Polack wars, and you from England,
Are here arriv'd, give order that these bodies
High on a stage be placed to the view;
And let me speak to th' yet unknowing world   390
How these things came about. So shall you hear
Of carnal, bloody, and unnatural acts;
Of accidental judgments, casual slaughters;
Of deaths put on by cunning and forc'd cause;
And, in this upshot, purposes mistook   395
Fall'n on th' inventors' heads. All this can I
Truly deliver.
   Fort.   Let us haste to hear it,
And call the noblest to the audience.
For me, with sorrow I embrace my fortune.

I have some rights of memory in this kingdom,   400
Which now to claim my vantage doth invite me.
   Hor. Of that I shall have also cause to speak,
And from his mouth whose voice will draw on more.
But let this same be presently perform'd,
Even while men's minds are wild, lest more mischance   405
On plots and errors happen.
   Fort.   Let four captains
Bear Hamlet like a soldier to the stage;
For he was likely, had he been put on,
To have prov'd most royally; and for his passage
The soldiers' music and the rites of war   410
Speak loudly for him.
Take up the bodies. Such a sight as this
Becomes the field, but here shows much amiss.
Go, bid the soldiers shoot.

       Exeunt marching; after the which a peal of ordinance
                                    are shot off.

NOTES

This scene takes place on a high 'platform'—a paved terrace—before the Castle at Elsinore (Helsingör). See i, 2, 213, 252.

2. **Nay, answer me.** *Me* is emphatic. Bernardo, in hailing Francisco, instinctively uses the sentinel's formula. Francisco, with a touch of humour, suggests that it is rather his business to ask this question of Bernardo than Bernardo's to ask it of him. Cf. l. 14.—**unfold:** disclose.

3. **Long live the King!** Not, apparently, the watchword or countersign but merely a customary exclamation. Francisco, who is expecting Bernardo, recognizes his voice.

9. **sick at heart:** depressed; in low spirits.

13. **rivals:** partners.

15, 16. **the Dane:** the Danish king.—**Give:** God give.

19. **A piece of him.** A mildly humorous affirmative. Cf. *Titus Andronicus*, iv, 2, 51–54:

> *Nurse.*   Good morrow, lords.
> O, tell me, did you see Aaron the Moor?
> *Aaron.* Well, more or less, or ne'er a whit at all!
> Here Aaron is; and what with Aaron now?

Beaumont and Fletcher, *Thierry and Theodoret*, iii, 2:

> *Bawdber.* De Vitry, I take it.
> *De Vitry.* All that's left of him;

Southern, *The Maid's Last Prayer*, 1693, iv, 3, p. 44:

> *Lady Susan.* Mr. Granger! is 't you?
> *Granger.* The best part of him, Madam.

Horatio is a sedate person, constitutionally prone to such mild pleasantries. Cf. i, 5, 125, 126; iii, 2, 93, 94, 290, 296; iv, 6, 7; v, 2, 162, 163.

23–26. **fantasy:** imagination.—**of us:** by us.—**along:** i.e., to come along. Ellipsis of a verb of motion is very common.

29. **approve our eyes:** prove the trustworthiness of our eyes.
—**speak to it.** They have not ventured to speak to the Ghost,
for it was thought dangerous to address an apparition, except
in due form. Cf. *Merry Wives*, v, 5, 51: 'They are fairies. He
that speaks to them shall die'; *Macbeth*, iv, 1, 89: 'Listen, but
speak not to't.'

33. **What . . . seen.** This clause is the object of *assail your
ears*, i.e., 'force you to hear' (with the suggestion of an attempt
to convince): 'may make one more attempt to get a hearing
from you for our account of what we have seen.'

37. **his:** its; the regular genitive of the neuter pronoun. See
i, 2, 216, note.

42. **Thou art a scholar,** etc. Commonly but erroneously explained in accordance with Douce's note, 'that the exorcisms
of troublesome spirits were usually performed in Latin.' Horatio is not asked to drive away the apparition, but to question
it, in order to discover what it is and why it appears. To accost
the spirit was hazardous, for it might be a demon. Horatio,
as a scholar, knows how to address the apparition in the right
way, so as neither to offend it nor to subject himself to any evil
influence. His language is formal and solemn, but he uses no
Latin and utters no exorcism. See also ll. 126–139.

48, 49. **Denmark:** the King of Denmark. Cf. l. 61; i, 2, 28,
69, 125; iv, 3, 60, 67.—**sometimes:** sometime, formerly.

56–58. **might:** could.—**the . . . eyes:** the testimony of my
own eyes, which is a matter of the senses and must be true.

61. **Norway:** the elder Fortinbras (ll. 80–86).

62. **parle:** parley; conference between hostile leaders.

63. **smote.** The parley broke up in a battle, in which the
King smote (routed) the Polanders. Cf. *Judges*, iii, 13: 'And
he . . . went and smote Israel.'—**the sledded Polacks:** the
Polanders, who ride in sledges. See Textual Notes.

65. **jump:** exactly, precisely. Cf. v, 2, 386; *Othello*, ii, 3, 392.

68. **in . . . opinion:** in the general view or range of my
opinion (as opposed to any precise thought). *Gross and scope*
is hendiadys for 'gross scope.' Cf. 'law and heraldry' for
'heraldic law' (l. 87).

70. **Good:** my good friend. Cf. *Comedy of Errors*, iv, 4, 22; *Winter's Tale*, v, 1, 19; *Antony and Cleopatra*, i, 2, 25; i, 3, 78.—**tell . . . knows:** Let him who knows tell me.

72. **subject.** Collective for 'subjects.' Cf. i, 2, 33.

74. **foreign mart:** dealing with foreign countries; negotiations abroad.

75. **impress.** Shipcarpenters were impressed (conscripted) in time of war.

77. **might be toward:** could be in preparation, in the offing.

81. **image:** exact likeness. Cf. iii, 2, 248; *Winter's Tale*, v, 1, 127.

83. **emulate pride:** pride of rivalry; a proud desire to rival him.

86. **compáct.** Accented on the second syllable.

87. **law and heraldry:** heraldic law, i.e., a decree made and ratified by the heralds of both countries; equivalent to what we call 'international law.' The Second Quarto reads 'heraldy,' which is an old form of the noun.

89. **seiz'd:** possessed (a regular law term).

90. **a moiety competent:** an adequate portion (of his own lands). *Moiety* was not confined to the sense of 'half.'

91, 92. **gagèd:** engaged; i.e., pledged, staked.—**had** (subjunctive): would have.—**inheritance:** possession.

93. **comart:** mutual bargain. The Folio reads *Cou'nant* (i.e., covenant).

94. **carriage . . . design'd:** the purport of the agreement drawn up. The *carriage* of any document is 'that which it carries,' its 'bearing' or 'tenour.'

96. **unimproved:** unused. To *improve* anything often means to 'utilize it,' 'put it to profitable use.' Cf. 'improved land,' 'unimproved real estate.'—**mettle:** high spirit, valour.

98. **Shark'd up:** picked up without distinction, as the sharkfish collects his prey' (Steevens).—**lawless.** So the Second Quarto (*lawelesse*). The Folio reads 'Landlesse.' *Lawless* may even mean 'outlawed,' as in Munday, *The Downfall of Robert Earl of Huntington* (Collier's Dodsley, XIII, 17).—**resolutes:** bravoes, desperadoes.

99. **some.** This suggests that he enlisted his desperadoes without telling them just what the enterprise was.

100. **That hath a stomach in't:** that affords one an opportunity to show valour. The present tense gives the effect of quoting the very words used by Fortinbras.

101. **our state:** our government; our administration.

103. **terms compulsatory.** Synonymous with *strong hand*.

105. **motive:** moving cause. Cf. i, 4, 76; ii, 2, 587; iv, 7, 16.

106. **head.** The same as *source* in meaning (cf. *wellhead*, *fountainhead*).

107. **romage:** intense general activity. Cf. Capt. Nathaniel Boteler, *Dialogues*, 1634 (ed. Perrin, 1929, pp. 229, 230): '*Admiral.* What doth your word *Rummage* imply? *Captain.* It is to remove any goods or luggage, from one place or part to another, either betwixt the decks or elsewhere; but most commonly this term is appropriated to the removing or clearing of any goods or lading in the ship's hold, that so they may handsomely be stowed or ordered.'

108-125. In the Quartos but not in the Folios. Some think that Shakespeare omitted these splendid lines in revising the play because he had in the meantime written *Julius Cæsar*; but that is no reason. Their omission seems to be merely a 'cut.' Whether such cuts were made by Shakespeare or not we have no means of knowing.

108. **be.** The subjunctive in indirect discourse—an ancient construction. The *be* does not express any special doubt in the speaker's mind.

109. **Well may it sort:** It may well be in accord with this state of things.

112. **mote:** a speck of dust. Cf. *Matthew*, vii, 3.

113. **palmy:** flourishing, triumphant.

116. **squeak.** Alluding to the horribly thin and strident voice ascribed to spectres—the 'vox exigua' of the Æneid, vi, 492, 493. So in *Julius Cæsar*, ii, 2, 24: 'Ghosts did shriek and squeal about the streets.' Cf. Dryden, *Don Sebastian*, ii, 1:

> Sometimes, methinks, I hear the groans of ghosts,
> Thin, hollow sounds, and lamentable screams.

117. **As.** *As* may mean 'as also,' 'as well as'; i.e., 'and so likewise there were.' But the ellipsis would be harsh. Perhaps a line has dropped out before *As*. The substance of the lost line would be 'Prodigies appeared in the heavens.' Some critics have been rash enough to compose a verse to fill the gap.[1]— **trains of fire.** Among the 'wonderfull signes' that foretold the death of Cæsar, Plutarch mentions 'fires in the element [i.e., the sky], and spirites running vp and downe in the night' (North, ed. 1595, p. 787).—**dews of blood.** An oft-reported prodigy. Cf. *Julius Cæsar*, ii, 2, 21: 'Which drizzled blood upon the Capitol.'

118. **Disasters:** threatening signs. *Disasters* in its astrological sense includes any threatening phenomena in the heavenly bodies.—**moist star:** the moon. Cf. 'the moonshine's wat'ry beams' (*Romeo and Juliet*, i, 4, 62); 'the wat'ry star' (*Winter's Tale*, i, 2, 1); 'the wat'ry moon' (*Midsummer Night's Dream*, ii, 1, 162); 'That night-wandering, pale, and watery star' (Marlowe, *Hero and Leander*, i, 107). According to the old science, which divided all things according to the four categories—moist, dry, hot, cold—the moon was moist by nature. Hence it was not only 'the governess of floods' (*Midsummer Night's Dream*, ii, 1, 103) but had much to do with dew, mist, and fog.

119. **Upon . . . stands:** by whose influence the sea is controlled (in its tides).

120. **doomsday.** Clark and Wright cite *Matthew*, xxiv, 29: 'The moon shall not give her light.'—**eclipse.** There were several eclipses of sun or moon in Shakespeare's time.

121. **precurse:** forerunning; indication in advance.—**fierce:** terrible.

122. **harbingers.** A harbinger was an officer who went ahead

[1]Tschischwitz (1869) shifted the lines, putting ll. 121-125 between l. 116 and l. 117. The same change was suggested in 1872 by Gerald Massey (*The Secret Drama of Shakespeare's Sonnets*, Supplement, p. 46) and is adopted by Wilson (1934). But the preterite tense *was* (in l. 120) suffices to show that ll. 117-120 refer to Roman history and not to contemporary Denmark.

to arrange for the lodgings of a king and his suite. The word
is here used with a recollection of this sense.—still: ever, always; for the fates, Horatio implies, never come unannounced.

123. **omen:** dire event.

125. **climature:** clime, country. Dyce's emendation for the
Quarto reading (*Climatures*).

126. **soft!** The regular interjection to check discourse:
'hush!' 'hold!' 'enough!' Cf. i, 5, 58; iii, 1, 88; iii, 2, 410;
iv, 2, 3; v, 1, 240.

127. **I'll cross it, though it blast me.** Horatio crosses the
Ghost's path so as to pass directly before its face, calling upon
it to stay. The apparition then stands still and he adjures it to
speak. The Ghost is about to obey when the cock crows. Horatio's courage comes out strongly here, for to cross a spirit,
or to let it cross you, was even more dangerous than to speak
to it.—**Spreads his arms.** Not in the Folios. The Second
Quarto (in the margin opposite ll. 127, 128) has '*It spreads his*
[i.e., its] *armes.*' The Quarto of 1676 and Rowe are probably
right in letting Horatio make this gesture.

128-139. Horatio shows a scholar's knowledge in his enu-
meration of the causes that send ghosts back to earth. He mentions (1) some good action which remains undone; (2) some
disclosure for the benefit or protection of surviving friends;
(3) the revelation of buried treasure. Abundant illustration of
all three points occurs in European folklore. See Marlowe,
The Jew of Malta, ii, 1 (ed. Dyce, I, 263); Dekker, *Newes
from Hell*, 1606 (ed. Grosart, II, 111); Henry More, *The
Præexistency of the Soul*, 1647, stanzas 19, 20; Glanvil's *Sadu-
cismus Triumphatus*, 1681, Part II, pp. 235-242, 276-287;
Brand's *Popular Antiquities*, ed. Hazlitt, III, 117-119.

131. **do ease:** relieve thy conscience and let thee rest in peace.
—**grace to me:** be set to my credit as a virtuous action. Only
on this condition does Horatio promise to carry out the apparition's wishes, for he cannot be sure that it is not a malignant ghost or even a demon.

133, 134. **thy country's fate.** Cf. ll. 108-111, 122.—**happily:**
haply, perhaps.

139. **Stay.** The Ghost starts as if to go. Then the cock crows, and it stalks away. Horatio forgets his learning in his excitement and calls upon Marcellus, whom the spirit must pass in its course, to 'stop it,' though that is impossible.

140. **partisan:** halberd, pike.

146. **malicious mockery:** a hollow mockery of doing harm; a mere imitation of injury.

151. **lofty:** high-pitched.

152. **at his warning:** when the cock's crow warns them of sunrise. Ghosts, trolls, devils, and the like, according to a very old belief, cannot endure the sunlight (cf. *Midsummer Night's Dream*, iii, 2, 380 ff.). Farmer cites the first hymn of Prudentius 'At Cockcrow' (*Ad Galli Cantum*), ll. 37–40:

> Ferunt vagantes daemones,
> Laetos tenebris noctium,
> Gallo canente, exterritos
> Sparsim timere et cedere.

See H. J. Schmitz, *Die Bussbücher*, II (1898), 442.

154. **extravagant:** out of bounds; escaped from its *confine* or assigned limits.—**erring:** wandering. Cf. *Othello*, i, 1, 137: 'an extravagant and wheeling stranger.'

156. **object:** sight. In Elizabethan English all that the eye can take in at one view may be called an *object.*—**probation:** proof.

158. **'gainst:** just before.

162. **wholesome:** free not only from witchcraft and demonic influences, but from contagion, which was commonly ascribed to the night air. Cf. *Julius Cæsar*, ii, 1, 265, 266:

> To dare the vile contagion of the night,
> And tempt the rheumy and unpurged air.

—**strike.** Regularly used of the sudden malignant action ascribed to an evil planet (so also *sunstruck, moonstruck*). Cf. *Titus Andronicus*, ii, 4, 14: 'If I do wake, some planet strike me down'; *Coriolanus*, ii, 2, 117, 118:

> And with a sudden reinforcement struck
> Corioles like a planet;

Dekker, *Old Fortunatus* (Pearson ed., I, 116): 'If your wit be not planet strucken, if your brains lie in their right place, you are well inough.'

163. **takes:** bewitches, enchants. All kinds of ill effects were ascribed to malicious fairies and elves—from 'pinching black and blue' (*Comedy of Errors*, ii, 2, 194; cf. *Merry Wives*, v, 5, 49) to idiocy, madness, and even death (*Merry Wives*, v, 5, 51). Cf. John Webster, *The Displaying of Supposed Witchcraft*, 1677, p. 323: 'The comon people, if they chance to have any sort of Epilepsie, Palsie, Convulsions, or the like, do presently perswade themselves that they are bewitched, forespoken, blasted, fairy-taken, or haunted with some evil spirit'; *Gammer Gurton's Needle*, i, 2 (ed. Manly, II, 98):

> There they syt as still as stones in the streite,
> As though they had ben taken with fairies or els with some il sprite.

164. **gracious:** full of divine grace; blessed.
165. **in part.** Horatio speaks with his habitual caution.
166. **in russet mantle clad.** The dawn is cloudy or misty. *Russet* was a kind of coarse homespun, either brown or grey in colour. Cf. *Love's Labour's Lost*, v, 2, 413; Peele, *Essex his Welcome*, l. 15 (ed. Bullen, II, 270): 'thy rude tire and grey russet coat.'
173. **loves.** These gentlemen are Hamlet's personal friends. The plural of abstract nouns is common when two or more persons are mentioned. Cf. i, 2, 251, 254; ii, 2, 14, 289.

Scene II.

This scene takes place on the same day as scene i. The time is still the forenoon, for Horatio, Marcellus, and Bernardo enter at l. 159 (cf. i, 1, 174, 175). The stage direction in the Second Quarto is: *Florish. Enter Claudius, King of Denmarke, Gertrad the Queene, Counsaile* [i.e., Council]: *as Polonius, and his Sonne Laertes, Hamlet, Cum Alijs.* The text follows the Folio. The 'Lords Attendant' provides for the 'Counsaile.'

Wilson thinks that Hamlet enters after all of the other 'court figures,' but this would be a strange distortion of ceremony. One cannot imagine Polonius as allowing his son and daughter to precede the Prince.

1-39. This speech deserves careful study with reference to the character of Claudius, which is often misconceived. Its artificial style and balanced antithesis are not the effects of hypocrisy, but merely of ceremony. Being the King's first speech from the throne since his coronation, it is formal and dignified, especially so through l. 16—the end of the King's acknowledgment of the aid of his advisers. Then follows, in a style still dignified but less stilted, an account of the business for which this particular council has been assembled. Lines 17-25 sum up facts already known to the Council, and the rest of the speech concerns the dispatching of Voltemand and Cornelius as ambassadors to Norway. The whole address is appropriate, skilfully constructed, and even eloquent. It gives the audience a high idea of the intellectual powers of the King, whom we as yet have no reason to suspect or to dislike.

2. be: is. The subjunctive after *though* accords with the old idiom.—**that:** though that; though. *That* is common in repeating a particle just used.—**us:** all of us. Not the 'royal *we*.'—**befitted:** would befit.

4. of woe: woful, mournful. Cf. 'thieves of mercy' for 'merciful robbers' (iv, 6, 18).

5. discretion: wise moderation (which teaches us to restrain our natural grief).

7. ourselves: myself and all of you. A suggestion that the marriage was not merely a personal affair, but an advantage to the whole state. If Claudius had meant 'myself' only, he would have said 'ourself.'

8. our: my. The royal *we*.

9. jointress: a widow who has *jointure*, an estate which falls to her on the death of her husband.

10. defeated: 'destroyed, annulled' (Child).

11. auspicious: of happy aspect or expression. The line, as Steevens remarks, is 'only the ancient proverbial phrase, "to cry with one eye and laugh with the other." ' He quotes *Winter's Tale*, v, 2, 79 ff.: 'But, O, the noble combat that 'twixt joy and sorrow was fought in Paulina! She had one eye declin'd for the loss of her husband, another elevated that the oracle was fulfill'd.' Cf. Alanus de Insulis, *Anticlaudianus*, viii, 1: 'Alter lascivit oculus dum profluit alter'; Massinger, *The Old Law*, ii, 1 (ed. Gifford, 1813, IV, 491):

> I have known a widow laugh closely, my lord,
> Under her handkerchief, when t'other part
> Of her old face wept like rain in sunshine.

12, 13. **mirth:** cheerfulness.—**dole:** grief.

14-16. **barr'd:** shut out; left unconsulted.—**Your better wisdoms:** not, 'your judgment, which is better than mine,' but 'your wise counsel as to what it was better for me to do,' 'your wise preference.' So in *Captain Thomas Stukeley* (ed. Simpson, I, 171):

> I'll send for a friend or two of mine
> And take their better counsels in the matter.

Cf. *As You Like It*, ii, 7, 45: 'your better judgments'; *Timon*, iii, 6, 52: 'Let it not cumber your better remembrance' (i.e., 'your memory of pleasanter things'). For the plural cf. i, 1, 173, note.—**freely . . . along:** heartily agreed with me throughout this affair.

17. **that you know:** what you already know. The Councillors are acquainted with the demand of young Fortinbras, but not with the King's purposed reply (ll. 26-33).

18. **our worth:** my ability to govern.

20. **Our state:** my royal administration.—**disjoint and out of frame.** Synonymous: 'disjointed,' 'broken in its structure.' Such fulness of phrase is still characteristic of the official style.

21. **Colleagued . . . advantage:** with no ally except his false notion that this is a favourable moment for him. *Dream* is emphatic.

22. **to pester us with message:** to *annoy* me with *frequent* messages. *Pester* carries both senses.

24. **bands:** bonds; binding covenants and decisions.

28. **Norway:** the King of Norway. See i, 1, 48, note.

29. **impotent:** feeble.—**bedrid:** confined to his bed—literally, ridden (i.e., carried) on a bed.

31–33. **gait:** procedure.—**levies, lists, full proportions.** Three synonyms.—**subject.** Collective: 'subjects.' Cf. i, 1, 72.

37. **To business:** to negotiate.

38. **dilated:** expressed in full; detailed. *Delated*, the Quarto reading, is merely a variant spelling of *dilated* (like the old *devide* for *divide*) and is not equivalent to 'delivered,' 'handed over.'—**allow.** The verb is attracted into the plural by the plural noun *articles*. Cf. iii, 2, 207.

39. **and let . . . duty:** and let your promptness express, in action, the usual formula of farewell. This would be 'We commend our duty to your Highness,' i.e., 'We offer our devoted service' (cf. v, 2, 189, and note). See Kenyon, *Philological Quarterly*, I (1922), 71–73.

40, 41. **duty.** The repetition is intentional and effective: the ambassadors submissively echo the words of the King.—**nothing:** not at all.

42 ff. **And now, Laertes,** etc. Ceremony over, and the state business dispatched, Claudius falls gracefully into a familiar strain, which becomes still more intimate as he proceeds. At l. 45 he abandons the royal *we* and the formal *you* for the personal and affectionate *I* (*my*) and *thou*. He is affable as well as kingly, and Shakespeare clearly meant to depict him as endowed with distinct charm in speech and bearing.

44. **the Dane:** the Danish king.

46. **my offer, not thy asking:** something granted before it is asked.

47–49. **native to:** naturally associated with; bound by ties of nature to.—**instrumental:** serviceable.—**thy father.** Polonius is a noble of the highest rank. Claudius is obviously indebted to him for assistance in procuring his election as King. Both Claudius and the Queen are genuinely fond of the old councillor, slightly bored though they may sometimes be by his occasional prosing. Cf. iv, 1, 12.

51. leave and favour: gracious permission. Hendiadys.

56. pardon: permission to depart. Cf. iii, 2, 329; More, *Richard III* (ed. Lumby, p. 76): 'When the duke had this leaue and pardon to speake, then waxed he bolde.'

58–60. wrung . . . consent. Omitted in the Folios.

62, 63. Take thy fair hour. A graceful adaptation of the familiar *Carpe diem*: 'Thy life is now at its most delightful season. Be it thine to enjoy!'—**graces:** good qualities (of every kind). The verses combine permission for Laertes to enjoy his youth while it lasts ('Time be thine') with the wish that such enjoyment may be guided by the best qualities of his nature.

64. cousin. Often used for 'uncle,' 'nephew,' etc.

65. more than kin, etc. Hamlet catches up the King's words and continues them, under his breath, with bitter irony: 'Yes, nephew and son both!—a little more than normal kin, and yet not quite kindly in my feelings toward you.' He is applying to his own case an old proverbial antithesis, of which Steevens and Collier quote three good examples: 'The neerer we are in bloud, the further wee must be from loue; and the greater the kindred is, the lesse the kindness must be' (Lyly, *Mother Bombie*, iii, 1; ed. Bond, III, 195); 'In kinde a father, not in kindliness' (*Gorboduc*, i, 1, 18); 'I would he were not so neere to us in kindred, then sure he would be neerer in kindness' (Rowley, *A Search for Money*, 1609; Percy Society ed., p. 5). Cf. Bastard, *Epigrams*, 1598, iii, 29: 'Neuer so many cosins: so fewe kynde'; Webster, *Duchess of Malfy*, iv, 2, 288–290 (ed. Lucas, II, 101):

> You have bloodely approv'd the auncient truth,
> That kindred commonly doe worse agree
> Then remote strangers;

Thynne, *Emblemes and Epigrames*, 1600 (ed. Furnivall, p. 50):

> Straungers to our kinde and to our bloode,
> Then our owne kinde and kinn, do vs more good;

Macbeth, ii, 3, 146, 147:

> There's daggers in men's smiles; the near [i.e., nearer] in blood,
> The nearer bloody;

Matthew, x, 36: 'A man's foes shall be they of his own house-
hold' (from *Micah*, vii, 6).

67. **Not . . . sun**: The clouds do not hang on me. I am only
too much in the sun—more in the position of a *son* than I wish
I were! Thus Hamlet bitterly refuses the title which the King
has emphasized. Before Claudius can reply, the Queen interposes and thus gives him a chance to ignore Hamlet's taunt.
He is glad to let it pass, for he is determined, for her sake, to
be on friendly terms with his stepson.

69. **Denmark**: the King of Denmark. Cf. i, 1, 48.

70. **vailed**: downcast.

72, 73. **common**: universal.—**nature**: natural life.

75. **particular**: personal, as if it were an individual experience.

79. **windy . . . breath.** A scornfully elaborate phrase for
'heavy sighs.' 'Windy sighs' was a regular phrase (Peele,
David and Bethsabe, i, 3, 87, and Kyd, *Spanish Tragedy*, iii, 13,
165, ed. Manly, II, 433, 564).

80. **fruitful**: teeming, abundant.

81, 82. **haviour**: bearing, appearance.—**moods**: moody appearances. See Textual Notes.

84. **play.** Spoken with bitter emphasis. See ll. 145–149.

85. **passeth show**: surpasses all mere *signs* of grief.

87. **cómmendable.** Accented on the first syllable.

90. **bound.** The subject of the verb is *that father*; the object
is *survivor*. 'That father, by dying, laid his surviving son (your
father) under an obligation to mourn for him.'

92. **obsequious sorrow**: sorrow befitting obsequies (funeral
rites).—**perséver**: persevere.

93. **obstinate condolement**: mourning that refuses to be com-
forted.

95. **incorrect to heaven**: uncorrected—not brought into submission to God's will.

99. **As any . . . sense**: as anything that is the commonest
object of sight or hearing.

100. **peevish**: childish, foolish.

101, 102. **a fault . . . nature**: a triple fault, involving (1) rebellion against God's will; (2) unfilial feelings (as if one

blamed one's father for dying); (3) revolt against the established order of nature (for death is as natural as life).

103–105. whose. The antecedent seems to be *nature* rather
than *reason*.—**common theme:** for the natural order of things
proclaims that death must be the universal lot of mankind.—
still: ever, always.—**he.** Good Elizabethan grammar.

106. We. The royal *we* appropriately introduces the sentence
relating to succession to the throne. In l. 112 the more familiar
and affectionate *I* is fitly used. Then, in l. 114, the formal style
of royalty is resumed in the expression of a request that is in
fact a command.

107. unprevailing: unavailing.

108–117. Thus the King solemnly proclaims Hamlet his heir;
and, even in this elective monarchy, such an announcement
would go far to determine the succession. Cf. iii, 2, 355–359.
We must not regard his words as hypocritical. He loves the
Queen passionately, and she is devoted to her son. Besides,
Claudius is not an habitual or hardened criminal, nor does he
wish to increase his guilt by further offences. He hopes to live
at peace with Hamlet and to atone for past wrongs by kindness
in the days to come. That this cannot be, is a part of the
tragedy. It is the King's nemesis that the good he purposes
turns to evil in his hands.

110. nobility of love: distinguished affection.

112. impart: express myself. Cf. Henry Porter, *Two Angry
Women of Abington*, 1599 (Malone Society, ll. 257, 258):
'With all the parts of neighbor loue I [do] impart my selfe to
maister Goursey.'—**For:** as for.

113. school: your university studies. The university of Wittenberg (founded in 1502, united with that of Halle in 1817)
was at the height of its reputation in Shakespeare's day and
was much esteemed in England because of its connection with
Luther and the Reformation. Chettle in his tragedy of *Hoff-
man* (*ca.* 1602) speaks of 'Wittenberg, where wit growes'
(ed. 1631, C r°). Nashe, however, attacks the institution in
The Unfortunate Traveller, 1594 (ed. McKerrow, II, 247 ff.).

114. retrograde: contrary; literally, moving backward. Cf.

Chapman, *May Day*, iii (Pearson ed., II, 373): 'Come, be not retrograde to our desires.' *Retrograde*, as an astronomical term, describes the motion of a planet when it seems to move backward, i.e., in a direction contrary to the order of the signs of the zodiac.

115. **bend you:** bow your will; submit your inclination.

116. **our eye:** my royal presence; at court. Cf. iv, 4, 6; iv, 7, 45.

117-119. **son.** The King, with unruffled dignity, repeats the words of l. 64, emphasizing once more that title (*son*) which has provoked Hamlet's bitter jest (l. 65). The Queen interposes again (as in l. 68), thus preventing any further taunts and enabling Hamlet to obey *her* rather than his stepfather. She shows herself a skilful peacemaker.—**thy . . . thee.** The familiar and affectionate form of address. The King has used the more formal *you*.

121. The King does not fail to note that Hamlet has ignored him and addressed his reply to the Queen; but he is ready to accept the answer as satisfactory. He tries to persuade himself that all will be well.

122. **Be as ourself:** Regard yourself as King to all intents and purposes.

124. **Sits . . . heart:** gives me heartfelt satisfaction.—**grace:** honour.

125. **Denmark.** Cf. i, 1, 48.

127. **rouse:** drink, draught; especially, a deep draught—one that empties the beaker. The spelling *rouce* (in the Folios) shows the pronunciation. *Rouse* is a clipped form of *carouse* (German *gar aus*, 'quite out'). See v, 2, 300.—**bruit again:** report again, reëcho. The King, who wishes to honour his stepson, but is working out his own fate, selects a kind of tribute that is particularly repugnant to Hamlet, educated at a foreign university and constitutionally averse to the coarser manners of the Scandinavians, especially to their heavy drinking. Cf. i, 4, 13-38. In 1490, when James IV of Scotland and his wife were entertained at Baahus Castle in Norway, 'at the table the toasts of the King, the Queen, and some other noble persons were

drunk, each toast accompanied with six cannon shots' (A. H. Millar, *Scottish Review*, XXI [1893], 160).

129. **too too.** A very common reduplication of *too*. The accent seems to have been *too'too*, with no pause between the words.—**solid.** The Folio reading. The Second Quarto reads 'this too too sallied flesh'; the First, 'this too much grieu'd and sallied flesh.' *Sallied* may well be a form of *solid*, due to confusion of pronunciation between ŏ and ă. Cf. such forms as *farren* for *foreign*; *clatpole* for *clotpole*; *quandam* for *quondam*; *asprey* for *osprey*; *arras* for *orris*. George MacDonald's interpretation of *sallied* as 'sullied' is eloquently defended by Wilson. *Sallied* would be an easy misprint for *sullied*, and *sallies* for *sullies* occurs in the Second Quarto in ii, 1, 39, and *vnsallied* for *unsullied* in *Love's Labour's Lost*, v, 2, 352 (Folio). But the explanation of *sullied* as indicating that Hamlet regards his own flesh as defiled by his mother's incest is far-fetched, and *solid* is obviously correct. Hamlet wishes that one who, like himself, is tired of life could melt away with a wish, or that suicide were not forbidden by God's law: 'Thou shalt not kill.' What follows explains why he is life-weary. There is a curious coincidence of phraseology (*weary*, *solid*, and *melt*) in *2 Henry IV*, iii, 1, 47–49:

> And the continent,
> Weary of solid firmness, melt itself
> Into the sea!

132. **canon:** divine law.

134. **uses.** Either 'customs' or (better) 'enjoyments,' i.e., 'advantages to be derived from life in this world.'

135. **an unweeded garden.** Cf. Rowlands, *Hell's Broke Loose*, 1605 (Hunterian Club ed., p. 3): 'In this vn-weeded Garden of the World.'

137. **merely:** entirely, utterly.

140. **Hyperion:** the sun god, the most beautiful of the divinities. The manly beauty of the elder Hamlet is several times emphasized; as by Marcellus in i, 1, 143, by Horatio in i, 2, 186, and by Hamlet in his famous speech to his mother: note especially 'Hyperion's curls' (iii, 4, 55–63).

141. **might not beteem:** could not allow.

147. **or ere.** Both *or* and *ere* mean 'before,' and the combination simply emphasizes the idea. This *or* is not the conjunction *or* but a form related to the Anglo-Saxon *ǣr* (*ere*). Cf. l. 183.

150. **discourse of reason:** the process or faculty of reasoning. To *discourse* is an old word for to 'pass from premises to conclusions.' The noun *discourse* (with or without the added phrase *of reason*) is used for either the process or the faculty. Cf. iv, 4, 36–39.

153. **Than I to Hercules.** A suggestion as to Hamlet's personal appearance. He is strong and active—a good fencer—but not stalwart.

154. **unrighteous:** because they were insincere.

155. **left the flushing:** allowed the redness to disappear.— **galled:** irritated, inflamed. *Salt*, *flushing*, and *galled* all emphasize the same idea. Cf. *Troilus and Cressida*, v, 3, 55: 'Their eyes o'ergalled with recourse of tears.'

157. **dexterity:** speed, eager haste.

158. **nor it cannot.** Such double negatives are common.

160. **I am glad,** etc. A courteous greeting, mechanically uttered before Hamlet sees who it is. The next line is spoken in enthusiastic recognition of his friend.

161. **myself.** Emphatic. Hamlet will not forget Horatio so long as he remains conscious of his own identity, for Horatio is his *alter ego*, his second self.

163. **change:** exchange. I will not call you 'servant,' nor shall you call me 'lord': we will call each other 'friend.'

164. **And what make you?** And what are you doing?— **from:** away from.

165–167. Hamlet's courtesy to his inferiors is charming. It is not without reason that Ophelia calls him 'the glass of fashion and the mould of form' (iii, 1, 161). This makes the rudeness which he puts on when he is counterfeiting madness all the more deceptive.

169. **A truant disposition:** a feeling that I should like to run away from school. Horatio, in his mildly humorous way, replies as if Hamlet had said *makes*, and gives himself a character

quite at variance with his real nature. *Disposition* often means (as here) a 'mood' or 'fancy.'—my lord. Practically a single word (cf. French *milord*) and often preceded by an adjective.

174. your affair. Emphatic: 'your actual business.'

175. to drink deep. Cf. i, 4, 8–22, where Hamlet expresses his dislike of the Danish habit of heavy drinking.

180. Thrift: mere economy. A bitter jest. The only reason for such haste was, he says, to save the remnants of the funeral feast.—bak'd meats: pasties. Elaborate funeral feasts are an old and universal custom, only recently fallen into disuse. The Scandinavian funeral feasts (or *arvals*) are often mentioned in the sagas: but of these Shakespeare knew nothing; he is simply reporting the manners of his own time. See Viscount Dillon, *The Antiquary*, XXVI (1892), 11–14.

181. coldly: when cold; in a cold state. Adverbs in -*ly* were often used to express, not *manner* (as in modern English), but *condition* (like adjectives).

182. dearest. The formula devised by Clark and Wright to cover the Elizabethan meanings of this word cannot be improved: '*Dear* is used of whatever touches us nearly either in love or hate, joy or sorrow.' *My dearest foe* is, then, 'my bitterest enemy.' The whole speech has a proverbial cast; there is no allusion to any particular person.

183. Or ever: before ever. Cf. l. 147, note.

186. once. Horatio, though a Dane (v, 2, 352), was not a courtier; but he has once before visited the Danish court, doubtless as Hamlet's guest in some university vacation. His words in i, 1, 60–63, need not imply that Horatio was with the elder Hamlet in the Norwegian and Polish combats.—goodly: handsome. Cf. i, 1, 47–49.

187, 188. He was . . . again. The Folio puts a comma after *man*, a colon after *all*; the Second Quarto lacks both The Quarto text would mean, as Clark and Wright interpret it, 'He was, take him for all in all, a man upon whose like I shall not look again.' Cf. Mabbe, *Celestina* (ed. *Tudor Translations*, p. 96): 'Take him all together, and for all in all, you shall not finde such another.' For the loose (but common) construction, cf. Ford and Dekker, *The Sun's Darling*, iii, 1, 2, 3:

> Thou hadst a body the four elements
> Dwelt never in a fairer;

Greene, *The Defence of Conny Catching*, 1592 (ed. Grosart, XI, 88): 'Such foolish affection towards one she knew not what he was, nor whither he would.'—**a man.** Cf. *Julius Cæsar*, v, 5, 73–75:

> His life was gentle, and the elements
> So mix'd in him that Nature might stand up
> And say to all the world, 'This was a man!'

190. Horatio has been startled by Hamlet's 'Methinks I see my father.' Hamlet is equally surprised by Horatio's words.

192. **Season your admiration:** Moderate or control your astonishment.

193. **deliver:** report, relate. Cf. l. 209.

198. **the dead vast.** *Vast*, the reading of the First Quarto, is generally preferred by editors to *wast* (i.e., *waste*), the reading of the Second Quarto and the Folio. *Waste* describes the night as a great void, and suggests illimitable darkness. *Vast* expresses the second of these ideas clearly and suggests the first. Cf. *Tempest*, i, 2, 327: 'that vast of night.'

200. **at point:** completely.—**cap-a-pe:** from head to foot. Cf. *Winter's Tale*, iv, 4, 761.

203. **oppress'd:** overwhelmed by the horror of the sight.—**fear-surprised:** seized upon by fear. *Surprise* usually means to 'take captive,' 'arrest,' 'seize,' literally or figuratively.

204, 205. **his truncheon's length.** The truncheon was a short staff or baton, carried as a sign of military command. Cf. *Troilus and Cressida*, v, 3, 52, 53:

> The hand of Mars
> Beck'ning with fiery truncheon my retire.

—**distill'd:** dissolved, disintegrated.—**with the act of fear:** by the action of fear.

207. **In dreadful secrecy:** as a dread secret; under a solemn pledge of silence. Cf. *2 Henry VI*, iii, 2, 158: 'A dreadful oath, sworn with a solemn tongue!'

216, 217. **it head:** its head. Three forms for the genitive case of *it* were in use: *his*, the ancient form for both masculine and neuter; *its* or *it's*, a form adopted under the influence of a feeling that *his* is exclusively masculine; *it*, a compromise form. Of these *his* is by far the commonest in Shakespeare. Cf. v, 1, 244.—**did address . . . speak:** began to make such movements as indicated that it meant to speak.—**address:** apply.

224. **Indeed, indeed, sirs:** Quite right, gentlemen. 'This is Hamlet's courteous acknowledgment of Horatio's last remark, and indicates his approval of the conduct of his friends' (Child). See note on ll. 165–167.

230. **beaver:** visor. Helmets differed much in the construction of the movable front or 'face-guard.' If this consisted of two parts, the upper (the visor) was shoved up, and the lower (the beaver) down, when the helmet was open. If the face-guard was single, it was called either *visor* or *beaver* indifferently, and was so adjusted as to be lowered in some helmets, raised in others, and in still others either raised or lowered at will.

232. **countenance:** expression (of the face).

235. **constantly:** unswervingly.

236. **amaz'd you:** confused your thoughts. Horatio does not mean merely that Hamlet would have been astonished, but that he would have been unable to think at all—would not have known what to think of the nature and purpose of the apparition. Cf. ii, 2, 591, 592; iii, 2, 339; iii, 4, 112.

238. **tell:** count.

240. **grizzled:** grey. 'A sable silver'd' means exactly the same thing: 'black with white hairs intermixed.' Horatio varies the phrase instead of answering baldly 'yes.' So he does in i, 4, 1, 2:

> *Ham.* The air bites shrewdly; it is very cold.
> *Hor.* It is a nipping and an eager air.

244. **assume.** Hamlet does not know whether the apparition was his father's ghost or a demon that had taken the shape of his father. See Introduction.

245. **gape.** Hell-mouth was a familiar figure in mediæval art (e.g., in the Anglo-Saxon *Cædmon* manuscript), in the religious pageants, and on the Elizabethan stage. It was an enormous wide-open mouth with huge teeth. 'One hell-mouth' ('j Hell mought') is an item in an inventory of the properties of the Lord Admiral's Players in 1599 (*Henslow Papers*, ed. Greg, p. 116). Cf. Harsnet, *Declaration*, 1603, p. 71: 'The little children were neuer so afrayd of hell mouth in the old plaies painted with great gang teeth, staring eyes, and a foule bottle nose.'[1]

246. **hold my peace.** Hamlet is thinking of the danger of speaking to a demon. Cf. i, 1, 42, and note.

247. **conceal'd.** So Hamlet infers from Horatio's words in ll. 206, 207.

248. **Let it be tenable:** Regard it as something that must be held.

254. **Your loves, as mine to you.** Another mark of Hamlet's courtesy. He will not allow Horatio and the rest to call themselves his servants and offer him their duty. Let them rather regard him as their friend and give him their love. Cf. ll. 162, 163; i, 5, 191.—**loves.** Cf. i, 1, 173.

256. **I doubt some foul play:** I suspect that something is wrong. *Foul play* did not to the Elizabethans, as to us, suggest exclusively murder. Hamlet has no definite suspicion of the truth until the Ghost reveals it (i, 5, 25, 26).

---

[1] See Hearne's ed. of Fordun, p. 1403 (two plates); Hone, *Ancient Mysteries Described*, 1823, p. 138 (plate); Thomas Sharp, *A Dissertation on the Pageants anciently performed at Coventry*, 1825, pp. 61–63, and plates 5–8; Henry Ellis, *Account of Cædmon's Metrical Paraphrase*, 1833, plates iv, xi; Fairholt, *Lord Mayor's Pageants*, I (1843), xxix ff. (with figure); Halliwell, *Outlines of the Life of Shakespeare*, 6th ed., II, 289; *The Buggbears*, iv, 2, 78–80 (ed. Bond, *Early Plays from the Italian*, p. 127); *Arden of Feversham*, iv, 3, 1–3 (ed. Tucker Brooke, *The Shakespeare Apocrypha*, p. 24); Yarington, *Two Tragedies in One*, 1601 (ed. Bullen, *Old English Plays*, IV, 92); *The Tryall of Cheualry*, 1605 (same, II, 285); Middleton, *More Dissemblers besides Women*, iv, 2, 129–131 (ed. Bullen, VI, 453); Tourneur, *The Revenger's Tragedy*, i, 3 (ed. Collins, II, 29).

Scene III.

The Ghost has appeared at one o'clock in the morning (i, 1, 39). Scene ii provides for the forenoon of the same day, scene iii for the afternoon. Thus there is a fitting interval between scene ii and the beginning of scene iv—after midnight, when Hamlet and his friends are watching for the Ghost.

3. convoy: means of conveyance.

6. fashion: a habit of young men or young princes.—**a toy in blood:** a caprice of youthful passion.

7. violet. Cf. Chapman, *Revenge for Honour*, v, 2 (Pearson ed., III, 351): 'the prime virgins of the Spring, the violets.'—**in . . . nature:** in the early prime (the springtime) of life. This passage is enough to settle the question of Hamlet's age, and its testimony is confirmed by 'young' (l. 124) and 'blown youth' (iii, 1, 167).—**primy.** Cf. *The Repentance of Robert Greene*, 1592 (ed. Grosart, XI, 179): 'Oh were I now to begin the flower of my youth, were I now in the prime of my yeares, how far would I bee from my former follyes.'

8. The metre of this verse is exquisite. *Sweet*, if dwelt upon in pronunciation, gives the effect of two syllables, since the pitch of the voice will vary in the vowel.—**Forward:** early. Cf. *Two Gentlemen*, i, 1, 45: 'the most forward bud.'

9. The perfume . . . minute: something that makes a passing minute sweet and fills it up; the pleasant pastime of a minute.

10. No more but so? Only that and nothing more? Not spoken in plaintive accents; for Ophelia does not doubt Hamlet, nor, gentle as she is, has she any lack of spirit. Her question is merely an acknowledgment that she is listening to her brother's sermon, much as if she had said 'Ah?' 'Indeed?' or 'Well?' The actress's foreknowledge of Ophelia's doom should not overshadow this scene. Ophelia is full of the joy of living; and she is rather more than a match for her brother, as we shall see presently (ll. 45–51).

11. nature crescent: a man's nature (or being), as it grows.

12. **thews:** sinews.—**this temple:** the body. The metaphor
is carried out in the next lines: 'As the body (the temple)
grows larger, the services conducted therein by the mind and
soul (the priests of the temple) grow more extensive and
elaborate,' i.e., 'greater and greater objects occupy the thoughts
and affections.' The figure is Biblical. See *1 Corinthians*, vi,
19: 'Know ye not that your body is the temple of the Holy
Ghost which is in you?' In *Macbeth*, ii, 3, 73, the King's body
is called 'the Lord's anointed temple.'

14. **withal:** at the same time.

15, 16. **soil:** foul thought.—**cautel:** wile, deceit.—**will:**
desire.

17. **His greatness weigh'd:** when his high rank is taken into
consideration.

18. Omitted in the Quartos.

20. **Carve for himself:** indulge his own fancy; choose for
himself. Cf. *Othello*, ii, 3, 173, 174:

> He that stirs next to carve for his own rage
> Holds his soul light; he dies upon his motion;

Lyly, *Mother Bombie*, i, 3 (ed. Bond, III, 178, 179): 'Neither
father nor mother . . . shalbe her caruer in a husband.' The
figure (which had become a mere idiom) alludes to the carver's
opportunity to select some special tidbit.

21. **safëty.** Trisyllabic. The Folio reads *sanctity*. Wilson
accepts Theobald's conjecture, *sanity*.—**health:** welfare.

23. **voice and yielding:** authority and assent.

26. **in . . . place:** acting as he must in his special circumstances and under the restrictions of his rank.

28. **main:** mighty, powerful; not, chief.—**goes withal:**
agrees therewith.

34. **affection:** feelings. Do not let yourself go so far forward
as your natural feelings, if unrestrained, might lead you. The
military metaphor is carried out in the next line. Laertes, like
his father, is fond of elaborate figures of speech and rather
plumes himself upon his elegant language.

36. **chariest:** most sparing; most cautious and circumspect.

39, 40. **canker:** the rose caterpillar; called 'a worm i' th' bud' in *Twelfth Night*, ii, 4, 114. This *galls* (gnaws) the heart of the young roses 'before the buds (French *boutons*) are unclosed.' Early flowers are called 'the first-born infants of the spring' in *Love's Labour's Lost*, i, 1, 101. Cf. *Two Gentlemen*, i, 1, 45, 46:

> The most forward bud
> Is eaten by the canker ere it blow;

Day, *Law Tricks*, 1608, ii, 1 (ed. Bullen, II, 31):

> Do not let despaire,
> Like the ranke cancker bred by sultrie aire,
> Eate this young Rose of beautie in the bud.

44. **Youth . . . near:** Youth, in its natural ardour, often rebels against itself (acts contrary to its better nature), even if no tempter is at hand. The impulses and passions that rise against reason and self-control are often described as rebels or insurgents. Cf. iii, 4, 82-85; *All's Well*, v, 3, 6-8:

> Natural rebellion, done i' th' blaze of youth,
> When oil and fire, too strong for reason's force,
> O'erbears it and burns on;

Antony and Cleopatra, i, 4, 31-33:

> As we rate boys who, being mature in knowledge,
> Pawn their experience to their present pleasure
> And so rebel to judgment.

45-52. Ophelia is quietly amused at the wise airs of her brother, who resembles his father in his fondness for holding forth. She receives the sermon demurely; and then, when he is least expecting a retort, she bids him take a leaf out of his own book. The effect is diverting: Laertes suddenly remembers that he is in a hurry.

45. **th' effect:** the purport, the substance.—**lesson:** with a mischievous suggestion that Laertes is 'reading a lesson' like a preacher.

47. **ungracious:** graceless.

49. **Whiles:** whilst, while.—**libertine:** free-liver.

50. **primrose path.** So in *Macbeth*, ii, 3, 21: 'the primrose way to th' everlasting bonfire.' Cf. *Matthew*, vii, 13, 14.— **dalliance:** pleasure, self-indulgence.

51. **recks not his own rede:** heeds not his own counsel.— **O, fear me not!** O, don't fear for me! don't worry about me! Cf. iii, 4, 7.

53. **A double blessing . . . grace:** To receive two blessings (at parting from one's father) is a double favour from heaven.

54. **Occasion smiles . . . leave:** Opportunity treats me kindly in granting me this second good-bye.

57. **There.** Polonius lays his hand on his son's head and gives him his blessing.

58 ff. Rushton (*Shakespeare's Euphuism*, 1871, p. 46) long ago observed that these precepts resemble the advice of Euphues to Philautus (Lyly, *Euphues*, ed. Bond, II, 31). He quotes:

Be not lauish of thy tongue. . . .

Euery one that shaketh thee by the hand, is not ioyned to thee in heart. . . .

Be not quarrellous for euery lyght occasion: they are impatient in their anger of any equal, readie to reuenge an iniury, but neuer wont to profer any: they neuer fight without prouoking, and once prouoked they neuer cease. . . . It shal be there better to heare what they say, then to speak what thou thinkest.

Polonius's advice is sound and sensible—not more 'worldly-wise' than the occasion warrants[1]; and it concludes with a precept which raises the whole speech to a high ethical standard. Compare the Countess's farewell to her son in *All's Well*, i, 1, 70–79:

Be thou blest, Bertram, and succeed thy father
In manners, as in shape! Thy blood and virtue
Contend for empire in thee, and thy goodness
Share with thy birthright! Love all, trust a few,
Do wrong to none. Be able for thine enemy

[1] For similar precepts see Hesiod, *Works and Days*, 707–716; 'Rabbi Bilesie's Farewell to his Son' in *Greene's Mourning Garment* (ed. Grosart, IX, 137–139); Greene, *James IV*, iv, 1, 149–166 (ed. Collins, II, 93, 94); Greene, *The Carde of Fancie* (ed. Grosart, IV, 21–23); *Florio's Second Fruites*, 1591, Chap. vi, pp. 92–105; Massinger, *A New Way to Pay Old Debts*, i, 2, 129 ff. (ed. Gayley, *Representative Comedies*, III, 338).

> Rather in power than use, and keep thy friend
> Under thy own life's key. Be check'd for silence,
> But never tax'd for speech. What heaven more will,
> That thee may furnish, and my prayers pluck down,
> Fall on thy head!

59. **chárácter:** engrave, inscribe. Cf. i, 5, 98–104.

60. **unproportion'd:** unsymmetrical; out of harmony with reason and good conduct.—**his:** its. See i, 2, 216, note.

61. **vulgar:** indiscriminate in friendship.

64, 65. **But do not dull . . . comrade:** But do not make thy palm so callous by shaking hands with everybody that it can no longer feel the difference between a true friend and a chance acquaintance.—**entertainment:** reception, welcoming.—**comrade.** The Folio reading. The Quartos have *courage*, which Wilson retains, explaining it as 'spark,' 'brave,' 'blood'; but the passage that he quotes from the *New English Dictionary* does not confirm this reading. Furthermore, the metre requires the word to be accented on the second syllable, and this is a known accent for *comrade* (*1 Henry IV*, iv, 1, 96) but unlikely for *courage*. Finally, *courage* is an obvious misprint for *comrague*, i.e., 'fellow-rogue.' Cf. Sir Edward Hoby, *A Curry-combe for a Coxe-combe*, 1615, p. 69: 'his poore Camragues of Doway.'

65–67. **Beware . . . of thee.** Cf. Castiglione, *Il Cortegiano* (in Sir Thomas Hoby's version, *The Courtier*, ed. 1577, sig. Dv r°):

Neither let him runne rashly to these combates, but when hee must needes to saue his estimation withall. . . . But when a man perceyueth that he is entred so farre that hee cannot draw back withoute burthen, hee must, both in such thinges he hath to do before the combate, and also in the combat be utterly resolued with hymselfe, and alwayes shew a readinesse and a stomacke.

—**Bear't:** Conduct the affair.—**that:** so that.—**opposèd:** opponent.

68. **voice:** suffrage, recommendation, approval.

69. **censure:** judgment, opinion. Cf. iii, 2, 92.

70, 71. **Costly.** The advice of Euphues is quite different (ed. Bond, II, 227): 'For thy dyet, be not sumptuous, nor yet

simple: For thy attyre, not costly, nor yet clownish, but cutting thy coat by thy cloth.'—**express'd in fancy:** showing its
costliness by anything fantastic about it. The next phrase repeats the idea.

72. **the apparel . . . man.** Proverbial. Cf. Fynes Moryson,
Itinerary (1599), II, 46: 'The Wise man hath taught vs, that
the apparrell in some sort shewes the man.'

74. **Are most . . . in that:** show their fine taste and their
gentlemanly instincts more in that than in any other point of
manners. The Second Quarto reads 'Or of a most select and
generous, chiefe in that'; the Folio, 'Are of a most select and
generous cheff in that.' The correction is due to Rowe. See
Textual Notes.

76. **loan . . . friend.** An old saw runs:

I had my			And my	
I lent my	} syluer {		To my	} frynde.
I asked my			Of my	
I loste my			And my	

See Kaluza, *The Romaunt of the Rose*, I, 81, note; Rimbault,
A Little Book of Songs and Ballads, 1851, p. 42.

77. **borrowing . . . husbandry:** A habit of borrowing makes
one less keen about economy.

78–80. **This above all . . . any man.** Thus Polonius rises
from his salutary precepts of worldly wisdom to one great
general truth which includes and ennobles them all.

81. **season this:** ripen this advice; bring it to fruition in
good conduct. Cf. ii, 2, 145: 'She took the fruits of my
advice.'

83. **tend:** are waiting.

94. **put on me:** brought to my notice.

98. **Give me up the truth:** Tell me the whole truth.

99. **tenders:** offers.

102. **Unsifted:** untried, inexperienced.

106–109. Polonius puns on *tender* in the sense of 'an offer'
(l. 106), of 'hold' or 'regard' (l. 107), and finally of 'furnish'
or 'afford' (l. 109): 'Hold yourself at a higher rate,—don't
make yourself so cheap,—or you'll furnish me with a fool for

a daughter (by making a fool of yourself).'—**crack the wind
. . . phrase:** make the poor word pant and wheeze like an
over-ridden horse.—**Running it thus.** Cf. *Comedy of Errors*,
iv, 1, 57: 'Fie, now you run this humour out of breath!';
Chapman, *An Humorous Day's Mirth* (Pearson ed., I, 65):
'Heres a poore name run out of breath quickly!'; Milton,
Animadversion upon the Remonstrant's Defence (Pickering
ed., III, 240): 'You thus persecute ingenuous men all over
your booke with this one over-tir'd rubricall conceit still of
blushing; but if you have no mercy upon them, yet spare your
selfe, lest you bejade the good galloway, your owne opiniaster
wit, and make the very conceit it selfe blush with spur-galling.'
—**Running.** Collier's emendation for *Wrong* (Second Quarto)
or *Roaming* (Folio).

110. In this and her next speech Ophelia speaks with gentle
dignity and defends herself with spirit, though with perfect
respect.—**impórtun'd.** The usual accent in Shakespeare.

112. **fashion:** in precisely the same sense in which Laertes
uses the word in l. 6.—**Go to.** Literally, 'Go away!' and, like
our colloquial *Go way!* (which is an old idiom), used to express reproof, expostulation, impatience, or incredulity. Sometimes it merely closes or shuts off discussion, like 'Very well!'
or 'Enough said!'

113. **countenance:** authority, confirmation.

115. **springes:** snares. The woodcock (though in fact an in-
telligent bird) served as a proverbial synonym for credulous
foolishness. It was even supposed to have actually no brains.
See v, 2, 317. Cf. Heywood, *Pelopæa and Alope* (Pearson ed.,
VI, 299):

> Mens flatteries
> Are just like Circes riches, which can turne
> Vain-glorious fooles to Asses, credulous Fooles
> To Woodcocks.

116. **prodigal:** prodigally, superabundantly.

117–119. **These blazes . . . a-making:** such flashes of youthful fancy, which have more show than substance, and whose
appearance and reality both die out suddenly, even while the
promise is being uttered. Polonius is embroidering the prov-

erb, 'Hot love soon cold.' Cf. Lyly, *Mother Bombie*, iv, 1 (ed.
Bond, III, 206): 'Bauins [i.e., fagots of brushwood] will haue
their flashes, and youth their fansies; the one as soon quenched
as the other burnt.'

122, 123. **Set . . . parley:** When a besieger appears before the
castle of your heart and summons you to a parley, do not immediately enter into negotiations (*entreatments*) for surrender.
The metaphor by which a woman or a woman's heart is identified with a castle or walled town defending itself against be-
siegers was common in the Middle Ages and had become
conventional long before Shakespeare's time.[1] It survives in
the phrase 'to lay siege to one's heart.' Cf. Greene, *Mamillia*,
1583 (ed. Grosart, II, 25): 'What? shall the beauty of Pharicles
enchant thy mynde, or his filed speech bewitch thy senses?
Wil not he thinke the castle wanteth but scaling, that yeeldeth
at the first shot; and that the bulwarke wanted but batterie,
that at the first parle becomes Prisoners?'; Chapman, *May
Day*, i, 1 (Pearson ed., II, 325): 'Well shee may hold out a
parlee or two, for 'tis a weake fort that obeyes at the first or
second summons'; Chapman, *The Blind Beggar of Alexandria*
(Pearson ed., I, 22):

> Prince of Arcadia, louely Doricles,
> Be not discouraged that my daughter heere,
> Like a well fortified and loftie tower,
> Is so repulsive and vnapt to yeelde.
> The royall siege of your heroycke partes
> In her acheeuement will be more renound,
> And with the greater merite is imployde.

The figure is elaborated, with an affectation of military detail,
in Howell's *Familiar Letters*, Book ii, no. 4 (ed. Jacobs, p. 379):

---

[1] See *Gentleman's Magazine*, New Series, III (1835), 199, 200; A.
Schultz, *Das Höfische Leben zur Zeit der Minnesinger*, 1889, I, 577,
fig. 171, and J. von Antoniewicz, *Romanische Forschungen*, V (1890),
248–251, for details and for illustrative figures from old ivory carvings.
For a pageant of such a Castle presented before Henry VIII in 1511 see
Edward Hall's *Chronicle* (ed. 1809, p. 526). For a similar show performed
before Queen Elizabeth for the entertainment of the French ambassadors
in 1581, see Nichols, *Progresses of Queen Elizabeth*, 2d ed., 1823, II,
310–329.

'There are some Beauties so strong, that they are Leaguer-proof, they are so barricado'd, that no Battery . . . can do good upon them. There are others that are tenable a good while, and will endure the brunt of a Siege, but will incline to parley at last; and you know, that Fort and Female which begins to parley is half won.'

126. **In few:** in short; in brief.

127. **brokers:** panders, procurers. Polonius defines the word in l. 129.

128. **Not . . . show.** Ophelia has described Hamlet's vows as 'holy.' Polonius retorts that their holiness is mere disguise; they wear the garb of innocence, but that, he says, is not their true colour.—**investments:** vesture, attire. Cf. 'Whose white investments figure innocence' (*2 Henry IV*, iv, 1, 45); 'In pure white robes, Like very sanctity' (*Winter's Tale*, iii, 3, 22, 23).

129, 130. **mere:** out-and-out.—**Breathing . . . bawds:** speaking in soft and persuasive accents, like hypocritical tempters. Cf. *As You Like It*, ii, 3, 13: 'sanctified and holy traitors'; *Merchant of Venice*, iii, 4, 27: 'I have toward heaven breath'd a secret vow.'—**bawds.** Theobald's emendation for the Quarto and Folio reading, *bonds*. Some editors retain *bonds*, interpreting it as 'vows' or 'pledges'; but bonds do not 'breathe.'

133. **slander:** disgrace; spend discreditably.—**moment:** momentary.

135. **Come your ways:** Come along. *Ways* is an old genitive used adverbially ('on your way'). Cf. iii, 1, 133.

Scene IV.

This scene takes place on the second night of the action and begins shortly after midnight. See i, 1, 174, 175; i, 2, 160 ff., 189, 225, 252, 253.

1. **shrewdly.** The literal meaning of *shrewdly* is 'cursedly,' 'wickedly,' but it is often used (like our *plaguily, confoundedly*) to strengthen a verb (especially one that denotes some disagreeable action).

2. **eager:** sharp. Horatio's method of saying 'yes' has already been noted (i, 2, 241, 242).

3. **hour.** Often dissyllabic and frequently spelled *hower* (so in the Folio here).

6. **the spirit.** Hamlet does not commit himself on the question whether or not the apparition is his father's ghost. Cf. i, 2, 199, 211, 244.—**pieces:** pieces of ordnance. For the old Scandinavian custom of cannon shot as an accompaniment to royal toasts see i, 2, 127 (and note); v, 2, 286–289.

8. **doth . . . rouse:** sits up late and drinks deep.

9. **upspring.** This was a dance or a dance-movement (figure), as Steevens proved from the old play of *Alphonsus*, wrongly ascribed to Chapman (Pearson ed., III, 238):

> We Germans have no changes in our dances—
> An Almain and an upspring, that is all.

Perhaps the upspring was identical, as Elze supposes, with the old German dance called the *hupfauf* (or *hüpfauf*), i.e., 'hop-up.' We are not to suppose that the King is dancing. He might 'open the ball,' perhaps, but would hardly go capering about the chamber! *Upspring* seems to be the subject of *reels*: 'That swaggering dance, the upspring, is reeling through the hall!' (Child).

11. **kettledrum.** Douce cites Cleveland, *Fuscara* (Works, ed. 1687, p. 3): 'As Danes Carowze by Kettle-drums.'

12. **The triumph of his pledge:** the splendid feat of health-drinking in which he drains the cup at a draught.—**Is it a custom?** The King was holding a drinking bout, of the sort for which all Germanic nations were once famous, and the Danes especially so in Shakespeare's day. Cf. Greene, *Mourning Garment* (ed. Grosart, IX, 136): 'Thou must bring home pride from *Spaine*, lasciuiousnesse from *Italy*, gluttony from *England*, and carowsing from the *Danes*.' This custom is distasteful to Hamlet, both by nature and by education, and he does not like it any better for knowing that Claudius is drinking his health (i, 2, 123–128). Horatio's question seems rather odd, if he is a Dane (v, 2, 352). Possibly Hamlet's father had given up the custom. At all events, one cannot agree with Wilson that Ham-

let's 'Ay, marry, is't' indicates that his father 'had also in-
dulged in heavy-headed revels.'

13. **Ay, marry, is't:** Yes indeed it is. *Marry*, originally an
oath ('by the Virgin Mary'), is used as a light expletive. The
dramatic purpose of the long speech that follows is to make
the coming cf the Ghost a surprise, both to Hamlet and to the
audience. There is a similar device before i, 1, 40, and i, 1, 126.

16. **More . . . observance:** more honourable to break than to
observe.

17, 18. **east and west:** far and wide; everywhere. The phrase
modifies 'traduc'd and tax'd.' The Folio omits 'This . . .
scandal' (ll. 17–38).—**tax'd:** taken to task, blamed.—**of:** by.

19, 20. **clip:** call (Anglo-Saxon *clypian*).—**with swinish
phrase:** by calling us pigs.—**Soil our addition:** sully our title—
our reputation.—**indeed.** Used (as almost always in Shakespeare) in the strong sense of 'in point of fact.'

21, 22. **at height:** at the full height (the acme) of possible
achievement.—**attribute:** honour, reputation.

23. **in particular men:** in the case of *individuals* (precisely as
in the case of whole *nations*, which so far Hamlet has been considering). It is interesting to compare Hamlet's eloquent
moralizing with Nashe's reflections on the same vice of drunk-
enness:

'A mightie deformer of mens manners and features, is this vnnecessary
vice of all other. Let him bee indued with neuer so many vertues, and
haue as much goodly proportion and fauour as nature can bestow vpon a
man: yet if hee be thirstie after his owne destruction, and hath no ioy
nor comfort, but when he is drowning his soule in a gallon pot, that one
beastly imperfection will vtterlie obscure all that is commendable in him;
and all his good qualities sinke like lead down to the bottome of his
carrowsing cups, where they will lie, like lees and dregges, dead and vn-
regarded of any man' (*Pierce Penilesse*, 1590, ed. McKerrow, I, 205).

24. **some vicious mole of nature in them:** some natural fault
which is a blemish. In what follows three ways are mentioned
in which this blemish may originate: (1) in their birth, i.e., by
inheritance; (2) by the over-development of some natural tend-
ency; (3) by some habit accidentally or thoughtlessly contracted.

26. **his:** its.

27. **the o'er-growth of some complexion:** the over-development of some part of their constitution. A man's *complexion* (temperament) was thought to be determined by the proportion of the four humours that existed in his physical make-up. These were called blood, phlegm, bile (red bile or choler), and black bile (or melancholy). According as one or another of these substances predominated, the man was sanguine, phlegmatic, choleric, or melancholy. If one of these four tendencies increased to an excessive degree, a fault might be the result—rashness, sloth, irascibility, or moroseness.

29. **o'erleavens:** pervasively modifies (as leaven changes dough).

30. **plausive:** pleasing, agreeable.

32. **nature's livery:** something by which the man is marked by nature. This covers both (1) any inherited peculiarity of temperament and (2) any such peculiarity as results from 'the o'ergrowth of some complexion.'—**fortune's star:** something determined by mere luck. This refers to the accidental forming of 'some habit.'

33. **Their virtues else:** all their other virtues; i.e., all their other qualities, however excellent. *Their* is Theobald's emendation for *His.*—**grace:** holiness

34. **may undergo:** can sustain or support. Human nature is incapable of infinite goodness, but the virtues of these men come as near perfection as humanity can sustain.

35. **Shall:** will be sure to; will inevitably.—**take corruption:** be infected (in the world's opinion). The world will see only their one fault and overlook their many virtues.

36–38. **dram:** small amount; little bit.—**e'il:** evil. The Second Quarto spells the word *eale.* It is a contraction, like *de'il* for *devil.* The Quarto has *deale* for *devil* twice in ii, 2, 627.—**often:** Steevens's emendation for the Quarto reading 'of a.'—**dout:** banish, nullify (literally, do out, put out). The Quarto spells the word *doubt;* as the Folio does in iv, 7, 193.—**To his own scandal:** to the utter disgrace of the man in question. Thus the sentence sums up the whole lesson of ll. 23–36:

'That modicum of evil (in the man) often nullifies (in the world's opinion of him) the whole substantial or underlying nobility of his nature, to his own utter disgrace.'

39 ff. Hamlet, like Horatio, is a scholar and knows how an apparition should be addressed. He understands the danger of speaking to a spirit (see note on i, 1, 42), and he is fully alive to the possibility that this may be a demon in his father's shape. Accordingly he begins by invoking the angels and all good spirits (the ministers or agents of God's grace) to protect him; and then, calling the apparition by his father's name, he adjures it to tell its errand. By using this form of words he avoids to some extent the danger involved in accosting it if it should be a demon; for in that case he has not, strictly speaking, addressed it at all.

40. **health**: salvation. Cf. Woodes, *The Conflict of Conscience* (ed. 1581, Hiij, lf. 2 v°):

> So doo the Diuels,
> Yet of their health they alway doe dispaire.

A *spirit of health* is, then, a good spirit, as opposed to a demon or *goblin damn'd*. The antithesis is carried out in the next two lines. Hamlet does not raise the question whether his father's soul is saved or lost, but whether this apparition is a spirit of good or of evil. If it is the ghost of his father, then he assumes that it has come with good intent.

42. **charitable**: good, benevolent.

43. **questionable shape**: a shape (that of my father) which prompts me to question thee.

44, 45. **Hamlet . . . Dane.** There is no climax in these words. Hamlet the scholar knows that a supernatural being should be called upon by all known names that may belong to it. The theory was that the right name would force or induce it to speak. The same idea is the basis of all such invocations as that which begins the third book of *Paradise Lost*: 'Hail, holy Light,' etc.—**royal Dane.** Hamlet pauses for a moment after these words; but the Ghost says nothing, and he calls upon it passionately for an answer.

47, 48. **canóniz'd**: sanctified, i.e., buried with all sacred rites. *Canónize* was the regular Elizabethan accentuation. Cf. Marlowe, *Faustus*, i, 1 (ed. Dyce, II, 13): 'Shall make all nations to canónize us.'—**hearsèd**: entombed. *Hearse* in Elizabethan English may mean 'bier,' 'monument,' or 'tomb.'—**cerements**: the waxed cloth in which the body was wrapped.

51. **may**: can.

52. **cómplete**. Such dissyllabic adjectives throw the accent back when the next syllable in the verse is accented. See Schmidt, *Shakespeare-Lexicon*, pp. 1413–1415. Cf. i, 5, 61; ii, 2, 491; iii, 2, 65; iv, 1, 1.

53. **Revisits**. A good Elizabethan form of the second person.—**the glimpses of the moon**. This suggests that the sky was broken by strips of cloud, so that the moon appeared only at intervals.

54–56. **and we fools of nature . . . souls**: and causing us (who are, in such a case, reduced to the condition of fools by our weak human nature) to agitate our frame of mind with thoughts which grasp at more than our souls can comprehend. —**we**. Common Elizabethan grammar for *us*.

57. **do**. Emphatic. Hamlet (like Horatio in i, 1, 130) thinks that the Ghost has come back to impose some duty on those who survive.

59. **impartment**: communication.

61. **waves**. So in the Second Quarto. The Folio has *wafts*.— **removed**: remote, distant.

62. **No, by no means!** Hamlet's friends still fear that the apparition is a demon. This comes out clearly in ll. 69–78. Hamlet knows the danger, but is determined to take the risk: he cares nothing for his *life*; and no demon can hurt his *soul*.

65. **a pin's fee**: the value of a pin.

67. **immortal**. This, as well as many other passages, shows that Shakespeare does not mean to represent Hamlet as questioning the main doctrines of Christianity.

72. **assume . . . form**: change its shape from that of your father to a form that shall be horrible. The sense may be

brought out by pausing after *other* and emphasizing *other* and *horrible*. Horatio fears that the apparition may take a fiend's shape and drive Hamlet to suicide. Precisely the same idea is expressed in *King Lear*, iv, 6, 67–72:

> *Edgar.* Upon the crown o' th' cliff what thing was that
> Which parted from you?
> *Gloucester.*   A poor unfortunate beggar.
> *Edgar.* As I stood here below, methought his eyes
> Were two full moons; he had a thousand noses,
> Horns whelk'd and wav'd like the enridged sea.
> It was some fiend.

73. deprive your sovereignty of reason: take away the sovereign control which your reason exercises over you; dethrone your reason.

75–78. The very place . . . beneath. Omitted in the Folio. The poverty of Elizabethan stage scenery made such descriptive passages necessary and thus incalculably enriched the drama. Compare the famous description of Dover Cliff in *King Lear*, iv, 6, 11–24.

75. toys of desperation: desperate fancies or impulses. Horatio refers to what is known as 'altitude fascination'—the impulse to throw one's self down from the edge of a dizzy height. Cf. *King Lear*, iv, 6, 22–24:

> I'll look no more,
> Lest my brain turn, and the deficient sight
> Topple down headlong.

76, 77. motive: moving cause. Cf. i, 1, 105; ii, 2, 587; iv, 7, 16.—**fadoms:** fathoms.

78. waves: beckons, with a motion towards the distance. The Folio reads 'wafts.'

81. My fate cries out. Hamlet feels instinctively that this is the supreme moment of his life. The Ghost speaks to him, as it were, with the tongue of destiny.

82. artire. The same word as *artery*; here in the sense of 'sinew.'

83. Némean. Usually accented on the penult. To kill the lion of Nemea (a valley in Argolis) and fetch his skin was one of the Twelve Labours of Hercules.—**nerve:** sinew.

85. **lets:** hinders.
89. **Have after:** Come on, let's follow.
90. **state:** government, administration.

Scene V.

The Ghost, followed by Hamlet, leaves the stage by one door at l. 86 of scene iv; Horatio and his companions follow, and the stage is left empty for a moment. Then the Ghost and Hamlet reënter by the other door. At l. 112 of scene v Horatio and Marcellus are heard calling from without, and they enter by the same door by which Hamlet and the Ghost had reentered. We are to imagine that the whole interval between the end of scene iv and l. 112 has been occupied in the attempt of Horatio and Marcellus to find Hamlet.

1. **no further.** Hamlet is still uncertain whether the apparition is a ghost or a demon.

3. **flames:** not of hell, but of purgatory, as is shown by ll. 10–13.

6. **bound:** in duty bound; obliged (in reason and charity).

12. **foul crimes.** We are not to think of Hamlet's father as a criminal. He is simply expiating the ordinary sins of mortality, which now appear to him in a more serious light than when he was alive. *Crime* is common in the general sense of 'fault,' 'sin.' Cf. l. 79; ii, 1, 43; iii, 3, 81.

16. **young.** Cf. i, 3, 7, note.

17. **thy two eyes.** The formality of this dual fits the solemnity of the Ghost's address.—**like stars . . . spheres.** Each planet (according to the Ptolemaic astronomy) was fixed in a hollow sphere concentric with the earth and revolving about it as a centre.

18. **knotted . . . locks.** Another suggestion of a detail of Hamlet's personal appearance. Cf. iii, 4, 121: 'your bedded hairs.'

19, 20. **an end:** on end.—**porpentine:** porcupine.

21. **this eternal blazon:** this proclamation or disclosure of the secrets of eternity, i.e., of the world beyond the grave.

23. **If thou didst . . . love.** This adjuration, with Hamlet's reply, suggests the tender affection which existed between father and son.

26. **Murther?** Hamlet's horrified exclamation shows that up to this time he had no definite suspicion of the truth. See i, 2, 256, note.

30, **meditation:** thought. Cf. *Wily Beguiled*, Prologue: 'Ile make him fly swifter then meditation.'

31. **apt:** ready, prompt.

32. **shouldst thou be:** wouldst thou assuredly be.

33. **rots.** Thus the Folios; the Quartos read 'rootes.' The very existence of a slimy water-weed seems to be decay; it thrives in corruption and 'rots itself' through its lazy, stagnant life. Cf. *Antony and Cleopatra*, i, 4, 44–47:

> This common body,
> Like to a vagabond flag upon the stream,
> Goes to and back, lackeying the varying tide,
> To rot itself with motion;

Otway, *The Orphan*, i, 2, 24–26:

> I would be busy in the world, and learn,
> Not like a coarse and useless dunghill weed,
> Fixt to one spot, and rot just as I grow;

Shelley, *The Sensitive Plant*, iii, 94; 'the weeds which were forms of living death.'—**Lethe:** the river of oblivion, one draught of which makes the departed spirit forget his life in this world. Cf. *2 Henry IV*, v, 2, 72: 'May this be wash'd in Lethe and forgotten?'; Drayton, *Queen Isabel to Mortimer*: 'Those black weeds on Lethe banks below.'

35. **my orchard:** i.e., the palace garden; not merely 'a plantation of fruit trees,' as in modern usage. The word is a form of *wort-yard*.

36–38. For the death of Hamlet's father in the old story see Introduction.—**process:** account.—**abus'd:** deceived.

40. **O my prophetic soul!** My soul, by its abhorrence of my uncle, foreshadowed this revelation. To suppose that Hamlet had definitely suspected the **murder destroys the dramatic force** of the Ghost's message (l. 25).

42. **adulterate:** adulterous. Hamlet had not suspected adultery. He had been shocked and grieved by the 'o'er-hasty marriage' (which the Church regarded as incestuous), but what he now learns comes with all the horror of an unsuspected enormity. Note especially l. 105.

43. **witchcraft of his wit.** Claudius, then, had a keen intellect (*wit*) and seductive gifts of mind and manner. Cf. *Othello*, ii, 3, 378: 'Thou know'st we work by wit, and not by witchcraft.' But Claudius's wit *is* witchcraft: he has bewitched the Queen.

50. **decline:** fall back.

54. **a shape of heaven:** a heavenly shape; an angelic form.

58. **soft!** See i, 1, 126, note.

61. **sécure:** unheeding; free from anxiety and suspicion (Latin *securus*, 'without care'). Cf. *King John*, iv, 1, 130: 'Pretty child, sleep doubtless and secure.' For the accent see i, 4, 52, note.

62. **hebona:** ebony, the sap of which was thought to be rank poison. So in Marlowe, *The Jew of Malta*, iii (ed. Dyce, I, 298), 'the juice of hebon' is mentioned as deadly.

63. **ears.** Lightborn in Marlowe's *Edward II* (ed. Dyce, II, 274, 275) boasts that he learned various secret methods of murder in Naples—'to poison flowers,' for example,

> Or, whilst one is asleep, to take a quill
> And blow a little powder in his ears.

Iago uses a metaphor which recalls this passage in *Hamlet*: 'I'll pour this pestilence into his ear' (*Othello*, ii, 3, 362).

64. **leperous.** Cf. l. 72.

68, 69. **posset:** curdle, coagulate. A posset was a curdled drink made of spiced wine or ale, hot milk, grated biscuit, pulp of apples, etc. The compound was something like a custard, and was often said to be 'eaten.'—**eager:** sour, acid.

71. **bark'd:** covered (as with the bark of a tree).

72. **lazar-like:** like a leper. The word is derived from *Lazarus*, the beggar in the parable (*Luke*, xvi, 20).

75. **queen.** *Queen* is the acme of the climax, as in the King's

soliloquy (iii, 3, 55).—**at once:** all at the same time.—**dispatch'd:** instantly deprived.

76. **sin:** sinfulness (in general). There is no reference to any particular deed. Cf. iii, 3, 81: 'With all his crimes broad blown, as flush as May.'

77. **Unhous'led:** not having received the Eucharist (administered by the priest shortly before death).—**disappointed:** unprepared (for death), as by confession and absolution.—**unanel'd:** without extreme unction (A.-S. *ele*, 'oil').

80. **O, horrible!** In the Quartos and Folios this line is a part of the Ghost's speech. An old conjecture gives the line to Hamlet, 'in whose mouth it is a proper and natural exclamation; and who, according to the practice of the stage, may be supposed to interrupt so long a speech' (Johnson). The next line is clearly the Ghost's reply to Hamlet's exclamation.

83. **luxury:** lasciviousness.—**damned.** Dissyllabic.

85. **Taint not,** etc. The Ghost does not accuse the Queen of complicity in the murder; indeed, the context seems to exonerate her in that regard. But Hamlet, when he considers the matter, is still in doubt, and he is not satisfied of her innocence until iii, 4, 30, when her words and bearing prove that she has no suspicion that Claudius is a murderer.

89, 90. **the matin:** the dawn.—**his uneffectual fire:** its fire which gives no heat and which dies out entirely and becomes of no effect as soon as day dawns. Cf. *The Distracted Emperor* (ed. Bullen, *Old Plays*, III, 170): 'As uneffectuall as the gloaworms fyer'; Nashe, *Strange Newes*, 1592 (ed. McKerrow, I, 260): 'A number of Apes may get the glowworme in the night and thinke to kindle fire with it, because it glisters so, but, God wote, they are beguiled, it proves in the end to be but fools fire.'

93. **hell?** Hamlet invokes all the powers of the universe to aid him in his revenge; and he even thinks of calling upon the hosts of hell if they should be needed. Lady Macbeth expressly summons the demons of murder to assist her in killing Duncan (i, 5, 41-51).—**Hold, hold, my heart!** Before this the

Second Quarto and the Folio insert 'O fie.' The text follows
Capell in omitting it. Probably it was an actor's 'gag.'

97. **this distracted globe.** He grasps his head with both
hands, as if it were bursting.

98. **table:** tablet. Small ivory tablets were used for memoranda. Cf. l. 107.

99, 100. **fond:** foolish.—**recórds.** Accented on the second
syllable.—**saws of books:** wise sayings extracted from books.
—**forms:** ideas.—**pressures:** impressions.

107. **My tables!** In his excitement, Hamlet instinctively follows habit and jots down the 'happy thought' that has occurred
to him.—**Meet:** fit, proper.

110. **my word:** my motto; that which expresses the guiding
principle of my life henceforth. Dover Wilson aptly compares
the 'words' or mottoes of the knights in *Pericles*, ii, 2.

113. **Heaven secure him!** Thus Horatio once more expresses
his fear that the apparition may be a demon. Cf. i, 4, 69 ff.

114. **So be it!** An instinctive 'Amen!'

116. **Hillo . . . bird, come.** The halloo of Marcellus reminds Hamlet of the falconer's call in summoning a hawk.
In what follows he speaks flippantly of the Ghost and its
errand. This does not mean that he wishes to conceal the
seriousness of the whole matter from his friends; for that
would be idle, and the end of the scene shows that he has no
such intention. Nor is this light tone a symptom of madness.
It is merely revulsion of feeling after an emotional crisis. The
fearful strain to which Hamlet has been subjected demands
relief, and in such cases the relief may come either in tears or
in laughter and reckless jesting. When he recovers his self-
possession, he speaks soberly and coherently (ll. 165 ff.).

127. **circumstance:** ceremony; especially, ceremonious talk.

136. **by Saint Patrick.** Hamlet still speaks rather wildly,
swearing by a saint whom a Dane would not be expected to
adjure. There is no allusion (as some have thought) to 'blun-
ders and confusion'; nor is it likely that Hamlet is thinking
of St. Patrick's Purgatory—a cave in Ireland supposed to afford an entrance to the world beyond the grave.

137. **offence.** Hamlet's play upon Horatio's word is obvious. He picks it up and applies it in a different sense.

138. **an honest ghost:** a straightforward, honourable ghost; i.e., just what he pretends to be, and not a demon in my father's shape. The emphasis is on *ghost*.

139. **what is between us.** Later, Hamlet confides the secret to Horatio, and to Horatio alone. See iii, 2, 81, 82.

140. **as you may:** as best you can.

141. **soldiers.** Trisyllabic.

147. **Upon my sword.** The hilt of his sword forms a cross, upon which each is to lay his right hand when he swears. Cf. Malory, *Morte Darthur*, x, 18 (ed. Sommer, p. 442): 'He made them to swere on the crosse of a suerd'; Munday, *The Death of Robert Earl of Huntington*, v, 1 (Collier's Dodsley, XIII, 82): 'by the cross of my good blade.' Sometimes the hilt was kissed when such an oath was taken (Collier's Dodsley, VIII, 424). The sword-oath in various forms goes back to ancient Germanic paganism. It is recorded of the Quadi, for instance, that, 'drawing their swords (*quos pro numinibus colunt*) they swore perpetual fealty' (Ammianus Marcellinus, xvii, 12, 21). See Grimm, *Deutsche Mythologie*, 4th ed., I, 169, 170; III, 73; Vordemfelde, *Die Germanische Religion*, 1923, pp. 43, 44.—**sworn . . . already:** since 'in faith' is an oath.

150. **truepenny:** honest old boy. Cf. *The ·Return from Parnassus* (ed. Macray, p. 101): 'What haue we heere, old trupenny come to towne?'

156. **Hic et ubique:** Here and everywhere—a wanderer's motto.

163. **pioner:** miner, digger. Pioners or pioneers were foot-soldiers who dug trenches and mines. Cf. *Henry V*, iii, 2, 91 ff.: 'How now, Captain Macmorris? Have you quit the mines? Have the pioners given o'er?'

165. **as a stranger give it welcome.** It was a point of good manners, when receiving strangers into one's house, not to question them about themselves.

167. **dreamt of** (emphatic): even *dreamt* of.—**your philosophy:** this philosophy that people make so much of. *Philosophy*,

not *your*, is the emphatic word. It means 'natural philosophy' —what we call 'science'—which takes no account of ghosts and spirits. Cf. ii, 2, 384–385: 'There is something in this more than natural, if philosophy could find it out.' For *your* cf. iv, 3, 21 ff.

172. **put . . . on.** A clear allusion to his purpose of counterfeiting madness.—**antic:** fantastic.

174. **encumb'red:** folded, with an air of solemn importance, as of one who knows more than he cares to tell and hugs a secret to his breast.

176–178. **an if:** if.—**be.** A common old form of the plural. —**might:** were allowed to speak.—**giving out:** utterance.— **note:** indicate.

180. **grace:** God's grace. The line is an elaboration of 'So help you God!'—the ordinary form of oath.

184. **commend me to you:** protest my devotion to you. The phrase means literally 'hand myself over to you.'

185. **so poor.** Hamlet alludes to his uncle's having obtained the election to the kingship which would naturally have fallen to *him*. Cf. iii, 2, 354–359.

188. **still:** always.

189. **O cursed spite.** This phrase, in Elizabethan usage, was equivalent to the modern 'What an infernal nuisance!' though more dignified than our idiom. Hamlet is resolved to avenge his father, but he is too highly civilized to welcome the duty that the savage code of his nation and time imposes. Thus he differs from the stock 'revenger' in the old plays, who (in Senecan fashion) revels in bloodthirstiness.

191. **together** (emphatic): i.e., as friends and equals. This is Hamlet's protest against the ceremonious respect which his companions strive to pay him. They stand back to let him go first, as if they were his attendants; but he insists on their walking by his side. Cf. i, 2, 253, 254.

Act II. Scene I.

Between Act I and Act II the interval cannot be more than six or eight weeks. Since the departure of Laertes (i, 3, 87) time enough has elapsed for his father to think a remittance seasonable and for Ophelia to have 'repelled' Hamlet's letters and 'denied his access' to her (ll. 108–110). The interval cannot be long, for when the play begins Hamlet's father had been dead for about two months and scene ii in Act III takes place only four months after the murder (l. 136). In the meantime Hamlet has been acting the madman and Rosencrantz and Guildenstern have been summoned in haste (ii, 2, 4).

1. **notes:** memoranda—in continuation, no doubt, of the 'precepts' in i, 3, 59 ff.

3. **marvell's:** marvellous, wonderfully. Cf. iii, 2, 312.

6. **Marry.** Used colloquially for 'why,' 'indeed,' or almost any similar expletive. See i, 4, 13.

7. **me.** Literally 'for me'; but used colloquially without any special significance.—**Danskers:** Danes.

8. **how:** how they come to be there.—**who:** of what rank.—**means:** supply of money.—**keep:** resort.

9, 10. **finding:** if you find.—**By this . . . question:** by this roundabout means and by giving your conversation this turn. *Question* may mean either 'conversation' or 'enquiry.'

11, 12. **come.** Indicative, not imperative: 'Then you come nearer (to the information you are seeking) than you can do by any personal questions'; and Polonius proceeds to show how this may be done—namely, by making remarks that shall tempt the hearer to tell what he may have observed.—**more nearer.** Such double comparatives and superlatives are common.

19, 20. **put on him:** lay to his charge.—**forgeries:** inventions; imaginary faults.—**rank:** flagrant.

22–24. **wanton:** gay—in the modern colloquial sense; practically synonymous with 'wild.'—**liberty:** freedom from restraint.

25. **fencing.** Not discreditable in itself, but a valued accomplishment (see iv, 7, 72–103). The fencing schools, however,
were frequented by wild young bloods, and to spend much
time in such places might be a sign of dissipation. So Gosson,
The Schoole of Abuse, 1579, fol. 30 rº: 'Fencing is growne to
such abuse, that I may well compare the Schollers of this
schoole, to them that prouide Staues for their owne shoulders;
that foster snakes, in their owne bosoms; that trust Woolues,
to garde their sheepe.' Cf. Greene, *The Debate betweene Follie
and Love*, 1587 (ed. Grosart, IV, 218): 'Hath not Follie
inuented a thousand deuices to drawe a man from idlenesse,
as Tragedies, Comedies, Dancing schooles, Fencing houses,
wrastling places, and a thousand other foolish sportes?'

26. **Drabbing:** licentiousness.

28. **season it in the charge:** modify or soften the accusation
in the very act of bringing it.

30. **incontinency:** immoderate indulgence in any of these
wild courses.

31–35. **breathe . . . quaintly:** suggest his faults so delicately—
with such delicate reticence.—**taints of liberty:** faults incident
to lack of restraint. Cf. l. 24.—**unreclaimed:** not recalled from
a state of wild nature; untamed by age and experience.—**Of
general assault:** attacking everybody; to which all young men
are exposed.

37, 38. **my drift:** my meaning.—**a fetch of warrant:** a war-
rantable device.

40. **soil'd i' th' working:** soiled by the experiences that accompany growth from youth to manhood. The figure comes
from the marks that one's hands leave on delicate material.

43. **Having ever seen:** if he has ever seen.—**crimes:** faults.
Very common in this general sense. Cf. i, 5, 12; iii, 3, 81.

44. **breathe of:** make these suggestions about. Cf. iii, 4, 198.

45. **He closes . . . consequence:** He will be sure to agree with
you, following up your remark as follows.

47. **addition:** title; mode of address.

49. **'a:** he.

50. That Polonius loses the thread of his discourse here

should not lead us to undervalue the wisdom of his advice to his son in i, 3, 58 ff.

58, 59. o'ertook in's rouse: surprised or overcome (by intoxication) in his drinking.—**rouse.** See i, 2, 127, and note. —**falling out:** quarrelling.

63. carp. Merely used to carry out the figure with Polonian thoroughness. Any other fish would do as well.

64. we of wisdom and of reach: we wise and far-reaching persons. Cf. *Wily Beguiled*, i, 2 (ed. Hawkins, III, 301): 'Thus men of reach must look to live'; Heywood, *2 Edward IV* (ed. de Ricci, M 4 r°): 'a iudgement of such reach.'

65. windlasses: roundabout ways. Cf. Mabbe, *Celestina* (ed. *Tudor Translations*, p. 90): 'What a wind-lace hast thou fetcht, with what words hast thou come upon me?'—**assays of bias:** indirect attempts. A figure from bowling. The *bias* is the curve which the bowl makes in reaching its goal—like a 'curve' in baseball.

66, 67. by . . . out: by indirect means discover truths. Polonius forces the sense of *directions* a little for the sake of the formal antithesis.—**lecture and advice:** lesson and instructions.

68. You have me: You catch my meaning. Cf. the modern slang phrase, 'You get me?'

70. Good my lord! Merely a polite phrase of leave-taking, accompanied by a bow, like the French 'Monsieur!'

71. in yourself: by yourself; on your own part. Reynaldo is to use his own eyes and not to rely altogether on 'windlasses and assays of bias.'

73. And let him ply his music. Merely a parting direction to Reynaldo to see that Laertes does not neglect his practice of music—an art in which every gentleman was expected to have some skill. Cf. Sir Philip Sidney's letter to his brother, 1580 (ed. Arber, *An English Garner*, I, 308): 'Now, sweet Brother, take a delight to keep and increase your music. You will not believe what a want I find of it, in my melancholy time.' For Polonius, as Reynaldo is leaving the room, to call after him with this detail is true to the nature of anxious parents.

77. **closet:** private sitting room, boudoir. Cf. iii, 2, 343.

78. **doublet:** a close-fitting jacket. Doublet and hose (breeches) were the regular essentials of masculine attire.—**unbrac'd:** unlaced. The doublet was laced or buttoned from the bottom nearly to the top. At the top it was left open for a short distance, so as to show the shirt. To leave it 'all unbrac'd' was a great disorder in attire, like leaving one's waist-coat unbuttoned now-a-days. Cf. Marston, *What You Will*, i, 1, 21 (ed. Halliwell, I, 226), where Jacomo, in love, enters 'unbraced, and careles drest.'

79. **No hat.** Hats were often worn in-doors. Ophelia would have expected to see Hamlet at the door with his hat on, but he would remove it as he crossed the threshold.—**foul'd:** soiled.

80. **down-gyved:** dangling like gyves or fetters round his ankles. Cf. *Two Gentlemen*, ii, 1, 78-83: 'You chid at Sir Proteus for going ungarter'd. . . . He, being in love, could not see to garter his hose.'

84. **horrors.** The line appears to lack a syllable in the middle, but this was supplied by trilling the last *r* in *horrors*. Furness asks, 'Why not let Ophelia's strong emotion shudderingly fill up the gap?' This confounds sentiment with metre. It might perhaps be maintained that the verse is left incomplete in order, by a kind of discord, to produce the effect of strong emotion; but it has yet to be shown that shudders can count for metrical feet.

85. **Mad.** Hamlet had already begun to 'put an antic disposition on' (i, 5, 172), and Polonius, like the King and Queen, was concerned to discover the cause (cf. ii, 2). Now he thinks he has it.

91. **As:** as if.

92. **shaking of mine arm:** shaking my arm. *Of* is often used in this participial construction.

95. **As:** that.—**his bulk:** his whole body,—literally, the trunk. Cf. *1 Jeronimo*, i, 3, 6, 7 (in Kyd, ed. Boas, p. 304): 'I haue mischiefe Within my breast, more then my bulke can hold.'

96. It is at this moment that Hamlet decides that he must renounce Ophelia and give up all thought of marriage and happiness. To involve an innocent girl in such a revenge as he contemplates would have been a crime. His study of Ophelia's face is but the long look in which he says farewell to his hopes. Some critics, however, imagine that he is trying to discover whether Ophelia is strong enough to stand by him in his plans, and that, reading weakness in her countenance, he renounces her for ever. Such a theory ignores the obvious fact that Hamlet cannot for a moment have wished to make Ophelia his accomplice in a deed of blood.

102. **ecstasy:** madness.

103. **Whose . . . itself:** which has this property when it is violent—that it destroys itself (i.e., the person who suffers from it). Cf. Burton's *Anatomy of Melancholy*, iii, 2, 4 (ed. 1638, p. 538): ' "For if this passion continue," saith Ælian Montaltus, "it makes the blood hot, thick and black, and if the inflammation get into the braine, with continuall meditation and waking, it so dries it up that madness followes, or else they make away themselves." '

112. **quoted:** noted, observed.

113. **beshrew my jealousy!** plague take my suspicious nature! *Beshrew* means literally 'curse.'

114, 115. **proper to:** characteristic of.—**To cast beyond ourselves:** to overshoot ourselves; to err by going too far. It is characteristic of the young not to see all there is in a matter; of the old, to see more than there is in it. Cf. Greene, *Mamillia*, 1583 (ed. Grosart, II, 110): 'You knowe olde men are verye suspitious: . . . wee are colde of complexion, and therefore fearefull by nature, and will quicklye spye a padde [i.e., a toad] in the strawe, and a snake in the grasse.'

118, 119. **which . . . love:** For us to conceal it might cause the King (and us) more sorrow than he will feel displeasure at learning that Hamlet loves you. Polonius, though of very high rank, does not believe that the King and Queen will approve Hamlet's marrying Ophelia. He is mistaken, as the Queen's words prove in v, 1, 267.—**close:** secret.

Scene II.

2. Moreover that: besides the fact that.

5-10. The King's language shows that Hamlet's appearance and behaviour since he has begun to play the madman are very different from what they were in scene ii of the First Act. Then he was merely sorrowful; now he looks and acts like a lunatic. The distinction was doubtless made much more striking on the Elizabethan stage than it usually is in our modern theatres. Cf. l. 150.

6, 7. Sith: since.—**that:** what.

11. of: from. Rosencrantz and Guildenstern are two young noblemen who had been selected, as the custom was, to be Hamlet's playfellows when he was a small boy, and to share his studies and sports until he went to the university.

12. so . . . haviour: so closely associated with his life and ways throughout his youth. The Folios read 'his youth and humour,' which would mean 'his actions and disposition as a young man.'

13. vouchsafe your rest: consent to remain.

14. companies. The plural of abstract nouns is common when two or more persons are thought of. So 'pleasures' in l. 28. Cf. i, 1, 173; i, 2, 251, 254; ii, 2, 290.

16. occasion: opportunity.

18. open'd: if it is disclosed. The King has a bad conscience, and may feel somewhat uneasy about Hamlet's madness; but we are not called upon to see anything in his words beyond their plain meaning. The Queen is distressed at her son's condition, and Claudius is anxious to make her happy. Her request to Rosencrantz and Guildenstern, we observe, is precisely the same as his.

21. more adheres: is more attached. Both the King and the Queen overestimate Hamlet's intimacy with these two noblemen. Hamlet treats them familiarly, to be sure, but he knows better than to trust them.

22. gentry: courtesy.

24. **the supply and profit:** the fulfilment and furtherance.

26–34. Shakespeare has purposely made Rosencrantz and Guildenstern, who always hunt in couples, indistinguishable in character, manners, and language. Their close likeness is amusingly shown in their replies, which are almost antiphonic: Rosencrantz utters a half-line, two whole lines, and a half-line; Guildenstern continues in a speech of exactly the same length and the same metrical arrangement. We note, too, the carefully regulated form of the thanks of the King and Queen, in which the names are so arranged that neither Rosencrantz nor Guildenstern shall feel that either has been more honoured than the other.

27. **of:** on, over.

28. **your dread pleasures:** your wishes as our revered sovereigns.—**into:** into the form of.

30. **in the full bent:** with full intention. The figure comes from the *bending* of a bow when one takes aim.

42. This speech shows the same style of friendly compliment in which the King habitually addresses Polonius, who is a very important person at court and in Danish politics. Both the King and the Queen have a genuine affection for 'the good old man' (as the Queen calls him in iv, 1, 12). *Thou* (instead of *you*) expresses this feeling.—**still:** always.

43–45. **Assure you:** assure yourself; rest assured.—**liege:** liege lord, sovereign.—**I hold . . . king:** I regard my duty both to God and to my king as highly as I value my soul.

47. **policy:** statecraft, statesmanship.

49. **lunacy.** Hamlet had begun to play the madman as soon as he appeared at court after his interview with the Ghost. His behaviour with Ophelia, then, did not first give Polonius the idea that Hamlet was mad, but merely furnished him with an explanation for his supposed madness.

52. **the fruit:** the dessert.

53. **grace:** honour. An introduction by Polonius would be more honourable to them than one by a minor court-official.

54, 55. **He tells me,** etc. The King, throughout the first part of the play, confides immediately to his wife anything that he learns about Hamlet. This is not without importance in determining the feeling of Claudius toward his stepson.—**head:** fountain head, origin.

56. **doubt:** suspect.—**the main:** the main thing; i.e., the general subject that has occupied his thoughts of late.

59. **Norway:** the King of Norway. Cf. i, 2, 28.

60. **greetings and desires:** i.e., the complimentary good wishes with which the Danish missive began.

61. **Upon our first:** as soon as we made known our business.

65-67. **your Highness.** Common for 'your Majesty.'—**griev'd:** aggrieved, offended, indignant.—**impotence:** feeble health. Cf. i, 2, 29.—**borne in hand:** deceived. The phrase implies not merely a single act, but a systematic course of deception.—**arrests:** writs of arrest, summoning him to the King's presence.

71. **To . . . arms:** to bring the question to the test of warfare.

73. **fee:** value. He gave him land which yields an income of three thousand crowns a year. The Quartos make it 'three-score thousand.'

79, 80. **On . . . set down:** on such conditions with regard to the public safety as are (in this document) submitted for your approval. *Allowance* is common in this sense.

80-82. **likes:** pleases.—**at our more consider'd time:** 'at a time when we have more leisure for consideration' (Clark and Wright).—**business.** Trisyllabic.

86-88. **My liege,** etc. Polonius begins a set speech, which has an exordium (ll. 86-105), a narrative part (ll. 106-146), and a peroration (ll. 147-151).—**expostulate:** discuss.—**Why day is day,** etc. Polonius declares that to explain the duties of subjects to their kings would be as superfluous as to define day or night.

90. **brevity is the soul of wit.** This, like many other lines of Shakespeare, has become a proverb in a sense different from that which it bears in its own context. *Wit* here signifies 'wisdom.' The whole remark means: 'The wise or instructive part of every speech may be put in a few words; and what often makes wisdom tedious is the ornaments or flourishes with which it is decked out.'

95. **More matter, with less art.** Not spoken impatiently, as often on the stage. The words combine a compliment to the eloquence of Polonius with a suggestion that the Queen is eager to hear the gist of the matter. The reply of Polonius shows that he takes her remark as a compliment: 'Art, madam? you do me too much honour! This is not *art*: it comes natural to me.'

104. **Thus . . . thus.** Here Polonius almost loses the thread of his discourse, as in his instructions to Reynaldo (ii, 1, 49).

105. **Perpend:** Mark my words and consider.

106. **have while she is mine.** The fondness for distinctions which characterizes the style of Polonius will not allow him to use even so simple a word as *have* without splitting hairs.

109–112. **To the celestial,** etc. Hamlet's love letter was written before he began to play the madman. Its stilted style has done him much harm in the esteem of modern readers. However, he is but following the fashion of Shakespeare's time. No suitor would have dreamed of beginning with so unceremonious a phrase as 'Dear Ophelia.' Compare the burlesque love letter in Middleton and Rowley's *Changeling*, iv, 3 (ed. Bullen, VI, 89).—**a vile phrase.** Hamlet has used *beautified* in the sense of 'endowed with beauties'—as an emphatic synonym for the ordinary word *beautiful*. Polonius censures it as affected and also, no doubt, as suggesting artificial aids to beauty.—**bosom.** Cf. *Two Gentlemen*, iii, 1, 248–250. 'Women anciently had a pocket in the fore part of their stays, in which they not only carried love-letters and love tokens, but even their money and materials for needle work' (Steevens).

116. **Doubt . . . fire.** Hamlet's poetry is poor, as he himself confesses; but it was expected that every lover should show his devotion in verse.

117. **that the sun doth move:** i.e., about the earth—the centre of the system according to the old (Ptolemaic) astronomy.

118. **Doubt:** suspect.

120, 121. **ill at these numbers:** a poor hand at this verse-making.—**to reckon my groans:** to express my love sorrows in the set forms of verse.

123. **whilst . . . him:** as long as this body remains his; as long as he lives. Hamlet thinks of his body as a complicated piece of mechanism to which his soul supplies the motive power. The advance of practical invention has made the word *machine* so familiar that it sounds hopelessly prosaic, but to Shakespeare's audience it was an 'elegant' term. Wordsworth's famous phrase 'the perfect pulse of the machine' (in 'She was a Phantom of Delight'), written in 1804, has been defended on the same ground, but with less reason. The word must have appeared in questionable taste even to Wordsworth's contemporaries.

126. **above:** besides.

131. **might:** could.

133, 134. **As I perceiv'd it.** Polonius (as he has told Ophelia in i, 3, 91–95) had been informed of Hamlet's suit by others. By this time, however, the old man has come to believe that he discovered it for himself.

136. **play'd . . . table book:** stored the matter away in my own mind, as one locks up letters in a desk or makes private memoranda in one's tablets or note-book.

137. **given . . . winking:** forced my heart to shut its eyes to what was going on.

138. **with idle sight:** with unintelligent or unperceiving eyes.

139. **What might you think?** Polonius implies that they could then have supposed him capable of intriguing to obtain a royal alliance for his daughter.—**round:** directly, without mincing matters. Cf. iii, 1, 191; iii, 4, 5.

140. **my young mistress:** this young lady here. Spoken with an air of affectionate jocularity.—**bespeak:** address.

141. **out of thy star.** In ordinary language this would be *out of thy sphere* (as in the Second Folio). Polonius likes to substitute for the usual word one not quite so exact but more novel. Osric in v, 2, has the same trick, but carries it much farther.

142. **prescripts:** definite orders; instructions. The Folio has *Precepts*.

145. **she . . . advice:** she carried out my advice. Good ad-

vice 'bears fruit' when it is carried out in action. See note on i, 3, 81.

147–150. In this account of the development of Hamlet's supposed madness Polonius indulges his imagination and follows the lead of his learning. Burton informs us that many authors 'make leannesse, want of appetite, want of sleepe, ordinary symptoms' of the melancholy of lovers, 'and by that meanes they are often brought so low, that . . . one scarce knows them to be the same men' (*Anatomy of Melancholy*, iii, 2, 3, 1, 4th ed., 1632, p. 509).

148. **watch:** sleeplessness. What we should call *insomnia*.

149. **declension:** decline; downward course (from bad to worse).

150. **raves.** Once more we have a clear distinction between Hamlet's melancholy in i, 2, and his present supposed lunacy. See note on ll. 5–10.

153–155. **Hath there been . . . otherwise?** A clear instance of Polonius's falling into dotage. The King's reply should not be spoken impatiently, but with indulgent courtesy.

159. **the centre:** the earth's centre, which was also the centre of the universe according to the Ptolemaic astronomy.

160. **four hours.** *Four* was used for an indefinite number, as we say 'three or four.' Cf. our use of *forty* and *forty thousand*. Many examples of this use of *four*, etc. (which is very old and not confined to English) are collected by Elze.[1] Cf. *Winter's Tale*, v, 2, 148; *Henry V*, v, 1, 43. Malone's example from Webster's *Duchess of Malfy*, iv, 1, 10 (ed. Lucas, II, 89), 'She will muse foure houres together,' is alone enough to show that Hanmer's emendation, *for*, is unnecessary.

163. **arras:** tapestry hanging on a frame at a little distance from the wall.

165. **thereon:** on that account. *On* and *upon* are very common in this causal sense.

170. **board:** accost, address.—**presently:** instantly; without delay.—**give me leave.** A courteous phrase of request for the

[1] *Jahrbuch der Deutschen Shakespeare-Gesellschaft*, XI (1876), 288–294.

departure of the King and Queen. It means 'permit me to be alone,' and so 'leave me.'

172. God-a-mercy: thank you. The phrase originally meant 'God have mercy!' but it became confused with *gramercy*, itself a corruption of the Old French *grant merci*, 'much thanks.'

174. You are a fishmonger. All sorts of attempts have been made to wring an occult sense out of this wild speech. Coleridge fancied that Hamlet means 'You are sent to fish out the secret.' But it is the business of fishmongers to sell fish, not to catch them. The remark is, in fact, merely a bit of Hamlet's pretended insanity. For him to call the elegantly dressed, dignified, and over-refined courtier—the pattern of all that is elaborate in manners—a fish-seller was the very maddest thing that he could say. The audience, too, would be infinitely amused by the presumed effect of such an announcement on Polonius himself. He receives it, however, with an indulgent smile.

182. a god. Warburton's emendation for 'a good' (Folio, Quarto). He cites *Cymbeline*, iii, 4, 166, where the sun is called 'common-kissing Titan.' Malone adds *King Edward III*, ii, 1, 438, 439 (ed. Tucker Brooke, *Shakespeare Apocrypha*, p. 79):

> The freshest summers day doth soonest taint
> The loathed carrion that it seemes to kisse.

On the ancient theory that the sun breeds maggots see Tilley, *Modern Language Review*, XI (1916), 462–464.

185. Let . . . sun: Keep her at home, away from the temptations of public resorts. Cf. Gosson's warning to ladies to avoid the publicity of the theatres: 'We walke in the sun many times for pleasure, but our faces are tanned before we returne' (*The Schooll of Abuse*, 1579, Shakespeare Society ed., p. 49). Hamlet uses *conception* in the sense of 'intelligence' or 'quickness of understanding,' and then proceeds to pun on the word. Cf. Spenser, *Faerie Queene*, iii, 6, 5–9; Middleton, *More Dissemblers besides Women*, ii, 3, 80, 81 (ed. Bullen, VI, 412):

> Sure if you prove as quick as your conceit,
> You'll be an excellent breeder.

187. **How say you by that?** Not 'What do you mean by that?' but 'What do you say to that?' A triumphant exclamation, like 'I told you so!' *By* in the sense of 'concerning' is very common.—**Still:** always.

195. **the matter.** Polonius means, 'What is the *subject matter* of the book?' But Hamlet chooses to take *matter* in the sense of 'the subject of a quarrel,' as if Polonius had said 'What's the row?' The joke is a very cheap one—well-worn in Elizabethan usage—and thus seems all the madder, since Hamlet was not in the habit of using stale witticisms.

204 ff. **honesty:** honourable conduct. Hamlet means that, although all these things are facts, yet it is not fair to mention them in satirizing old men, since the old are not to blame for their age. If they could 'walk backward,' they would quickly return to a time of life when none of these gibes would be true. For the crab's supposed gait, which had become proverbial, cf. Webster, *The Duchess of Malfy*, i, 1, 355 ff. (ed. Lucas, II, 46):

> Like the irregular Crab,
> Which though't go backward, thinkes that it goes right,
> Because it goes its owne way.

—**should be:** would undoubtedly be.—**old:** only as old.

211. **pregnant:** ready, quick-witted.

212. **happiness:** felicity; cleverness (of phrase or idea).

220. **withal.** At the end of a sentence or clause *withal* is often equivalent to 'with.'

223. **These . . . fools!** This fling may or may not be heard by Polonius, who is on his way out. Anyhow, Hamlet, whose normal manners are very courteous, feigns madness by being as rude as he can. Nobody takes offence at his rudeness, for all accept it as a symptom of insanity.

231. **As . . . earth:** like the general run of mortals.

235. **Neither:** not that either.

240. **strumpet.** Fortune is so called proverbially (as in ii, 2, 515; *King John*, iii, 1, 61: cf. *Henry V*, v, 1, 85; *Lear*, ii, 4, 52; *Cymbeline*, iii, 1, 31), because she grants favours to all men and is constant to none. Cf. Chaucer, *Troilus*, i, 843, 844:

Woost thou nat wel that Fortune is comune
To every manere wight in som degree?

241. the world's . . . honest. A stock joke. Cf. *1 Jeronimo*,
i, 3, 91, 92 (in Kyd, ed. Boas, p. 307):

Isabella. What newes, Ieronimo?
Jeronimo. Strange newes: Lorenzo is becom an honest man.

250. Then is the world one. Cf. *The Return from Parnassus*,
iii, 5 (ed. Macray, p. 126):

Why the wide world that blesseth some with wayle,
Is to our chayned thoughts a darkesome gayle;

Richard II, v, 5, 20, 21:

The flinty ribs
Of this hard world, my ragged prison walls.

251. A goodly one: a fine spacious one.—**confines:** cells.

258. your ambition. They suspect that Hamlet's secret trouble
is disappointment at not having succeeded to the throne, and
on this matter they insist on sounding him throughout the
interview. Hamlet soon discovers their theory, and he teases
them by giving them some ground for thinking they are right,
but no clear evidence.

264 ff. Which dreams, etc. Hamlet has intentionally wan-
dered from the point which Rosencrantz is trying to investi-
gate, and Guildenstern rather skilfully brings him back to it.
The result, however, is simply a quibbling dialogue on the
general subject of ambition. Thus Hamlet outwits his cross-
examiners.

270, 271. Then . . . shadows. This is simply an instance of
that paradoxical reasoning in which the wits of Shakespeare's
time delighted. Guildenstern has said, in effect, that ambition
is merely a shadow; Hamlet argues as follows: 'If ambition is
a shadow, our monarchs and heroes, who are entirely composed of ambition, must be shadows, and our beggars, the only
persons in the world who have no ambition, must alone be
composed of real substance. If, now, the beggars are the only

real bodies, and the monarchs and heroes are shadows, then the monarchs and heroes must be the shadows of the beggars, since there cannot be a shadow without a real body to cast it.' *Outstretch'd* suggests the fantastic length of a man's shadow. The hero seems very tall, but he is in fact only the ludicrously elongated shadow of some quite ordinary beggar.

272. **fay:** faith (Old French *fei*, modern *foi*).

273. **wait upon you:** escort you.

274. **No such matter!** No such thing! Not at all! As usual, Hamlet declines to allow his friends and associates to call themselves his servants. See i, 2, 162–163, 253–254.—**sort you with:** associate you with; put you in the same class with.

275, 276. **I am most dreadfully attended:** My attendants are a very poor lot.

278. **what make you?** what are you doing? (as in i, 2, 164). Hamlet appears to remember that he has neglected to ask the customary question. In reality, he is skilfully introducing, as if it were a mere 'by-the-way,' a cross-questioning which elicits from Rosencrantz and Guildenstern a confession that they *were* sent for.

280–282. **Beggar that I am.** This is intended to foster their belief that Hamlet is suffering from disappointed ambition.—**too dear a halfpenny:** too dear at the price of a halfpenny. His thanks are worthless, he implies, since he has no power in the state.

284. **justly:** honestly.

286. **What should we say?** Being unprepared for Hamlet's questioning, they betray themselves at once by their hesitation.

290. **your modesties.** For the plural cf. ll. 14, 28; i, 1, 173.

292–298. **To what end?** For what purpose? Why should we be sent for?—**That.** Emphatic.—**consonancy:** harmony; undisturbed friendship.—**by what . . . withal:** by anything more sacred still that a better talker might urge in appealing to you. *Propose* in the sense of 'talk' is common.—**withal:** with. Cf. l. 220.—**even:** frank.

301. **of you:** on you.

304–306. **So . . . feather:** Thus my answering my own question in advance will head off your confession, and so your promise of secrecy will not be broken in the least. *Prevent* in the sense of 'forestall' and *discovery* in the sense of 'disclosure' are both common.

307. **mirth:** cheerfulness.

308–310. **frame:** fabric, structure.—**a sterile promontory:** a barren rocky point jutting out into the sea of eternity. By a similar metaphor Macbeth speaks of human life as 'this bank and shoal of time' (i, 7, 6).—**brave:** splendid.

311. **fretted:** adorned with fretwork—like the ceiling of a magnificent hall. Clark and Wright compare Bacon, *Advancement of Learning*, ii, 14, 9: 'If that great Workmaster had been of an human disposition, he would have cast the stars into some pleasing and beautiful works and orders [i.e., patterns], like the frets in the roofs of houses; whereas one can scarce find a posture [i.e., arrangement] in square or triangle or straight line amongst such an infinite number.'

313, 314. **a man.** Some editors follow the Fifth Quarto and omit *a*, but the article is needed. Hamlet's meaning is not 'What a masterpiece is *mankind*!' but 'Look at *a man*, and see what a masterpiece he is!' It is the individual, not the race, that is in his mind, as the rest of the sentence proves. In l. 322 *man* is right, for there the negative is universal: 'No man delights me.'—**infinite in faculties.** Cf. Marlowe, *1 Tamburlaine*, ii, 7, 21–25:

> Our souls, whose faculties can comprehend
> The wondrous architecture of the world,
> And measure every wand'ring planet's course,
> Still climbing after knowledge infinite,
> And always moving as the restless spheres.

—**express:** precisely adapted to its purpose—like a delicately adjusted piece of mechanism.

317. **this quintessence of dust:** this finest extract or sublimation of dust.

328–330. **what lenten entertainment:** what a poor reception. —**coted:** passed.

333. **the adventurous knight:** the knight errant, wandering

in search of adventures. He was a common figure in certain Elizabethan dramas of an old-fashioned type which were the lineal descendants of the mediæval *romans d'aventure*. Good examples are Heywood's *Four Prentices of London* and the equally ludicrous *Sir Clyomon and Sir Clamydes* (written, perhaps, by Thomas Preston, the author of *Cambyses*). This class of plays is ridiculed in Beaumont and Fletcher's famous burlesque, *The Knight of the Burning Pestle*. See Schelling, *Elizabethan Drama*, 1908, I, 198-208.

334, 335. **target:** a small shield.—**the humorous man:** the eccentric man; the man with a dominant whimsey—another stock character in Elizabethan plays. A good example is Jaques in *As You Like It*, whose 'humour' or peculiar whim is satirical melancholy. The Elizabethan age, which gave every encouragement to individuality, abounded in what we call 'odd characters,' and the 'comedy of humours' was in high favour on the stage. Ben Jonson's *Every Man in his Humour* and *Every Man out of his Humour* illustrate the extreme development of this form of drama.

338. **whose lungs . . . sere.** As we might say 'whose risibilities have hair triggers.' The *sere* or *sear* is a part of the mechanism of a gun-lock; if it is *tickle* (delicately adjusted), the gun goes off at a touch. Cf. Nicholas Breton, *Pasquil's Fooles-Cap*, 1600, st. 9:

> And if thou chaunce to meete an idle Mate,
> Whose tongue goes all too glibbe vpon the seare,
> And chiefe delight is so much in his prate,
> As where hee comes, will be chiefe Prater there.

The lungs are often mentioned as the instruments of laughter. Cf. *As You Like It*, ii, 7, 30-33:

> My lungs began to crow like chanticleer
> That fools should be so deep contemplative;
> And I did laugh sans intermission
> An hour by his dial.

338, 339. **the lady . . . for't:** The lady shall speak her mind freely (as ladies like to do), even if that should spoil the regularity of the metre.—**halt:** limp.

344. **Their residence:** their remaining at the capital as a resident company.

346, 347. **their inhibition . . . innovation.** What hinders them (from remaining at the capital) is the new fashion. Hamlet, who has been absent from Denmark at the university, does not know what this new fashion is, as his next speech proves, and Rosencrantz explains: the novelty consists in having companies of boys act in public. All attempts to make the inhibition refer to any of the numerous decrees of the Lord Mayor and Aldermen of London prohibiting plays within the city limits have failed; nor does the context favour any such interpretation.

354, 355. **an eyrie:** a nest or brood—used only of birds of prey.—**eyases:** young or nestling hawks.—**cry . . . question:** shriek out their speeches in a key above that of natural talk—referring to the 'childish treble' of the youngsters' voices. *Question* often means 'talk' or 'conversation.' Cf. Armin, *A Nest of Ninnies*, 1608 (Shakespeare Society ed., p. 55): 'They cry it up in the top of question.'—**tyrannically:** boisterously. The stage tyrant was a proverbially noisy and violent character. Cf. Bottom's wish in *A Midsummer Night's Dream*, i, 2, 30–32: 'My chief humour is for a tyrant. I could play Ercles rarely, or a part to tear a cat in, to make all split.'

356. **berattle . . . stages:** In their plays these children berate the adult theatres, which they style contemptuously 'the common stages.' Cf. Chapman, *All Fools*, iii, 1 (Pearson ed., I, 148): 'Let me, then, schoole him; foot, ile rattle him vp'; Fletcher, *The Humorous Lieutenant*, iv, 1 (ed. Dyce, VI, 493): 'I never was thus rattled.'—**the common stages.** So in Middleton's play, *The Phœnix* (acted by the 'Children of Paules'), an adult actor is called 'a common player' (i, 4).

359, 360. **many . . . thither:** many gentlemen are so much afraid of satirical pens that they hardly dare visit an ordinary theatre lest the world think them behind the times. The *goose-quills* are the pens of the poets who, in writing plays for the child actors, insert speeches berating 'common stages' as unfit to be patronized by any person of taste.

362 ff. **escoted:** supported (financially).—**Will they pursue the quality,** etc.: Will they give up the stage when their voices change? If not, they must become 'common players' in course of time, and then they may well blame their authors for having put into their mouths satirical attacks on their own *succession*, i.e., on what they themselves are going to be by-and-by.—**the quality:** the (actor's) profession.

369. **much to do:** much ado; a great hubbub.—**on both sides.** The grown-up players had retorted by satirizing the child actors.

370–373. **tarre:** egg on, incite. Cf. *King John*, iv, 1, 116, 117:

> And, like a dog that is compell'd to fight,
> Snatch at his master that doth tarre him on.

—**argument:** plot.—**question:** dialogue. For a time no play was saleable unless it embodied a quarrelsome dialogue between a Poet and a Player (on the subject of the grown-up actors and the children's companies).

376. **carry it away:** carry off the booty; get the victory.

377. **Hercules and his load too.** The load of Hercules is the globe, which he bore upon his shoulders to relieve Atlas while Atlas fetched the apples of the Hesperides. The meaning is that the boys 'have won the whole world of playgoers,' 'they carry all before them'; but there may be (as Steevens thought) an allusion to the Globe Theatre and its sign, which is said to have been Hercules with his load (the globe) on his shoulders.

378, 379. **my uncle,** etc. Hamlet is still encouraging the theory of Rosencrantz and Guildenstern that his madness is due to disappointed ambition.—**mows:** grimaces, faces (French *moues*). The Second Quarto reads *mouths*. Cf. iv, 4, 50.

384, 385. **his picture in little:** a miniature of him.—**'Sblood:** by God's blood. Hamlet, in his rôle of madman, startles his companions by this tremendous oath, which fits the style of a swaggering ruffian. Cf. iii, 2, 386.—**philosophy:** science.

387. **Your hands.** Another bit of mad action. Hamlet gives a welcoming hand to his friends at the end—rather than the beginning—of their long conversation.

389–391. **comply . . . garb:** use compliments (or ceremony) with you in this style.—**my extent:** my display of cordiality. See ll. 440 ff. *Extend* in the sense of 'show' is common.—**show:** appear.—**entertainment:** welcome.

395. **In what?** Spoken eagerly, for now at last Guildenstern thinks Hamlet is about to tell what ails him; but the next speech is as baffling to the cross-questioners as ever.

397. **I know a hawk from a handsaw.** A proverb: 'I can distinguish between things that do not resemble each other at all'; 'I have some little common sense and discrimination.' Some think the proverb was taken from the sport of falconry and was originally 'to know a hawk (i.e., a falcon) from a *hernshaw* (a heron)'; but it has not been found in that form, and the corruption, if there be one, is probably older than Shakespeare's time. The speech sounds to Rosencrantz and Guildenstern like mere raving, but the audience understands Hamlet's hidden meaning: he is sane enough when the circumstances are suitable. He has, in fact, given few signs of insanity in the preceding dialogue, but as soon as Polonius enters he talks as wildly as in his previous conversation with the old courtier (ii, 2, 172 ff.).

402. **Happily:** haply, perhaps.

403. **an old man . . . child.** Cf. Latimer, *Second Sermon before Edward VI* (ed. Arber, p. 56): 'Al old men are twise chyldren, as the Prouerb is. *Senex bis puer.* An olde manne, twyse a child.'

406, 407. **You say right . . . indeed.** Addressed to Rosencrantz, in order to seem to be deep in conversation when Polonius comes up.

409. **I . . . you.** The pronouns are not emphasized. Hamlet simply repeats the words of Polonius, mimicking his tone.—**When Roscius . . . Rome.** Since Roscius lived in Cicero's time, the remark might well inform Polonius that his news is stale news; but the old man takes it as mere madness and goes on with the speech which Hamlet has interrupted.

412. **Buzz:** chatter! A rude exclamation signifying that Hamlet takes no interest in what Polonius says, and perhaps

also that his news is old news. Blackstone reports that *buzz* was once in use at Oxford 'when any one began a story that was generally known before.' *Buzzers* for 'idle talkers,' 'gossips,' 'busybodies' occurs in iv, 5, 90. To *buzz* is common in the sense of 'to speak idly or deceitfully.' Cf. Chapman, *The Widow's Tears*, ii, 1: 'Thinke 'twas but a Buzz [i.e., an idle tale] deuis'd by him to set your brains a-work, and diuert your eie from his disgrace.'

414. **Then . . . ass.** Spoken, or chanted, as if it were a line from an old song.

415 ff. **tragedy, comedy,** etc.: Polonius begins well. His first five terms are quite sober, and he very properly distinguishes the pure pastoral (like Guarini's *Pastor Fido* or Fletcher's *Faithful Shepherdess*) from such plays as *As You Like It*, which are comedies with a pastoral admixture. *Tragical-historical*, too, is an acceptable term for what we call 'historical tragedy' (like *Macbeth* or *Julius Cæsar*) as distinguished from 'history' (like *King John* or *Henry IV*). But the old man's tongue runs faster than his thoughts, and he ends his catalogue with a preposterous four-story adjective that never fails to bring down the house. See Textual Notes.

417, 418. **scene . . . unlimited:** dramas that observe the unities of place and time and also those which give no heed to such limitations. The Elizabethan critics were inclined to restrict the place and time in a drama in accordance with what they thought to be Aristotle's rules. Cf. Sidney, *The Defence of Poesy*, ed. Cook, p. 48: 'The stage should always represent but one *place*; and the uttermost *time* pre-supposed in it, should be, both by *Aristotle's* precept and common reason, *but one day*.' Sidney goes on to ridicule the changes of place that the English playwrights allowed.

. . . You shall have Asia of the one side, and Afric of the other; and so many under-kingdoms, that the player, when he comes in, must ever begin with telling where he is, or else the tale will not be conceived. Now, you shall have three ladies walk to gather flowers, and then we must believe the stage to be a garden. By-and-by we hear news of shipwreck in the same place, and then we are to blame if we accept it not for a rock. Upon the back of that, comes out a hideous monster with fire and smoke, and then the miserable beholders are bound to take it for a cave; while, in the mean time, two armies fly in, represented with swords and bucklers, and then, what hard heart will not receive it for a pitched field?

Shakespeare almost always wrote plays with 'scene unlimited,' but he was well aware of the so-called rules, and in *The Tempest* he has given us a specimen of what he could do when he chose to observe them. The action of that comedy is confined to one day and the place to a single island—though with some minor shifts.

418–420. Seneca. The favourite classical tragedian in Shakespeare's time. His plays had a profound effect on the English drama.—**Plautus.** The plot of *The Comedy of Errors* comes in the main from the *Menaechmi* of Plautus, but there is also substantial borrowing from his *Amphitruo*. Latin classical plays were often performed at the universities and public schools, both in the original and in translation. Polonius, like Hamlet, was a 'university man' (see iii, 2, 104 ff.).—**the law of writ:** plays composed according to the rules of writing—those that observe the three unities (of time, place, and action). —**the liberty:** plays which show complete freedom from such restrictions. Polonius is summing up what he has already said. —**only:** uniquely excellent.

421. Jephthah. See *Judges*, xi. The song (identified by Steevens) is one of a large class of Scriptural ballads. It was entered in the Stationers' Register in 1567 or 1568 and again in 1624 (Arber, I, 355; IV, 131) and occurs in a seventeenth-century black-letter broadside, in the Roxburghe collection, III, 201 (ed. Ebsworth, VI, 685, 686). The first stanza runs as follows in a manuscript copy of about 1600 (*Shirburn Ballads*, ed. Clark, p. 175):

> I read that, many yeares ago,
>   When *Jep*[*t*]*ha*, Judge of *Israel*,
> Had one faire Daughter, and no moe,
>   Whom he beloued passinge well,
>   And as by lot, God wot
>   It came to passe, most like it was,
>   Great warres there should be,
>   And who should be chiefe but he, but he.

424. What treasure had he? Polonius knows what the answer must be. He is humouring the supposed madman. Besides, he expects more evidence in support of his theory as to the cause of Hamlet's insanity.

427. passing: surpassingly.

428. Still: always. Cf. l. 187.

432. that follows not. Polonius understands this to mean 'That doesn't *logically* follow,' and takes the remark for mere insanity. There is no deep meaning in the passage: Hamlet is talking madly.

438. row: stanza.

439. my abridgment: the players, who cut short my quotation. If it were not for them, I would recite more of the 'pious chanson' for you.

440. masters: gentlemen.

442, 443. valanc'd: fringed with a beard. An old-fashioned bed had not only curtains attached to the bedposts and enclosing the sleeper, but also a 'valance'—drapery that hung from the bedstead to the floor.—**to beard me.** Cf. *Macbeth*, v, 5, 6: 'We might have met them dareful, beard to beard.'

443, 444. lady. Said to the boy who acted young women's parts. No actress appeared on a public stage till the revival of the theatre after the Restoration; but ladies of rank often played in masques at court.—**mistress:** madam.

445. chopine: a kind of wooden stilt, sometimes a foot or eighteen inches in height, placed under the sole of a woman's shoe to increase her stature. Chopines were much worn in the East and in Venice, and the fashion made some progress in England in the seventeenth century. See Bulwer, *Anthropometamorphosis*, 1653, pp. 550, 551; Fairholt, *Costume in England*, ed. Dillon, 1885, II, 72, 73, and fig. 37. Cf. Marston, *The Dutch Courtezan*, iii, 1 (ed. Bullen, II, 50):

> *Tysefew.* Dost not wear high cork shoes—chopines?
> *Crispinella.* Monstrous ones.

446. crack'd. A coin would not pass if it had a crack extending from the edge to a point inside the circle that surrounded the monarch's head or other device. Hamlet's pun is clear enough. He hopes that the boy's voice is not so cracked as to spoil its *ring*—that it is still 'as clear as a bell.'

447, 448. **We'll e'en to't:** We'll just go at it.—**French falconers.** Famous for their skill and for the excellent training of their falcons. George Turbervile credits the material of his elaborate *Booke of Faulconrie*, 1575, to two Italian and six French falconers.—**fly . . . see:** let the hawk fly in quest of any bird in sight; undertake anything, no matter how difficult.

451. **your quality:** your professional ability. Cf. l. 362.—**passionate:** emotional.

456. **caviary to the general:** a delicacy not appreciated by the general run of playgoers.—**caviary:** caviare—a Russian relish made of sturgeon's roe. It was a novelty in England in Shakespeare's time, and fondness for it was an 'acquired taste.' Nicholson quotes Nicholas Breton, *The Court and Country*, 1618 (D3, lf. 2):

> This [a Porpose Pye] was one of your fine dishes. Another, a great Lady sent him, which was a little Barrell of *Cauiary*, which was no sooner opened and tasted, but quickly made vp againe, was sent backe with this message, Commend me to my good Lady, and thanke her honour, and tell her we haue black Sope enough already; but if it be any better thing, I beseech her Ladyship to bestow it vpon a better friend, that can better tell how to vse it.

458–470. **cried in the top of mine:** were more authoritative than mine; literally, called out with a louder voice than mine. Cf. l. 355.—**set down:** written, composed.—**modesty:** moderation; artistic restraint; freedom from extravagance.—**cunning:** skill.—**sallets:** salads; hence, figuratively, highly seasoned or spicy passages.—**affectation.** The Folio reading. The Second Quarto has *affection*, which means the same thing.—**honest:** gentlemanly; in good taste.—**wholesome:** sound and clear.—**more handsome than fine:** elegant, but not gaudy or overdecorated.—**Priam's slaughter.** See Æneid, ii, 506 ff.

472 ff. Whether the passages that follow are actually quotations from some lost tragedy is an insoluble question. Probably not. At all events, there is no satire involved. To make the recited passages sound like histrionic recitation ('a fiction and a dream of passion') they must be sharply distinguished

from the blank-verse speeches in HAMLET itself; and this effect of declamation (as contrasted with natural passion) is produced by overcharging the style. The contrast is strengthened by putting the actual dialogue of the scene in prose. See A. W. von Schlegel, *Sämmtliche Werke*, ed. Böcking, VI, 251.[1]

472. **th' Hyrcanian beast:** 'th' Hyrcan tiger' (*Macbeth*, iii, 4, 101). Cf. *3 Henry VI*, i, 4, 155; Æneid, iv, 367 ('Hyrcanae tigres'). Hyrcania was a wild region in Asia.

473. **begins.** Emphatic. Though Hamlet has misquoted the passage, he has still made a good verse. We are thus prepared for his proposal in ll. 565 ff.

474 ff. As Steevens observed, there is a strong resemblance between the style of this speech and the language in which Marlowe tells the same story in his *Tragedy of Dido*, Act ii. Note particularly his description of Pyrrhus (ed. Dyce, II, 387):

> At last came Pyrrhus, fell and full of ire,
> His harness dropping blood, and on his spear
> The mangled head of Priam's youngest son;
> And, after him, his band of Myrmidons,
> With balls of wildfire in their murdering paws,
> Which made the funeral flame that burnt fair Troy.

476. **couched:** hidden.—**horse.** See Æneid, ii, 13 ff.

478, 479. **dismal:** ill-omened.—**gules:** the heraldic term for 'red.'—**trick'd:** adorned. Another heraldic word. Lines 479–486 afford a good example both of the power of this passage and of its intentionally overcharged style.

481, 482. **with:** by means of.—**parching.** The city was on fire.—**tyrannous:** savage, ferocious.

484, 485. **o'ersized:** glued over.—**coagulate:** coagulated, clotted.—**like carbuncles.** The carbuncle was thought to emit light by its own nature. Cf. Hawes, *Pastime of Pleasure*, xi, 33:

> Carbuncles in the most darke nyght
> Dothe shyne fayre with clere radiant beames.

---

[1]'Was in dem Schauspiele selbst wieder als dramatische Dichtung erscheinen sollte, musste gegen dessen würdige Poesie so wie theatralische Erhöhung gegen die einfache Natur abstechen.'

491. His antique sword: the sword which he had wielded long ago in his youth. See i, 4, 52, note. Cf. Æneid, ii, 509–511:

> Arma diu senior desueta trementibus aevo
> Circumdat nequiquam umeris, et inutile ferrum
> Cingitur, ac densos fertur moriturus in hostes.

495. the whiff and wind. Cf. *Troilus and Cressida*, v, 3, 40, 41:

> When many times the captive Grecian falls,
> Even in the fan and wind of your fair sword.

—**fell:** cruel, fierce.

496. unnerved: feeble in sinew. Cf. Marlowe, *Tragedy of Dido*, ii (ed. Dyce, II, 388):

> Whereat he lifted up his bedrid limbs,
> And would have grappled with Achilles' son,
> Forgetting both his want of strength and hands;
> Which he disdaining, whisk'd his sword about,
> And with the wind thereof the king fell down.

—**senseless:** having no feeling.—**Ilium.** Used in the mediæval sense of the *arx* (citadel) of Troy, not for Troy as a whole.

498. his: its.

499. Takes . . . ear. Here the overcharging of the style is unsuccessful, and the effect is that of bombast.

503. like . . . matter. *His will* means 'his purpose'; *his matter*, 'the accomplishment of his purpose.' As a neutral stands idle between two parties, so Pyrrhus paused midway between his purpose and its fulfilment.

505. against: just before.

506. rack: clouds. Dyce quotes Bacon's *Sylva Sylvarum*, § 115: 'The winds in the upper region, which move the clouds above, which we call the rack.' Cf. *Tempest*, iv, 1, 156.

507. the orb below: this round earth—'Tellus' orbed ground' (iii, 2, 166).

509. the region: the sky; the air. Cf. l. 606.

511. Cyclops'. The Cyclopes were the gigantic workmen of Vulcan (*Hephæstus*), the god of smiths' work and the manufacture of armour.

512. for proof eterne: to stand the test forever.

513. remorse: pity, compassion.

515. Out. An interjection of contempt and abhorrence.—
strumpet Fortune! See note on l. 240.

517. fellies: the 'rim' of the wheel.—**nave:** the hub.—**her
wheel.** The allegory of Fortune's wheel is current under two
forms, both known to Shakespeare. In the strictly classical
form, Fortune is represented as riding on her wheel, which
turns constantly. A variation is seen in the conception of
Fortune as standing 'upon the rolling restless stone' (*Henry V*,
iii, 6, 31). The second form, popular in the Middle Ages and
later, represents Fortune as sitting by a wheel which she turns
by means of a crank. On this wheel are mortals, who are therefore sometimes rising, sometimes at the summit, and sometimes declining or at the very bottom of their fate. It is this
latter figure which Edmund has in mind in *King Lear* (v, 3,
174) when he says, 'The wheel is come full circle; I am here,'
i.e., 'I began life at the very bottom; I have risen to the summit
of prosperity; and I have now descended to precisely the same
insignificance at which I began.' See Patch, *The Goddess
Fortuna*, 1927, Chapter V.

521. It shall . . . beard. Hamlet, who has been deeply moved
by the Player's tragic speech and action, is naturally irritated
at Polonius's criticism, and retorts with the freedom which
madness allows: 'Too long? So is your beard! We'll send
them both to the barber's together.' To Polonius this rude
gibe sounds like insanity, for it stands in marked contrast to
Hamlet's well-known courtesy of speech and manner (see
note on l. 223). Besides, like other jests which Hamlet makes
when talking with Polonius, it is a stock joke, and therefore
quite beneath Hamlet's dignity as a witty man. Cf. Middleton,
The Mayor of Queenborough, iii, 3 (ed. Bullen, II, 56):

> Call in the barber.—If the tale be long,
> He'll cut it short, I trust; that's all the hope.

522. a jig: a comic dialogue (or short farce) in song, much
like some of the 'turns' in our vaudeville shows (cf. iii, 2,

132). Jigs were a favourite form of entertainment on the stage and often followed the performance of a play. Cf. *Pasquil and Katherine* (ed. Simpson, *The School of Shakespeare*, II, 150): 'The Iigge is cal'd for when the Play is done.' Most of the old jigs are lost. For discussion and specimens see Baskervill, *The Elizabethan Jig*, 1929. Cf. W. J. Lawrence, 'The Elizabethan Stage Jig' (*Pre-Restoration Stage Studies*, 1927, pp. 79 ff.).

525. **mobled:** muffled. The word is unusual and strikes Hamlet as odd. Polonius, however, admires it just because it *is* unusual. He also wishes to soothe Hamlet's irritation by finding something to praise in the Player's speech.

529. **bisson rheum:** blinding tears.—**a clout:** a cloth.

531. **o'erteemed:** worn out by childbearing.

534. **state:** government of the world.

539. **Unless . . . at all:** unless the Epicurean doctrine be true, that the gods live in unruffled calm and are never disturbed by sympathy for mankind.

540, 541. **milch:** flowing with tears; literally, yielding milk. —**eyes:** the stars.—**passion:** strong emotion.

542, 543. **whe'r:** whether.—**in's:** in his.

545-550. **bestow'd:** lodged and otherwise provided for.— **abstract.** Always a noun in Shakespeare.—**you were better.** *You* is originally dative in this idiom: 'It would be better *for you.*' It was felt as a nominative, however, and '*I* (*thou, he*) were better' was used instead of *me* (*thee, him*). Cf. a similar confusion in 'if you like,' which meant originally 'if it like (i.e., please) you.'

552. **I will use them,** etc. Polonius means this as a compliment, for he has already expressed his admiration for these players.

553, 554. **God's bodykins.** A common grotesque oath. *Bodykins* means 'little body,' i.e., 'the host' or 'consecrated wafer.' Such vulgar swearing, being foreign to Hamlet's usual talk, helps to convince the Danish court that he is really mad. Cf. l. 384; iii, 2, 386.—**after:** according to.

562. **The Murther of Gonzago.** No such drama is known,

nor is it likely that it ever existed apart from the tragedy of
HAMLET. Plays within plays, however, were common—as in
A Midsummer Night's Dream, *The Tempest*, Kyd's *Spanish
Tragedy*, and Beaumont and Fletcher's *Knight of the Burning
Pestle* and *Four Plays in One*. See W. J. Lawrence, *Englische
Studien*, XXXIII (1904), 384–403.

566. **dozen or sixteen lines.** Much ingenuity has been wasted
in identifying Hamlet's dozen or sixteen lines, as if we were
to suppose that Shakespeare wrote *The Murther of Gonzago*
without them and then inserted them somewhere!

570. **mock him not.** Another indication of Hamlet's courtesy.
He himself can poke fun at Polonius, for his mockery will
pass as madness and is therefore not an insult. But it would
be quite another thing for the players to make sport of the old
nobleman, and Hamlet is alive to the temptation they might
feel to follow his own example, especially since they may not
have heard of his supposed madness.

574. **Good my lord!** Spoken with a low bow, as a courteous
phrase of leave-taking. Cf. ii, 1, 70.

576. **rogue:** poor creature; wretched fellow.

578–580. **dream.** Emphatic.—**passion:** strong emotion.—
Could . . . conceit: could force his soul into such accord with
his conception (of the part he played) that, by the operation
of his soul (upon his bodily powers), his whole face grew pale.

581–583. **aspéct.** Accented on the second syllable.—**his
whole function:** all the powers of his body—i.e., all those that
operate to express emotion. Cf. *Macbeth*, i, 3, 140, 141:
'Function Is smother'd in surmise.'—**forms:** appearances
(such as those mentioned in ll. 580–582).—**his conceit:** his
conception of the part.

584. **For Hecuba:** Priam's wife, whose passionate grief is
described in ll. 525 ff.

587. **the motive:** the moving cause, the incentive. Cf. i, 1,
105; i, 4, 76; iv, 7, 16.

590. **Make mad . . . free:** by his description of the crime
he would drive those spectators mad who had any such sin
on their conscience, and would horrify even the innocent.

591. **the ignorant:** those who had not intelligence enough to comprehend the actor's words—the 'groundlings,' for example, who (as Hamlet says in iii, 2) are unable to understand anything but pantomime and noise.—**amaze:** paralyze, stun. Cf. iii, 2, 339; iii, 4, 112.

594, 595. **A dull . . . rascal:** a stupid and poor-spirited wretch. *Mettle* (the same word as *metal*) is often used for one's 'material' or 'quality,' and so for one's 'spirit' or 'temper.'— **peak Like John-a-dreams:** go moping about like one in a dream. To *peak* is, literally, to 'pine away,' as in *Macbeth*, i, 3, 23: 'Shall he dwindle, peak, and pine.' *John-a-dreams* (i.e., 'of dreams') was a more or less proverbial name for a dreamy, absent-minded fellow. Collier quotes Armin, *A Nest of Ninnies*, 1608 (Shakespeare Society ed., p. 49): 'His name is John, indeede, saies the cinnick; but neither John a nods, nor John a dreames.'—**unpregnant of my cause:** with no real sense of the cause to which I should be devoted, heart and soul. Cf. *Measure for Measure*, iv, 4, 22, 23:

> This deed unshapes me quite, makes me unpregnant
> And dull to all proceedings.

597, 598. **property . . . life:** all that he possessed. He was robbed of his crown, of his queen—ay, of his very life!— **defeat:** destruction.

598 ff. **Am I a coward?** Hamlet rages against himself for stupid inactivity—not for hesitation or weakness of will. He has done nothing to avenge his father and seems incapable of doing anything. Why? Not, surely, because he is a coward! Yet even *that*, he exclaims, with bitter irony, is possible: otherwise he must have killed his uncle long ago. Thus he relieves his excitement by railing until, at the end of the soliloquy, he grows calm and expresses in the plainest language what the matter really is: *he needs evidence*. He must not kill a man on the word of an apparition, and thus far no other testimony has been procurable. He is angry at what he thinks his own stupidity and he calls upon his brains to go to work. They have, indeed, obeyed him before he spoke: 'The play's the

thing!' It will force the King to confession, and then Hamlet can act when once he 'knows his course.'

600. beard. The play contains several hints of Hamlet's personal appearance. We have already learned that he has 'knotted and combined locks' (i, 5, 18) and that he is not a Hercules (i, 2, 153).

601, 602. gives me ... lungs? 'You lie in your throat' was a greater insult than simply 'You lie,' because it implied that the lie was deliberate and not a casual lip-falsehood. 'As deep as to the lungs' is, then, 'in the superlative degree.' Cf. Webster, *The Devil's Law-case*, iv, 2, 643 (ed. Lucas, II, 306): 'Ile give the lye in the stomacke—that's somewhat deeper then the throat'; *The Birth of Merlin*, ii, 2, 99 (ed. Tucker Brooke, *Shakespeare Apocrypha*, p. 360): 'Thou liest beneath thy lungs'; Heywood (Pearson ed., IV, 160): 'Hee lies below his entrayles.'

603. 'Swounds: by God's wounds—our 'Zounds.'

604. pigeon-liver'd. The supposed gentleness of the dove was explained in the old physiology on the theory that it had no gall and hence no bitterness or capacity for resentment. 'He has no more gall in him than a dove' says Viola of her patient husband in Dekker's *Honest Whore* (Pearson ed., II, 10).

606. the region kites: the kites of the air. Cf. l. 509.

608. Remorseless: pitiless. Cf. l. 513.—**kindless:** unnatural.

610. brave: fine, noble.

611. father. First supplied in the Third Quarto (1611). See Textual Notes.

612. by heaven and hell. Heaven prompts him to revenge because his uncle deserves death; hell, because he is actuated by anger and hatred.

613. unpack: unload, relieve.

615. scullion. So the Folio. The Second Quarto reads 'stallyon.' No misprint is easier. Wilson accepts *stallion* in the sense of 'a male courtesan.' For *scullion* (kitchen wench) applied to a railing woman see *2 Henry IV*, ii, 1, 65.

616. About: Go to work!

617-620. guilty creatures ... malefactions. Several anecdotes of this kind were current. The German *Hamlet* (*Der Bestrafte Brudermord*) contains at this place such a story about a woman who had murdered her husband. Heywood, in his *Apology for Actors*, 1612 (G–G 2), tells of two such occurrences, one of which he says happened at Lynn in Norfolk when Lord Sussex's company was playing there, the other at Amsterdam during a visit of the English comedians.

618, 619. **cunning of the scene:** the skill with which the play was acted.—**presently:** instantly; on the spot.

621, 622. **For murther . . . organ.** The doctrine that 'murder will out' is strongly asserted in Chaucer, *The Nun's Priest's Tale*, B 4240 ff. (ed. Robinson, p. 240):

> O blisful God, that art so just and trewe,
> Lo, how that thou biwreyest mordre alway!
> Mordre wol out, that se we day by day.
> Mordre is so wlatsom and abhomynable
> To God, that is so just and resonable,
> That he ne wol nat suffre it heled be.
> Though it abyde a yeer, or two, or thre,
> Mordre wol out, this my conclusioun.

625. **tent:** probe.—**blench:** flinch.

626 ff. Coleridge (*Shakespearean Criticism*, ed. Raysor, I, 28) aptly quotes Sir Thomas Browne, *Religio Medici*, i, 37 (*ca.* 1635): 'I believe . . . that those apparitions and ghosts of departed persons are not the wandering souls of men, but the unquiet walks of devils, prompting and suggesting us unto mischief, blood, and villany.' A fine outspoken case of the belief that the devil may take the shape of a dead man occurs in *Every Woman in her Humour*, 1609 (ed. Bullen, *Old English Plays*, IV, 359, 360). See also Kyd, *Cornelia*, iii, 1, 128–147 (ed. Boas, pp. 125, 126); Tourneur, *The Atheist's Tragedy*, iii, 2 (ed. Nicoll, p. 218).

630. **As he is:** as [well may be the case, for] he is. The elliptical use of *as* is very common.—**such spirits:** such conditions of one's temperament. Cf. Fletcher, *Women Pleased*, iii, 4:

> I am not mad,
> Nor does the devil work upon my weakness;

The Night Walker, iii, 2, 5, 6:

> They say spirits appear
> To melancholy minds, and the graves open.

631. **Abuses:** deceives, deludes (by appearing in the likeness of my father and falsely accusing my uncle of murder).—**to damn me:** by persuading me to kill an innocent man.

632. **More relative:** referring back more surely from the evidence to the fact—hence, more positive and cogent, more conclusive. The First Quarto reads: 'I will haue sounder proofes.' Cf. D'Avenant, *The Platonic Lovers*, v (ed. 1872, II, 98):

> He doth proceed on grounds so relative
> As would persuade the wisest to a jealousy.

Act III. Scene I.

---

1. **by no drift of circumstance:** by no turn which you could give to the conversation (cf. i, 5, 127; ii, 1, 10). Thus the Folio; the Second Quarto reads 'conference.'

2. **puts on this confusion:** acts in this distracted way. *Puts on* means simply 'clothes himself with,' and does not suggest (as in modern usage) something *assumed* or *counterfeited*. Such figures from clothing are remarkably common in Shakespeare.

12. **disposition:** mood; inclination at the time (not, general disposition). Guildenstern is no fool, and he has seen the effort which it costs Hamlet to be cordial.

13, 14. **Niggard . . . reply:** He was not inclined to conversation, but he talked very freely in answer to any questions we asked. *Free* does not imply that Hamlet gave satisfactory answers (cf. ll. 5–10).—**question:** talk (not, interrogation). —**demands:** questions. The word does not carry any suggestion of peremptoriness.

14, 15. **assay . . . pastime:** try to attract him to any sport or amusement, in order to relieve his mind.

17. **o'erraught:** overtook and passed.

23. **the matter:** the subject matter; i.e., the performance.

24. **content:** please. Claudius is genuinely eager to live at peace with his stepson for two reasons—his own safety, and his love for the Queen, who is naturally distressed by the present situation. It is only after he learns that Hamlet knows of the murder, and that there can be no peace between them (that is, after the play within the play), that he takes measures to destroy Hamlet.

29 ff. Here again (as in ii, 2) the King confides his plans with respect to Hamlet to the Queen.—**closely:** privately.

31-35. **Affront:** meet face to face.—**espials:** spies.—**bestow ourselves:** station ourselves.—**encounter:** meeting, interview. —**frankly:** freely.—**as he is behav'd:** according as he behaves himself.

40-42. **So shall I hope,** etc. This conveys to Ophelia and her father a suggestion that the marriage which Polonius had thought impossible (ii, 2, 141, 142) would be quite agreeable to the King and Queen.

43. **Gracious:** my gracious lord.

44, 45. **bestow ourselves:** take our places [behind the arras]. —**book.** A prayer book (see l. 89) or some book of devotion, as the word *exercise* (for 'religious exercise') suggests. Cf. l. 48.—**colour:** give a specious (colourable) pretext to.

46, 47. **to blame:** blameworthy, culpable. Polonius does not mean that Ophelia is doing wrong. He simply moralizes the situation in a general way. A young woman with a prayer book, but not praying, is a good emblem for the hypocrisy of us mortals.—**prov'd:** found true by experience.

49-54. **'tis . . . burthen!** This remark of the King's is an aside and is therefore perfectly sincere: it is, in fact, a thought, not a speech. Claudius, like Macbeth, has sinned hideously under the influence of temptation, and his conscience, like Macbeth's, torments him incessantly. Herein he differs from such deliberate villains as Iago and Edmund (in *King Lear*). His words prepare us for the wonderful scene (iii, 3) in which he tries in vain to repent and makes a hopeless attempt to pray.

52. **to:** in comparison with. The haggard cheek under the paint is ugly in contrast with the paint that beautifies it.

56–88. In this famous soliloquy Hamlet is often thought to be dallying with the purpose of suicide as a means of escape from his duty. But this view overlooks the facts of the situation and does violence to Hamlet's own words. He has formed his plan to make the King betray himself, has written his 'dozen or sixteen lines,' and is eager to try the crucial experiment. Meanwhile there is a wearisome interval in which he can do nothing but wait for nightfall. Inaction brings depression of spirits, and the thought recurs to him that death would be a relief. All men have such thoughts at such moments, and to all men—as to Hamlet—they lead to the further reflection that every one has the power of life or death in his own hands. But reflections are not purposes. By *the question* Hamlet does not mean 'the question for me to decide now, in my own case,' but rather the question which, as it seems to him, must sooner or later force itself upon every man: 'Is it nobler to live miserably or to end one's troubles by a single stroke?' The answer, he says, would be obvious if death were only a sleep. The whole course of his argument is general, not personal. He is not suffering from the scorn of the world, the law's delay, or the insolence of office.

57. **in the mind.** This modifies *nobler*, not *suffer*: 'Does it show a nobler quality of mind to submit or to resist?'

59, 60. **to take arms,** etc. When troubles come like an onrushing sea, suicide is like the act of a warrior who runs to meet the waves, sword in hand, thus opposing them until they close over his head and his troubles are ended. Ingleby compares Abraham Fleming's translation of Ælian, xii, 23 (*A Registre of Hystories*, 1576, fol. 127 v°):

> Some of them [i.e., of the Celts] are so boulde or rather desperate, that they throw themselues into ẙ fomey floudes with their swordes drawne in their handes, and shaking their Iauelines, as though they were of force and violence to withstand the rough waues, to resist the strength of the streame, and to make the floudes affraide least they should be wounded with their weapons.[1]

[1] See also *New Shakspere Society Transactions*, 1887–92, pp. 49*–52*.

63. **a consummation:** a final settlement of everything. Cf. Montaigne, *Essais*, iii, 12 (Florio's translation, ed. 1603, p. 627): 'If it be a consumation of ones being, it is also an amendement and entrance into a long and quiet night. Wee finde nothing so sweete in life, as a quiet rest and gentle sleepe, and without dreames.'

65. **the rub:** the impediment, the difficulty. A metaphor from bowling. A *rub* is any obstruction which hinders or deflects the course of the bowl.

67. **shuffled . . . coil:** disentangled ourselves from the tumult of human affairs. *Coil* carries not only the sense of 'turmoil' (the only sense in Shakespeare elsewhere) but probably also, as 'shuffle off' suggests, that of 'something that entangles us' —'is coiled about us' (like a rope). These two uses of *coil* are really different words of distinct derivation, but in Shakespeare's time they must have been regarded as the same word in two strangely different senses.

68. **respect:** consideration. Cf. iii, 2, 193.

69. **of so long life:** so long-lived; so lasting. If it were not for this impediment, Hamlet argues, no one would endure calamity long.

70. **time:** the times; the world we live in.

72. **The pangs . . . love.** Cf. John Heywood, *The Play of Love*, ll. 62, 63 (ed. Brandl, *Quellen*, p. 162):

> Of all paynes the most incomparable payne
> Is to be a louer not louyd agayne.

—**déspis'd.** For the accent see i, 4, 52, note. For *despis'd* (Second Quarto) the Folio reads *dispriz'd*.

75. **his quietus make:** settle his own account. *Quietus est* is an old formula for 'He is quit'; 'his account has been settled.' The phrase (as well as the noun *quietus*) was common in the sense of 'death wound.' Thus in Fletcher, *The Chances*, ii, 1, Antonio, wounded by Don John, says: 'H'as given me my *quietus est*.' In the present instance the word suggests the quiet of sleep and the grave. There is an old proverb: 'He that dies pays all debts' (*Tempest*, iii, 2, 140). Cf. *1 Henry IV*, iii, 2, 157: 'The end of life cancels all bands' (i.e., bonds).

76. **a bare bodkin:** a mere stiletto or poniard.—**these fardels:** these burdens. The Second Quarto omits 'these.'

77. **grunt:** groan. Not an undignified word in Elizabethan times. Cf. Dekker, *The Gull's Horn-Book*, 1609 (ed. Grosart, II, 216): 'sicke gruntinge patients.'

79. **undiscover'd:** unexplored — therefore, mysterious. — **bourn:** boundary. Cf. Marlowe, *Edward II* (ed. Dyce, III, 288):

> Weep not for Mortimer,
> That scorns the world, and, as a traveller,
> Goes to discover countries yet unknown.

80. **No traveller returns.** Critics have worried over this, since, they remark, the Ghost had returned. But Hamlet is thinking of human beings, not of ghosts.—**puzzles:** confounds—so that it cannot act.

83. **conscience.** Here again Hamlet is speaking in general terms, not thinking especially of himself. Blakeway cites *Richard III*, i, 4, 137 ff., where the Murderer complains that conscience 'makes a man a coward. A man cannot steal, but it accuseth him; a man cannot swear, but it checks [i.e., rebukes] him. ... It fills a man full of obstacles.' Cf. the same, v, 3, 180, 310. A less probable interpretation takes *conscience* to mean 'that of which we are conscious': 'It is this knowledge that makes us all cowards' (Child).

84. **And thus.** Hamlet is speaking still more generally. He has abandoned the theme of suicide and the life after death, and is extending his observations to the whole subject of *irresolution* as caused by *fear of the consequences* of any act. This does not apply to him in particular, for nobody has suggested that he is *afraid* to strike the King. He is merely philosophizing, as he has already done in i, 4, 23–38—a passage which no sane critic regards as having a personal application.—**native.** The natural complexion of resolution is ruddy or sanguine.

85. **cast:** shade (of colour).—**thought:** melancholy, despondency. Cf. iv, 5, 188.

86. **pith:** importance. The Folio reading. The Second Quarto reads *pitch*, i.e., 'height,' 'elevation'—especially, 'the highest

point reached by a soaring falcon.' Cf. *Richard II*, i, 1, 109:
'How high a pitch his resolution soars!'

87. **With this regard:** on this account.

88. **Soft you now!** Hold! Hush! Cf. i, 1, 126.

89. **Nymph.** A courtly way of addressing a lady, not un-
common in the old language of compliment. Cf. l. 44.

91. **many a day.** This (like 'long' in l. 94) indicates that
some time has elapsed since i, 3, 132–136. The interval has not
been long, though it may seem so to Ophelia.

92. **well, well, well.** Apparently the repetition is meant to
express low spirits—not (as Dowden thinks) impatience or
(as Wilson suggests) indifference.

95. From this point Hamlet talks as insanely as he knows
how. Ophelia replies with the gentle firmness which one
might use to a refractory child, until Hamlet's feigned madness grows so distressing that she can only pray to heaven for
his relief. No doubt Hamlet suspects that somebody is listening, and he cannot afford to take chances. Whether or not
Ophelia is acting under instructions, it is necessary that she
should share the general opinion that he has lost his mind.
Indeed, it is far more merciful to her to confirm that impression
than to let her think that he is sane and does not love her.
As for taking her into his confidence, that is manifestly impossible. He cannot think for a moment of making her his
accomplice in a deed of blood. Love and marriage are not
for him until his revenge is accomplished. If ever he emerges
triumphant from the difficulties that surround him and takes
his seat upon the throne of Denmark, explanation will be
easy enough.

103. **honest:** chaste.

109. **commerce:** intercourse, association.

111–115. **translate:** transform.—**his:** its.—**sometime:** once;
formerly.—**now . . . proof.** Hamlet is thinking of his mother's
sin, which well might make him feel that there is no purity
left in the world.

117. **Indeed . . . so.** The actress who plays Ophelia should
not turn this gentle and spirited rejoinder into a wail of misery.

119. **cannot so inoculate our old stock:** cannot, by grafting, so change our sinful nature (inherited from Adam) that we shall not still have some flavour of it. The figure is that of a crabtree (a wild apple) in which a bud or shoot of a better sort has been set as a graft. The fruit, Hamlet says, will still taste of the old stock. Cf. *Coriolanus*, ii, 1, 205, 206:

> We have some old crabtrees here at home that will not
> Be grafted to your relish.

121. **I was the more deceived.** See note on l. 117. Ophelia has no doubt of Hamlet's love; nor should this line be so rendered as to indicate that she has. His madness is what distresses her.

123. **indifferent honest:** tolerably virtuous.

125. **ambitious.** Whether or not Hamlet suspects that Ophelia is a decoy, or that there are listeners, he is prudent enough to encourage the notion that Rosencrantz and Guildenstern had formed—that thwarted ambition is the cause of his madness (ii, 2, 258). Soon, however, he assigns another cause (l. 152). The result is confusion, which is what he designed.

133, 134. **We:** we men.—**Go thy ways:** Go along; literally, on your way. Cf. i, 3, 135.

134. **Where's your father?** An awkward question for Ophelia, but she does not hesitate to give the only possible answer. She must not reply, 'My lord, he is behind the arras.' Hamlet, she thinks, is insane, and she is acting under the orders of those whom she regards as most interested in his cure. Hence she does not scruple to treat him, in this matter of telling the truth, as madmen must often be treated. Nor has Hamlet any reason to be angry with Ophelia, even if he knows that Polonius is behind the arras; for, by counterfeiting lunacy, he has forfeited the right to be treated as sane. It is possible that he has seen the arras shake, or even that he has caught sight of Polonius for a moment. Note, however, that in what follows he treats Ophelia no more harshly than before. Indeed, he merely follows the train of thought already begun in l. 122 ('Get thee to a nunnery!'). As to the stage action, however, one thing is certain. Polonius undoubtedly shows his head for

a moment to the audience; for such is the regular convention when a character is in hiding—whether behind the hangings, or behind a screen, or in a chest. And he must withdraw his head precipitately when he hears Hamlet's question—to the amusement of the audience, who are further diverted by realizing that the old courtier must hear himself called a fool. The comic effect would be heightened if Hamlet had his back turned to Polonius when the head appeared. On the whole, then, we may feel reasonably certain that Hamlet does not see Polonius but has merely a vague suspicion that he is within earshot.

145. monsters. Alluding to the favourite Elizabethan jest of the horns supposed to grow upon a man's head if his wife is unfaithful. Cf. *Othello*, iv, 1, 63: 'A horned man's a monster and a beast.'

148. your paintings: i.e., those of you ladies in general. Painting the face appears to have been an almost universal fashion amongst Elizabethan ladies, and the dramatists and satirists are never weary of attacking it. Here, in what follows, Hamlet is talking about women in general, and it never occurs to Ophelia to take his words as meant for her in particular: they are too absurdly inapplicable. Her only feeling is sorrow at his pitiable condition.

150 ff. jig . . . amble. Two kinds of affected gait. Cf. *The Return from Parnassus*, iv, 1, 1353, 1354 (ed. Macray, p. 67): 'Each mincinge dame, Each ambling minion.'—**lisp:** applied to any kind of affected softness of pronunciation. Cf. Chaucer's famous lines (*Prologue*, 264, 265):

> Somewhat he lipsed, for his wantownesse,
> To make his Englissh sweete upon his tonge.

—you nickname . . . ignorance: You give new and affected names to ordinary things (instead of 'calling a spade a spade') and then pretend that this affectation of yours is due to ignorance—that you really do not know what these vulgar objects are called. *Wantonness* often means 'affectation'; as, for example, in Elyot's *Governour* (ed. Croft, I, 35): 'Omittinge no letter or sillable, as folisshe women often times do of a wantonesse.'—**moe:** more. Not a clipped form of *more* but another formation from the same root.

156. all but one. The audience (but not Ophelia) knows that Hamlet means the King. Probably the three words are uttered in a whisper, inaudible to the listeners behind the arras.

158-162. This passage proves that Hamlet is not naturally of a melancholy temperament. Ophelia dwells not only on his intellectual accomplishments but on the charm of his manners and address. He is courtier and soldier, as well as scholar. In short, he is the first gentleman of Denmark. For *soldier* cf. v, 2, 406-411.

159. The courtier's, etc.: the courtier's eye, the scholar's tongue, the soldier's sword. The order of words is a favourite one in the Elizabethan fine style. See Textual Notes.

160, 161. Th' expectancy . . . state: the hope and the adornment of our country, which is made fair by him.—**fair:** proleptic. Cf. *Macbeth*, i, 6, 1-3.—**glass:** mirror.—**the mould of form:** 'the model by whom all endeavoured to form themselves' (Johnson). *Form* refers especially to deportment, courtly behaviour.

162. of: by.

163. deject: cast down.

165. most sovereign. Since the reason should govern all the faculties. Cf. Ford, *The Broken Heart*, iv, 2 (ed. Gifford and Dyce, I, 288, 289):

> Depos'd the empress of her soul, her reason,
> From its most proper throne.

166. jangled. Cf. Fletcher, *The Pilgrim*, iv, 3, 4, 5:

> Like bells rung backward,
> They are nothing but confusion and mere noises.

167. blown: full-blown, in full blossom. This is decisive as to Hamlet's age. His youth has come to full flower—he is arrived at early manhood. Cf. Mabbe, *The Rogue* (ed. *Tudor Translations*, I, 164): 'Her yeeres were rather shorter, then full seventeene, being so well growne in the bud, that she was now ready for the blowing.'

168. **ecstasy**: madness.

170. **affections**: feelings, inclinations. Cf. Marlowe, *The Jew of Malta*, ii (ed. Dyce, I, 276):

> Be thou void of these affections,
> Compassion, love, vain hope, and heartless fear.

172. **madness.** The King is always uncommonly keen. Hamlet acts the madman well enough to deceive the others, but Claudius is not quite convinced, and henceforth he is tormented by the fear that Hamlet's insanity is assumed for some sinister purpose.

174, 175. **doubt**: fear.—**prevent**: forestall.

177. **to England.** The quick-witted and resourceful King has already formed a plan to get rid of the possibly dangerous Hamlet for a season. It does not appear, however, that he yet intends him to be killed on his arrival. That idea comes later, when he has learned (from the play within the play) that Hamlet knows about the murder. We do not hear of this purpose until iv, 3, 60-70. If it were now in the King's mind, that fact would be revealed to the audience in a soliloquy or an aside.

180, 181. **variable objects**: the variety of sights incidental to travel.—**something-settled**: somewhat settled. Cf. iii, 2, 79. —**matter**: subject of thought.

182, 183. **Whereon . . . himself**: the constant beating of his brains on which subject (whatever it is) makes him act unnaturally. The subject of *puts* is not *brains*, but the whole idea in the phrase 'whereon his brains still beating.'

184. **It shall do well**: It will be certain to help. The King's prescription of foreign travel is, in fact, a good one, and neither Polonius nor the Queen sees anything objectionable or suspicious in it.

186. **neglected**: that met with no response.

191. **round**: outspoken (without mincing matters).

193. **find him not**: do not discover his secret trouble.

Scene II.

This scene comes in the evening of the same day as scene i: namely, on the day after ii, 2. See ii, 2, 565.

1 ff. Hamlet's advice to the players has always been understood—and rightly—to embody Shakespeare's own views on the art of acting. These are distinguished by moderation and common sense—not by novelty. The marvel is, the *style*.

2. **trippingly**: easily—i.e., without exaggerated emphasis or any excessive deliberation or roundness of utterance; with an approach, therefore, to the language of real life.—**mouth it.** To *mouth* a word is to hold it long in the mouth before allowing it to pass the lips. 'Stagey' declamation is, amongst other things, distinguished by this dwelling on the vowel sounds.

3-14. **live**: lief.—**the town crier.** Since the town crier wishes to be heard distinctly at some distance, he must mouth his words, and the result is a kind of loud singsong.—**temperance**: self-control, moderation.—**robustious**: boisterous. Cf. *Henry V*, iii, 7, 159: 'robustious and rough.'—**periwig-pated.** Actors of course wore wigs, but these were not the fashion in society.—**the groundlings**: spectators who sat or stood in the pit (called 'the yard'), which was the cheapest place in the theatre. Cf. Dekker, *The Gull's Horn-Book*, 1609 (ed. Grosart, II, 247): 'Your Groundling . . . buyes his sport by the penny.'—**capable of**: able to appreciate.—**inexplicable dumb shows.** The dumb show (a scene of action without words) was an important element in early plays, but was losing caste when Shakespeare wrote. For examples, see the Third Act of *Locrine*. Such pantomimes, Hamlet intimates, appeal more strongly to the groundlings, who enjoy guessing at puzzles, than to the *élite*, who take the drama seriously. Hamlet does not condemn dumb shows in general, but only such of them as are 'inexplicable'—such as rather confuse one and disturb the attention than illuminate the plot.—**noise.** Cf. Heywood, *Love's Mistress*, iv (Pearson ed., V, 146): 'The Vulgar are best pleas'd with noyse and showes.'

15. **Termagant . . . Herod.** In the Middle Ages all Moham-

medans were thought to be idolaters, and the romances give
them, as deities, Termagant (or Tervagant), Mahound, etc.
Mahound is *Mohammed*, but the origin of *Tervagant* is unknown. Since the Saracens were regarded as a ferocious race,
their gods were described as violent in word and deed. The
god or fiend Termagant seems to have been a character in certain old English plays (now lost), and his part was undoubtedly acted with plenty of sound and fury. Bishop Bale in his
Actes of English Votaries (quoted by Ritson) speaks of certain
persons as 'grennyng' (i.e., grinning savagely) 'like terma-
gauntes in a playe' (Part II [1550]; ed. 1560, sig. Oiiii, lf. 1 r°).
Herod was, of course, a well-known character in the English
Biblical dramas, and his part was that of a raging tyrant. Thus
in a Coventry pageant Herod exclaims, 'I stampe, I stare, I loke
all abowt,' and we have the stage direction: 'Here Erode ragis
in the pagond [i.e., on the wagon on which the play was acted]
and in the strete also' (Thomas Sharp, *A Dissertation on the
Pageants*, 1825, p. 107).

18 ff. **too tame,** etc. Cf. Heywood, *Apology for Actors*, 1612,
C3 r°:

> It [acting] instructs him [the scholar] to fit his phrases to his action,
> and his action to his phrase, and his pronunciation to them both. . . .
> And this is the action behoouefull in any that professe this quality
> [i.e., acting], not to vse any impudent or forced motion in any part of the
> body, no rough or other violent gesture, nor on the contrary, to stand like
> a stiffe starcht man, but to qualifie euery thing according to the nature of
> the person personated: for in oueracting trickes, and toyling too much in
> the anticke habit of humors, men of the ripest desert, greatest opinions, and
> best reputations, may breake into the most violent absurdities. I take not
> vpon me to teach, but to aduise, for it becomes my Iuniority rather to be
> pupild myselfe, then to instruct others.

21-25. **modesty:** moderation.—**from.** Emphatic: 'away
from'; 'contrary to.'—**at the first:** i.e., when the art of acting
was first invented.—**to hold . . . nature.** 'Nowe,' say the
imagined defenders of plays, according to Gosson's *Schoole of
Abuse* (1579), 'are the abuses of the worlde reuealed, euery
man in a playe may see his owne faultes, and learne by this
glasse to amende his manners [i.e., his morals]' (sig. B5, 1 r°).

—**feature:** form—literally, 'make.'—**the very age and body
of the time:** the times exactly as they are. A person's general appearance is determined in the main by two things—
his *age* and his *body* (i.e., his form or 'build'). Cf. Cicero,
in his oration in defence of Roscius of Ameria (16, 47):
'Etenim haec conficta arbitror a poetis esse, ut effictos nostros
mores in alienis personis expressamque imaginem vitae coti-
dianae videremus.'—**his:** its.—**pressure:** shape—literally, impression, as in wax.

31–33. **come tardy off:** not executed with sufficient spirit and
vigour.—**the unskilful:** the injudicious or undiscriminating
among the audience. *Skill* for 'judgment,' 'discrimination,' is
common.—**the censure of the which one:** the opinion of a
single one of whom.—**in your allowance:** in winning approval
of your acting. *Allow* frequently means 'approve.'

35. **not to speak it profanely.** Hamlet apologizes for his apparent flippancy in comparing the Creation with the work of a
master mechanic and his journeymen. Cf. Dekker, *Northward
Ho*, iv, 1 (Pearson ed., III, 45): 'Here's a swaggering fellow,
sir, that speakes not like a man of Gods making'; *As You Like
It*, iii, 2, 216: 'Is he of God's making?'

39. **abominably.** Spelled *abhominably* in the Folios and
Quartos. The word was thought to be derived from *ab homine*
and carried the special sense of 'in a way contrary or repellent
to what is natural in man.' See *Love's Labour's Lost*, v, 1,
27, 28.

40. **indifferently:** pretty well. Cf. iii, 1, 123.

43–50. **clowns:** rustic fellows and buffoons.—**speak no more,**
etc. The Elizabethan clowns used to improvise freely, and
sometimes even to engage in conversation with the audience.
At this point the First Quarto gives specimens of such 'gag-
ging': 'Cannot you stay till I eate my porrige? and, you owe
me a quarters wages: and, my coate wants a cullison: and,
your beere is sowre.'—**there be of them:** there are some of
them.—**quantity:** small quantity. Cf. iii, 4, 75; v, 1, 293.—
barren: dull, stupid.—**villanous:** vulgar.—**fool:** actor who
plays the fool's (i.e., jester's) part (with an obvious pun).—

uses: practises.—**make you ready:** dress; put on your costumes.

52. **presently:** at once. Cf. ii, 2, 170.

58. **sweet.** Very common merely in the sense of 'dear.'

59. **just.** Often used in the sense of 'exact,' 'accurate.' Hamlet means that Horatio is a 'well-balanced person,' 'a symmetrical character.' What follows is a fine description of this philosophical and unruffled student.

60. **conversation:** association.—**cop'd withal:** dealt with. The whole clause means 'as ever I have associated with.'

63. **revénue.** Accented on the second syllable.

65. **candied.** Cf. *1 Henry IV*, i, 3, 251, 252:

> Why, what a candy deal of courtesy
> This fawning greyhound then did proffer me!

—**ábsurd.** For the accent cf. i, 4, 52, note.

66. **pregnant hinges:** readily moving (supple) joints.

67. **thrift:** thriving, prosperity, worldly advantage.

68. **was ... choice:** had the power of discriminating.

74–76. **blood and judgment:** impulse and discretion. Men who act on mere impulse or who, on the other hand, deliberate until the right moment is past, are alike exposed to the caprices of Fortune.—**To sound what stop she please:** to play upon as she likes; to treat as her caprices dictate. Horatio possesses both impulse and judgment in a well-balanced combination. Thus he neither acts over-hastily, nor delays when action is needed. For *stops* cf. ll. 372–376.

78. **in my heart of heart:** in the very heart of my heart. An emphatic repetition of 'in my heart's core.'

79. **Something too much of this.** Hamlet feels that his frank praise of Horatio has gone so far as to be embarrassing to them both. *Something* is adverbial, like *somewhat*. Cf. l. 359; iii, 1, 181.

81. **circumstance.** Collective. We should now use the plural.

82. **have told thee.** Thus we learn, for the first time, that Hamlet has told Horatio the Ghost's story.

84. **with . . . soul:** with observation so keen as to absorb

every faculty of thy soul. Not merely Horatio's *mind*, but his *whole soul*, is to concentrate its powers in the single act of watching the King.

85. **occulted:** craftily hidden.

86. **in one speech:** the 'dozen or sixteen lines' which Hamlet had written for the express purpose (ii, 2, 566).

87. **a damned ghost:** a demon—not my father's spirit. Cf. ii, 2, 626–631.

88. **my imaginations:** i.e., my belief in my uncle's guilt and in the other dreadful things which the apparition told.

89. **stithy:** forge, smithy. *Stith* means anvil. Since Vulcan is the god of smiths, his forge must be sooty above all others.

92. **In censure of his seeming:** in passing judgment on his appearance and behaviour. Cf. i, 3, 69.

93. **If he steal aught.** Once more Horatio replies with a touch of mild humour. See note on i, 1, 19. We observe that, as he has shared Hamlet's scruples about the apparition (i, 4, 69–74), he agrees with him that a test is necessary.

95. **idle:** foolish or insane in my words and actions. Cf. iii, 4, 11. Hamlet never feigns madness when he is alone with Horatio, who is in his confidence. Here he expressly tells his friend that it is time to act the madman again, since the others are coming.

97. **cousin:** nephew. The King does not call Hamlet *son* (as in i, 2, 64), not wishing to irritate him.

99. **the chameleon's dish,** etc.: When I ought to be on the throne myself, can I be satisfied with such promises as you have made me? Cf. ll. 354–359; i, 2, 108–112. The chameleon was supposed to live on air. Hamlet's reply is meant to foster the belief that disappointment about the kingship is the cause of his insanity (ii, 2, 258; iii, 1, 125). Cf. Fenton, *Tragicall Discourses*, 1567, fol. 232 rº: 'I in the meane tyme accordynge to the Cameleon lyvynge with the breathe of the ayre doo feede but vppon the offer of vayne ymaginacions.'

101, 102. **I have ... this answer. These ... mine:** I have nothing to do with this answer; your reply does not fit my question. Hamlet has twisted the sense of *fare*, as if the King had asked about his diet. The King calls his attention to this incoherence and, at the same time, implies a general denial of any thoughts or purposes that could make Hamlet's answer pertinent.

103. **No, nor mine now.** 'A man's words, says the proverb, are his own no longer than he keep them unspoken' (Johnson).

104. **i' th' university.** All the great European universities produced plays on festal occasions. Cf. Heywood, *Apology for Actors*, 1612: 'In the time of my residence in *Cambridge*, I haue seene Tragedyes, Comedyes, Historyes, Pastorals, and Shewes, publickly acted, in which the Graduates of good place and reputation haue bene specially parted [i.e., furnished with rôles]: this is held necessary for the emboldening of their *Iunior* schollers, to arme them with audacity, against they come to bee imployed in any publicke exercise' (C3 v°). Milton satirizes this custom in a famous passage:

In the Colleges so many of the young Divines, and those in next aptitude to Divinity have bin seene so oft upon the Stage, writhing and unboning their Clergie limmes to all the antick and dishonest gestures of Trinculo's, Buffons, and Bawds; prostituting the shame of that ministery which either they had, or were nigh having, to the eyes of Courtiers and Court-Ladies, with their Groomes and *Madamoisellaes*. There while they acted, and overacted, among other young scholars, I was a spectator. They thought themselves gallant men, and I thought them fools; they made sport, and I laught, they mispronounc't, and I mislik't, and to make up the *atticisme*, they were out, and I hist (*Apology against A Modest Confutation*, Works, Pickering ed., III, 267, 268).

108. **Capitol.** The assassination of Cæsar took place in the *curia Pompei* (Pompey's Senate House). Shakespeare's play shifts the place to the Capitol. See *Julius Cæsar*, ii, 1, 211.— **Brutus kill'd me.** Polonius would not have added this bit of superfluous information if he had not been treating Hamlet as a lunatic.

110. **a brute part,** etc. A stock pun. Hamlet's use of so coarse and stale a witticism accords with his acting the madman. Such talk (like that in ii, 2, 172 ff.; iii, 1, 92–157) is quite at variance with his character as a gentleman and a scholar. Of course

Polonius takes no offence.—**part.** Common for 'act,' 'deed.'
—**calf.** Cf. *Love's Labour's Lost*, v, 2, 247–255.

114. **stay . . . patience:** await your leisure.

121. **my head upon your lap.** This appears to have been
common at private theatrical entertainments. Steevens quotes
Fletcher, *The Queen of Corinth*, i, 2 (ed. Dyce, V, 408):
'Ushers her to her coach, lies at her feet At solemn masques.'

132. **your only jig-maker:** the nonpareil of all writers of
comic songs. See ii, 2, 522, and note. Cf. Ford, *Love's Sacrifice*,
ii, 1 (ed. Gifford and Dyce, II, 30): 'Petrarch was a dunce,
Dante a jig-maker . . . to me.'

135. **'s two hours:** this two hours.

136. **twice two months.** Four months have passed since the
King's death. This scene, then, is to be dated at least two
months later than Hamlet's interview with the Ghost, which
took place a month or two after the murder. See i, 2, 138 ff.

137, 138. **I'll have a suit of sables:** I'll throw off my mourning and wear the richest furs that can be found. By *black*
Hamlet refers to his 'customary suit of solemn black' (i, 2, 78).
Sable often means 'black'; but Hamlet says *sables*. These are
mentioned as splendid and dignified attire (not mourning)
in iv, 7, 81.

140–145. **by'r Lady:** by our Lady (the Virgin Mary).—
suffer not thinking on: submit to being forgotten.—**hobby-
horse.** The hobby-horse was a very ancient character in May
games and morris dances. In Shakespeare's time, however, he
was frequently omitted, partly because the Puritans regarded
him as a remnant of heathen superstition. Hence the popular
saying quoted by Hamlet, which occurs also in *Love's Labour's
Lost*, iii, 1, 30.

145. **dumb show.** It has caused remark that after Hamlet's
fling at 'inexplicable dumb shows' (l. 14) he should have allowed such a pantomime in this play. There are three good
reasons. First, the dumb show suits the old-fashioned and
stilted character of *The Murder of Gonzago* (see note on ll.
165 ff.). The second reason is even more important. The
centre and focus of interest during the acting of *The Murder*

of Gonzago must be—for Shakespeare's audience—not the actors in that play, but the guilty Claudius. We should therefore be enabled to follow the plot without attending too much to the players—and in this we are assisted by the dumb show, which is by no means 'inexplicable' but gives a clear summary of the plot. Finally, the dumb show is meant to torture King Claudius, and thus to help in making him reveal his 'occulted guilt.' It is the first turn of the thumbscrew.

146. **What means this?** Ophelia may need enlightenment, but King Claudius cannot fail to perceive that the play will come close to the facts of his crime. Yet he must not betray himself by objecting or by leaving the hall: he must stand the torture, if he can, without wincing. And, indeed, he shows amazing self-control. He does not flinch until the very moment when Lucianus uses the poison, and even then his actions do not reveal his secret, except to Hamlet and Horatio, who already know it.

147, 148. **miching malhecho:** sneaking crime. To *mich* (in modern dialect, *meech*) is to 'sneak' or 'skulk' (cf. *micher* for 'truant schoolboy' in *1 Henry IV*, ii, 4, 451), and *malhecho* is Spanish for 'misdeed.' Ophelia, who thinks that Hamlet is raving, tries to soothe him by remarking quietly, 'No doubt this show indicates the plot of the play.'

152. **keep counsel:** keep a secret. Cf. iv, 2, 11.

158. **naught:** naughty. Ophelia reproves Hamlet gently for his loose talk.

162. **the posy of a ring:** the short rhyming motto on a ring. *Posy* is a contraction of *poesy*. A long list of posies, from a manuscript of about 1596, may be found in Arber's *English Garner*, I, 611–619. Examples are: 'There is no smart Can turn my heart'; 'As true in love As turtle dove'; 'In thee my choice I do rejoice.' See also *Archæological Journal*, XVI (1859), 307 ff.; *Love's Garland, or Posies for Rings*, etc., 1624 (in Halliwell's *Literature of the Sixteenth and Seventeenth Centuries*, pp. 223 ff.).

165 ff. The same necessity to make the style of the 'play within the play' distinct from the style of the play itself exists

in the case of 'The Mousetrap' as in the case of the Pyrrhus declamation (see ii, 2, 472, note). Here the difference is marked by the use of rhyme and by the elaborately sententious manner.

165–170. Cf. Greene, *Alphonsus*, iv, 1, 1152–1156 (ed. Collins, I, 113):

> Thrise ten times *Phœbus* with his golden beames
> Hath compassed the circle of the skie,
> Thrise ten times *Ceres* hath her workemen hir'd,
> And fild her barnes with frutefull crops of Corne,
> Since first in Priesthood I did lead my life;

and also iv, 2 (I, 116):

> Thrise *Hesperus* with pompe and peerelesse pride
> Hath heau'd his head forth of the Easterne seas,
> Thrise *Cynthia*, with *Phœbus* borrowed beames,
> Hath shewn her bewtie throgh the darkish clowdes,
> Since that I, wretched Duke, haue tasted ought,
> Or drunke a drop of any kinde of drinke;

Selimus, Emperour of the Turkes, ll. 37 ff. (Malone Society ed., p. 1):

> Twice fifteene times hath faire *Latonaes* sonne
> Walked about the world with his great light:
> Since I began, would I had nere begunne,
> To sway this scepter.

—**Phœbus' cart:** the chariot of the sun.—**Neptune's salt wash:** the surging waves of the sea.—**Tellus' orbed ground:** this globe; the earth. Cf. ii, 2, 507.—**borrowed:** i.e., from the sun. Cf. Marlowe, *1 Tamberlaine*, i, 1 (ed. Dyce, I, 14): 'Before the moon renew her borrow'd light.'

175. **I distrust you:** I am anxious about you.

176. After this line the Second Quarto inserts 'For women feare too much, euen as they loue,' and begins the next verse with 'And.' The other Quartos agree.

177. **holds quantity:** maintain proportion; correspond in amount. When women love much, they feel great anxiety; when they feel slight anxiety, it is a sign that their love is small.

179. **proof:** experience.

184. **My operant powers:** the physical forces that work in

the functions of life; my vital forces. Cf. Webster, *Appius and Virginia,* v, 2, 108, 109 (ed. Lucas, II, 222):

> This sight has stiffned all my operant powers,
> Ic'd all my blood, benum'd my motion quite.

184. leave to do: cease to act.

187. O, confound the rest! O, may God destroy that which you were about to say! may it never come to pass! With the Queen's protestations in ll. 187 ff., 226 ff., compare the heroics of Cornelia in Kyd's *Cornelia,* Act ii, ll. 1 ff. (ed. Boas, pp. 111 ff.)—a translation of Garnier's *Cornélie.*

189. In ... accurst! If I take a second husband, may he prove a curse to me!

190. None ... first! Let no woman wed a second husband unless she has murdered her first husband! Hamlet watches his mother, for he suspects her of complicity in the murder. The Ghost, interrupted by the approach of dawn, has left this point doubtful (i, 5, 85–88), and Hamlet's suspicion is not relieved until iii, 4, 27–30.

192, 193. instances: causes, motives.—**move:** prompt.—**respects of thrift:** considerations of worldly welfare or profit. Cf. iii, 1, 68.

194. I kill my husband dead: I kill my dead husband a second time, as it were, by this act of unfaithfulness.

198–201. Purpose ... memory: We cannot hold fast to our purposes when we have forgotten what prompted them; if memory fails, no purpose can last long.—**validity:** strength, vigour.—**like fruit ... be:** A purpose holds until the moment for action comes, as fruit hangs on the tree so long as it is unripe; but one's purposes fail of their own accord when the moment for action arrives.

203. To pay ourselves: A purpose is an obligation laid upon us by ourselves; and we readily excuse ourselves for neglecting it, for a man is an indulgent creditor to himself.

206, 207. The violence ... destroy: When either grief or joy is violent, it exhausts itself by its own force, and thus the resolutions formed under its impulse come to naught.—**Their own**

enactures: their purposed acts.—**destroy.** Attracted into the plural by the plurals that precede. Cf. i, 2, 38.

208, 209. **Where:** in persons in whom, etc.; i.e., in persons of an emotional temperament.—**on slender accident:** as a result of any trifling occurrence. *On* was common in this causal sense, which survives in *on compulsion, on purpose.*

216. **hitherto:** so far; up to this point in human history. In other words, 'Such has always been the experience of mankind.'

218, 219. **who in want ... enemy.** An insincere friend is an unripe foe. He needs only to be put to the test at a crisis to be ripened into an avowed enemy.

221, 222. **contráry.** Note the accent.—**devices:** plans, purposes.—**still:** constantly.

228–229. Omitted in the Folio.—**An anchor's cheer:** an anchorite's (hermit's) fare. Steevens would read 'chair,' in support of which he quotes Hall, *Satires,* iv, 2 (ed. Singer, p. 86): 'Sit seven yeres pining in an Anchore's chair.' Wilson reads *cheere* (with the Second Quarto) and interprets it as 'chair.' But cf. 'wedding cheer' (*Romeo and Juliet,* iv, 5, 87); 'royal cheer' (*Timon,* iii, 6, 56).—**my scope:** the limit of my enjoyment of life.

230. **blanks the face of joy:** either 'blanches joy's face,' 'turns it pale' (the proper hue of joy being rosy-red; cf. *Comedy of Errors,* iv, 2, 4: 'Look'd he or red or pale, or sad or merrily?'); or, perhaps better, 'turns it to a blank,' 'deprives it of all expression'—almost equivalent to 'blasts.'

232. **here and hence:** in this world and the next.

236. **My spirits grow dull:** My vitality is at a low ebb. The King has a feeling of physical depression; he does not mean that he is despondent in mind.

240. **doth protest.** Queen Gertrude calmly criticizes the exaggerated style of the speech. She shows no such disturbance of mind as might indicate a guilty conscience.

242. **the argument:** an outline of the plot. When a play was presented at court, it was customary to submit such an outline beforehand in order to avoid incidents that might be offensive. The King's question shows how well he is controlling himself.

He knows what torture the play has in store for him (for he has seen the dumb show), but he does not betray himself, even by a tone or a look. To the courtiers his question seems to concern merely some resemblance between the play and the Queen's second marriage. Hamlet's reply is meant to give another turn to the screw, but even then Claudius shows no distress. He merely asks (l. 246), with an air of polite interest, what the *title* of the play is.

242-245. **no offence:** nothing offensive. Hamlet picks up the King's words and twists the sense: 'There's no crime in the play—nothing but a little playful poisoning.'—**in jest:** not in fact, but merely in the play. His words sound insane to the courtiers.

247. **'The Mousetrap':** the thing in which he'll 'catch the conscience of the King.'—**Tropically:** by a trope; metaphorically.

248. **the image:** the exact representation. Sarrazin (*Shakespeare Jahrbuch*, XXXI [1895], 169) supposes the source to be an historical event, the murder of the Marchese Alfonso Gonzaga of Castelgoffredo in 1592, at his country house, by eight ruffians in the pay of his nephew.

252, 253. **free:** free from guilt, innocent.—**gall'd jade.** To *gall* is to 'rub off the skin so as to make a sore spot'; *jade* is a common disrespectful term for 'horse.'—**winch:** wince. Clark and Wright compare Lyly, *Euphues* (ed. Bond, I, 257): 'Well I knowe none will winch excepte shee bee gawled, neither any bee offended vnlesse shee be guiltie.' Tilley (No. 525) adds, from the same (II, 151): 'Rubbe there no more, least I winch, for deny I wil not that I am wroung on the withers.' The proverb is common. Cf. *The Pryde and Abuse of Women, ca.* 1550 (ed. Hazlitt, *Early Popular Poetry*, IV, 243):

> Rubbe a galde horse on the backe,
> And he wyll kicke and wynse;

Rowlands, *Martin Mark-all*, 1610 (Hunterian Club ed., p. 15): 'It is not good medling with galled Iades, least they winch and

kicke.'—**withers:** the ridge between a horse's shoulders.—
unwrung: not chafed, and therefore not sensitive. Our con-
sciences are clear.

255. **a chorus:** a character in a play whose business is to
make explanations to the audience. Father Time in *The Winter's Tale* (iv, 1) is a good example. In *Henry V* the Chorus
speaks a Prologue to each act and a final Epilogue. Cf. *Romeo
and Juliet*, i, ii. Gower is the Chorus in *Pericles*.

256, 257. **I could . . . dallying:** If I could look on at a scene
of dalliance between your lover and you, I could tell what it
meant. By the *puppets* Hamlet means Ophelia and her
imagined lover. Puppet shows, which were very common,
regularly had an interpreter, who sometimes sat on the stage.

261. **better, and worse:** keener as to wit, but worse as to
meaning. Ophelia does not resent Hamlet's indecency, since
she thinks him mad.

262. **So:** i.e., for better, for worse.—**you:** you women.—
must take. So the First Quarto. The other Quartos and the
Folios read *mistake*—a word formerly common in the sense of
'take wrongly (or wrongfully),' 'take (something) to which
one has no right.' Attempts to justify this reading amount to
something like the following interpretation : 'According to the
marriage service you take your husbands "for better, for
worse"; that is, promising to be faithful wives in all the
changes of fortune; but, in fact, your "taking" is "mis-taking"
(fraudulent taking), since you do not keep your marriage
vows.' But this is to torture language unmercifully.

263. **Pox:** Plague on it!

264, 265. **the . . . revenge.** Simpson notes Hamlet's quotation from an old play, *The True Tragedy of Richard III*, 1594
(Malone Society ed., ll. 1892, 1893):

> The screeking Rauen sits croking for reuenge.
> Whole heards of beasts comes bellowing for reuenge.

267. **Confederate . . . seeing:** the time being in league with
me (since this is a favourable moment), and nobody except my
confederate, the time, seeing what I am about.

268. **midnight weeds.** Poisonous and magic herbs were thought to derive additional power from being collected at some special time, as, for example, at midnight.

269. **With Hecate's ban:** by the curse (the evil spell) of Hecate, the goddess of witchcraft and black magic. See *Macbeth*, iii, 5 (a scene not written by Shakespeare).

272-275. **He poisons him,** etc. Hamlet says this without any show of excitement, as if he were merely explaining the play to spectators who were not at all touched in conscience by its incidents.

276. **rises.** The King has endured the dumb show without flinching, and also the whole course of the play until this moment. Even now, when the details of his secret crime are enacted before his eyes, he does not betray himself except to Hamlet and Horatio, who have learned the facts already. To the others (including the Queen) Claudius seems merely to be suddenly indisposed. Cf. ll. 310-315.

277. **false fire:** the harmless discharge of a gun loaded with powder only. Cf. Gosson, *Apology for The School of Abuse* (ed. Arber, p. 75): 'When I spare not to greete them with poulder and shot, answeares mee againe with a false fire'; Defoe, *Captain Singleton*, 1720, p. 149: 'We saw Lions and Tigers, and Leopards every Night and Morning in Abundance; . . . if they offer'd to come near us, we made false Fire with any Gun that was uncharged, and they would walk off as soon as they saw the Flash.'

280. **some light!** The King calls for the torchbearers to conduct him to his chamber. See the stage direction before l. 95.

282, 283. **strucken . . . ungalled.** Hamlet repeats the idea already expressed in ll. 252, 253.

286-289. **this:** this declamation; the way in which I have spoken these verses. Hamlet has relieved his excitement by a bit of theatrical spouting. We may compare his apparent flippancy in i, 5, 116-163. The feathers and razed shoes are allusions to actors' costumes.—**turn Turk:** apostatize (like a Christian who becomes a Mohammedan); play me false.— **Provincial roses:** huge rosettes. Clark and Wright note that

Rosa Provincialis was a name for the damask rose. Provins, a French town, was famous for its roses.—**raz'd:** slashed; ornamented by cross-cuts in a pattern. Hunter quotes Henry Peacham, *The Truth of Our Time*, 1638, pp. 61, 62: 'Shootyes that goe under the name of Roses, from thirty shillings to three, foure, and five pounds the paire. Yea, a Gallant of the time not long since, payd thirty pound for a paire.'—**a cry:** a pack—used ordinarily of hounds, but here jocosely of actors.

290. **Half a share.** Horatio speaks with his customary mild humour (see i, 1, 19). In Shakespeare's time each regular member of a company of players had his proportion of the receipts instead of a salary. Some had a full share, some half a share. Cf. Dekker, *The Wonderfull Yeare*, 1603 (ed. Grosart, I, 100): 'The worst players Boy stood vpon his good parts, swearing . . . he would . . . be half a sharer (at least).'

295. **pajock:** peacock. The peacock had an evil reputation for cruelty and lust in the natural history of Shakespeare's day, and perhaps the poet had this in mind.

296. **rhym'd:** i.e., by saying *ass* instead of *pajock*.

302. **recorders:** a sort of flageolet.

303, 304. **For . . . perdy.** This sounds like an echo of Kyd's *Spanish Tragedy*, a very popular play (iv, 1, 196, 197; ed. Boas, p. 87):

> And if the world like not this Tragedie,
> Hard is the hap of olde Hieronimo.

—**belike:** probably.—**perdý.** An old-fashioned oath (*par dieu*), used colloquially for 'assuredly.' *Perdý* and *comedý* made a good rhyme in Elizabethan pronunciation.

312. **distemper'd:** out of sorts physically.

314. **drink.** Cf. i, 2, 124–128, 175; i, 4, 8–22. Claudius was no habitual drunkard, though he sometimes drank deep, according to the Danish custom. Hamlet, who hates both the King and the custom, calls him 'the bloat King' (iii, 4, 182).

315–319. **choler:** bile. In the speech that follows Hamlet puns on the word. The King pretends to be suffering from a sudden attack of indigestion, causing dizziness—from what we still call a 'bilious attack.'—**should:** would surely.—**for**

. . . purgation. One continuous pun. *Purgation* means (1) 'purging by means of medicine' and (2) 'purification of the soul by confession and penance.' Cf. *As You Like It*, v, 4, 44. *Choler* means both 'bile' and 'anger.'

320. **frame:** structure, coherent form. Hamlet's speech sounds to Guildenstern like madness.

327, 328. **wholesome:** sane, rational.—**your pardon.** Cf. i, 2, 56, note.

334–337. **But, sir,** etc. Hamlet pretends to make a strong effort to fix his wandering wits upon the subject.—**to the matter!** Let us return to the subject!

338, 339. **your behaviour.** This does not refer particularly to anything that Hamlet had said or done during the play-scene, but to his general wildness of speech and manner. The summons from the Queen merely carries out the suggestion made by Polonius before the play began (iii, 1, 189–193).—**amazement and admiration:** confusion of mind and wonder. Cf. ii, 2. 591; iii, 4, 112.

343. **closet:** private room; boudoir. Cf. ii, 1, 77.

346. **trade:** business. The word was common in this sense, and conveys no suggestion that Rosencrantz and Guildenstern are mercenary agents. Cf. *2 Henry IV*, i, 1, 173, 174:

> His forward spirit
> Would lift him where most trade of danger rang'd.

—us. Hamlet's intentional use of the royal *we* reminds Rosencrantz of the idea that his madness sprang from thwarted ambition, and he accordingly makes one more attempt to induce him to reveal the cause of his insanity (cf. ii, 2, 258).

349. **by these pickers and stealers:** by these ten fingers; by this hand (with a gesture). The phrase, as Whalley notes, comes from the catechism of the Church of England, where the catechumen is told to keep his hands from 'picking [i.e., pilfering] and stealing.'

350–354. **distemper:** disorder of mind.—**liberty.** Rosencrantz hints that Hamlet may be put under restraint (as a lunatic) if he stubbornly refuses to tell what ails him. Cf. iii, 1, 194; iv, 1, 14: 'His liberty is full of threats to all.'—**I lack**

advancement. Hamlet recurs to the cause already discussed with Rosencrantz and Guildenstern (ii, 2, 249 ff.). Cf. i, 5, 185; iii, 1, 125.

355. the voice of the King. Claudius has proclaimed Hamlet his successor in i, 2, 109.

358, 359. while the grass grows—: While the grass is growing, the horse starves. Hamlet implies that to wait for 'advancement' that is so far off is very unsatisfying. The proverb was common, and English examples have been cited from the sixteenth century; but it is far mustier than that, for Petrus de Vineis quotes it in a letter written before 1249: 'Dum herba crescit, equus moritur' (*Epistles*, ii, 53).—**something:** somewhat. Cf. l. 79.—**musty:** and therefore too trite to be quoted in full.

360–362. To withdraw: to step aside so as to be out of the hearing of the players. Hamlet withdraws to one side of the stage with Rosencrantz and Guildenstern, as if he had something of moment to confide to them.—**go about:** undertake, try.—**to recover . . . of me:** to get to the windward of me.—**into a toil.** Cf. Fletcher, *The Woman's Prize*, iv, 4:

> How daintily and cunningly you drive me
> Up like a deer to the toil!

363–365. if my duty . . . unmannerly: If, in my devotion to your interests, I am too bold in questioning you, it is my love that causes this breach of good manners. Hamlet, assuming an air of vacancy, pretends to find this apology unintelligible.

371. touch. Cf. *Richard II*, i, 3, 163–165:

> Or like a cunning instrument cas'd up
> Or, being open, put into his hands
> That knows no touch to tune the harmony.

372. as easy as lying. A proverbial phrase, conveying no personal suggestion, though Rosencrantz and Guildenstern are at liberty to put the coat on if it fits them. The word *lying* should not be emphasized.—**ventages:** wind-holes—the 'stops' mentioned in l. 376.

386. organ: musical instrument.—**'Sblood.** This oath is rapped out with startling unexpectedness and almost makes Guildenstern jump. See note on ii, 2, 383.

388. fret. Frets are small bars of wire or wood on a guitar or the like, to guide the fingering. Hamlet puns on the sense of 'worry,' 'agitate.' Cf. Dekker, *The Gull's Hornbook* (ed. Grosart, II, 254): 'Theres no musick without frets'; Dekker, *The Honest Whore*, i, 2 (Pearson ed., II, 10): 'Musitian will he never be (yet I find much musicke in him), but he loues no frets.'

391. presently: without delay.

393–399. Polonius is merely humouring the supposed madman. There is nothing absurd in his conduct. As to the shifting shapes of clouds cf. *Antony and Cleopatra*, iv, 14, 2–11:

> Sometime we see a cloud that's dragonish;
> A vapour sometime like a bear or lion,
> A tower'd citadel, a pendent rock,
> A forked mountain, or blue promontory
> With trees upon't that nod unto the world
> And mock our eyes with air. Thou hast seen these signs;
> They are black Vesper's pageants. . . .
> That which is now a horse, even with a thought
> The rack dislimns, and makes it indistinct
> As water is in water.

400, 401. Then. The false appearance of logic given by the use of *then* is a part of Hamlet's counterfeit madness.—**by-and-by:** immediately.—**They . . . bent.** Spoken aside, in self-congratulation on his success in playing the madman: 'They indulge my folly—humour me in my supposed madness—as completely as I can wish.'—**bent.** An idiom from archery.

406–417. Hamlet's imaginative nature pictures him to himself as capable of any atrocity in the way of revenge. We are not, however, to suppose that there was any danger of his killing his mother. Indeed, the Ghost has expressly warned him not to harm her (i, 5, 85–88). One purpose of this speech is to enlighten the audience, so that, when Hamlet threatens the Queen in scene iv (ll. 18–21), they may know that he does not mean to do her any harm.

408. **Contagion.** Two ideas combine in this poetic figure. In the night, evil spirits and malign influences were supposed to have more power than by day; and at the same time the night air was regarded as charged with actual contagion. Cf. *Julius Cæsar*, ii, 1, 265: 'the vile contagion of the night'; *2 Henry VI*, iv, 1, 3–7:

> And now loud-howling wolves arouse the jades
> That drag the tragic melancholy night,
> Who with their drowsy, slow, and flagging wings
> Cleep [i.e., surround] dead men's graves, and from their misty jaws
> Breathe foul contagious darkness in the air.

410. **Soft!** Cf. i, 1, 126.

412. **Nero:** who murdered his mother.

415. **be.** Subjunctive: 'Let my tongue and soul be hypocrites.' His soul is to pretend a savage purpose which it does not feel, and his words are to express it.

416. **How . . . somever:** howsoever much.—**shent:** berated; violently reproved.

417. **To give them seals:** to confirm or fulfil them by action.

Scene III.

---

1. **I like him not:** I do not like the way he is acting.—**with us.** The royal *we*—'with me the King.'

3. **your commission.** Rosencrantz and Guildenstern are to 'bear the mandate' (iii, 4, 202–204)—a sealed letter addressed to the King of England ordering him to put Hamlet to death (iv, 3, 60–70; v, 2, 19–25). This is what is called 'their grand commission' (v, 2, 18). Whether King Claudius tells them its contents we are nowhere informed. Probably not; for he is secretive by disposition, and now, if ever, secrecy is the best policy. The audience does not learn what the mandate prescribes until iv, 3, 60–67. Ostensibly Hamlet is sent as ambassador (iii, 1, 177, 178; iv, 6, 9, 10). His own suspicions are vague (iii, 4, 202 ff.; iv, 3, 50).—**dispatch:** cause to be drawn up.

5. **The terms of our estate:** the condition of my royal rank. A stately phrase for 'my kingly office.'

11. **peculiar:** individual, private.

13. **noyance:** harm, injury.

14. **depends and rests.** A singular verb with a plural subject is especially common when the verb precedes or when the subject has a collective sense.

15. **cesse:** cessation, decease. The Folio reads 'cease.'

16. **a gulf:** a whirlpool.

17 ff. **a massy wheel,** etc. This stilted and inconsistent figure is a fine instance of courtly rhetoric. Rosencrantz fixes his wheel 'on the highest mount' because a king occupies an exalted position; but he has no definite idea of the mechanics of the structure and (in l. 19) takes refuge in the vaguest of all words—'things.' Then he abandons his specific metaphor of the wheel and emphasizes the *fall* ('ruin') of the structure.

22. **ruin:** downfall.

24. **Arm you:** prepare yourselves; make ready.

25. **fear.** *Fear* includes both the ordinary meaning and the sense 'object of fear' (i.e., Hamlet).

27. **closet.** Cf. iii, 2, 343.

28. **convey myself:** slip quietly, without being seen.

29. **the process:** what is said; their conversation.—**tax him home:** take him to task soundly. *Home* comes from the sense of 'a home thrust.' Cf. iii, 4, 1.

30. **as you said.** The suggestion had come from Polonius, but the King had accepted it (iii, 1, 189–195).

33. **of vantage:** from a favourable position.

37. **the primal eldest curse.** See *Genesis*, iv, 10–12.

39. **Though inclination . . . will:** though I not only *wish* to pray, but feel a strong *impulse* toward prayer.

41. **bound:** in duty bound.

43. **neglect:** omit; leave undone.

46, 47. **snow.** Cf. *Isaiah*, i, 18.—**Whereto . . . offence?** For what purpose does God's mercy *exist*, if not to confront a man's guilt when that appears as accuser before the Great Judge, and thus to procure his pardon?

48–50. this twofold force, etc.: 'Lead us not into temptation,' and 'Forgive us our trespasses.'

54. effects: things obtained; gains.

55. mine own ambition: the satisfaction of my lust for power.—**my queen.** Note that 'my queen' is the acme of the climax (cf. i, 5, 75). The murder was a 'crime of passion.'

56. th' offence: that which has been gained by the crime; the booty.

57. the corrupted currents: the evil courses; the 'ways of the world.'

58. Offence's gilded hand: the guilty hand, if lined with gold.

59, 60. the wicked prize . . . law: a part of the booty may be used to bribe the judge.—**'tis not so above.** Cf. Ford, *Love's Sacrifice,* iii, 2 (ed. Gifford and Dyce, III, 62): 'Heaven is an unbrib'd justice.'

61–64. There. Emphatic.—**there the action . . . nature:** *There* (in God's court) the suit must be brought in its true nature—in exact accord with the facts. An action at law is said to *lie* when it may legally be brought.—**we . . . evidence:** We must meet our sins face to face, for they are present in court to accuse us; and thus we are forced to testify against ourselves. Supply *are* before *compelled.*—**What rests?** What remains? What is there left for me to do?

65, 66. can: can accomplish.—**what can it:** i.e., even *it.*

68, 69. limed soul. The figure is that of a bird caught by alighting upon a twig smeared with the sticky substance called birdlime. The harder it struggles, the more it is besmeared and ensnared ('engag'd'). Thus the King's soul, in its efforts to find some escape from guilt, merely succeeds in convincing itself that no escape is possible—since he can neither pray nor repent. Cf. Ariosto, *Orlando Furioso,* xxiii, 105: 'Like the heedless bird that finds itself caught in a net or in birdlime: the more it beats its wings and strives to get loose, the more it entangles itself.'

69. Make assay. Addressed by the King to himself: 'Though prayer seems impossible, yet make the attempt.'

73. **pat:** readily, conveniently.—**praying:** and therefore off his guard.

74. **now.** Here Hamlet draws his sword, which he sheathes again at l. 88.

75. **That would be scann'd:** That point needs scrutiny.

79. **this is hire and salary:** This would be to act as if I had hired him to murder my father and were now paying him his wages. The text follows the Folios. The Quartos read 'this is base and silly.'

80. **grossly:** in a gross condition; not purified by repentance, confession, and absolution. Cf. i, 5, 76–79.—**full of bread:** in the full flush of worldly pleasures (as opposed to prayer and fasting). Malone aptly quotes *Ezekiel*, xvi, 49: 'Pride, fulness of bread, and abundance of idleness.'

81. **crimes:** faults, sins—not in the special sense of 'criminal offences.' Cf. i, 5, 12; ii, 1, 43.—**broad blown:** in full bloom. Cf. i, 5, 76: 'Cut off even in the blossoms of my sin.'—**flush:** full of life and vigour.

82. **audit:** final account (in the book of judgment).

83. **in our ... thought:** judging as well as our circumstances allow, and letting our thoughts take their natural course, we must conclude, etc. 'Our course of thought' is contrasted with God's complete knowledge; and what makes the difference is 'our circumstance,' i.e., the fact that we are mere men.

85. **in the purging of his soul.** Contrasted with *grossly* in l. 80.

86. **season'd:** ripened, matured; i.e., thoroughly prepared. —**his passage:** from this world to the next.

88–93. **Up, sword, ... hent:** Back, sword, into thy sheath, and be thou seized by me at a more horrid moment—when his death will involve his damnation.—**relish:** taste, trace.—**that his heels,** etc.: so that he may fall headlong to hell.

88–95. See Introduction.

96. **This physic:** the considerations which lead me to postpone revenge. Wilson interprets *physic* as 'prayer,' comparing l. 85.

Scene IV.

1, 2. straight: straightway, immediately.—**lay home to him:** tax him home (iii, 3, 29); assail him with home truths.—**broad:** free, lawless. Cf. 'broad words' (*Macbeth*, iii, 6, 21).

4. heat: anger (on the King's part).—**silence me:** stop talking and hide myself. The Second Quarto and the Folios read 'silence'; the First Quarto has 'shrowde my selfe.' Hanmer reads *'sconce*, i.e., 'ensconce'—a not improbable emendation. Cf. *Merry Wives*, iii, 3, 96: 'I will ensconce me behind the arras.'

5. round: outspoken. Cf. ii, 2, 139; iii, 1, 191.

7. fear me not: Do not be afraid that I shall spare him. Cf. i, 3, 51.

9–14. Note the line-for-line arrangement of the speeches (*stichomythia*).—**idle:** foolish. Cf. iii, 2, 95.

14. Have you forgot me? Have you forgotten who I am?

17. those. A threat is implied. The Queen turns to leave the room, as if to summon Claudius; but Hamlet detains her.

19. a glass: a mirror.

21. What wilt thou do? The Queen's alarm is caused by some menace in Hamlet's action. He has forced her to sit down and stands over her in a threatening attitude. See note on iii, 2, 406–417. In the First Quarto the Queen, in reporting the interview, says:

> Whenas he came, I first bespake him faire,
> But then he throwes and tosses me about,
> As one forgetting that I was his mother:
> At last I call'd for help.

23. a rat? Cf. *The Hystorie of Hamblet*, 1608, Chap. iii: 'He cried, A rat, a rat! and presently drawing his sworde thrust it into the hangings.' The exclamation is not found in Belleforest's *Histoire*, of which *The Hystorie* is a translation. See Introduction.—**for a ducat:** I'll bet a ducat.

25. Is it the King? So Hamlet supposed when he made the thrust. In the interval between scenes iii and iv, then, there has been time enough for the King to reach the Queen's apartment and conceal himself.

28. **As kill . . . brother.** A plain accusation that the Queen was an accomplice in the murder of her husband. Her astonishment convinces Hamlet of her innocence; and he makes no further allusion to such complicity, even when she asks 'What have I done?' in l. 39. There are resemblances between this scene and that in which Edward III accuses his mother of murdering her husband in Marlowe's *Edward II* (ed. Dyce, II, 288–289). In Belleforest and the prose *Hystorie* the Queen declares her innocence in emphatic terms, adds that her second marriage was the effect of fear, and joins Hamlet in his plans for revenge. Cf. the First Quarto:

> *Queene.* But as I haue a soule, I sweare by heauen,
> I neuer knew of this most horride murder. . . .
> *Ham.* And mother, but assist mee in reuenge,
> And in his death your infamy shall die.
> *Queene.* Hamlet, I vow by that maiesty,
> That knowes our thoughts, and lookes into our hearts,
> I will conceale, consent, and doe my best,
> What stratogem soe're thou shalt deuise.

33. **too busy:** too much of a busybody; too meddlesome.

37, 38. **custom.** Cf. ll. 161 ff.—**braz'd it:** plated it with brass; made it impenetrable to shame.—**proof:** armour. Cf. *Richard III*, v, 3, 220: 'armed in proof.'—**sense:** feeling.

40. **Such an act.** Hamlet upbraids his mother for her adultery. He no longer accuses her of murder.

41–44. **grace:** beauty.—**the rose.** Cf. Milton, *Paradise Lost*, viii, 619: 'rosy red, love's proper hue.'—**a blister:** a brand of infamy. Cf. iv, 5, 118–120.

46. **contraction:** the obligation of the marriage contract.

47. **religion:** the marriage vow. Cf. *King John*, iii, 1, 229: 'with all religious strength of sacred vows.'

48. **A rhapsody of words:** mere senseless verbiage.—**glow.** Cf. *King John*, iv, 1, 113, 114: 'blush and glow with shame.'

49. **this solidity.** Cf. *Troilus and Cressida*, i, 3, 113: 'all this solid globe.'—**compound mass.** Our globe is conceived as an harmonious compound of the four elements.

50. tristful: sad, gloomy. The Folio reads 'tristfull'; the Second Quarto has 'heated.'—**against the doom:** at the approach of the Day of Judgment.

51. thought-sick: sick at heart. *Thought* is often used in the sense of 'melancholy,' 'despondent thought.' Cf. iii, 1, 85; iv, 5, 188; *Twelfth Night*, ii, 4, 115.

52. the index. Cf. *Othello*, ii, 1, 263, 264: 'an index and obscure prologue.' The *index* of a book meant the 'table of contents,' which precedes the text of a volume.

53. this picture. *Station* ('attitude in standing') in l. 58 is enough to prove that this portrait was full-length, and if so, the portrait of Claudius was doubtless of the same sort. Miniatures have often been substituted on the stage. Cf. *Two Noble Kinsmen*, iv, 2. In the old German *Hamlet* (*Der Bestrafte Brudermord*), iii, 5, Hamlet speaks of the portraits as 'dort in jener Gallerie.'[1]

54. counterfeit presentment: representation in portraiture. Cf. *Merchant of Venice*, iii, 2, 115: 'Fair Portia's counterfeit!'

56. Hyperion. See i, 2, 140.—**front:** forehead.—**Jove.** Cf. iii, 2, 294.

58. station: posture in standing. No paraphrase does justice to the alert activity expressed by the original word.

62. a man. Cf. i, 2, 187, 188.

65. his: its.

---

[1] For portraits (real or imaginary) hanging on a wall see Webster, *The Devil's Law-Case*, iii, 3, 379 ff. (ed. Lucas, II, 284); Middleton, *Blurt, Master Constable*, ii, 1, 174 ff.; ii, 2, 85 ff., 110 ff., 159–162; iii, 1, 1 (ed. Bullen, I, 33, 37, 38, 40, 50); Heywood, *If You Know Not Me*, Part II (Pearson ed., I, 275 ff.). Small portraits (miniatures or the like) are common in stage business. See Marlowe, *Edward II*, i, 4, 127 (ed. Dyce, II, 185; ed. Charlton and Waller, p. 92); *A Merry Knack to Know a Knave*, 1594 (Hazlitt's Dodsley, VI, 565); Fletcher, *The Custom of the Country*, v, 3, 17, 18; Fletcher, *The Humorous Lieutenant*, v, 5, 28 ff.; Dekker, *Satiromastix* (Pearson ed., I, 157); Ford, *The Lover's Melancholy*, ii, 1; iv, 3; v, 1 (ed. Gifford and Dyce, I, 37, 86, 98); Brome, *The Novella*, iv (Pearson ed., I, 147); Brome, *The Queen's Exchange* (Pearson ed., III, 474, 475); *The Puritaine Widow*, i, 1, 135–138 (ed. Brooke, *Shakespeare Apocrypha*, p. 222). On the whole question see W. J. Lawrence, *Pre-Restoration Stage Studies*, 1927, pp. 111–116.

66, 67. **leave:** cease.—**batten:** gorge yourself.

68. **at your age.** To Hamlet, a very young man, his mother seems too old to feel passionate love. We should not be misled into exaggerating the Queen's age. She is in what we should call the prime of life.

69, 70. **The heyday in the blood:** the liveliness of youthful passion; 'the compulsive ardour' (l. 86).—**tame:** under control.—**waits upon:** defers to.

71-81. **Sense sure you have,** etc.: You have life and the faculty of motion. Hence I infer that you have also the faculty of perception by the senses. But surely all your five senses must be paralyzed. Mere insanity could not cause you to make such a mistake in choosing; for madness never so thoroughly suspended the action of the five senses as not to leave some fragment of one of them—enough to enable you to choose where the difference was so enormous ('to serve in such a difference'). That *sense* means 'sensuous perception' in ll. 71, 74 (as in l. 80), not 'intellect,' is clear from Hamlet's appeal to sight, feeling, hearing, and smell. Cf. *Venus and Adonis*, 433-444. *Motion* means 'normal bodily motion,' as contrasted with paralysis: she 'lives and moves and has her being.'

74. **ecstasy:** madness. Cf. l. 138; iii, 1, 168.

75. **quantity.** Emphatic: 'small quantity,' 'modicum.' Cf. iii, 2, 45; v, 1, 293.—**choice:** the power to choose; discrimination.

76. **To serve:** enough to serve.

77. **cozen'd:** cheated, tricked.—**hoodman-blind:** blindman's buff. The Queen, Hamlet implies, had made her choice with as little discrimination as that shown by the *hoodman* (or blinded person) in blindman's buff, who seizes upon anybody within reach and cannot tell one from another.

78-81. Omitted in the Folios.—**sans:** without.—**so mope:** be so dull and torpid.

82, 83. **Rebellious hell.** The baser elements in our nature are conceived as rising in mutiny against our nobler selves. The figure is similar to that in the warning of Laertes to Ophelia: 'Youth to itself rebels' (i, 3, 44).—**matron's.** Emphatic: 'even in a matron's frame.'

86. **gives the charge:** makes the attack.

88. **reason panders will:** reason, which should control desire, becomes basely subservient to it.

90, 91. **grained:** dyed in grain, i.e., in fast colours. *Grain* was a kind of scarlet dye-stuff (cochineal).—**leave their tinct:** give up their colour.

92. **enseamed:** soaked in grease.

95. **daggers.** Cf. iii, 2, 414.

96. **A murtherer.** To the Queen this word sounds like a mere abusive epithet. To the end she remains in ignorance of the murder.

97. **the tithe:** the tenth part.

98. **a vice of kings:** a rascally buffoon among kings. The *vice* in the old morality plays was a comic character.

99. **cutpurse.** Properly, 'one who steals money by cutting a hole in the purse' (worn at the girdle); then, 'a pickpocket' in general; here, 'a sneaking thief.' Claudius is not a usurper. He has been legally elected King in Hamlet's absence; and thus, as Hamlet says to Horatio in calmer and more literal language, he has 'popp'd in between th' election and [Hamlet's] hopes' (v, 2, 65).

101. **Enter the Ghost.** There is no room for discussion whether this is a 'subjective' or an 'objective' ghost—whether it is a figment of Hamlet's brain or an actual apparition. Ghosts had the power, it was believed, of appearing and speaking to one person while remaining invisible and inaudible to all others present. The fact that a speech is given to the Ghost settles the question. If he were a delusion, Hamlet would merely imagine that he heard his words, and, if the audience needed to know what Hamlet imagined he heard, he would himself repeat them. There is a similar situation in Chapman's tragedy *The Revenge of Bussy d'Ambois*, v, 1 (Pearson ed., II, 166). Guise and Clermont are conversing when the ghost of Bussy appears, calls for vengeance, and vanishes. Clermont, Bussy's brother, sees and hears the ghost, but Guise perceives nothing.

Guise. Why stand'st thou still thus, and applyest thine eares
And eyes to nothing?

> *Clermont.*   Saw you nothing here?
> *Guise.* Thou dream'st, awake now; what was here to see?
> *Clermont.* My Brother's spirit, vrging his reuenge.
> *Guise.* Thy Brother's spirit! Pray thee, mocke me not.

Clermont convinces Guise that the apparition is not imaginary;
but Hamlet does not convince his mother. Since she thinks
him insane, his seeing the Ghost is, to her, a symptom of his
insanity.—**in his nightgown.** These words are in the First
Quarto only. The Ghost appears, not (as in Act I) in armour,
but 'in his habit as he lived'; in his dressing gown, attire suitable for the privacy of his own apartment.

102. **A king of shreds and patches!** Often taken as alluding
to the motley attire of a fool or jester; but apparently Hamlet
means merely that Claudius's royalty is a threadbare, out-at-
elbows, patched-up thing. He has compared him to a clown,
then to a pickpocket and sneak-thief; now he compares him
to a ragged vagabond. Cf. the First Quarto: 'a king of clowts,
of very shreads.'

103, 104. **Save me ... guards!** Cf. i, 4, 39.

107, 108. **laps'd in time and passion:** 'having suffered time
to slip and passion to cool' (Johnson). Literally, *laps'd* means
'having slipped or failed.'—**important:** momentous.

110. **Do not forget.** Cf. i, 5, 91.—**This visitation.** Since the
Ghost has a private message of vengeance, intended only for
Hamlet's ear, he shows himself to Hamlet alone. His message
is interrupted (at l. 112) by his sympathy for the Queen's distress. Cf. i, 5, 84–88.

112. **amazement:** utter confusion of mind. Cf. ii, 2, 591; iii,
2, 339.

114. **Conceit:** imagination (which forms, in the Queen's
mind, a vivid image of her guilt).

118. **incorporal:** bodiless.

119. **spirits.** In moments of excitement the *spirits* or 'vital
forces' were thought to come, as it were, to the surface, and
to cause various symptoms of agitation, such as a wild glare
in the eyes.

120. **th' alarm:** the call to arms (*all' arme*).

121. **bedded hairs:** 'thy knotted and combined locks' (i, 5, 18).—**excrements:** in the literal sense of 'outgrowths.' The hair and nails, being not exactly a part of the body but rather something growing out of it, were often so called.

122. **an end.** Cf. i, 5, 19.

123, 124. **distemper:** distraction.—**patience:** calmness, self-control.

127. **capable:** capable of feeling and emotion.

128, 129. **convert:** change utterly.—**effects:** deeds.

135. **as he liv'd:** as he was dressed when alive; not, as if he lived.

138, 139. **ecstasy:** madness.—**cunning:** skilful.

144. **gambol from:** not merely 'wander from,' but 'wander away from in a fantastic way.'—**for love of grace:** for God's sake.

145. **flattering unction:** soothing ointment. Hamlet urges his mother to take his reproofs and exhortations seriously and not as the ravings of a maniac.

147–149. **skin . . . unseen.** For the metaphor cf. Thomas Hughes, *The Misfortunes of Arthur*, ed. 1587, iii, 1 (sig. C4–D):

> I neuer yet sawe hurt so smoothly heald,
> But that the skarre bewraid the former wound:
> Yea, where the salue did soonest close the skinne,
> The sore was oftner couered vp than cur'de.
> Which festering deepe and filde within, at last
> With sodaine breach grew greater than at first.

152–155. **Forgive me . . . good:** I must ask you to forgive my action in thus upbraiding you, though it is a good action (a virtue) on my part; for, in these corrupt times, the virtuous cannot chide the vicious without asking pardon for the liberty —indeed, they must bend the knee (*curb*) and beg for leave to benefit them by such needed reproof. Hamlet feels some compunction at his own harsh language, but he justifies it in the very act of apologizing.—**fatness . . . times.** Hamlet compares the corrupt times to a body that is unhealthily corpulent (*pursy*). Cf. Heywood, *Apology for Actors*, 1612, sig. B r°:

'In the fatnes and ranknes of a peacable Common-wealth';
Chapman, *Byron's Conspiracy*, i, 1 (Pearson ed., II, 191):

> Peace must not make men Cowards, nor keepe calme
> Her pursie regiment [i.e., government] with men's smootherd breaths.

160. **Assume . . . not.** This has become a proverb in a sense
different from that which it bears in the context. *Assume*
means, not 'counterfeit' or 'pretend,' but 'Take to yourself
in practice': 'Force yourself to act virtuously, even if you are
not virtuously inclined.'

161–165. **That monster . . . put on.** Custom, who is a monster
because he takes away our feeling of the badness of evil habits,
is yet an angel in this point, namely, that he likewise makes
good actions easy. *Monster* and *angel* stand in antithesis. The
Folios omit the passage. The Second Quarto reads *deuill* for
evil. The emendation was suggested to Theobald by Thirlby.
Many editors retain *devil*; but *evil* is necessary to mark the
antithesis between bad habits and good, and *monster* makes a
satisfactory antithesis to *angel*.—**frock or livery.** With a slight
pun on *habits*.—**That aptly is put on:** that is easy to wear.
Obviously the figure is not meant to suggest fraud or the con-
cealment of evil intent under a cloak of virtue.

166. **shall:** will certainly.

167–170. **the next . . . potency.** Omitted in the Folios.

168, 169. **use:** habit.—**can . . . nature.** For, as the proverb
runs, 'habit is a second nature.' Cf. Nashe, *The Unfortunate
Traveller* (ed. McKerrow, II, 302): 'Vse is another nature.'—
either master, etc.: The devil in a man (the evil in his character) may be kept under control by good habits or may even
be quite eradicated thereby. *Maister* was first supplied in the
Third Quarto (1611), which omits *either*. The Second Quarto
has 'And either the.' See Textual Notes.

171, 172. **And when . . . you:** And when you show some
sign of wishing for the blessing of heaven, I will be once more
your dutiful son and ask your blessing at parting, as I used to
do. Cf. i, 3, 53, 57, 81.—**you.** Emphatic.—**For:** as for.

174. **To punish me with this.** Hamlet sees that the King will

at once perceive that he killed Polonius by mistake for him, and will take measures accordingly. See l. 211; iv, 1, 13-15.—**and this**: and this dead man.

175. **their scourge and minister**: heaven's scourge (of punishment) and heaven's agent—minister of divine retribution. *Their* refers to heaven (l. 173). The use of a plural pronoun to refer to the singular noun *heaven* is common.

176. **bestow him**: stow him away; dispose of him.

178. **cruel.** Hamlet's harsh treatment of his mother still troubles him.

179. **Thus . . . behind**: Thus, in this interview, I have made a bad beginning (by killing Polonius when I meant to kill the King); but there is worse to come: that is, worse for you and Claudius; for I shall kill him sooner or later. The Queen does not understand this vague threat. Perhaps she thinks that *bad* refers to her son's treatment of her. *Thus* is the Folio reading. The Quartos have *This,* which Wilson retains, thinking that it refers to the dead body of Polonius.

182. **bloat**: bloated with drinking. See note on i, 4, 12.

183. **mouse.** A common pet name. Cf. *Love's Labour's Lost*, v, 2, 19.

184, 187. **reechy**: nauseous—literally, smoky. Cf. *reek*.—**ravel . . . out**: disentangle, explain.—**essentially**: really; in fact.

190. **paddock**: toad.—**gib**: tomcat. The word is a contraction of *Gilbert* and was common as a cat's name. The animals here mentioned were regarded as unclean or uncanny. Cf. *Macbeth*, i, 1, 8, 9; iv, 1, 14, 15.

191. **Such dear concernings**: matters of such importance to one's self. For *dear* see i, 2, 182, note.

193-196. **Unpeg the basket.** The fable cited, though it has not been found elsewhere, is easy to reconstruct. An ape finds a basket full of birds on the housetop and opens it. The birds fly away. The ape gets into the basket and jumps out in an attempt to fly, but falls from the roof and breaks his neck.—**To try conclusions**: to try an experiment.—**down**: by the fall. Cf. Nashe, *The Unfortunate Traveller*, 1594 (ed. McKerrow,

II, 291): 'My owne mother gaue I a boxe of the eare too, and brake her necke down a paire of staires.'

200. **I must to England.** The King does not announce this voyage to Hamlet until iv, 3, 48, and then Hamlet pretends to take it as a novelty. The present passage shows that he had already learned of the project—how, Shakespeare does not say, but it is easy to imagine; for Hamlet was not destitute of friends among the King's counsellors and he was ever on his guard.—**Alack!** Merely a natural expression of sorrow at the coming separation. The Queen has no suspicion of the King's evil purpose.

202. **There's letters seal'd.** See iii, 3, 3 (note); iv, 3, 66; v, 2, 18. The Folio omits ll. 202–210.

203. **adders fang'd:** adders with fangs—whose fangs have not been extracted. *Fang'd* is an adjective, not a participle.

205. **knavery:** some crime against myself. The precise nature of the plan Hamlet does not discover until they are at sea, when he opens the commission (see v, 2, 17–25).

206. **enginer:** engineer. The Elizabethan accent was on the first syllable, as in other words in *-eer*; *pioner, mutiner, muleter.*

207. **Hoist:** hoisted, blown up.—**petar:** petard—a kind of bomb used especially for blowing gates open.

209. **at the moon.** There is grim humour in the use of *at* instead of *to.*

210. **When . . . meet.** Another figure from warfare. Hamlet imagines two plotters (the King and himself) as digging a mine and a countermine and suddenly coming face to face in their excavations.

211. **packing.** With a pun: (1) lugging; carrying a load on my back; (2) leaving the country in haste (on account of his death).

214. **most grave.** An obvious pun. Cf. *Romeo and Juliet,* iii, 1, 101, 102, where Mercutio, mortally wounded, says to Romeo, 'Ask for me to-morrow, and you shall find me a grave man.' Hamlet's levity of tone is, as on previous occasions, due to excitement and revulsion of feeling. Cf. i, 5, 116 ff., 150 ff.; iii, 2, 282 ff.

216. **to draw . . . with you:** to come to the end of my business with you. A regular phrase when one is approaching the end of a long speech. Cf. Latimer, *Seventh Sermon before Edward VI* (ed. Arber, p. 202): 'But to drawe towarde an ende.' From this point, in the old story, the Queen heartily assists Hamlet in his plans of revenge.

Act IV. Scene I.

The Quarto of 1676 is the oldest text to begin a new Act here. That Rosencrantz and Guildenstern enter with the King has excited some surprise among the moderns. Obviously the Queen enters by one door, from her apartment; the King and his companions at the other door, from a conference in which Rosencrantz and Guildenstern have probably received their commission and have announced their readiness to depart. See iii, 3, 3, 24–26.

1. **matter:** meaning.—**prófound:** 'deep, literally, and deep in significance' (Corson). For the accent see i, 4, 52, note.

4. **Bestow this place on us:** give it up to us; leave us.

7. **Mad.** Despite Hamlet's protestations in iii, 4, 139 ff., the Queen still believes that he is mad, and that he was really trying to kill a rat behind the arras. His seeing the Ghost and talking with it has confirmed this opinion. Thus she can conceal his protestation of sanity without being false to her husband.

11, 12. **brainish apprehension:** insane notion.—**good old man.** The regard of the King and Queen for Polonius is evident throughout the play. It should teach the actor who plays the part that the old Councillor, though at times ridiculous, is not to be made a mere ancient buffoon.

13. **It had been so with us.** The King immediately perceives what the Queen cannot know—that Hamlet had intended to kill him when he thrust his sword through the tapestry; and henceforth he has no doubt that Hamlet is sane and that he is his mortal enemy.—**us:** me. The 'royal *we*.'

14, 15. **His liberty.** Cf. iii, 1, 194, 195; iii, 2, 351, 352.—
to us: to me.

16. **answer'd:** accounted for, explained—i.e., to the public.
The King does not exaggerate the danger to the royal family
that may result from the violent death of so great a noble as
Polonius. See iv, 5, 96 ff.

17. **to us:** not, 'to you and me,' but 'to me, the King.' So
also *our* in l. 19.—**providence:** foresight.

18. **short:** on a short leash; under control.—**out of haunt:**
away from the society of others.

20. **We would not.** So people will say.

22. **divulging:** coming to light.

25, 26. **ore:** precious metal (especially gold).—**mineral:**
mine or metallic vein.

27. **He weeps.** This white lie of the Queen's has so misled
actors that Hamlet is often made to sob violently over the body
of Polonius at the end of the preceding scene. She is exaggerating in her eagerness to spare Hamlet as much as possible.
Cf. iii, 4, 173.

31, 32. **We must . . . excuse:** I must defend with all my
royal authority and excuse with all my skill.

33. **with some further aid.** Henceforth, until Hamlet em-
barks for England, he is always under surveillance, though his
guards are not always seen by the audience. Thus he has no
opportunity to attack the King. Cf. iv, 3, 14.

40. **And what's untimely done.** Both Second Quarto and
Folio omit the rest of this line and the Folio omits ll. 41–44
(through *air*). The text accepts Capell's conjecture, which is
an improvement on Theobald's 'For, haply, Slander.'

41, 42. **o'er . . . diameter:** across the whole breadth of the
world.—**As level:** with as sure an aim.—**his blank:** its mark.
The *blank* is literally the white circle or spot at the centre of
the target.

44. **woundless:** invulnerable. Cf. i, 1, 145.

45. **My soul . . . dismay.** A sincere expression of the turmoil in the King's mind. The death of Polonius is, he knows,
a serious matter, likely to shake his throne. See iv, 5, 98 ff.

Scene II.

1. Safely stow'd. Hamlet has not yet recovered from the excited mood in which we saw him at the very end of the preceding act. Hence the flippancy of his language.

6. whereto 'tis kin. See *Genesis*, iii, 19.

11, 12. keep your counsel: keep your secrets. Cf. iii, 2, 152. Hamlet suggests that he knows well enough (but will not tell) what they and the King have in mind with regard to him. Cf. iii, 4, 202-210.—**demanded of:** interrogated by.—**replication:** formal answer.

15 ff. Take you me for a sponge? Rosencrantz appears to understand *sponge* in the literal sense, regarding Hamlet's words as mere madness. Hamlet explains. The figure (as Caldecott notes) is derived from a passage in Suetonius (*Vespasian*, 16): 'Creditur etiam procuratorum rapacissimorum quemque ad ampliora officia ex industria solitus promovere, quo locupletiores mox condemnaret; quibus quidem vulgo pro spongiis dicebatur uti, quod quasi et siccos madefaceret et exprimeret umentes.' Cf. Andrewes, *Sermon at Saint Mary's Hospital*, 1688 (Oxford ed., 1841-1843, V, 23, 24): 'A practice it hath been . . . to use wealthy citizens as spunges, to roll them up and down in moisture till they be full, and then to wring all out of them again'; Mabbe, *The Rogue* (ed. *Tudor Translations*, ii, 34): 'Your scandalous and offensive persons, whom we properly compare unto Sponges, who what they sucke in one place, have it wrung from them in another.'—**countenance:** favour.

18. like an ape: as an ape keeps things which he intends to devour. The text follows the Folio. The First Quarto has 'as an Ape doth nuttes.' The Second Quarto reads 'like an apple,' which Wilson retains, regarding it as an allusion to the apple-eating groundlings in the theatre. But the peculiar style of eating suggests apes rather than theatregoers.

24, 25. A knavish speech . . . ear. Not in the general sense, but simply '*My* knavish speech sleeps in (is not understood by) your foolish ear.'

28, 29. **The body ... body.** Mere nonsense, designed to carry out Hamlet's pretence of madness.

31. **Of nothing.** Whalley cites the Prayer Book Version of *Psalm* cxliv, 4: 'Man is like a thing of naught: his time passeth away like a shadow.' The phrase had become an idiom to express the utmost contempt, as in Gabriel Harvey, *Foure Letters*, 1592 (ed. Grosart, I, 184): 'A silly bullbeare, a sorry puffe of winde, a thing of nothing.' Wilson's suggestion is possible—that Hamlet is also hinting that the King has not long to live.

31. **Hide fox, and all after!** Omitted in the Quartos. Doubtless the formula of a child's game similar to hide-and-seek. One person (the fox) hides, and the other players are to find him if they can. As he speaks, Hamlet runs off as if he were the fox ('Catch me if you can!'), and is followed by Rosencrantz and Guildenstern. Cf. Moros, the silly character in Wager's comedy *The Longer Thou Livest, the More Fool Thou Art, ca.* 1559 (Aii, 3 r°): 'When we play and hunt the fox, I outrun all the boyes in the schoole.'

Scene III.

---

1. The Folio has the stage direction '*Enter King*'; the Second Quarto, '*Enter King, and two or three.*' The King's opening speech (like that at the end of the scene) is obviously a soliloquy, as the Folio would make it. If there are 'two or three' with him, they must be Attendants, who stand back and are not supposed to listen. They can hardly be the 'wisest friends' mentioned in iv, 1, 38.

4, 5. **of:** by.—**distracted:** turbulent. Note the wildness of the mob described in iv, 5, 99–108.—**multitude.** Hamlet's popularity is one reason why the King has to be cautious in putting him out of the way. Another reason is the Queen's love for her son.—**in:** in accordance with.

7. **bear:** manage.

9–11. **Deliberate pause:** the outcome of careful thought.—**Diseases ... at all.** Proverbial. Cf. Nashe, *Christs Teares over*

Ierusalem, 1593 (ed. McKerrow, II, 20): 'To desperate diseases must desperate Medicines be applyde.'

12. **bestow'd:** deposited, hidden.

14. **guarded.** See iv, 1, 33, note.

21-24. **politic:** skilled in statecraft. Shakespeare may have remembered 'the Diets of the Empire convoked at Worms' (Singer).—**e'en:** just now; at this moment.—**Your worm ... table.** Brandes compares Montaigne's *Essays*, ii, 2 (Florio's translation, 1603, p. 266): 'The heart and life of a mighty and triumphant Emperour, is but the break-fast of a seely-little Worme.'—**Your.** See i, 5, 167, note.—**variable service:** two ways of serving the same kind of food.

28-30. *King.* **Alas . . . that worm.** Omitted in the Folios.

33. **progress:** a journey of state undertaken by a monarch from one part of his realm to another. Queen Elizabeth and James I were fond of such progresses.

38. **indeed.** In the emphatic sense: 'in fact,' 'to speak plainly.'—**shall nose him:** will be sure to smell him.

43. **Which . . . grieve:** which we tender as dearly (hold at as high a rate) as we dearly (deeply) grieve. For *dearly* see note on i, 2, 182.

46, 47. **at help:** favourable.—**Th' associates:** Rosencrantz and Guildenstern.—**tend:** await your convenience.—**bent:** ready. A figure from archery.

50. **I see a cherub,** etc. A mad-sounding remark, meaning simply 'I have some notion of what they are.' Heaven's cherubim, of course, see everything.

51, 52. **dear mother.** The maddest speech that Hamlet has yet made. The Queen is not present. The King corrects Hamlet patiently in his reply, which carries us back to i, 2, 64, 110-112.

56. **at foot:** 'at his heels,' as we say.—**tempt him:** coax him. The King deprecates any disturbance.

58, 59. **seal'd . . . affair.** This makes it clear enough that Rosencrantz and Guildenstern do not know the contents of the sealed mandate that they carry to the English king. See note on l. 66.—**leans on the affair:** appertains to the business.

60. **England**: King of England. Cf. ii, 2, 59.—**at aught**: at any value. We still use the negative 'set at naught.'

61. **As . . . sense**: as [well thou mayst, for] my great power may well give thee a feeling thereof (i.e., of the value of my favour). Cf. iv, 7, 159.

63, 64. **thy free . . . us**: though technically free, yet thou standest in awe of me and payest homage accordingly.— **coldly set**: regard indifferently.

65. **process**: instructions, mandate.

66. **letters**: a letter (Lat. *litterae*). See iii, 4, 202–204. This sealed mandate to the English king is quite distinct from the 'commission' given to Rosencrantz and Guildenstern (iii, 3, 3). Its contents are a secret. Their commission gives them custody of the mandate and of Hamlet and directs them to deliver it and him. They are ignorant of its contents.—**con- gruing to**: congruent with; in complete agreement with. The Folio reads *coniuring*, i.e., calling upon him solemnly.—**effect**: purport.

67. **present**: instant, immediate. Thus, for the first time, we learn of the King's purpose.

68. **the hectic**: a continuous (as opposed to an intermittent) fever.

70. **Howe'er my haps**: whatever fortune I may have had or may have in the future.

Scene IV.

3. **conveyance**: escort. Danish heralds would accompany the troops of Fortinbras to certify that they come marching through the kingdom by royal license (see ii, 2, 77–80).

6. **in his eye**: in his royal presence. Cf. i, 2, 116.

8. **softly**: slowly.

9–66. The omission of these lines in the Folio is a mere 'cut' to shorten the play when acted. It would not do to delete Fortinbras altogether at this point, for something was needed to account for his indispensable presence at the end of the play.

9. **powers:** forces, troops.

14. **Norway.** Cf. i, 1, 48.

15. **the main:** the whole country.

17. **speak.** Emphatic, and so with a prolonged vowel which, with the change of pitch in utterance, gives the necessary dissyllable. Cf. 'O' in l. 65. Pope reads 'speak it.'

19. **the name.** Emphatic: 'the mere *name* of conquest.'

20. **To pay . . . farm it:** I would not take it on lease at a rental of five ducats a year.

22. **A ranker rate:** a higher rate. If the plot of ground were sold outright (in fee), the price would not yield an annual income of more than five ducats.

26. **debate:** fight out; settle by combat.

27. **imposthume:** internal abscess or ulcer. Hamlet means that such wars are the result of the corruption which comes from too much peace and luxury. It was an old theory that war is the natural exercise or gymnastics of the body politic, and that a country long at peace develops faults in the national character analogous to the diseases that idle luxury breeds in the human body. Cf. Bacon's essay *Of the True Greatness of Kingdoms and Estates*: 'No body can be healthful without exercise, neither natural body nor politic; and certainly, to a kingdom or estate, a just and honourable war is the true exercise. A civil war, indeed, is like the heat of a fever; but a foreign war is like the heat of exercise, and serveth to keep the body in health; for in a slothful peace, both courages will effeminate and manners [i.e., morals] corrupt.'

32. **inform against me:** denounce me.

34. **market of his time:** 'that for which he sells his time' (Johnson); what he gets in payment for his time.

36, 37. **discourse:** faculty of reasoning.—**Looking before and after:** as one must do in reasoning logically—passing from premises to conclusions. See i, 2, 150, note.

38. **capability and godlike reason.** Hendiadys: 'that capability of godlike reason.'—**godlike:** since reason makes us akin to the gods and distinguishes us from beasts.

39. **fust:** grow musty from lack of use.

40. **Bestial oblivion:** forgetfulness like that of the beasts (which do not remember their parents long).

41. **thinking ... event:** considering too carefully what the outcome may be.

45. **Sith:** since.

46, 47. **gross:** literally, 'large'—hence (as here) 'easily seen,' 'obvious to the eye.'—**charge:** expense.

50. **Makes mouths at:** makes faces at; holds in contempt. Cf. ii, 2, 381.—**event:** outcome, result.

53-56. **Rightly ... stake:** True nobility of soul is—to restrain one's self unless there is great cause for resentment, but nobly to recognize even a trifle as such a cause when honour is involved. Hamlet rings the changes on the word 'great.' *Greatly* in l. 55 means 'nobly,' 'as a great soul should.'

61. **a fantasy:** a fancy, a whim, a mere notion.—**trick of fame:** trifle of reputation; a matter affecting one's reputation in the very slightest degree.

63, 64. **Whereon ... cause:** not big enough to hold the men needed to settle the case by combat.—**continent:** receptacle (that which *contains*).

65. **O.** Prolonged in utterance. Cf. l. 17.

Scene V.

1-20. The text follows the Second Quarto except in l. 16 ('Let her come in'), which the Quarto gives to Horatio. The Folio gives it to the Queen, to whom it also assigns (erroneously) ' 'Twere good ... minds.' The Gentleman is expunged in the Folio, which gives his rôle to Horatio.

5, 6. **tricks:** plots and deceits.—**Spurns enviously at straws:** takes offence angrily at trifles.

8, 9. **the unshapèd ... collection:** The formless, disconnected way in which she speaks prompts the hearers to gather up and patch together her distracted utterances—as one is always tempted to try to make sense out of the ravings of a delirious patient.—**aim:** guess.

10. **botch . . . thoughts:** patch the words together so as to adapt them to their own ideas, i.e., to the suspicions they already have about the sudden death of Polonius.

11-13. **Which.** The antecedent is *words*. 'These words,' says the Gentleman, 'uttered as they are with an accompaniment of nods and winks and gestures, *do* appear to give some ground for suspicion.' Note the very cautious way in which he expresses himself: 'might indeed make one think that one might imagine—nothing *certain*, but many unhappy things.'

14, 15. It is significant that Horatio is a trusted (though unofficial) adviser at court.—**ill-breeding:** breeding evil; prone to evil thoughts.

18. **toy:** trifle.—**amiss:** misfortune.

19. **artless jealousy:** unreasonable and unwise suspicion.

20. **spills:** destroys. The excessive suspicion which guilt brings with it often causes the guilty person to act in a way that rouses suspicion in others. Thus the Queen's avoidance of Ophelia might have caused that very suspicion which she wished to avoid.—**Enter** *Ophelia* **distracted.** So in the Folio. The Second Quarto has simply '*Enter Ophelia*' (after l. 16). The First Quarto reads '*Enter Ofelia playing on a Lute, and her haire downe singing.*'

22. **How now?** Merely a courteous greeting like 'How do you do?'

23 ff. The fragments that Ophelia sings appear to be bits that would be familiar to the Elizabethan audience, but only three lines (23, 24, 187) have been found that antedate the play. Coleridge rightly bids us note 'the conjunction here of these two thoughts that had never subsisted in conjunction, the love for Hamlet and her filial love, and the guileless floating on the surface of her pure imagination of the cautions so lately expressed and the fears not too delicately avowed by her father and brother concerning the dangers to which her honour lay exposed' (*Shakespeare Criticism*, ed. Raysor, I, 33, 34).

23, 24. These lines resemble the Walsingham song, popular in Shakespeare's time. Cf. the version preserved in the Percy MS.:

'As yee came from the holy Land
    Of Walsingham,
Mett you not with my true loue
    By the way as you came?'

'How shold I know your true loue,
    That haue mett many a one
As I came from the holy Land,
    That haue come, that haue gone?'[1]

—**your true-love:** your affianced lover.

25. **cockle hat and staff.** The signs of a pilgrim. A cockle shell stuck in the hat was originally a sign that the wearer had been on a pilgrimage to the famous shrine of St. James at Compostela in Spanish Galicia. See *All's Well*, iii, 4, 4; iv, 3, 57 ff. That lovers are pilgrims and their lady-loves are saints was a common metaphor. See *Romeo and Juliet*, i, 5, 95 ff.; and cf. *Merchant of Venice*, i, 1, 119, 120; ii, 7, 39, 40; *Two Gentlemen*, ii, 4, 145; *Sonnets*, xxvii, 6.

28. **Say you?** Is that what you wish me to tell you? Cf. l. 47.

37, 38. **Larded:** bedecked.—**did not go.** All the Quartos and Folios have 'not.' We are to regard it as Ophelia's insertion in the verse. She suddenly remembers that the words of the song do not quite agree with the facts of her father's burial, which was hasty and without the usual ceremonies. See ll. 83–84, 213–215. For this reason *not* (omitted by Pope and most editors, but defended by Caldecott) is retained by Dowden and Wilson.

41. **God dild you!** God yield (i.e., repay) you!—**the owl.** Douce tells the following story as popular in Gloucestershire:

Our Saviour went into a baker's shop where they were baking, and asked for some bread to eat. The mistress of the shop immediately put a piece of dough into the oven to bake for him; but was reprimanded by her

---

[1] See *Bishop Percy's Folio Manuscript*, ed. Hales and Furnivall, III, 465 ff.; Delaney's *Garland of Good Will*, Percy Society ed., p. 111; Beaumont and Fletcher, *The Knight of the Burning Pestle*, ii, 8; Child, *English and Scottish Ballads*, IV (1857), 191 ff.; Chappell, *Popular Music of the Olden Time*, I, 236, 237; *The Pepys Ballads*, ed. Rollins, II, 22, and VIII, 9.

daughter, who insisting that the piece of dough was too large, reduced it to a very small size. The dough, however, immediately afterwards began to swell, and presently became of a most enormous size. Whereupon, the baker's daughter cried out, 'Heugh, heugh, heugh,' which owl-like noise probably induced our Saviour for her wickedness to transform her into that bird. This story is often related to children, in order to deter them from such illiberal behaviour to poor people.[1]

44. God be at your table! In her madness Ophelia uses a form of blessing that might be spoken by one who enters and finds a company at dinner.

45. Conceit: imagination—'Her mind is running on her father.'

48. To-morrow . . . day. 'This song alludes to the custom of the first girl seen by a man on the morning of this day being considered his Valentine or true-love' (Halliwell). See Douce, *Illustrations of Shakespeare*, 1839, pp. 470–473; Rose, *Folk-Lore*, XXX (1919), 63–70. In her madness Ophelia sings a song that she has heard in childhood. Her nurse, as Strachey suggests, may well have been as free-spoken as Juliet's. Everybody knows what happens in the way of indecorous speech when delirium stirs up the dregs of memory and puts an end to reticence.

49. betime: early.

53. dupp'd: opened. *Dup* is a contraction of *do up* (cf. German *aufmachen*); so *doff, don,* and *dout* ('do out'). Cf. Edwards, *Damon and Pythias* (Collier's Dodsley, I, 231): 'Iche weene the porters are drunke, wil they not dup the gate to-day?'

58. By Gis: a common contraction of 'by Jesus.' Cf. Preston, *Cambises,* l. 237 (ed. Manly, II, 171): 'What, man, I will not sticke for that, by Gisse!'

61. Cock. A vulgar substitute for *God* in oaths. Cf. Justice Shallow in *2 Henry IV*, v, 1, 1: 'By cock and pie, sir.'

---

[1] For versions of this folk-tale see Halliwell's Folio Shakespeare; *Journal of the Gypsy Lore Society*, 2d Series, I (1907), 90; Leland, *The English Gipsies*, 1873, p. 16. Cf. Fletcher, *The Nice Valour*, iii, 3, 9–11 (and Dyce's note).

69. **cannot choose but weep:** cannot help weeping. Cf. iv, 7, 66.

76, 77. **this is the poison . . . death.** That it is Claudius who speaks must not blind us to the fact that this sentence is meant to sum up for us—the audience—the meaning of the madness that precedes, as the Gentleman's 'She speaks much of her father' (l. 4) prepares us to understand it. Laertes agrees with the King's diagnosis (ll. 156 ff.). Disappointed love and Hamlet's madness had no doubt made Ophelia 'deject and wretched' (iii, 1, 163), but it is the mysterious tragedy of her father's death that has driven her mad. In her madness, thoughts of love and marriage of course recur and take strange shapes in their utterance.—**this is.** Pronounced as one syllable (with prolonged *s*). Often written *this* (without *is*).—The Second Quarto inserts 'and now behold' after 'death' in l. 77.

77-96. The King feels genuine sorrow for Polonius and Ophelia; and, besides, their fate has involved him in such difficulties that he seems to be hemmed in by troubles which are ever drawing nearer.

78, 79. **When . . . battalions.** The King's eloquent (and characteristic) elaboration of the familiar proverb. See iv, 7, 165, 166. Cf. Webster, *The Devil's Law Case*, ii, 1 (ed. Lucas, II, 260): 'One mischiefe never comes alone.'

81. **muddied.** The muddy bottom of the people's minds has been stirred up by angry suspicions, and their thoughts are roiled and turbid.

83, 84. **we:** I—not, you and I.—**done but greenly:** acted with childish folly.—**In hugger-mugger:** in haste and secrecy. Polonius had been buried without the ceremonies that befit his rank. See ll. 213-215.

89. **Feeds . . . clouds:** Instead of trying to discover the facts about his father's death, Laertes does nothing but wonder about it, making such wonder his only food for thought. Thus he keeps himself in a state of wilful uncertainty and confusion of mind.

90. **wants not buzzers:** lacks not persons who buzz or whisper in his ear; scandalmongers. Cf. *No-body and Some-body*,

l. 1912 (ed. Simpson, I, 352): 'Strange rumors and false buzz-
ing tales'; Greene, *Orlando Furioso*, ii, 1, 527–529 (ed. Collins,
I, 238):

> Here see thou buzze into the Counties eares
> That thou hast often seene within these woods
> Base Medor sporting with Angelica;

1 Jeronimo, ii, 2, 28–30 (ed. Boas, p. 312):

> Moreouer, I will buze Andreas landing,
> Which, once but crept into the vulgar mouthes,
> Is hurryed here and there, and sworne for troth.

92–94. **necessity, of matter beggar'd.** The necessity of making up a good story without materials drives these scandalmongers to accuse the King.—**nothing stick:** by no means
scruple.—**our person:** me the King, as personally responsible
for the death of Polonius—as his actual murderer. Cf. ll. 127,
149–152.—**In ear and ear:** now in one of his ears, now in the
other. These 'buzzers' surround him.

95. **a murd'ring piece:** a kind of mortar loaded with a variety of missiles and intended to scatter its shot; also called
a *murderer*. Cf. Chapman, *Bussy d'Ambois*, iii (Pearson ed.,
II, 59): 'like a murthering peece, making lanes in armies.'
Steevens quotes Fletcher, *The Double Marriage*, iv, 2, 5–7:

> A father's curses hit far off, and kill too;
> And, like a murdering piece, aim not at one,
> But all that stand within the dangerous level.

97. **my Switzers.** In Shakespeare's time the Swiss furnished
bodyguards to many foreign princes. The Pope has still such
a guard in the Vatican. Probably the most famous Swiss body-
guard known to history was that butchered by the populace
on the outbreak of the French Revolution while defending
Louis XVI. In honour of their heroic death the Lion of Lu-
cerne has been erected. In Fletcher, *The Double Marriage*,
iv, 1, the Duke of Sesse, disguised as a Swiss, declares:

> 'Tis the profession
> Of all our nation to serve faithfully
> Where th' are best paid.

99-101. overpeering of his list: when it towers (literally, looks) above its boundary or limit (high-water mark). Cf. *King John*, iii, 1, 23: 'Like a proud river peering o'er his bounds.'—**the flats:** the low country near the sea.—**head:** armed band.

103-106. And . . . 'Choose we!' And, as if—with no remembrance of ancient institutions and no knowledge of settled custom—the world were to begin at the present moment, they, the rabble, assuming the right to ratify and support any and every suggestion that takes their fancy, cry out 'Let *us* choose!' *Ratifiers and props* refers to *they*, the rabble.

109 ff. In this terrifying situation the Queen appears as a fearless and high-spirited woman, passionately in love with her guilty husband; and Claudius himself meets the furious mob with calm dignity and splendid courage.

110. counter. A hound 'hunts counter' (*contre*, *contra*) when he follows the scent backward—away from the animal pursued.

113. give me leave: leave me and let me go in alone. Cf. ii, 2, 170.

114. We will. The fact that Laertes has the mob under control makes him all the more terrifying and emphasizes the King's fortitude.

115 ff. Henceforth Laertes appears as the typical avenger. He serves as a complete foil to Hamlet in this regard. He assumes that the King is somehow guilty of Polonius's death and acts accordingly, without weighing the evidence. Then, informed that Hamlet was the slayer, he joins in the King's plot without scruple and violates his own code of honour. Witness his confession in v, 2, 324 ff.

118. brands. Cf. iii, 4, 44.

122. Let him go, Gertrude. The Queen has caught hold of Laertes to prevent his attacking the King. Claudius controls the crisis with a master hand.

124, 125. peep to: look at from a distance. Traitors can get no nearer a king than the hedge or protecting barrier which 'divine right' builds about him; through this they can *peep*, but that is all. The word and the figure are intentionally grotesque, expressing contempt.—**his:** its.

132. **grace:** regard for God's laws.

134–136. **both the worlds.** He cares not what may happen to him, either in this world or the next, if only he can avenge his father's death. Contrast Hamlet's scruple in ii, 2, 626 ff.— **throughly:** thoroughly.

137. **My will . . . world!** Nothing shall stop me—not even the whole world—until I have had my will.

142, 143. **That swoopstake . . . loser:** that you are determined to include in your revenge both friend and foe, as if, in gaming, you were to sweep from the board all the money in sight, whether it belonged to the winner or to the loser. Cf. Heywood, *2 Edward IV* (ed. de Ricci, sig. O4 r°): 'I would the deuil were there to crie swoope-stake [i.e., I take them all]'; Middleton, *Your Five Gallants*, iv, 2 (ed. Bullen, III, 198): 'the old servingman swooped up all [in gaming].'

146. **pelican.** The mother pelican was supposed to draw blood from her own breast to feed her young. Cf. Henry Medwell, *Nature* (ed. Brandl, *Quellen*, p. 76):

> Who taught the pellycan her tender hart to carue
> For she nolde suffer her byrdys to dye;

Mabbe, *Celestina* (ed. *Tudor Translations*, pp. 89, 90): 'The Pellicane, with her beake breaketh up her owne brest, that she may give her very bowels and intrals to her young ones to eat'; *Edward III*, iii, 5, 110–113 (ed. Brooke, *Shakespeare Apocrypha*, p. 90):

> A Pellican, my Lord,
> Wounding her bosome with her crooked beak,
> That so her nest of young ones may be fed
> With drops of blood that issue from her hart.

See Lauchert, *Geschichte des Physiologus*, 1889, pp. 8, 169–171, 211.

151. **as level:** with as sure an aim.—**pierce:** i.e., through all doubts and obscurities—as the sun pierces the clouds and mists.

153. **Enter** *Ophelia.* Rowe adds 'fantastically drest with Straws and Flowers': Wilson reads 'with flowers in her hand.'

154 ff. We get the impression that this is the first time Laertes has seen Ophelia since she went mad. At all events, her entrance at this crisis revives and intensifies his rage against the unknown murderer, and threatens to undo all that Claudius has accomplished in the way of controlling him.

155. **virtue:** faculty.

161–163. Dr. Johnson's paraphrase is (as usual) highly satisfactory: '*Love*, says *Laertes*, is the passion by which nature is most exalted and refined, and as substances refined and subtilised, easily obey any impulse, or follow any attraction, some part of nature, so purified and refined, flies off after the attracting object, after the thing it loves.' *Nature* is 'human nature.' *Instance* combines the two common meanings of 'sample' and 'proof.' Ophelia's nature has sent her 'wits' after her father (into the grave), as a precious part of itself in proof of love.

170, 171. **A-down . . . a-down-a.** For this chorus or burden cf. Deloney, *The Garland of Good Will*, Song 3:

> Whenas King *Edgar* did govern this Land,
>   *adown, adown, down, down, down,*
> And in the strength of his Years he did stand,
>   *call him down-a.*

—**the wheel:** the spinning wheel, to whose rhythmic motion songs and ballads were often sung. Cf. *Twelfth Night*, ii, 4, 45–47:

> The spinsters and the knitters in the sun
> . . . .
> Do use to chant it.

—**becomes it:** suits the ballad and its tune. Cf. iv, 7, 79, note.— **It is . . . steward.** The song tells the story of the false steward. The ballad is unknown.

174. **This . . . matter:** This random talk of hers is more significant (of what she has suffered) than sane speech could be.

175 ff. Whether Ophelia actually brings flowers and herbs on the stage or simply imagines them, nobody can tell for cer-

tain. That she has culled precisely those that she mentions is
out of the question. There is no indication in the old stage
directions how the distribution (real or imagined) was made.
Editors are pretty well agreed, however, that she gives rosemary and pansies to Laertes (as if he were her true-love),
fennel and columbines to the King, and rue to the Queen—
saving some for herself. The daisy remains in doubt. Perhaps
she gave it to the King or the Queen. Wilson thinks she kept
it (as well as the pansies) for herself. For the old 'language
of flowers' see Clement Robinson, *A Handfull of Pleasant Delites*, 1584, and the first few pages of Greene's *A Quip for an
Upstart Courtier*, 1592 (ed. Grosart, XI, 213 ff.).

175–179. **that's for remembrance.** The smell of rosemary was
thought to strengthen the memory. Cf. Greene, *Never Too
Late* (ed. Grosart, VIII, 198): 'Shee hath giuen thee a Nose-
gay of flowers wherin as a top gallant for all the rest, is set in
Rosemary for remembrance.'—**thoughts.** *Pansy* comes from
the French *pensée*. Cf. Chapman, *All Fools*, ii (Pearson ed.,
I, 139):

> *Cornelio.* I pray, what flowers are these?
> *Gazetta.* The Pancie this.
> *Cornelio.* O, thats for louers thoughtes.

—**A document in madness!** A piece of instruction given to
me in this mad talk! What the instruction is we learn from
the next sentence: 'Thoughts and remembrance would indeed
be fitting for me now.'

180. **fennel:** a symbol of flattery and deceit. Malone quotes
Florio's dictionary, *A Worlde of Wordes*, 1598, p. 96: 'Dare
pinocchio, *to giue fennell*, . . . *to flatter, to dissemble*.' Nares
quotes Greene, *A Quip for an Upstart Courtier*, 1592 (A 3, lf.
1 r°; ed. Grosart, XI, 214): 'Vppon a banke bordring by,
grewe womens weedes, Fenell I meane for flatterers.' Steevens
notes that columbine is called a 'thankless flower' by Chapman
(*All Fools*, ii; Pearson ed., I, 139); but it does not appear
whether this justifies us in ascribing that meaning to the flower
as a symbol.

181 ff. **rue.** Since rue is bitter, and since its name coincides

with the verb *rue*, the herb became a symbol for sorrow or repentance. Its name *herb of grace* was associated with the idea of repentance for one's sins. Hence Ophelia thinks it a good Sunday name for the herb. Cf. *Richard II*, iii, 4, 104–107:

> Here in this place
> I'll set a bank of rue, sour herb of grace.
> Rue, even for ruth, here shortly shall be seen,
> In the remembrance of a weeping queen.

—**with a difference.** An heraldic term for a variation (usually slight) in a family coat of arms, indicating that the wearer belonged to a younger branch of the family. Ophelia means merely that the Queen's cause of sorrow differs from hers; but the Queen, and the audience, feel that rue should mean 'grief' in Ophelia's case, 'repentance for sin' in the Queen's. Henley quotes Greene, *A Quip for an Upstart Courtier*, 1592 (ed. Grosart, XI, 216): 'Some of them smild and said Rue was called herbe grace, which though they scorned in their youth, they might weare in their age, and it was neuer too late to say *Miserere*.'

183. **a daisy.** Henley quotes Greene, *A Quip for an Upstart Courtier*, 1592 (A 3, lf. 2 r°; ed. Grosart, XI, 218): 'Next there grewe the dessembling daisie, to warne such light of loue wenches not to trust euery faire promise that such amorous batchelers make them.' Dyce suggests that 'Ophelia means that the daisy is for herself' (cf. iii, 1, 117–121); but the next sentence indicates (unless 'you' is emphasized or is addressed to the company in general) that she gives it to somebody. Clark and Wright think she gave it to the King or the Queen.
—**violets.** Malone quotes Clement Robinson's *Handfull of Pleasant Delites*, 1584 (ed. Rollins, p. 4): 'Violet is for faithfulnesse.'

187. **For . . . joy.** From an old song known to the mad Jailer's Daughter in *The Two Noble Kinsmen*: 'I can sing "The Broom" and "Bonny Robin"' (iv, 1, 107, 108). See Chappell, *Popular Music of the Olden Time*, I, 233, 234.

188, 189. **Thought:** melancholy thought, sorrow. Cf. iii, 1, 85.—**passion:** passionate grief.—**favour:** beauty.

190 ff. **For the tune** see Chappell, I, 236, 237.

200. **And . . . souls.** An old formula of prayer.—**of:** on.—
God b' wi' you: good-bye.

202. **commune.** Accented on the first syllable.

206, 207. **collateral:** indirect.—**touch'd:** i.e., with guilt in
the death of Polonius.

213. **óbscure.** For the accent see note on i, 4, 52.

214, 215. **trophy:** anything that serves as a memorial or as
a mark of honour.—**hatchment:** a tablet, with coat of arms
and mourning emblems, set up on a tomb or a house-front, or
over a gate.—**formal ostentation:** due and proper ceremony.

216, 217. **as . . . earth:** as if by a direct summons from God.—
That: so that.

218. **the great axe:** the axe of vengeance. This line may have
been in Milton's mind when he wrote the famous verses in
Lycidas, 130, 131:

> But that two-handed engine at the door
> Stands ready to smite once, and smite no more.

Scene VI.

7, 8. **Horatio's reply** accords with custom. Cf. Robert Tailor,
The Hog hath Lost his Pearl, iii (Collier's Dodsley, VI, 368):

> *Haddit.* My young lord, God save you.
> *Young Lord Wealthy.* And you also.

But there is a touch of Horatio's mild humour (see i, 1, 19);
for the sailor (who doubtless looks like the pirate that he is)
may well need God's blessing.—**'A:** He.—**an't:** if it.

12–30. **overlook'd:** read over.—**means:** means of access.—
appointment: equipment.—**thieves of mercy:** merciful robbers.—**they knew what they did:** they knew what they were
about; they understood what was for their own interest.—
a good turn. Hamlet has promised to procure their pardon and,
probably, to get them commissions in the navy.—**too light . . .
matter.** A figure from gunnery: 'not weighty enough to do the

subject justice.'—**good fellows.** Humorously ambiguous; for this phrase was often equivalent to 'thieves.'

32. **give you way:** procure you access. For other indications that Horatio stands well with the King and Queen see iv, 5, 14–16; v, 1, 316.

Scene VII.

In the interval occupied by scene vi Claudius has explained to Laertes that Hamlet had killed Polonius by mistake for the King. Laertes has not taken time to consult his 'wisest friends' (iv, 5, 204).

5. **Pursued my life.** Cf. iii, 4, 24, 25; iv, 1, 13.

6. **proceeded:** i.e., by bringing Hamlet to trial for murder and treason.—**feats:** deeds, acts.

8, 9. **your safety:** regard for your own safety.—**mainly:** strongly, powerfully.—**reasons.** These two reasons were obviously genuine. The Queen's love for her son and the King's love for the Queen are strong motives in the drama, and the necessity of taking the Danish people into account has just been proved by their insurrection under the lead of Laertes.

13. **be it either which:** whichever of the two you may choose to call it.

14, 15. **conjunctive:** closely joined, dear.—**in his sphere:** i.e., in its hollow crystalline sphere, concentric with the earth (in accordance with the Ptolemaic astronomy).

16–18. **motive:** moving cause; reason. Cf. i, 1, 105; i, 4, 76; ii, 2, 587.—**count:** accounting, judgment, trial.—**might:** could.—**the general gender:** the common people. Cf. iv, 3, 3, 4:

> Yet must not we put the strong law on him.
> He's lov'd of the distracted multitude.

20. **the spring ... to stone.** Reed notes the Dropping Well at Knaresborough (Yorkshire), described by Camden, *Britannia* (1590, p. 564): 'Sub quo fons est in quem ex impendentibus rupibus aquae guttatim distillant, vnde *Dropping Well*

vocant, in quem quicquid ligni immittitur, lapideo cortice
breui obduci, et lapidescere obseruatum est.' Nearer home for
Shakespeare were the baths of King's Newnham (Warwick-
shire), for which Dowden refers to Harrison's *Description of
England*, ii, 23 (ed. Furnivall, I, 348, 349). Cf. Greene, *The
Carde of Fancie*, 1587 (ed. Grosart, IV, 136): 'As though I
had drunke of the Riuer *Lincestis* in *Bohemia*, which presentlie
turneth whatsoeuer it toucheth into stones.'

21. **Convert . . . graces:** change his fetters to honours.

26. **terms:** condition. Cf. Lyly, *Endymion*, v, 3 (ed. Bond,
III, 75): 'I founde him in most melancholie and desperate
termes.' *Terms* is very vaguely used in Elizabethan English:
so *in good terms, in fair terms*, etc., for 'in a good way,' etc.

27. **if . . . again:** if I may commend her for what she was
before she lost her mind.

28, 29. **Stood challenger . . . perfections:** was exalted above
the whole contemporary world, challenging it to bring forward
any other woman to equal her in excellence. Moberly detects
an allusion to 'the coronation ceremony of the Emperor of
Germany as King of Hungary; when on the Mount of De-
fiance, at Presburg, he unsheathes the ancient sword of state,
and shaking it towards north, south, east, and west, challenges
the four corners of the world to dispute his rights.'

30–35. Here the King shows for the first time a feeling of
bitter enmity toward Hamlet.—**flat and dull:** tame and without spirit; incapable of resenting an injury.—**shall hear more:**
i.e., when the news comes from England.—**I . . . we.** The
King changes from the strictly personal *I* to the royal *we*.

41. **Of:** from.

46, 47. **your kingly eyes.** A formal and courtly phrase (like
'High and Mighty') masking Hamlet's scorn and hatred. Cf.
i, 2, 116: 'in the cheer and comfort of our eye'; iv, 4, 6: 'We
shall express our duty in his eye'; and similar expressions in
which *eye* is used for 'the royal presence.'—**pardon:** permission.

51. **abuse:** deceit, delusion.—**no such thing:** not what it
seems to be; not a reality.

52. **character:** handwriting. Cf. i, 3, 59.

59. **how . . . otherwise?** How can it be true that he has returned? And yet, on the other hand, how can it be otherwise
than true? The King finds it hard to believe that Hamlet has
come back; yet he cannot explain the letter upon any other
supposition.

60, 61. **Will you be rul'd by me?** Even in his horrified per-
plexity, the mind of Claudius works with its usual clearness
and promptitude. He has already formed another plan to destroy Hamlet.—**Ay.** Dissyllabic. Cf. note on *speak* in iv, 4, 17.
—**So:** provided that.

63. **checking at his voyage:** refusing to continue his voyage.
A falcon is said to check 'when she forsakes her proper game,
and follows some other of inferior kind that crossed her in her
flight' (Dyce).—**that:** if that; if. Cf. l. 160.

66. **shall not choose but fall:** cannot help falling. Cf. iv,
5, 69.

68. **uncharge the practice:** acquit the plot of being a plot.

71. **the organ:** the agent.—**It falls right:** The circumstances
fit your wish.

73-77. **a quality:** an accomplishment.—**Your sum of parts:**
the sum total of your accomplishments.—**siege:** rank—literally, seat.

78. **A very riband . . . youth:** a mere ornament of youth. It
was the fashion for courtiers to wear a jewel or ribbon on the
cap.

79-82. **youth no less becomes,** etc. In modern English we
should invert the phrase: 'The light and trivial sports that
characterize youth are just as becoming to the young as the
serious and dignified pursuits of sober years are to their elders.'
Cf. iv, 5, 172. Shakespeare is fond of metaphors from clothes.
—**sables.** See iii, 2, 138.—**weeds:** attire.—**Importing health
and graveness:** signifying due care for health and a proper
regard for dignity. *Health* is contrasted with *light*, and *graveness* with *careless*. Young men dress lightly and carelessly;
their elders wear warmer and more stately attire.

85. **can well on horseback:** are skilful riders. Feats of horse-

manship, over and beyond mere riding, were a highly esteemed accomplishment with gentlemen of Shakespeare's time.

88–91. **As:** as if.—**incorps'd:** incorporated; made into one body.—**demi-natur'd:** so united as to form with the animal a Centaur—half man and half horse. Cf. Sidney, *Arcadia*, ii, 5, 3 (ed. 1590, fol. 122 r°): 'as if Centaurlike he had bene one peece with the horse.'—**brave:** fine, noble.—**topp'd my thought:** surpassed anything that I could even think.—**in forgery of shapes and tricks:** in imagining feats of horsemanship.—**did.** Emphatic: 'actually performed.'

96–98. **He made confession of you:** He admitted that he knew you as an accomplished gentleman.—**art and exercise:** skill in both theory and practice. In *Troilus and Cressida*, iv, 4, 80, the 'Grecian youths' are described as 'flowing o'er with arts and exercise.'—**defence:** fencing.

101. **scrimers:** fencers (French *escrimeurs*).

104. **with his envy.** The King is going beyond the truth, but no doubt Hamlet piqued himself somewhat on his fencing.

108. **was your father dear to you?** The treacherous revenge which the King is about to propose is so abhorrent to what he knows to be the feelings of a gentleman that he fears some urging may be necessary. The savage exclamation 'To cut his throat i' th' church!' convinces him that Laertes will have no scruples (l. 127).

111–124. These reflections are curiously similar to the moralizing of the Player King in iii, 2, 196–209. Claudius cannot get 'The Mousetrap' out of his head—and no wonder!

112–114. **that:** because.—**passages of proof:** facts of experience.—**qualifies:** weakens.

115–124. Omitted in the Folios.

115–117. **There lives . . . it:** The very intensity of love serves to abate it, as the flame of a lamp makes the snuff (the charred piece of wick) that deadens the flame and reduces the light.—**still:** always, forever.

118. **plurisy:** excess, plethora—used especially of an excess of blood in the system. Cf. Greene, *Mamillia*, 1583 (ed. Grosart, II, 41): 'His nature seemes very precious, and yet very

perillous: euen like the patient, which by ouer much blood falleth into the Plurisie'; *Two Noble Kinsmen*, v, 1, 62–66.

119. **his own too-much**: its own excess.—**That**: what.

120. **this 'would'**: our will to act.

123, 124. **And then . . . easing**: when we have lost the will to do a thing, and yet say to ourselves 'We *should* do it!' this acknowledgment relieves our conscience somewhat, but weakens our moral fibre, since we rest content with merely confessing our duty instead of doing it. Similarly, a sigh is a relief, but (according to the old notion) it draws blood from the heart and thus weakens it. Cf. *Midsummer Night's Dream*, iii, 2, 97: 'With sighs of love, that costs the fresh blood dear'; *3 Henry VI*, iv, 4, 22: 'bloodsucking sighs.'—**to the quick o' th' ulcer!** Let me probe the sore to the quick. Let me put the crucial question without further talk.

127. **To cut his throat i' th' church!** The readiness of this reply is welcome to the King; but its crude ferocity produces in his mind that contempt which an intellectual villain must feel for mere brute rage. Yet he suppresses his disgust, and with admirable suavity assents to the principle of unscrupulous vengeance.

132. **We'll put on those shall**: We'll incite, instigate, persons who shall.

135. **remiss**: careless; unsuspicious by nature.

136, 137. **generous**: noble-minded. The frankness of the King's praise of Hamlet for qualities that are the opposite of those here shown by Laertes, indicates how sure he now feels of his accomplice.—**peruse**: scrutinize.

138. **shuffling**: trickery; sleight of hand.

139. **unbated**: not blunted. Rapiers for practice were blunted but had no button on the point.—**a pass of practice**: a thrust with this treacherous weapon. *Practice* means 'plot,' 'treachery' (as in l. 68). Cf. the words of the repentant Laertes in v, 2, 327–329:

> The treacherous instrument is in thy hand,
> Unbated and envenom'd. The foul practice
> Hath turn'd itself on me.

141. **I'll anoint my sword.** This is Laertes at his worst. He forgets his own code of honour in his reckless pursuit of revenge, although he is aware that Hamlet killed Polonius by mistake for the King. The idea, however, of fencing with poisoned swords is not unknown in Elizabethan literature. Cf. *Soliman and Perseda*, i, 3, 29–33 (ed. Boas, Kyd, p. 169):

> In Italy I put my Knighthood on,
> Where, in my shirt, but with my single Rapier,
> I combated a Romane much renownd,
> His weapons point impoysoned for my bane;
> And yet my starres did bode my victory.

142. **unction:** ointment.—**mountebank:** quack.

144, 145. **cataplasm:** poultice.—**Collected from:** composed of.—**simples:** medicinal plants.—**virtue:** medicinal efficacy.

146, 147. **Under the moon:** i.e., anywhere on earth. An idiomatic phrase: cf. *King Lear*, iv, 6, 26; *Antony and Cleopatra*, iv, 15, 68. It modifies *all* rather than *virtue*.—**withal:** with it.

148. **gall:** scratch; break the skin; draw blood. Cf. iii, 2, 252.

151. **fit us to our shape:** adapt us (in our actions) to our plan.

152. **that . . . performance:** if our intention should show itself because of our failure to carry it out adroitly.—**that:** if that; if. Cf. ll. 63, 160.

155. **did blast in proof:** should burst (fail) when put to the test. A 'metaphor taken from the trying or proving of firearms or cannon' (Steevens).—**Soft!** Wait a minute!—literally, slowly.

156. **solemn:** formal.—**your cunnings:** your skill as fencers. Cf. iii, 4, 139.

158–161. **dry:** thirsty.—**As make,** etc.: 'as [hot and dry you must become, for] make your bouts,' etc. Cf. iv, 3, 61.—**that:** when that; when. Cf. ll. 63, 152.—**for the nonce:** for that express purpose.

162. **stuck:** thrust. What Sir Toby calls 'the stuck-in' (*Twelfth Night*, iii, 4, 304). It is the vernacular equivalent of

stoccado (*Merry Wives*, ii, 1, 234). Cf. *Romeo and Juliet*, iii, 1, 77: 'Alla stoccata'; Marston, *Antonio's Revenge*, i, 2, 72 (ed. Bullen, I, 111): 'I would pass [i.e., thrust] on him with a mortal stock.'

165, 166. One woe . . . follow. Cf. iv, 5, 78, 79.

168 ff. The Queen's speech is lyrical rather than dramatic. It is Shakespeare the poet that speaks rather than Shakespeare the dramatist. But it is a masterpiece of its kind and any dramatic loss is our gain.

168. aslant. So the Folio. The Quarto reading, *ascaunt*, means the same thing.

169. hoar: grey—as the leaves of the willow are on the under side.

170. There . . . come. So the Folio. The Second Quarto reads 'Therewith fantastique garlands did she make Of Crow-flowers,' etc. Wilson follows the Quarto, remarking that the willow is 'the emblem of disconsolate love.' But the context shows that the Folio is right.

171–173. crowflowers. Two or three different flowers are so called.—**long purples:** orchids.—**liberal:** licentious in their talk.—**cold:** chaste.—**dead men's fingers.** Cf. *Roxburghe Ballads*, ed. Chappell, I, 261: 'Dead-man-thumb.'

174. coronet: woven into wreaths for the head.

175. envious: malicious.

179, 180. tunes. So the Folio and the First Quarto. The Second Quarto reads *laudes*, i.e., 'hymns or psalms of praise.'—**incapable of:** insensible of; having no feeling for. Cf. iii, 4, 127.

181. indued: adapted by nature.

187 ff. Too much, etc. This speech seemed far less artificial to Shakespeare's contemporaries than it does to us, for such punning expressions had come to be natural in Elizabethan style and were by no means inconsistent with deep feeling.

189. It is our trick: To shed tears is a natural human trait.

191. The woman will be out: All the womanish qualities of my nature will have spent themselves, and I shall be remorseless in my vengeance. The convention that 'tears are womanish' (*Romeo and Juliet*, iii, 3, 110) recurs in great variety of expression. Cf. *As You Like It*, iii, 4, 3; *Henry V*, iv, 6, 28-32; *Richard III*, i, 2, 164; *Coriolanus*, v, 6, 45; *Antony and Cleopatra*, iv, 2, 34-36. See *Macbeth*, iv, 2, 29, and note.

193. this folly douts it: this natural weakness (my weeping) puts it out. Laertes can no longer control himself. He rushes from the stage in a passion of tears.—**douts.** The Second Quarto reads *drownes*. Cf. i, 4, 37.

ACT V. Scene I.

1-5. Clowns: rustics, boors—an elderly sexton and his young helper.—**in Christian burial.** A regular phrase; not a mistake of the Clown's. Cf. *Martin's Month's Minde*, 1589 (ed. Grosart, Greene, I, 194, 195): 'They might not therefore burie him in Christian buriall.'—**when she . . . salvation:** when she wilfully seeks to go to heaven before her time.—**straight:** straightway, immediately.—**crowner.** A regular pronunciation of *coroner*; not a blunder.

6, 7. in her own defence. The Clown knows that self-defence is a justification for homicide, and he ludicrously infers that it may justify suicide also.

9. *se offendendo:* in self-offence—the Clown's blunder for *se defendendo*, 'in self-defence.'

11 ff. The Sexton's logic (as Sir John Hawkins suggests) may be an echo of arguments elaborated in a lawsuit of 1554— a case resulting from the death of Sir James Hales, who had committed suicide by walking into a river.

Walsh [one of the counsel] said that the Act [of self-destruction] consists of three Parts. The first is the Imagination, which is a Reflection or Meditation of the Mind, whether or no it is convenient for him to destroy himself, and what Way it can be done. The second is the Resolution, which is a Determination of the Mind to destroy himself, and to do it in this or that particular Way. The third is the Perfection, which is the Execution of what the Mind has resolved to do. And this Perfection consists of two Parts, viz. the Beginning and the End. The Beginning is the doing of the Act which causes the Death, and the End is the Death, which is only a Sequel to the Act (Plowden's *Reports*, translation, 1779, p. 259).

In summing up, the judge remarked:

Sir James Hales was dead, and how came he to his Death? It may be answered, by drowning; and who drowned him? Sir James Hales. And when did he drown him? In his Lifetime. So that Sir James Hales being alive caused Sir James Hales to die; the Act of the living, was the Death of the dead Man. And for this Offence it is reasonable to punish the living Man, who committed the Offence, and not the dead Man (p. 262).

13. **argal.** The Clown's corruption of *ergo*, 'therefore,' a word often used in formal reasoning. Cf. *All's Well*, i, 3, 53.

17. **will he nill he**: will he or will he not; willy-nilly; whether he will or no.—**nill.** A contraction of *ne* (the negative) *will*. Cf. *The Taming of the Shrew*, ii, i, 273.

25. **quest**: inquest.

26. **an't**: on't; of it.

29-31. **there thou say'st**: You're right in that!—**count'nance**: authorization. The Clown ludicrously speaks of the liberty to commit suicide as one more unfair advantage which the aristocracy have over the common people.—**even-Christen**: fellow Christian. Equivalent, in colloquial use, to 'fellow creature,' 'neighbour.'

36, 37. **Was he a gentleman?** The Clown is startled to hear Adam styled a gentleman, for he is familiar with the old rhyme:

> When Adam delved and Eve span,
> Where was then the gentleman?

Cf. Dekker, *The Wonderfull Yeare*, 1603 (ed. Grosart, I, 77): 'Though he haue no more Gentilitie in him than Adam had (that was but a gardner).' See also John Heywood, *The Spider and the Flie* (1556), xliv, 27; *Songs and Carols* (ed. Thomas Wright, Warton Club), p. 2; Lydgate, *Minor Poems*, ed. Mac-Cracken, II, 823.—**'A**: he.

44, 45. **confess thyself—**: Confess thyself an ass; or perhaps, as Malone suggests, 'Confess thyself and be hanged.' 'Confess and be hanged' was a common proverb. Cf. *Othello*, iv, 1, 38. —**Go to!** Enough! A protesting exclamation—literally, 'Go away!' 'Get out!'

49. **frame**: structure.

51, 52. **does well**: is a pretty good answer to my conundrum.

59. **unyoke**: unyoke your team of oxen; call it a day's work.

62. **Mass.** A common oath. Cf. ii, 1, 50.

63-68. **your.** See note on i, 5, 167: 'your philosophy.'—
Yaughan: Yohan, Johan. Some alehouse keeper in the neigh-
bourhood.—**a stoup**: a big cup or mug.

69 ff. **In youth**, etc. The Sexton, as Theobald noted, sings
mangled fragments of a poem printed in Tottel's *Miscellany*,
1557, and entitled 'The aged louer renounceth loue' (ed. Rollins, pp. 165, 166):

> 1 I Lothe that I did loue,
>   In youth that I thought swete:
>   As time requires for my behoue
>   Me thinkes they are not mete,
>
>   . . . .
>
> 3 For age with stelyng steppes,
>   Hath clawed me with his c[r]owche,
>   And lusty life away she leapes,
>   As there had bene none such.
>
>   . . . .
>
> 8 A pikeax and a spade,
>   And eke a shrowdying shete,
>   A house of claye for to be made,
>   For such a gest most mete.
>
>   . . . .
>
> 13 For beauty with her bande
>   These croked cares hath wrought:
>   And shipped me into the lande,
>   From whence I first was brought.

71. **contract**: shorten; make it pass pleasantly.—**a.** Clark
and Wright explain these *a*'s as indicating the singer's 'drawl-
ing notes.'—**behove**: behoof, advantage.

76. **hath made . . . easiness**: has made for it (has given it)
an easy quality in his case; has made it a commonplace occu-
pation which leaves his mind at ease.

77, 78. **The hand . . . sense:** The hand that is unaccustomed
to manual labour has more sensitiveness, is less callous.

80, 81. **clawed**: seized.—**hath . . . land:** has stopped my
voyage and sent me ashore.—**intil**: in to.

84. **jowls:** dashes.

85. **that.** The antecedent is *Cain's*: 'the jawbone of Cain, who,' etc. Skeat, however, thinks that *jawbone* is the antecedent and reports an old tradition that Cain's weapon was the jawbone of an ass (6 *Notes and Queries,* II [1880], 143; *Academy,* October 26, 1895, p. 343).

87, 88. **o'erreaches:** gets the better of.—**one . . . God:** one who was clever enough, while he lived, to disregard God's laws and apparently to escape unscathed.

96–100. **chapless:** jawless—i.e., lacking the lower jaw.—**mazzard.** Like *pate,* an old cant word for 'head.'—**trick:** special skill; knack.—**loggets:** little logs—a game in which the players throw pieces of hard wood at a stake or wooden wheel.

103. **For and.** This means 'and'; *but and* is often used in the same way.

107, 108. **quiddits:** hair-splitting definitions, such as those attempted in ll. 10–13. *Quiddity* (*quidditas*) is an old scholastic word for the 'whatness' of anything, i.e., its essential nature.—**quillets:** quibbles, subtle distinctions. Cf. Mabbe, *Celestina* (ed. *Tudor Translations,* p. 69): 'some quillet or quirke of Law.'—**tenures:** holdings of real estate.

109. **sconce.** Another cant term for 'head.'

111–121. **buyer of land.** There are constant references in Elizabethan and older literature to the ambition of persons not belonging to the 'landed gentry' to purchase estates and thus make themselves gentlemen. In this case it is a successful lawyer that Hamlet imagines as the purchaser.—**statutes.** Statutes merchant and statutes staple are 'particular modes of recognizance or acknowledgement for securing debts, which thereby become a charge upon the party's land' (Ritson). Cf. *Histriomastix,* iv, 1 (ed. Simpson, II, 56):

> Whilst slaves tye fast our Lands
> In Statute Staple, or these Marchants bands.

—**the fine . . . his recoveries:** the final outcome of his fines and the total acquired by his recoveries. 'Fine and recovery' was a legal process for changing an entailed estate into an estate

in fee simple (absolute possession).—**double vouchers.** A recovery with 'double voucher' was so called because two persons
were '*vouched* or called upon, to warrant the tenant's title'
(Ritson).—**his fine pate:** his subtly clever head.—**indentures:**
agreements or contracts. These were drawn up in duplicate on
a single sheet of paper or parchment and were then cut apart
in a zigzag (indented) line. Their fitting together at this line
was proof of genuineness.—**conveyances:** deeds.—**inheritor:**
possessor, owner.—**ha?** An interrogative 'huh?' 'eh?'

126. **sirrah?** A form of *sir*, used (as here) in addressing an
inferior or to express anger or contempt; often (to boys) as a
playful and affectionate term.

131–140. Hamlet uses the familiar *thee* and *thou* to the
Sexton, but the Sexton uses the respectful *you* in reply. The
inevitable pun on *lie* is elaborated into a game of repartee.
The Sexton wins by punning on *quick*, which Hamlet has used
in the sense of 'living.'

146. **rest her soul:** God give her soul repose!

148–155. **How absolute the knave is!** How the fellow insists
upon accuracy in language!—**by the card:** by the compass,
observing every point; punctiliously.—**equivocation:** ambi-
guity.—**picked:** choice, exquisite, refined.—**that the toe . . .
courtier:** that the peasant has become almost as polished in
language and manners as the courtier.—**galls his kibe:** follows
him so closely that he rubs and irritates the chilblain on the
courtier's heel. Cf. iii, 2, 252. So D'Avenant, *The Cruel Brother*
(ed. Maidment and Logan, I, 174):

> But I'll follow your heels so close, as I'll
> Go near to tread upon your kibes.

157. **Fortinbras.** See i, 1, 80–95; i, 2, 17–25.

170. **as mad as he.** The supposed eccentricity of Englishmen
gave rise to the notion on the Continent that they were a nation of madmen. Clark and Wright quote Marston, *The Mal-
content*, iii, 1, 96 ff. (ed. Bullen, I, 258): 'Your lordship shall
ever find . . . amongst an hundred Englishmen, fourscore and
ten madmen.'

177. thirty years. This figure and the 'three-and twenty' in l. 191 involve a problem as to Hamlet's age. See Introduction.

183. year. A good old form of the plural.

187. your. Cf. i, 5, 167; iv, 3, 21 ff.

191. you. The 'ethical dative,' which gives a colloquial touch to the style but adds nothing to the sense.

199. Yorick. Futile attempts have been made to explain this name as Danish; but, until it can be shown that Polonius, Claudius, Ophelia, Marcellus, and Bernardo are also Danish names, we need not trouble about the matter. So far as its form goes, *Yorick* looks like a corruption of *York*, but Jerick is a German peasant in the old play of *Alphonsus* (wrongly ascribed to Chapman) and Joris is the Duke of Brunswick's fool in Rowlands, *A Fooles Bolt*, 1614, pp. 22 ff.

205. it: the mere thought of it, i.e., of his bearing me on his back.

213. chapfall'n: lacking the lower jaw, chapless (l. 97); with a pun on the sense of 'down in the mouth,' 'disconcerted.'

215. favour: appearance of the face.

227. too curiously: with unreasonable ingenuity.

231. modesty: moderation, reasonableness.

236–240. An impromptu bit of versification by Hamlet. Cf. iii, 2, 282–285, 292–295.—**Imperious:** imperial.—**soft!** enough! hush! Cf. i, 1, 126.

241. Who is this? Hamlet has not heard of Ophelia's death or even of her madness, and this fact must be remembered in judging his passionate behaviour at the grave. There is nothing strange in his ignorance. He has not yet gone to court, and Horatio would not blurt out the sad news as soon as he met him at the pier.

244. Fordo: destroy.—**it:** its. See note on i, 2, 216.—**estate:** rank.

245. Couch we: Let us conceal ourselves.

247. noble: referring not to the character of Laertes but to his rank.

250–254. doubtful. Though Ophelia fell into the stream by accident (iv, 7, 175), yet her demeanour, and the fact that she

did not call for aid or attempt to save herself, had made the
clergy fear that she had committed suicide.—**great ... order.**
The King's command has prevailed against the usual rule of
the Church.—**For:** instead of.—**shards:** potsherds, bits of
broken pottery.

255. **crants:** garland. The word (spelled also *cranse,
craunce, corance*) is singular, not plural. It comes from the
Dutch *crans* or the German *kranz*. Such garlands, at the burial
of maidens, were carried to the grave and afterwards hung up
in the church.[1] In Middleton's play, *A Chaste Maid in Cheap-
side*, v, 4, Moll's coffin is 'adorned with a garland of flowers,
and epitaphs pinned on it, attended by many matrons and
maids.' Cf. a letter of 1668–9: 'Many have died this winter;
... and the Church is full of garlands, hung up for those who
died in youth' (*Diary and Correspondence of Dr. John Worth-
ington*, II, 304).

256. **strewments.** See ll. 266–269. Rolfe cites *Cymbeline*, iv,
2, 285. Cf. *Romeo and Juliet*, iv, 5, 79–80, 89; v, 3, 281;
Winter's Tale, iv, 4, 127–129 (Clark and Wright).—**the bringing home:** to the grave—her 'long home' (*Ecclesiastes*, xii, 5)
—as a bride was brought (escorted) to her new home by her
friends. For the marriage rites as 'sadly parodied' by the
funeral of a maiden, Clark and Wright compare *Romeo and
Juliet*, iv, 5, 84–90.

260. **a requiem.** So the Second Quarto. The Folio reads
'sage *Requiem*,' i.e., 'a requiem in due form.'

271. **thy most ingenious sense:** thy mind, endowed by nature with the finest faculties.

276, 277. **Pelion.** The lofty mountain upon which the Giants
piled Mount Ossa in their attempt to scale Mount Olympus,
which rose to the home of the gods in the sky.

279. **Conjures:** lays a spell upon. The word may be accented

[1] For descriptions and pictures see Jewett, *The Reliquary*, I (1860), 5–11;
XXI (1881), 145–148; Syer Cuming, *Journal of the British Archæological
Association*, XXI (1875), 190–195; Minns, *Papers and Proceedings of the
Hampshire Field Club*, IV (1905), 235–239; Burne, *Shropshire Folk-Lore*,
pp. 310–313; *Denham Tracts*, II (1895), 33; *New Shakspere Society
Transactions*, 1887–1892, p. 180.

on either syllable.—**the wand'ring stars:** the planets. *Planet* means 'wanderer' ($\pi\lambda\alpha\nu\acute{\eta}\tau\eta\varsigma$).

280, 281. **This . . . Dane.** 'Hamlet here asserts himself as rightful King of Denmark' (White). Cf. i, 2, 44. Only the First Quarto has the stage direction: *Hamlet leapes in after Leartes.*

282–286. Hamlet's calmness is not self-possession, but violent self-restraint in the attempt to be calm.—**splenitive and rash.** Synonymous: 'excitable and quick-tempered.' Cf. *Romeo and Juliet*, iii, 1, 162, 163:

> Could not take truce with the unruly spleen
> Of Tybalt deaf to peace.

The spleen was regarded as the seat of any sudden fit of wrath, laughter, or excitement.

290. **wag:** move up and down—such motion being the last sign of life in a dying man.

291. **what theme?** The Queen regards Hamlet as raving mad. His language, however, shows no incoherency until l. 313.

293. **their quantity:** their little bit. Spoken contemptuously. Cf. iii, 2, 4; iii, 4, 75.

296. **forbear him.** Addressed to Laertes: 'Let him alone,' 'Do not harm him.'

297, 298. **'Swounds.** See ii, 2, 603.—**thou't:** thou'lt, thou wilt.—**Woo't:** wilt. The form is a contraction of *wolt*, the *l* having become silent like the *l* in *would*. It was either rustic or colloquial, and its use here expresses angry contempt. The whole speech is a kind of passionate parody of the style of Laertes in ll. 274–277.

299. **drink up esill:** drain bumpers of vinegar. The word *esill* (Old French *aisil*) was associated, in everybody's mind, with the draught of vinegar and gall given to Christ at his crucifixion (*Matthew*, xxvii, 34). This, though intended as an anæsthetic, was regarded as an additional torment. Cf. *Kalender of Shepheardes*, 1506 (ed. Sommer, III, 156): 'Than was he nayled on the crosse, . . . and than gaue hym eysell and gall

to drynke.'[1] Dowden notes that vinegar was supposed to increase melancholy, and Lucas (*Times Literary Supplement*,
XXIX [1926], 512) detects an allusion to the hypocritical tears
which crocodiles were supposed to shed (cf. *Othello*, iv, 1,
256, 257). But assuredly Hamlet does not mean that the
sorrow of Laertes needs stimulus or that it is not genuine:
he is merely piling up extravagant hyperboles.

302. **quick:** alive.

305. **the burning zone:** that zone or belt of the celestial sphere
that is bounded by the Tropics of Cancer and Capricorn.

306, 307. **mouth . . . rant.** Synonymous. Cf. iii, 2, 3, 4.

307-310. **mere:** utter, stark.—**patient:** calm.—**couplets:**
twins.—**disclos'd:** hatched.

313. **But it is no matter.** At this point Hamlet recollects
himself. In his excitement he had quite forgotten that madness is his cue and he does not realize that his words to Laertes
have seemed insane to the hearers. Hence he now reverts to
his habitual style when counterfeiting insanity. Lines 314, 315,
therefore, are not to be brought into logical connection with
what precedes or with the situation at all. Certainly Hamlet
does not mean 'Laertes must have his whine and his bark.
If Hercules cannot silence dogs, much less I, who am little like
that hero' (Dowden) or 'Bluster away, my young Hercules:
but poor Hamlet's time will come' (Verity).

315. **the dog . . . day.** A familiar proverb. The King may
or may not regard Hamlet's words as a veiled threat.

317, 318. These two lines are heard by Laertes only.—
patience: calm endurance under stress of emotion.—**in . . .
speech:** by thinking of what we said last night (with regard
to your revenge). See iv, 7, 124 ff.—**to the present push:** to
the immediate attack or onset; into immediate action.

---

[1]Cf. also *The Castell of Perseverance*, sts. 269, 290 (*Macro Plays*, pp.
170, 177); *The Frere and the Boye*, ll. 1-3 (ed. Hazlitt, *Early Popular
Poetry*, III, 60); *The Prophesies of Rymour*, ll. 625, 626 (ed. Murray,
Thomas of Erceldoune, p. 61); Skelton, *Now Synge We*, ll. 38-40 (River-
side ed., I, 169); Gabriel Harvey (ed. Grosart, II, 71); Tobias Venner, *Via
Recta ad Vitam Longam*, 1620, p. 97. See especially Tolman, *Modern Language Notes*, IX (1894), 241-247; Hart, the same, XI (1896), 29.

320–322. At l. 319 the Queen starts to follow Hamlet. Lines 321 and 322 are (like ll. 317, 318) heard by Laertes only.— **a living monument.** If the Queen hears this, she will take *living* in the sense of 'lifelike.' Cf. Tourneur, *The Atheist's Tragedy*, iii, 1, 1, 2:

> Set downe the body. Pay Earth what shee lent.
> But shee shall beare a liuing monument.

To Laertes, however, the words mean that Hamlet shall be sacrificed as an offering to Ophelia's memory. Compare the sacrifice of Alarbus, demanded by Lucius 'ad manes fratrum' in *Titus Andronicus*, i, 1, 96 ff.

Scene II.

1, 2. **this.** Hamlet has just finished telling Horatio certain early incidents of the voyage.—**the other:** the rest of the story. —**the circumstance:** the details which I have told you.

6. **mutines:** mutineers.—**bilboes:** a kind of portable stocks carried on board ship. They consisted of a heavy horizontal bar of iron, to which were attached rings for the ankles. 'The punishment at the bilboes is when a delinquent is put in irons, or in a kind of stocks made for that purpose, the which are more or less heavy and pinching, as the quality of the offence is found to be, upon good proof' (Capt. Nathaniel Boteler, *Dialogues*, 1634, ed. Perrin, p. 17).—**Rashly:** obeying a sudden impulse.

7–11. **And . . . will.** Parenthetical.— **let us know:** let us recognize as a fact of experience.—**pall:** fail; come to naught. —**our ends:** the outcome of our plans.

15. **Finger'd:** laid hold on.

17. **to:** as to.

18. **Their grand commission.** See iii, 3, 3, and note.

20, 21. **Larded:** garnished, tricked out.—**Importing:** signifying.—**health:** welfare.

22. **hoo!** An interjection expressing fright.—**such bugs . . . life:** interspersed with such outbursts as to the danger of leaving a terrible creature like me alive.—**bugs:** bugbears.

23. **on the supervise:** as soon as the document had been read over (by the English king).—**no leisure bated:** no time for delay being subtracted from the immediacy of the execution. The idea is expressed from an odd point of view, and indeed, the whole speech is in a vein of fierce and bitter humour.

24. **No ... axe.** Hamlet's own words—not a quotation from the mandate. So (in l. 47): 'not shriving time allow'd.'

30. **Or:** a by-form of *ere*. Hamlet means that before he could prepare his brains, they had begun to act in carrying out a plan. He is thinking, perhaps, of the difficulty he had found in devising a scheme to force the King to confess, and of the play that he finally used for that purpose.

32–34. **fair:** in legible script (proper for a clerk or secretary). There is no special thought of the Italian or 'Roman' hand (*Twelfth Night*, iii, 4, 31).—**statists:** statesmen.—**A baseness:** a plebeian accomplishment. Cf. Heywood, *The Witches of Lancashire* (Pearson ed., IV, 189): 'It hath been held that it is the part of a Gentleman, to write a scurvy hand'; Claudius Hollyband, *Campo di Fior*, 1583 (ed. Byrne, *The Elizabethan Home*, 1925, p. 14):

Maurice. He said that there was no shorter waye to learne much, then to write faire and swifte.
Mendoza. But our noble men for the most parte, doe not obeye this commandement: which thinketh it a good and an honorable thing not to write well—thou wouldest saye it were the scratching of hennes.

36, 37. **yeoman's service:** substantial service, though in a humble capacity.—**effect:** purport.

39–42. Hamlet burlesques the words of his own document, which he had composed in the formal and stately style used by the King in the original.—**wheaten garland:** since agriculture can flourish only in time of peace.—**a comma:** as a connecting link. The language is scornfully grotesque. 'The *Comma* is the note [i.e., mark] of *connection* and continuity of sentences; the *Period* is the note of *abruption* and *disjunction*' (Johnson).

43. **as's of great charge.** A standard pun on *ass* and *as*. Cf. *Twelfth Night*, ii, 3, 184, 185; Lyly, *Mother Bombie*, iv, 2 (ed. Bond, III, 212):

> *Stellio.* I wyll talke with Memphios sonne; but as for Riscio—!
> *Memphio.* As for Dromio—!
> *Halfpenny.* Asse for you all foure!

Charge means 'burden' (as applied to the *asses*) and 'earnest conjuration' (as applied to the *as's*).

45, 46. **debatement:** discussion or consideration.—**sudden:** instant, immediate.

47. **shriving time:** even time enough for confession and absolution. It would be as absurd to take this passage literally, and to infer that the services of a priest were denied to Rosencrantz and Guildenstern, as it would be to suppose that the King's message contained an order not to grind the axe (l. 24). Hamlet merely emphasizes the idea of immediate death—of 'giving the men short shrift.'

48. **ordinant:** operative in controlling events; practically equivalent to 'foreordaining.' Hamlet recurs to the thought of the 'divinity that shapes our ends' (l. 10).

50–52. **model:** copy.—**writ:** writing, document.—**impression:** i.e., of the seal.

53. **changeling.** Spoken with bitter humour. A *changeling* is an elf or imp, often hideously ugly and always ill-tempered and malicious, substituted by the fairies for a baby stolen from the cradle. In the present instance Hamlet's changeling is fair to look upon, but its character is evil enough. Cf. Spenser, *Faerie Queene*, i, 10, 65.

56. **to't:** to their death. Cf. Heywood, *2 Edward IV*, ii, 4 (1599; ed. de Ricci, sig. R r°):

> *Keeper.* The men are patient, and resolude to die;
> The captaine and that other gentleman
> Haue cast the die whether shall suffer first.
>   *Brackenbury.* How fell the Lot, to Stranguidge or to him?
>   *Keeper.* The guiltlesse passenger must first go toot.

57–62. Horatio has not meant to suggest that there was anything wrong in Hamlet's counterplot. Indeed, he feels some satisfaction in the poetical justice that has overtaken the King's agents. But Hamlet, who is less calm by nature, is sensitive on that point, and feels that he must justify himself to his friend, as he has already justified himself to his own conscience.

58, 59. **defeat:** destruction.—**their own insinuation:** their own act in worming themselves into this affair. Cf. iii, 3, 3, note. Though Rosencrantz and Guildenstern did not know the contents of the 'grand commission' (l. 18), they had put themselves into the King's hands unreservedly and could expect no mercy from Hamlet. Cf. iii, 4, 31–33:

> Thou wretched, rash, intruding fool, farewell!
> I took thee for thy better. Take thy fortune.
> Thou find'st to be too busy is some danger.

60–62. **baser.** Hamlet speaks as a prince, conscious of his royalty and convinced of the difference between kings and common men. *Baser* is not used in a moral sense, but refers to rank and dignity. These lines indicate the proper position of Claudius in the drama. He is the 'mighty opposite,' the great antagonist, of Hamlet, and no contemptible foe. The struggle between him and his stepson is a battle of the giants. —**pass:** thrust.—**fell:** fierce.

63. Hamlet's constitutional disinclination to deeds of blood is still strong. In ll. 63–70 he sums up all the reasons why the King deserves death and adds that he ought to be killed to prevent his doing further mischief.—**thinks't thee:** seems it to thee. Cf. *methinks*, 'it seems to me.'—**stand me now upon:** is incumbent upon me, is my duty.

65–70. **Popp'd.** Contemptuously familiar language. Compare what Hamlet says of the King's 'stealing the diadem from a shelf and putting it in his pocket' (iii, 4, 100, 101).—**election.** See iii, 4, 99, and note.—**my proper life:** my own life.—**To quit him:** to pay him off.—**canker:** eating sore, cancer or ulcer. —**In:** into.

68–80. Omitted in the Second Quarto.

71, 72. **It must . . . there.** Horatio, tacitly accepting Hamlet's argument, suggests that immediate action is necessary and will be merely self-defence.

74. **A man's life's . . . 'one.'** Wilson detects an allusion to a

rapier thrust. He compares l. 291 and *Romeo and Juliet*, ii, 4, 23: 'One, two, and the third in your bosom.' The meaning depends (as so often in spoken speech) on tone and action. Delivered in one way, the line would be only a pensive reflection: 'What meaning has "shortly," after all? For what can be shorter than this life of ours?' Delivered in another way, the line is a menace to the King's life.

76–79. **I forgot myself.** Hamlet's own account of his behaviour refutes the theories both of those critics who think he was then acting the madman and of those who think that he was really insane.—**For . . . his.** A clear indication that Laertes the revenger was meant to be the foil to Hamlet the revenger. —**court.** The Folio has *count*; corrected by Rowe.—**bravery:** ostentation.

81 ff. The language and manners of Osric are a good-natured satire on the affectations of many young gentlemen at the English court. One of the peculiarities of his style is the use of words in a forced or unusual sense. Polonius has a touch of the same affectation. Compare the language of Emulo in Dekker, Chettle, and Haughton's *Patient Grissil* (1599).

84. **waterfly:** an unsubstantial creature, all wings and iridescence, skimming along the surface of life. Cf. *Troilus and Cressida*, v, 1, 37–39: 'Ah, how the poor world is pest'red with such waterflies—diminutives of nature!'

86–89. **Thy state . . . gracious:** Thy condition is the more virtuous.—**his crib . . . mess.** A disrespectful way of saying 'He will be sure to be admitted to the King's table.'—**a chough:** a silly, chattering creature. The term *chough* (pronounced *chuff*) was applied to the jackdaw and other noisy birds of the same family. Cf. *All's Well*, iv, 1, 22: 'Chough's language—gabble enough, and good enough.'

91. **I should:** I was to.

95 ff. In this conversation Hamlet beats Osric at his own game; but no harm is done to Osric (who is really a good fellow), for he never suspects that Hamlet is laughing at him.

96. **bonnet:** cap. The contest in courtesy is won by Osric, who holds his cap in his hand to the last, as we see from l. 109.

100-104. indifferent: rather.—**complexion:** temperament.—
I cannot tell how: somehow or other. Theobald points out the
resemblance to Juvenal, iii, 102, 103:

> Igniculum brumae si tempore poscas,
> Accipit endromidem: si dixeris 'Aestuo,' sudat.

109. for mine ease. A common phrase when one politely
insists on standing hat in hand. Such a contest in courtesy
is well illustrated by a model dialogue between two gentlemen,
Giordano and Edward, in Florio's manual of Italian and English conversation (cited by Malone):

> G. Why do you stand barehedded? you do yourself wrong.
> E. Pardon me good sir, I do it for my ease.
> G. I pray you be couered, you are too ceremonious.
> E. I am so well, that me thinks I am in heauen.
> G. If you loue me, put on your hat.
> E. I will doe it to obay you, not for any plesure that I take in it (*Florios
> Second Frutes*, 1591, Chap. vii, p. 111).

109-150. Sir, here . . . unfellowed. This is cut down to a
single sentence in the Folio: 'Sir, you are not ignorant of
what excellence *Laertes* is at his weapon.'
110-116. absolute: perfect, finished.—**differences:** qualities
or talents that distinguish him from others; accomplishments.
—**soft society:** agreeable manners.—**great showing:** splendid
appearance.—**feelingly:** with a due sense of his merits.—**card
or calendar of gentry:** a guide or model of courtly manners.
As one consults a card (compass) or a calendar for accurate
information and sure guidance, so every gentleman may learn
how to behave by observing Laertes. Cf. v, 1, 149.—**the continent . . . see:** the sum total of whatever qualities one gentleman would like to find in another. A *continent* is literally 'that
which contains.' Cf. iv, 4, 64.
117-120. definement: definition.—**perdition:** loss.—**to divide . . . sail:** To make an inventory of his fine qualities would
stagger the reckoning power of one's memory, and yet, after
all, the inventory would come far short of his real excellence.

The excellence of Laertes is a fast boat that sails steadily on; the inventory is another boat, which tries to overtake the leader, but *yaws* continually and thus falls far behind. A boat yaws when she steers badly, so that she does not hold her course but swings her bow from side to side and thus loses headway.— **dozy**: confuse, stagger.—**neither**: after all.—**in respect of**: in comparison with.

120-125. **in . . . extolment**: to give him the praise he truly deserves.—**of great article**. An *article* is an 'item,' but the word is here used collectively: 'with great qualities'; 'with a great amount of fine traits.'—**his infusion**: the nature with which he is infused or endowed.—**of such dearth and rareness**: of such rare excellence. *Dearth* and *rareness* mean the same thing: 'rarity.'—**his semblable is his mirror**: the only person who resembles him is his own image in the looking glass.—**who else would . . . more**: Anybody else who wishes to keep pace with him, can do so only as the shadow follows the substance.

128, 129. **The concernancy, sir?** What is the purport of all this?—**Why . . . breath?** Why do we attempt to describe the gentleman in our words, which are too crude to do him justice? 'Words,' as the Queen has told us, are 'made of breath' (iii, 4, 197).

131-136. **Is't . . . tongue?** Does Osric find it impossible to understand his own lingo when another man speaks it?— **do't**: win the game; succeed in nonplussing Osric.—**nomination**: naming, mention.—**All's**: all his.

141, 142. **yet . . . approve me**: If you, who are yourself a fool, supposed me not to be ignorant, that belief of yours would not be much evidence in my favour. The remark does Osric no harm; for he does not understand it, nor does Hamlet mean that he should.

145-150. **I dare not . . . excellence**: I dare not say that I know how excellent Laertes is, for such an assertion would be an implied claim of equal excellence on my own part, since only the excellent can judge of excellence.—**to know a man,** etc.: 'No man can completely know another, but by knowing himself, which is the utmost extent of human wisdom' (Johnson).

—**himself:** one's self.—**weapon.** Affectedly used as a plural.—
imputation: reputation.—**them:** i.e., his weapons.—**meed:**
deserts, excellence.

152. **Rapier and dagger.** In fencing it was common to carry
a dagger in the left hand to assist in warding off the blows or
thrusts of one's opponent.

153. **two.** A mere quibble on Hamlet's part: he is calling
attention to Osric's affected use of *weapon* as a plural.—**but
well:** but never mind.

154-160. **Barbary horses.** Proverbially excellent in Shakespeare's day.—**impon'd:** staked, wagered.—**assigns:** appurte-
nances.—**hangers:** straps attaching the sword to the belt.—
dear to fancy: tastefully designed; pleasing to the fancy.—
responsive to the hilts: corresponding to (harmonious with)
the hilts in design.—**of very liberal conceit:** very elegantly conceived, i.e., designed.

162, 163. **edified by the margent:** instructed by a marginal
note. This remark is omitted in the Folio.

164-166. **carriages.** This use is an affectation of Osric's and,
as such, is humorously criticised by Hamlet, to whom the word
suggests a gun carriage, the wheeled frame that *carries* a
cannon.

173-176. **laid:** wagered.—**a dozen passes.** The terms of the
wager seem clear enough. There are to be a dozen passes, or
'bouts,' and the King bets that the total score of Laertes shall
not exceed Hamlet's by three hits. Thus if the score stood 7
for Laertes and 5 for Hamlet, the King would win; so also if
it stood 6 to 6, or 6 to 4 with two draws. But if it stood
Laertes 8, Hamlet 4, the King would lose; so also if it stood
7 to 4, with one draw. *Twelve for nine*, however, cannot by
any twist be brought into accord with these terms. Many attempts have been made to clear up the passage, but they are
not worth repeating. As Dr. Johnson sensibly remarks, 'The
passage is of no importance; it is sufficient that there was a
wager.'—**vouchsafe the answer:** kindly consent to meet Laertes
in this match. Hamlet purposely misunderstands Osric and
thus forces him to explain.

180-185. **the breathing time of day with me:** the time of day when I take my exercise. To *breathe* or to *breathe one's self* was common in this sense.—**I will gain.** This is not a case of *will* for *shall*. Hamlet means 'I am willing to gain nothing,' i.e., 'I shall not object to receive no reward but the disgrace and the extra hits.'

186. **redeliver you:** carry back your reply.

189-192. **I commend my duty:** I offer my devoted service; I declare myself your humble servant. See i, 2, 39, note. Hamlet puns on *commend*, which meant also (as now-a-days) 'to praise.'—**Yours, yours.** Spoken, not slightingly, but in a courteous tone and with a polite gesture.—**for's turn:** for his purpose.

193-201. **This lapwing . . . head.** A mere jest at Osric's juvenile self-sufficiency: 'This young fellow is as forward as the lapwing, which begins to run before it is fairly out of the shell.' The lapwing was proverbially precocious. Cf. Chapman, *Revenge for Honour*, ii, 1 (Pearson ed., III, 304):

> Boldnesse inforces youth to hard atchievements
> Before their time, makes them run forth like Lapwings
> From their warm nest, part of the shel yet sticking
> Unto their downie heads.

—**away:** i.e., from the nest.—**comply:** use compliments, i.e., ceremonious language.—**the drossy age:** the degenerate present, in contrast with the Golden Age. In this sentence Hamlet more or less unconsciously continues to speak in the style that he has adopted in his talk with Osric.—**outward habit of encounter:** the fashionable habits of society. Doubtless there is (as often) a pun on *habit* in the sense of 'dress,' 'attire.' *Encounter* means 'meeting.'—**yesty collection:** frothy mess.—**carries . . . opinions:** These accomplishments, trivial as they are, make them thoroughly acceptable even to persons of the choicest and most refined judgment. *Fann'd* and *winnowed* are identical in sense. To emphasize and explain a word by adding *and* with a synonym is one of the commonest of rhetori-

cal devices.[1] Tollet aptly cites *Troilus and Cressida*, v, 3, 41:
'Even in the fan and wind of your fair sword.' Cf. the same,
i, 3, 27, 28:

> Distinction, with a broad and pow'rful fan,
> Puffing at all, winnows the light away.

The Second Quarto reads 'prophane and trennowed'; the
Folio, 'fond and winnowed.' *Fann'd* is Warburton's correction. Wilson calls it 'tautological' and accepts Tschischwitz's
profound, which involves an extraordinarily mixed metaphor.
Moberly explains *fond and winnowed* as 'absurd and over-
refined,' but this misrepresents the sense of *winnowed*.

203, 204. **commended him:** sent a message with his compliments.

209. **If his fitness speaks:** if his convenience calls for the
match.

214. **In happy time:** very opportunely—a mere phrase of
courtesy, like 'I am glad to hear it.'

214, 215. **to use . . . entertainment:** to meet Laertes in a
cordial and friendly way. *Entertainment* often means 'welcome' or 'reception.' Cf. ii, 2, 392.—**fall to play:** begin to fence.

221. **in continual practice.** Very significant. Cf. ii, 2, 308.

222–228. **how ill . . . heart:** how uneasy I feel. Hamlet has
a presentiment of evil. *Ill* is regularly used of any uneasy or
uncomfortable physical feeling. As everybody knows, such
presentiments are often accompanied by physical symptoms.—
gaingiving: misgiving.—**obey it.** Neither Hamlet nor Horatio suspects a plot; for, though they distrust the King, they
believe Laertes to be a man of honour, and the presence of
the Queen is an additional security. Yet Horatio, the philoso-
pher, urges Hamlet to obey his instinctive reluctance of mind;
for he knows that such feelings sometimes come from ideas

---

[1]Cf. 'high and palmy' (i, 1, 113); 'rank and gross' (i, 2, 136); 'free
and bounteous (i, 3, 93); 'traduc'd and tax'd' (i, 4, 18); 'knotted and
combined' (i, 5, 18); 'whiff and wind' (ii, 2, 495); 'deject and wretched'
(iii, 1, 163); 'holy and religious' (iii, 3, 8); 'delicate and tender' (iv,
4, 48).

that are well-founded, though too indistinct to be expressed at the moment.

230. **we:** i.e., men like you and me, who believe in God's providence.

231. **sparrow.** *Matthew*, x, 29: 'Are not two sparrows sold for a farthing? and one of them shall not fall on the ground without your Father.' Cf. *Luke*, xii, 6.—**it:** death.

234, 235. **is all:** is the only important matter.—**Since . . . betimes? Let be:** 'Since *no man knows aught of* the state of life which *he leaves*, since he cannot judge what other years may produce, why should he be afraid of *leaving* life betimes? Why should he dread an early death, of which he cannot tell whether it is an exclusion of happiness or an interception of calamity? I despise the superstition of augury and omens, which has no ground in reason or piety; my comfort is, that I cannot fall but by the direction of providence' (Johnson). Brandes notes the resemblance of Hamlet's reflections to Montaigne's Essay (i, 19) on 'Learning how to Die.'[1] The Second Quarto reads 'since no man of ought he leaues, knowes what ist to leaue betimes, let be'; the Folio, 'since no man ha's ought of what he leaues. What is't to leaue betimes?' The text follows Dr. Johnson's emendation but keeps 'Let be,' which he and the Folio omit (see Textual Notes). Wilson accepts the Quarto reading and paraphrases: 'Since no man can tell from anything on earth ("of aught he leaves") what is the right moment to die, why trouble about it?' But *to die betimes* certainly means 'to die young.'—**Let be:** Let it go. Do not try to dissuade me.

237 ff. 'I wish Hamlet had made some other defence; it is unsuitable to the character of a good or a brave man to shelter himself in falsehood' (Johnson). It is odd that Dr. Johnson failed to see that Hamlet's particular falsehood here is inseparable from the general falsehood involved in his counterfeiting madness. If his conduct here is to be reprehended, the blame

---

[1] 'No man dies before his time. The time you leave behinde was no more yours, than that which was before your birth, and concerneth you no more' (Florio's translation, ed. 1603, p. 38).

should go farther back and attach itself to his whole stratagem, and no one has ever taken ethical ground against that.

239. This presence: the King and Queen, in whose presence I speak. Cf. l. 251.

242. exception: objection, resentment.

249. faction: party.

251. this audience: this royal audience. Cf. l. 239.

253, 254. so far ... That: so far that you may believe that, etc.

255-261. 'A piece of satire on fantastical honour. Though *nature* is satisfied, yet he will ask advice of older men of the sword, whether *artificial honour* ought to be contented with Hamlet's submission' (Steevens). This explanation is sound, but the passage is not satirical. The distinction between *nature* (i.e., natural affection) and *honour* (the punctilio of society and convention) has already been made by Hamlet himself in l. 242. Cf. Nashe, *Have with You to Saffron-Walden*, 1596 (ed. McKerrow, III, 21): 'After the same manner that one of these *Italionate* conferences about a *Duell* is wont solemnly to be handled, which is when a man, being specially toucht in reputation, or challenged to the field vpon equall tearmes, calls all his frends together, and askes their aduice how he should carrie himselfe in the action.'

259, 260. masters: experts in these questions.—**a voice ... peace:** a decision that may serve as a precedent for reconciliation.

261-263. ungor'd: unscathed; free from disgrace.—**But ... wrong it.** The monstrous hypocrisy of these words, spoken as they are by a young nobleman whose instinct and training are honourable, shows the blind ruthlessness of the doctrine of revenge and stands in marked contrast to Hamlet's caution and conscience in his own case.

264. frankly: freely; with a heart free from rancour.

266. your foil. A courteous pun. *Foil* often means 'a bit of tinsel placed under a gem to enhance its brilliancy,' and so, 'that which sets off something by contrast.'

268. Stick fiery off: stand out in brilliant contrast. Cf. Chapman, *The Maske of the Middle Temple and Lincoln's Inn*

(Pearson ed., III, 93): 'The humble variety whereof, stucke off the more amplie the Maskers high beauties.'

272. **odds:** i.e., in the value of the stake. The King's stake is much greater than that of Laertes.

274. **is better'd:** has improved since he went to France.—**odds:** i.e., in the terms of the wager. Laertes may score two points more than Hamlet and still lose the match.

275, 276. **let me see another.** Laertes picks out the unbated and poisoned foil.—**likes:** pleases, suits.

277. Nothing can be less warranted than the idea (which Wilson 'assumes' from l. 317) that Osric is an accomplice in the plot. If that were the case, dramatic method would have made his guilt clear.

278-280. **stoups:** big goblets.—**quit . . . exchange:** repay Laertes (score a hit) in the third bout.

283. **an union:** a great and flawless pearl. See Textual Notes.

286, 287. **kettle:** kettledrum.—**the cannoneer.** See i, 2, 125–128; i, 4, 7–12.

298. **shall:** will surely.—**fat.** This adjective has given unnecessary trouble. The Queen, who understands sport (as her metaphor in iv, 5, 109–110 shows), sees that Hamlet is panting and perspiring a little and remarks that he is fat, i.e., 'not in perfect training,' 'not quite trained down.' A modern trainer might use the same word, or he might say that Hamlet is 'rather soft.' *Fat* does not here mean 'corpulent.' Nobody who remembers how *fat* was used by old people in New England sixty years ago will be misled by this adjective.[1]

---

[1] For Shakespeare's time and later cf. Sidney, *Arcadia*, i, 16, 5 (ed. 1590, fol. 69 v⁰): 'very faire, and of a fatnes rather to allure, then to mislike'; Greene, *Never Too Late*, 1590 (ed. Grosart, VIII, 187): 'a louely fat paire of cheekes'; *The London Prodigall*, 1605 (B 3, leaf 2 r⁰): 'fat, faire, and louely'; Heywood, *The Wise Woman of Hogsdon*, iv (Pearson ed., V, 328): 'fat, fresh and fayre'; Defoe, *Roxana* (Cripplegate ed., XII, 20): 'They saw me . . . thin and looking almost like one starved, who was before fat and beautiful.' Wilson accepts the suggestion of Bieber (*Anglistische Arbeiten*, III [1913], 69), Tilley (*Journal of English and Germanic Philology*, XXIV [1925], 315 ff.), and W. H. Dunn (*Times Literary Supplement*, May 26, 1927) that *fat* means 'sweaty.' Cf. E. v. Schaubert, *Anglia*, LII (1928), 93–96.

299. **napkin:** handkerchief.

300. **carouses:** drinks a full draught. See i, 4, 8.

301. **Good madam!** With a gesture, in courteous acknowledgment of the Queen's toast.

304. **dare not.** Hamlet has no suspicion that the cup is poisoned. He means that he does not think it wise to drink (in response to the Queen's toast) until the match is over.

307. **almost . . . conscience.** This aside makes the confession of Laertes in ll. 324–331, 338–342, sound less like too sudden a conversion.

309, 310. **pass:** thrust.—**make a wanton of me:** treat me indulgently; play with me (instead of doing your best to win). A wanton is 'a spoiled child.'

312. **Nothing neither way.** Thus ends the third bout: the score is, two hits for Hamlet (ll. 292, 297) and one draw.

313. The First Quarto has the stage direction: *They catch one anothers Rapiers, and both are wounded, Laertes falles downe, the Queene falles downe and dies.* The other Quartos have no stage direction. The Folios read *In scuffling they change Rapiers.* Just how this trick of exchange was managed on the Elizabethan stage is uncertain. In fencing with rapiers only (i.e., without daggers), there was a recognized series of plays in which each fencer seized the other's sword at the hilt and the result was such an exchange. The movements are shown in a series of cuts in Sainct-Didier's *Traicté* (1573), reproduced by Egerton Castle (*Schools and Masters of Fence,* 1885, pp. 59, 60, figs. 30–33). Perhaps Hamlet and Laertes drop their daggers and fence with foils only, thus carrying out the aforesaid series of manœuvers.

317. **as . . . springe:** like a fool, caught in my own snare. A woodcock, in its stupid curiosity, was supposed to fumble with the snare and thus achieve its own capture. See i, 3, 115, note.

319. **She . . . bleed.** Claudius is panic-proof. See iv, 5, 120 ff. —**sounds:** swounds, swoons.

328. **Unbated.** Cf. iv, 7, 139.—**practice:** plot.

332. **too:** i.e., not only 'unbated' (as he now sees) but also 'envenom'd.'

333. Thus Hamlet's vengeance is, to all intents and purposes, self-defence.

335. **hurt:** wounded.

337. **Drink off this potion!** 'It is probable, that the expression is figurative; and spoken upon making the King, who had declar'd he was only "hurt," taste again of his "sword"' (Capell). Line 339, then, must also be figurative; but anything is better than to make Hamlet force the dying King to drink. Capell supports his explanation by a reference to l. 353.

339. **temper'd:** mixed, compounded.

346. **mutes:** players who have no speaking parts in the drama.

347, 348. **as ... arrest:** as [I have not, for] this fierce sergeant, etc.—**sergeant:** a sheriff's officer. Cf. Peele, *Edward I*, i, 1, 62, 63 (ed. Bullen, I, 88, 89):

> They cannot scape th' arrest of dreadful death,
> Death that doth seize and summon all alike.

351. **the unsatisfied:** those who are uninformed.

364. **o'ercrows:** overcomes. The figure is from cockfighting, and the word (like the sport) was common in Elizabethan times.—**spirit:** vital force, vitality, life.

366, 367. **th' election.** Cf. l. 65.—**voice:** suffrage, vote. The crown of Denmark was elective (within limits), but nomination by the reigning king had much influence in determining his successor, and Hamlet is, for a moment, practically King of Denmark. We may infer that Fortinbras is related to the Danish royal family. Cf. ll. 400, 401.

368, 369. **occurrents:** occurrences.—**solicited:** brought on (this tragedy).

375. **This . . . havoc:** These dead bodies proclaim that a massacre has taken place. *Quarry* is the regular word for the game killed in a hunt. *Havoc* was the old battle cry for 'No quarter.' Cf. *Julius Cæsar*, iii, 1, 270 ff. *Cries on* means simply 'cries out,' 'shouts,' not 'calls for' or 'exclaims against.' Cf. *Othello*, v, 1, 48: 'Whose noise is this that cries on murther?'

376. **toward:** in preparation. Cf. i, 1, 77. Scandinavian warriors believed that, if slain in battle, they were translated to

Valhalla (*Valhöll*), Odin's palace in the sky, where they were to spend their time in feasting and fighting. Though Shakespeare may have known nothing about this pagan creed, the present passage accords with it and sounds appropriate in the mouth of young Fortinbras. Cf. *1 Henry VI*, iv, 5, 7: 'Now thou art come unto a feast of death.'

386. **jump:** exactly, opportunely. Cf. i, 1, 65.

393. **accidental judgments:** judgments of God brought about by means apparently accidental. This refers particularly to the death of the Queen and of Laertes. Cf. l. 318. *Casual slaughters* merely repeats the idea.

394. **put on:** instigated, prompted. These deaths, Delius thinks, were those of Rosencrantz and Guildenstern. If so, *cunning* describes Hamlet's cleverness in changing the death mandate, and *forc'd cause* indicates the necessity of self-defence which prompted him. Possibly, however, Horatio alludes to the death of Hamlet, to which Laertes was instigated by the King's craftiness and his own 'forced' (exaggerated) passion of revenge, and to the death of Laertes.—**forc'd.** Cf. *King Lear*, i, 1, 172: 'strain'd pride.'

400, 401. **rights of memory:** unforgotten rights.—**my vantage:** my presence (with troops) at this opportune moment.

403–406. **from his mouth.** See l. 367.—**more:** more voices, more suffrages.—**presently:** at once.—**On:** on account of.

406–414. In Elizabethan tragedy, the person of highest rank among the survivors regularly makes the speech which brings the play to a formal close. This necessity, indeed, accounts for the presence of Fortinbras in HAMLET. But for him, there would be no one left of sufficient rank to fulfil this office.

408, 409. **put on:** advanced to the kingship, and so put to the test.—**To have prov'd most royally:** to have shown himself every inch a king. This tribute from a fighter like Fortinbras should be a sufficient answer to those critics who regard Hamlet as a weak creature.—**passage:** death.

411. **Speak.** Subjunctive. 'Let the music, etc., speak.'

413, 414. **shows:** appears.—**ordinance:** ordnance.

TEXTUAL NOTES

[Qq indicates the exact agreement of four Quartos—Q₂ (1604; some copies dated 1605), Q₃ (1611), Q₄ (undated), Q₅ (1637). Q₂ without mention of the others indicates the agreement of the same four except in some detail of spelling. Q₁ (1603) is occasionally cited. Ff indicates the exact agreement of all four Folios—F₁ (1623), F₂ (1632), F₃ (1664), F₄ (1685). F₁ without mention of the others indicates agreement of the four except in some detail of spelling. The figures 1 and 2 (as in Dyce₁ and Dyce₂) indicate first and second editions. Conjectures are marked 'conj.'; omissions, 'om.']

ACT i, Scene 1, 16 soldier] souldier (Q₁); souldiers (Q₂); Soldier (F₁).
21 *Mar.* (Q₁ Ff)] *Hora.* (Qq).
33 we two nights have] we haue two nights (Q₂); we two Nights haue (F₁).
43 it not (Q₁ Ff)] a not (Q₂); line om. Q₃ Q₄ Q₅.
45 Question it (Q₁ Ff)] Speake to it (Qq).
49 thee speak (F₃ F₄)] thee speake (Q₁ Q₂ F₁ F₂); thee, speak (Rowe).
51 thee speak] thee speake (Q₁ Qq); thee, speake (F₁).
61 he th' (Q₅)] he the (Q₁ Q₂ Q₄); hee the (Q₃); th' (Ff).
63 the sledded Polacks (Malone)] the sleaded pollax (Q₁ Q₂ Q₃); the sleaded Pollax (Q₄ Q₅); the sledded Pollax (F₁ F₂); the sledded Polax (F₃); the sledded Poll-Ax (Q 1683); the sledded Poleaxe (F₄); the sledded Polack (Pope).
68 my (Q₁ Ff)] mine (Qq).
73 why (Q₁ Ff)] with (Qq).
73 cast (F₃ F₄)] cost (Q₁ Qq); Cast (F₁ F₂).
87 heraldry] heraldrie (Q₁); heraldy (Q₂); Heraldrie (Q₄ F₁); Heraldry (Q₃ Q₅ F₂ F₃ F₄).
88 those (Q₁ Ff)] these (Qq).
91 return'd (Ff)] returne (Qq).
93 comart (Q₂)] Cou'nant (F₁).
94 article design'd] article desseigne (Q₂); articles deseigne (Q₃); Articles designe (Q₄ Q₅); Article designe (F₁); Article design'd (F₂ F₃ F₄).
98 lawless] lawlesse (Q₁ Q₃ Q₄ Q₅); lawelesse (Q₂); Landlesse (F₁).
103 compulsatory (Qq)] Compulsatiue (F₁).
108–125 I think . . . countrymen] om. Ff.
112 mote (Q₄ Q₅)] moth (Q₂ Q₃).
117 As . . . blood] As starres with traines of fier, and dewes of blood (Q₂); Stars shon with Trains of Fire, Dews of Blood fell (Rowe). See note, p. 135, above.
118 in (Qq)] veil'd (Rowe); dim'd (Capell).
121 fierce (Q₄ Q₅)] feare (Q₂); fearce (Q₃).
125 climature (Dyce₂)] Climatures (Qq).
127 *Spreads his arms*] *It spreads his armes* (Qq); *He spreads his arms* (Q 1676); om. Ff.
138 you (Q₁ Ff)] your (Qq).

140 at it (F$_2$ F$_3$ F$_4$)] it (Qq); at ir (F$_1$).

142 *Exit Ghost* (Ff)] om. Qq.

160 The (Q$_1$ Ff)] This (Qq).

161 dare stir] dare walke (Q$_1$); dare sturre (Q$_2$ Q$_3$); dare stirre (Q$_4$); dares stirre (Q$_5$); can walke (F$_1$).

164 the (Ff)] that (Q$_1$ Qq).

175 conveniently (F$_2$ F$_3$ F$_4$)] conueniently (Q$_1$ F$_1$); conuenient (Q$_2$).

Scene 2 (stage direction)] *Florish. Enter Claudius, King of Denmarke, Gertradt he Queene, Counsaile: as Polonius, and his Sonne Laertes, Hamlet, Cum Alijs.* (Q$_2$); *Enter King, Queene, Hamlet, Leartes, Corambis, and the two Ambassadors, with Attendants.* (Q$_1$). The text follows F$_1$, except for *Voltemand* and *Cornelius*, who, in the Folio, enter after l. 25.

11 an . . . a (Qq)] one . . . one (Ff).

17 Now follows, that you know, young (Theobald)] Now followes [followes, (Q$_5$)] that you knowe [know (Q$_3$ Q$_4$)] young [yong (Q$_5$)] (Qq); Now followes, that you know young (F$_1$).

34 Voltemand] *Valtemand* (Q$_2$ Q$_3$ Q$_4$); *Voltemand* (F$_1$ Q$_5$); *Voltimand* (F$_2$ F$_3$ F$_4$).

38 dilated (Ff)] delated (Qq).

41 (stage direction)] om. Qq.

58 He hath (Q$_1$ Ff Q$_3$ Q$_4$ Q$_5$)] Hath (Q$_2$).

58–60 wrung . . . consent] om. Ff.

65 *aside* (Theobald$_2$)] om. Qq Ff.

67 so (Ff)] so much (Qq).

67 i' th' sun] in the sonne (Qq); i' th' Sun (F$_1$).

77 good mother] coold mother (Q$_2$); could smother (Q$_3$ Q$_4$ Q$_5$); good Mother (Ff).

82 moods (Q$_4$ Q$_5$)] moodes (Q$_2$ Q$_3$); modes (Q 1683); Moods (Ff).

82 shapes (Q$_3$ Q$_4$ Q$_5$)] chapes (Q$_2$); shewes (F$_1$).

83 denote (Ff Q$_5$)] deuote (Q$_2$ Q$_3$); deuoute (Q$_4$).

85 passeth (Ff)] passes (Qq).

96 a mind (F$_3$ F$_4$)] or minde (Qq); a Minde (F$_1$); a Mind (F$_2$).

114 retrograde (F$_1$ F$_4$ Q$_5$)] retrogard (Q$_2$ Q$_3$); retrograd (Q$_4$); retro-garde (F$_2$ F$_3$).

129 solid (Ff)] sallied (Qq); sullied (Wilson, following George Mac-Donald's explanation of 'sallied'). Q$_1$ reads 'this too much grieu'd and sallied.'

132 self-slaughter] seale slaughter (Q$_2$ Q$_3$ Q$_4$); Selfe-slaughter (F$_1$); selfe-slaughter (Q$_5$).

133 weary (Ff Q$_5$)] wary (Q$_2$ Q$_3$ Q$_4$).

137 to this (Ff)] thus (Qq).

143 would (Q$_1$ Ff)] should (Qq).

149 even she] om. Qq.

175 to drink deep (F$_3$ F$_4$)] for to drinke (Qq); to drinke deepe (Q$_1$ F$_1$ F$_2$).

178 to see my (Q₁ Ff)] to my (Qq).

185 O] om. Qq.

186, 187 He . . . He] a . . . A(Qq); he . . . He (Q₁ Ff).

187, 188 all in all. | I] all in all | I (Q₂ Q₃ Q₄); all in all, | I (Q₁ Q₅); all in all: | I (Ff).

198 vast (Q₁ Q₄ Q₅)] wast (Q₂ Q₃ F₁); waste (F₂ F₃ F₄).

200 Armed . . . cap-a-pe] Armed at poynt, exactly *Capapea* (Q₂); Armed at poynt, [point, (Q₄)] exactly *Cap apea* (Q₃ Q₄); Armed at point, exactly, *Cap a pe* (Q₅); Arm'd at all points exactly, *Cap a Pe* (Ff).

213 watch'd] watch (Q₂); watcht (Q₃ Q₄ Q₅ Ff); watched (Q₁).

224 Indeed, indeed (Q₁ Ff)] Indeede (Q₂).

225, 227, 228 *Both.* (Ff)] *All.* (Q₁ Qq).

237 Very like, very like (Ff)] Yea very like, very like (Q₁); Very like (Q₂).

249 whatsoever (Q₅ F₂ F₃ F₄)] what someuer (Q₂); whatsoeuer (Q₁ Q₃ Q₄ F₁).

254 *Exeunt*] After l. 253 in Qq Ff.

257 Foul] fonde (Q₂); foule (Q₁ Q₃ Q₄ Q₅ F₁ F₂); foul (F₃ F₄).

Scene 3, 3 convoy is] conuay, in (Q₂ Q₃ Q₄); convay in (Q₅); Conuoy is (F₁).

9 perfume and] om. Ff.

10 so? (Rowe)] so. (Qq Ff).

12 bulk] bulkes (Qq); Bulke (F₁).

18 For . . . birth] om. Qq.

21 safety (Q₃ Q₅)] safty (Q₂); safetie (Q₄); sanetity (Ff); sanity (Theobald conj.; Hanmer).

26 particular act and place] particuler act and place (Q₂); peculiar Sect and force (Ff).

49 like a (Ff)] a (Qq).

51 (stage direction)] as in Ff; after 'rede' in Qq.

65 comrade] courage (Q₁ Qq); Comrade (Ff).

68 thine (Ff)] thy (Qq).

74 Are most select and generous, chief in that (Rowe)] Or [Ar (Q₃); Are (Q₄ Q₅)] of a most select and generous, chiefe [cheefe (Q₅)] in that (Qq); Are of a most select and generous cheff in that (Ff); Are of a most select and generall chiefe in that (Q₁).

75 be (Ff)] boy (Qq).

76 loan] loue (Q₂ Q₃ Q₄); love (Q₅); lone (F₁).

77 dulls the (Q₅ F₃ F₄)] dulleth (Q₂); dulleth the (Q₃ Q₄); duls the (F₁ F₂).

83 invites (F₂ F₃ F₄)] inuests (Q₂); inuites (F₁).

109 Running (Collier conj.; Dyce₁)] Wrong (Qq); Roaming (Ff); Wronging (Pope); Wringing (Warburton conj.; Theobald).

115 springes (Q₄ Q₅)] Springes (Q₁ F₁ F₂); springs (Q₂ Q₃); Springs (F₃ F₄).

123 parley (Ff Q₅)] parle (Q₂ Q₃ Q₄).
125 tether (Ff)] tider (Q₂); teder (Q₃ Q₄); tedder (Q₅).
129 implorators (Q₃ Q₄ Q₅ Ff)] imploratotors (Q₂).
130 bawds (Theobald conj.; Pope₂)] bonds (Qq Ff).
131 beguile (Q₃ Q₄ Q₅ Ff)] beguide (Q₂).

Scene 4, 2 a nipping (Ff)] nipping (Qq).
5 Indeed? I (Capell)] Indeede; I (Q₂ Q₃ Q₄); Indeed, I (Q₅); Indeed I (Q₁ Ff).
17–38 This . . . scandal.] om. Ff.
27 the (Pope)] their (Qq).
33 Their (Theobald conj.; Pope₂)] His (Qq).
36 e'il] eale (Q₂); ease (Q₃ Q₄ Q₅).
37 often dout (Steevens 1793)] of a doubt (Qq).
49 inurn'd] interr'd (Q₁ Q₂); enurn'd (F₁); Inurn'd (F₂ F₃ F₄).
53 Revisits] Reuisites (Q₂); Reuisits (F₁); Revisitst (F₂ F₃); Revisıt'st (Q 1683 F₄).
61, 78 waves (Q₅)] waues (Q₂ Q₃ Q₄); wafts (Ff).
63 will I (Q₁ Ff)] I will (Qq).
70 summit] somnet (Qq); Sonnet (Ff); Summit (Rowe).
75–78 The very . . . beneath.] om. Ff.
82 artire] arture (Q₂); artyre (Q₃); attire (Q₄); artery (Q₅); Artire (F₁ F₂ F₃); Attire (F₄).
87 imagination (Q₁ Q₃ Q₄ Q₅ Ff)] imagion (Q₂).

Scene 5, 20 fretful (F₄)] fretfull (Q₁ F₁ F₂ F₃); fearefull (Qq).
33 rots (Ff)] rootes (Q₁ Q₂ Q₃); roots (Q₄ Q₅).
43 wit (Pope)] wits (Qq Ff).
47 what a (Ff Q₅)] what (Q₂ Q₃ Q₄).
55 lust (F₄)] but (Qq); Lust (Q₁ F₁ F₂ F₃).
56 sate (F₁ F₂)] sort (Qq); seat (F₃ F₄).
62 hebona] Hebona (Q₁ Qq); Hebenon (Ff).
68 posset (Ff)] possesse (Qq).
77 unanel'd] vnanueld (Q₂); vn-anueld (Q₃ Q₄); un-anueld (Q₅); vnnaneld (F₁); unnanneld (F₂ F₃ F₄).
80 Ff Qq give this line to the Ghost. Rann and a few others assign it to Hamlet, following a conjecture recorded by Johnson and made independently by Paul Whitehead. Q₁ gives 'O horrible, most horrible!' to the Ghost, but adds '*Ham.* O God!'
84 howsoever (F₂ F₃ F₄)] howsomeuer (Q₂); howsoeuer (Q₁ F₁).
84 pursuest (Ff Q₅)] pursues (Q₂ Q₃ Q₄).
91 *Exit* (Ff)] om. Qq.
93 Hold, hold, my (Capell)] ô fie, hold, hold my (Q₂); O fie! hold, my (Q₃); O fie! hold my (Q₄ Q₅); Oh fie: hold my (Ff).
95 stiffly (F₃ F₄)] swiftly (Qq); stiffely (F₁ F₂).
96 while (Ff)] whiles (Qq).

113 *Hor. (within)*] Qq have *Enter Horatio, and Marcellus* after 'sworn't,' omit *within*, and give 'My Lord, my Lord' to Horatio. F₁ has (after 'sworn't') '*Hor. & Mar. within.* My Lord, my Lord. *Enter Horatio and Marcellus.*'

113 Heaven (F₂ F₃ F₄)] Heauens (Q₂); Heauen (F₁).

114 *Ham.* (Qq)] *Mar.* (Ff).

115 *Mar.* (Qq)] *Hor.* (Ff).

116 bird (Ff)] and (Qq).

122 my lord (Q₁)] om. Qq; my Lord (Ff).

123 ne'er (F₂)] neuer (Q₂); nere (F₁); ne're (F₃ F₄).

132 Look you, I'll] I will (Qq); Looke you, Ile (F₁).

150 Aha] Ha, ha (Qq); Ah ha (F₁ F₂ F₃); Ah, ha (F₄).

158, 159, 160] So arranged in Ff. In Qq the order is 158, 160, 159.

167 your (Q₁ Qq)] our (Ff).

170 soe'er] so mere (Q₂ Q₃ Q₄); so ere (Ff Q₅).

179 this not to do] this doe sweare (Q₂); this [This (Q₁)] not to doe [do (F₃ F₄)] (Q₁ Ff).

181 Swear] om. Qq; sweare (Q₁); Sweare (F₁).

Act ii, Scene 1 (stage direction)] as in Ff. Qq have *Enter old Polonius, [Polonius (Q₅)] with his man or two.*

28 no (Ff)] om. Qq.

38 warrant (Ff)] wit (Qq).

39 sullies (Q₃ Q₄ Q₅ F₄)] sallies (Q₂); sulleyes (F₁ F₂ F₃).

40 i' th' (Ff)] with (Qq).

52, 53 at 'friend . . . gentleman'] om. Qq.

55 closes (Qq)] closes with you (Ff).

58 there o'ertook] there, or tooke (Qq); there o'retooke (F₁).

63 takes (Ff Q₅)] take (Q₂ Q₃ Q₄).

74 Qq Ff put Reynaldo's exit after l. 73 and Ophelia's entrance before 'Farewell.'

91 he would (Ff)] a would (Qq).

99 help (F₃ F₄)] helps (Q₂); helpe (Q₁ F₁ F₂).

105 passion (Ff)] passions (Qq).

112 quoted (Ff)] coted (Q₂ Q₃ Q₄); coated (Q₅).

Scene 2 (stage direction)] *Florish. Enter King and Queene, Rosencraus and Guyldensterne* (Q₂); *Enter King, Queene, Rosincrane, and Guildensterne Cum alijs* (F₁).

1 Rosencrantz] *Rosencraus* (Qq); *Rosincrance* (F₁); *Rosincros* (F₂); *Rosincross* (F₃ F₄).

5 I call (Ff Q₅)] call (Q₂ Q₃ Q₄).

12 since (Ff)] sith (Qq).

12 haviour (Q₅)] hauior (Q₂); haur (Q₃); hauour (Q₄); humour (F₁).

17 Whether . . . thus] om. Ff.

20 are (Q₃ Q₄ Q₅ Ff)] is (Q₂).

43 Assure you (Ff)] I assure (Qq).

45 and (Qq)] one (Ff).

57 our o'erhasty] our hastie (Q₂); our o're-hasty (F₁).

58 (stage direction)] *Enter Embassadors* (Qq after l. 57); *Enter Polonius, Voltumand, and Cornelius* (F₁ after l. 57).

73 three (Ff)] threescore (Qq).

76 (stage direction)] om. Qq Ff; supplied by Malone.

90 since (Ff)] om. Qq.

97 he is (Ff)] hee's (Q₂).

110, 111 Qq make 'that's . . . heare: thus' a part of the letter. F₁ prints 'but you shall heare these in her excellent white bosome, these' as if it were all a part of Polonius's remarks. Corrected in Q 1683.

126 above (F₂ F₃ F₄)] about (Qq); aboue (F₁).

137 winking (Ff Q₅)] working (Q₂ Q₃ Q₄).

143 his (Q₃ Q₄ Q₅ Ff)] her (Q₂).

146 repulsed, a (F₂ F₃ F₄)] repell'd, a (Q₂ Q₅); repeld. a (Q₃); repel'd, a (Q₄); repulsed. A (F₁).

148 watch (Q₃ Q₄ Q₅)] wath (Q₂); Watch (Ff).

149 a (Ff Q₅)] om. Q₂ Q₃ Q₄.

151 'tis this (F₁ F₃ F₄ Q₅)] this (Q₂ Q₃ Q₄); tis this (F₂).

156 (stage direction)] *Pointing to his head and shoulder* (Pope₂; Theobald).

167 *reading on a book*] om. Qq.

170 (stage direction)] *Exit King and Queene* (Q₂ after l. 169); *Exit King & Queen* (F₁ after 'presently,' l. 170).

182 god] good (Qq Ff); God (Warburton).

186 but not as . . . to't] But as your daughter may conceaue, friend looke to't (Q₂); but not as your daughter may conceiue. Friend looke too't (F₁).

188, 189 He . . . He] a . . . a (Qq); he . . . he (Ff).

189 far gone, far gone (F₃ F₄)] farre gone (Q₂); farre gone, farre gone (F₁ F₂).

203 you yourself] your selfe (Qq); you your selfe (F₁).

206 should be old (Ff)] shall growe old (Q₂).

210 grave?] graue. (Q₂); Graue (F₁).

211 that is out o' th' (F₁)] that's out of the (Qq).

213 sanity] sanctity (Q₂); Sanitie (F₁).

214 and suddenly . . . him] om. Qq.

217 honourable] om. Qq.

218 most humbly] om. Qq.

219 sir] om. Qq.

220 more (Ff)] not more (Qq).

229 excellent (Ff Q₄ Q₅)] extent (Q₂); **exelent (Q₃).**

230 ye (F₁ F₃ F₄)] you (Qq); yee (F₂).

232 over-happy . . . cap we] euer happy on Fortunes lap, We (Q₂ Q₃ Q₄); ever happy on fortunes cap, We (Q₅); ouer-happy: on Fortunes Cap, we (F₁).

241 but that (Ff)] but (Qq).

243–276 Let me . . . attended] om. Qq.

280 even (Q₅ F₂ F₃ F₄)] euer (Q₂ Q₃ Q₄); euen (F₁).

284 Come (Ff)] come, come (Qq).

298 could charge (Ff)] can charge (Q₂ Q₃ Q₅); can change (Q₄).

312 no other thing to me than] nothing to me but (Q₂); no other thing to mee, [me, (F₂ F₃ F₄)] then [than (F₄)] (Ff).

313 a piece (Ff Q₅)] peece (Q₂ Q₃ Q₄).

313 a man (Q₂ Q₃ Q₄ Ff)] man (Q₅).

313 ff. how noble . . . a god!] how noble in reason, how infinit in faculties, in forme and moouing, how expresse and admirable in action, how like an Angell in apprehension, how like a God: (Q₂); how Noble in Reason? how infinite in faculty? in forme and mouing how expresse and admirable? in Action, how like an Angel? in apprehension, how like a God? (F₁). Q₃ Q₄ divide the clauses as in Q₂; but Q₅ accords with F₁.

318 no, nor woman] nor women (Q₂); nor woman (Q₃ Q₄ Q₅); no, nor Woman (Ff).

326 you (Ff)] yee (Q₂ Q₃ Q₄); ye (Q₅).

333 of me (F₂ F₃ F₄)] on me (Q₂ Q₃ Q₄); of mee (F₁ Q₅).

337, 338 the clown . . . sere] om. Qq.

338 tickle o' th' sere] tickled a' th' sere (F₁). 'Tickle' is Staunton's conjecture.

339 blank (F₃ F₄)] black (Q₂); blanke (Q₃ Q₄ Q₅ F₁ F₂).

352–377 *Ham.* How comes . . . load too.] om. Qq.

356 berattle] be-ratled (F₁); be ratle (F₂); be-rattle (F₃ F₄).

364 most like (Pope)] like most (Ff).

379 mows] mouths (Q₂ Q₃ Q₄); mouthes (Q₅); mowes (Ff).

385 (stage direction) as in Ff] *A Florish.* (Q₂).

388 come (Ff)] come then (Qq).

389 lest my (Ff Q₅)] let me (Q₂); let my (Q₃ Q₄).

406 so (Q₁ Ff)] then (Qq).

416, 417 tragical-historical, tragical-comical-historical-pastoral] om. Qq.

419 light. For . . . liberty, these] light for . . . liberty: these (Q₂ Q₃); light for . . . libertie: these (Q₄); light for . . . liberty; these (Q₅); light, for . . . Liberty [liberty (F₄)]. These (Ff); light. For . . . Liberty, these (Theobald).

424 What (S. Walker conj.; Dyce₂)] What a (Q₁ Qq Ff).

441 my old (F₂ F₃ F₄)] old (Qq); my olde (F₁).

444 By'r Lady] by lady (Q₂ Q₃); my Ladie (Q₄); my Lady (Q₅); Byrlady (F₁); Berlady (F₂ F₃ F₄).

448 French (Q₁ F₁)] friendly (Qq).

465 indict (Collier)] indite (Qq Ff).

466 affectation (Ff)] affection (Qq).

467, 468 as wholesome . . . fine] om. Ff.

468 One] one (Qq); One cheefe (F₁).

469 tale (Q₁)] talke (Qq); Tale (Ff).

469 where (Q₁ Ff)] when (Qq).

476 the (Ff)] th' (Qq).

478 heraldry] heraldy (Q₂ Q₃); Heraldy (Q₄); Heraldry (Q₁ Ff Q₅).

496 Then senseless Ilium] om. Qq.

501 reverend] reuerent (Q₂); Reuerend (F₁).

503 And, like] Like (Qq); And like (F₁ F₄); And lik'd (F₂ F₃).

510 Aroused (Collier)] A rowsed (Qq F₂ F₃ F₄); A ro wsed (F₁).

525 O who (Q₁ Ff)] a woe (Q₂ Q₃ Q₄); ah woe (Q₅).

527 Mobled . . . good (F₂ F₃ F₄)] om. Qq; Inobled . . . good (F₁).

537 husband's] husband (Q₂); husbands (Q₃ Q₄ Q₅ F₂); Husbands (F₁ F₃ F₄).

542 whe'r (Capell)] where (Qq Ff); whe're (Theobald).

544 of this (Qq)] om. Ff.

553 bodykins (F₁)] bodkin (Qq).

554 who should scape (Q₁ Ff)] who shall scape (Qq).

560 (stage direction)] *Exit Polonius with all the Players but the First.* (Dyce). Q₂ puts *Exeunt Pol. and Players.* after 'Elsinore' (l. 572); F₁ has *Exit Polon.* after 'sirs' (l. 559).

565 for a (Ff)] for (Qq).

566 dozen (F₃ F₄)] dosen lines (Qq); dosen (F₁ F₂).

575 God b' wi' ye] God buy to you (Qq); God [*or* god] buy'ye (F₁ F₂ F₃); god b' w' ye (F₄).

575 (stage direction) Clark and Wright] *Exeunt.* (Q₂ after l. 574); *Exit.* (Q₃ Q₄ Q₅ after l. 574); *Exeunt. Manet Hamlet.* (F₁ after l. 574).

580 his (Ff)] the (Qq).

580 wann'd] wand (Qq); warm'd (Ff).

581 in's (F₁ F₃ F₄ Q₅)] in his (Q₂ Q₃ Q₄); ins (F₂).

585 to Hecuba] to her (Qq); to *Hecuba* (Ff).

587 the cue] that (Qq); the Cue (Ff).

606 have (F₂ F₃ F₄ Q₅)] a (Q₁ Q₂); haue (Q₃ Q₄ F₁).

609 O vengeance] om. Qq.

611 a dear father murther'd (Capell)] a deere murthered (Q₂); a deere [deare (Q₅)] father murthered (Q₃ Q₄ Q₅); the Deere [dear (F₃ F₄)] murthered (Ff).

615 A scullion!] a stallyon, (Q₂); a scalion, (Q₁); a stallion, (Q₃); stallion, (Q₄ Q₅); A Scullion? (Ff).

616 brain] braine (Q₁); braines (Qq); Braine (F₁).

625 he but (Ff)] a doe (Q₂).

627 a devil . . . the devil] a deale . . . the deale (Q₂); a diuell . . . the diuell (Q₃ Q₄); a divell . . . the divell (Q₅); the Diuell . . . the Diuel (F₁).

Act iii, Scene 1, 1 circumstance (Ff)] conference (Qq).
6 he will (Ff Q₅)] a will (Q₂ Q₃ Q₄).
27 on to] into (Qq); on To (Ff).
28 too (Ff)] two (Qq).
32 (lawful espials)] om. Qq.
33 Will (Ff)] Wee'le (Q₂).
46 loneliness (F₄)] lowlines (Q₂); lowlinesse (Q₃ Q₄); lonelinesse (F₁ F₂ F₃ Q₅).
55 Let's] om. Qq.
55 *Exeunt*] om. Qq.
55 Enter *Hamlet*] *Enter Hamlet* (Qq after 'burthen'; Ff after *Exeunt*).
72 despis'd love, the] despiz'd loue, the (Q₂); office, and the (Q₃); office and the (Q₄); despised love, and the (Q₅); dispriz'd Loue, the (F₁).
76 these] om. Qq.
83 of us all (F₂ F₃ F₄)] om. Q₂; of vs all (Q₁ F₁).
86 pith (Ff)] pitch (Qq).
92 well, well, well (Ff)] well (Qq).
97 you know (Qq)] I know (Ff).
99 the (Ff)] these (Qq).
107 your honesty should (F₄)] you should (Qq); your Honesty should (F₁ F₂ F₃).
119 inoculate] euocutat (Q₂); euacaut (Q₃); euacuate (Q₄); evacuate (Q₅); innoculate (F₁); inocculate (F₂ F₃); inocualte (F₄).
122 to a (Ff)] a (Qq).
133 all (Q₁ Ff)] om. Qq.
141 Go] om. Qq.
147 O] om. Qq.
148 paintings too (Q₁)] paintings (Qq); pratlings too (F₁); pratling too (F₂ F₃ F₄).
150 You jig, you] you gig & (Q₂ Q₄); you gig and (Q₃); gig and (Q₅); you gidgs, you (Ff); you jig and (Q 1676).
150 you lisp; you] you list you (Qq); you lispe, [lisp, (F₄)] and (Ff).
151 your ignorance (F₂ F₃ F₄)] ignorance (Qq); your Ignorance (F₁).
153 no moe marriages (Q₅)] no mo marriage (Q₂ Q₃ Q₄); no more Marriages (Ff); no more marriages (Q₁).
159 The courtier's, scholar's, soldier's] So arranged by Hanmer. In Qq Ff the order is 'The Courtiers, souldiers, schollers' (Q₂). Q₁ reads 'The Courtier, Scholler, Souldier, all in him, All dasht and splinterd thence.'
160 expectancy (F₃ F₄)] expectation (Qq); expectansie (F₁ F₂).
164 music] musickt (Q₂ Q₃); Musicke (F₁ F₂ Q₅); Musick (Q₄ F₃ F₄).
165 that (Ff)] what (Qq).
166 jangled, out of tune and] iangled [jangled (Q₅)] out of time, and (Qq); iangled [jangled (F₃ F₄)] out of tune, and (Ff); jangl'd, out of tune and (Capell).
167 feature (F₂ F₃ F₄)] stature (Qq); Feature (F₁).
169 Here Qq mark *Exit*; om. Ff.

181 something-settled (Warburton)] something setled (Qq Ff).
196 unwatch'd (F₂ F₃ F₄)] vnmatcht (Q₂); vnwatch'd (F₁).

Scene 2, 3 our (Qq)] your (Q₁ Ff).
21 so overdone] so ore-doone (Q₂); so ouer-done (F₁).
24 her own feature] her feature (Qq); her owne Feature (F₁).
26 it make (Ff)] it makes (Qq).
32 the which one (F₂ F₃ F₄)] which one (Qq); the which One (F₁).
35 praise (Ff Q₅)] praysd (Q₂ Q₃); praisd (Q₄).
36 the accent (Ff Q₅)] th' accent (Q₂ Q₃ Q₄).
37 nor man (Qq)] or Norman (Ff); Nor Turke (Q₁).
41 sir] om. Qq.
50 *Exeunt Players*] om. Qq.
50 Entrance as in Ff; Qq put it after 'work.'
53 *Exit Polonius* (Ff)] om. Qq.
56 *Both.* We will . . . they two.] *Ros.* I my Lord. [Lord (Q₃)] *Exeunt*
they [*those* (Q₃ Q₄ Q₅)] *two* (Qq); *Both.* We will [will, (F₃ F₄)] my
Lord. *Exeunt.* (Ff).
69, 70 distinguish, her election Hath (Ff)] distinguish her election,
[election (Q₃ Q₄)] S'hath [Shath (Q₃ Q₄); Sh'ath (Q₅)] (Qq).
74 commingled (Dyce)] comedled (Qq); co-mingled (Ff).
93 he (Ff)] a (Qq).
94 detecting (Ff)] detected (Q₂ Q₃ Q₄); detection (Q₅).
94 (stage direction)] *Enter Trumpets and Kettle Drummes, King,*
Queene, Polonius, Ophelia. (Q₂); *Enter King, Queene, Polonius, Ophelia,*
Rosincrance, Guildensterne, and other Lords attendant, with his Guard
carrying Torches. Danish March. Sound a Flourish. (F₁).
121, 122 *Ham.* I mean . . . *Oph.* Ay, my lord.] om. Qq.
140, 141 he . . . he (Ff)] a . . . a (Qq).
145 (stage direction) as in Ff] *The Trumpets sounds* [*sound* (Q₃ Q₄*
Q₅)]. *Dumbe show followes.* (Qq).
145 (dumb show)] *Enter a King and a Queene, the Queene embracing*
him, and he her, he takes her vp, and declines his head vpon her necke, he
lyes him downe vpon a bancke of flowers, she seeing him asleepe, leaues
him: anon come in an other man, takes off his crowne, kisses it, pours
poyson in the sleepers eares, and leaues him: the Queene returnes, finds
the King dead, makes passionate action, the poysner with some three or
foure comes in againe, seeme to condole with her, the dead body is carried
away, the poysner wooes the Queene with gifts, shee seemes harsh awhile,
but in the end accepts loue. (Q₂); *Enter a King and a Queene, very louingly;*
the Queene embracing him. She kneeles, and makes shew of Protestation
vnto him. He takes her vp, and declines his head vpon her neck. Layes
him downe vpon a Banke of Flowers. She seeing him a-sleepe, leaues him.
Anon comes in a Fellow, takes off his Crowne, kisses it, and powres poyson
in the Kings eares, and Exits. The Queene returnes, findes the King dead,
and makes passionate Action. The Poysoner, with some two or three Mutes

comes in againe, seeming to lament with her. The dead body is carried away: The Poysoner Wooes the Queene with Gifts, she seemes loath and unwilling awhile, but in the end, accepts his loue. Exeunt (F₁).

147 this is (Ff)] This is (G₁); this (Q₂); tis (Q₃); it is (Q₄ Q₅).

147 miching malhecho] myching Mallico (Q₁); munching *Mallico* (Qq); Miching *Malicho* (Ff).

151 Enter *Prologue*.] After 'fellow' (Q₂); after l. 158 (Ff).

152 counsel (F₄)] om. Qq; counsell (Q₁ F₁ F₂ F₃).

153 he (Pope)] a (Qq); they (Ff).

154 you'll (F₂ F₃ F₄)] you will (Qq); you'l (F₁).

166 Tellus' orbed ground] *Tellus* orb'd the ground (Qq); *Tellus* Orbed ground (Ff).

174 your former (Q₃ Q₄ Q₅ F₂ F₃ F₄)] our former (Q₂); your forme (F₁).

176 After this line Qq have 'For women feare too much, euen as they loue, [even . . . love, (Q₅)]' om. Ff.

177 For . . . holds (Ff)] And . . . hold (Qq).

178 In neither (Ff)] Eyther [Either (Q₃ Q₄ Q₅) none, in neither (Qq).

179 love (Q₅ F₃ F₄)] Lord (Q₂ Q₃ Q₄; loue (F₁); Love (F₂).

181, 182 Where . . . grows there.] om. Ff.

191 Wormwood, wormwood!] O wormewood, wormewood! (Q₁); That's wormwood. (Qq); Wormewood, Wormwood. (F₁).

200 like (Ff)] the (Qq).

209 joys (F₄)] ioy (Q₂); ioyes (F₁); joyes (F₂ F₃).

228, 229 To . . . scope] om. Ff.

229 cheer] cheere (Qq; Wilson); chair (Steevens conj.).

233 If . . . wife] If once a widdow, euer I be wife (Q₁); If once a Widdow, euer I be Wife (F₁); If once I be [bee (Q₃)] a widdow, [widow, (Q₅)] euer [ever (Q₅)] I be a wife [be wife (Q₄)] (Qq).

237 *He sleeps*] om. Qq; *Sleepes* (F₁).

238 *Exit* (Ff)] *Exeunt* (Qq).

250 o' that (Ff)] A that (Q₁); of that (Qq).

253 (stage direction)] Here in Ff; after l. 254 in Qq.

260 my (Ff)] mine (Qq).

262 must take your husbands (Pope)] must take your husband (Q₁; White); mistake your husbands (Qq); mistake Husbands (F₁); mis-take husbands (Capell).

263 Pox (Ff)] a poxe (Q₁); om. Qq.

267 Confederate (Q₁ Ff)] Considerat (Q₂ Q₃); Considerate (Q₄ Q₅).

269 infected (Q₁ Q₃ Q₄ Q₅ Ff)] inuected (Q₂).

271 (stage direction)] om. Qq.

271 usurp] vsurps (Q₁ Q₂); vsurpe (F₁).

272 He (Q₁ Ff)] A (Qq).

272 for's (F₁ F₃ F₄)] for his (Q₁ Qq); fors (F₂).

277 *Ham.* What, . . . fire?] *Ham.* What, . . . fire. (Ff); *Ham.* What, . . . fires? (Q₁); om. Qq.

281 *All.* (Ff)] *Pol.* (Qq).

287 two (Ff)] om. Qq.

289 sir] om. Qq.

315 rather (Ff)] om. Qq.

319 far (Q₄)] om. Qq; farre (F₁ F₃ F₂).

321 start ... from (Ff)] stare ... from (Q₂ Q₃ Q₄); stare ... upon (Q₅).

330 of my (Ff)] of (Q₂ Q₃ Q₄); of the (Q₅).

332 *Guil.*] *Guild.* (Ff); *Ros.* (Qq).

359 (stage direction)] *Enter the Players with Recorders.* (Qq after 'Denmark,' l. 357); *Enter one with a Recorder.* (Ff after 'musty,' l. 359).

373 fingers and thumbs] fingers, & the vmber (Q₂); fingers, and the thumb (Q₃); fingers, & the thumb (Q₄); fingers and the thumbe (Q₅); finger and thumbe [thumb (Q₄)] (Ff).

382 to the top of my (Ff)] to my (Qq).

388 can fret me (Ff Q₅)] can frett mee (Q₁); fret me not (Q₂ Q₃ Q₄).

389 (stage direction)] as in Capell; after 'sir' (l. 390) in Qq Ff.

395 'tis like (Q₅)] 'tis, like (Q₂); tis like (Q₃ Q₄); it's like (F₁).

397 back'd (Ff)] back't (Q₁); backt (Q₂); black (Q₃ Q₄); blacke (Q₅).

400–417 Qq give all these lines to Hamlet (Q₂ Q₃ by a catchword, Q₄ Q₅ by a speech heading). They put 'Leave me, friends' before 'I will say so.' They omit *Exit* after 'say so.' The Ff give the right adjustment.

400 will I (Ff)] I will (Qq).

404 I will say so. (Ff)] I will, say so. (Q₂ Q₃ Q₄ Q₅).

405 (stage direction)] as in Clark and Wright; om. Qq Ff.

407 breathes (Q₅ F₃ F₄)] breakes (Q₂ Q₃); breaks (Q₄); breaths (F₁ F₂).

409 bitter . . . day] busines as the bitter day (Q₂); bitter businesse [business (F₃ F₄)] as the day (Ff Q₅).

414 daggers (Q₅)] dagger (Q₂ Q₃ Q₄); Daggers (Ff).

Scene 3, 6 near us] neer's (Q₂ Q₃ Q₄); neare us (Q₅); dangerous (Ff).

7 lunacies] browes (Qq); Lunacies (Ff); Lunes (Theobald); brawls (Wilson); braves (anon. conj.; Parrott and Craig).

17 It is (Ff)] or it is (Qq).

18 summit] somnet (Qq); Somnet (Ff); Summit (Rowe).

22 ruin] raine (Qq); Ruine (Ff).

23 with (Ff)] om. Qq.

25 upon (F₂ F₃ F₄)] about (Qq); vpon (F₁).

26 *Both.* (Ff)] *Ros.* (Qq).

35 (stage direction) (Capell)] *Exit* (Qq F₂ F₃ F₄ after 'know'); om. F₁.

50 pardon'd (Ff)] pardon (Qq).

58 shove (F₂ F₃ F₄)] showe (Q₂); shoue (F₁).

72 *He kneels.*] om. Qq Ff; *hee kneeles* (Q₁).

73 it pat, now he is praying (Ff)] it, but [bot (Q₃)] now a is a-praying [is praying (Q₅)] (Qq).

74 he goes (Ff)] a goes (Q₂ Q₄ Q₅); goes (Q₃).

75 reveng'd (F₂ F₃ Q₅)] reuendge (Q₂ Q₃); reuenged (Q₄); reueng'd (F₁); revenged (F₄).

79 hire and salary] base and silly (Qq); hyre and Sallery (F₁); bait and salary (Wilson); a benefit (Q₁).

80 He (Ff)] A (Qq).

81 flush (Qq)] fresh (Ff).

89 drunk asleep (F₂ F₄)] drunke, a sleepe [asleep (Q₅)] (Qq); drunke asleepe (F₁ F₂).

91 At gaming, swearing (Ff)] At game [game, (Q₂ Q₄ Q₅)] a swearing (Qq).

Scene 4, 1 He will (Ff)] A will (Qq).

4 silence (Qq Ff)] 'sconce (Hanmer). Q₁ reads 'I'le shrowde my selfe behinde the Arras.'

5 with him] om. Qq.

6 *Ham. . . . mother*] om. Qq.

7 warrant (Ff Q₅)] wait (Q₂); waite (Q₃ Q₄).

8 Enter *Hamlet*] So placed in Ff; after 'round' in Qq.

20 inmost (Ff)] most (Qq).

22 Help, help (F₃ F₄)] Helpe (Qq); Helpe, helpe (F₁ F₂).

22 help, help, help (F₃ F₄)] helpe (Qq); helpe, helpe, helpe (F₁ F₂).

23 *Makes . . . Polonius.*] om. Qq; *Killes Polonius.* (F₁ after 'slain').

31 (stage direction) (Dyce₁)] om. Qq Ff.

38 it is (Ff)] it be (Qq).

48 doth (Ff)] dooes (Q₂ Q₃); does (Q₄ Q₅).

48, 49 glow; Yea, this] glowe Ore this (Q₂); glow Ore this (Q₃ Q₄); glow, Yea this (Ff); glow Yea this (Q₅).

50 tristful (F₄)] heated (Qq); tristfull (F₁ Γ₂ F₃).

52 That . . . index] Qq give the line to Hamlet. Corrected in Ff.

59 heaven-kissing (F₂ F₃ Q₅)] heaue, a kissing (Q₂ Q₃ Q₄); heauen kissing (F₁); Heaven kissing (F₄).

71-76 Sense . . . difference] om. Ff.

78-81 Eyes . . . mope] om. Ff.

88 And . . . panders] And . . . pardons (Qq); As . . . panders (Ff).

89 mine . . . soul] my very eyes [eies (Q₄)] into my soule (Qq); mine eyes into my very soule (F₁).

90 grained (Ff)] greeued (Q₂).

91 As . . . their] As will leaue there their (Q₂); As will not leaue their (F₁).

95 mine (Ff Q₅)] my (Q₂ Q₃ Q₄).

97 tithe] kyth (Qq); tythe (Ff).

101 (stage direction)] *Enter the ghost in his night gowne.* (Q₁ before 'Save me'); *Enter Ghost.* (Q₂ F₁ after 'No more'; Q₃ Q₄ Q₅ after 'pocket').

121 hairs] haire (Qq F₁ F₂); hair (F₃ F₄); Hairs (Rowe).

139 Ecstasy?] om. Qq.

143 And I (Ff Q₅)] And (Q₂ Q₃ Q₄).

158 live (F₂ F₃ F₄)] leaue (Q₂); liue (F₁).

161–165 That . . . on] om. Ff.
162 evil (Thirlby conj.; Theobald)] deuill (Q₂ Q₃); Deuill (Q₄) divell (Q₅).
165 Refrain to-night] to refraine night (Q₂ Q₃ Q₄); refraine to nigh (F₁); refrain to night (Q₅).
167–170 the next . . . potency] om. Ff.
169 And either master the (Jennens)] And either the (Q₂); And Maister the (Q₃); And master the (Q₄ Q₅); And exorcise the (Wilson conj.).
179 Thus (Ff Q₅)] This (Q₂ Q₃ Q₄).
180 One . . . lady] om. Ff.
202–210 There's . . . meet] om. Ff.
215 foolish (Q₁ F₁)] most foolish (Qq).
217 (stage direction)] *Exit Hamlet with the dead body.* (Q₁); *Exit.* (Qq); *Exit Hamlet tugging in Polonius.* (F₁).

Aᴄᴛ iv, Scene 1. The Quarto of 1676 is the earliest text to begin a new Act here. As stage direction Q₂ has *Eenter King, and Queene, with Rosen-craus and Guyldensterne.* F₁ has *Enter King.*
4 Bestow . . . while] om. Ff.
4 (stage direction)] om. Qq Ff; *Exeunt Ros. and* Guild. (Q 1676).
27 He (Ff)] a (Qq).
32 (stage direction)] after 'skill' (Qq); after 'excuse' (Ff).
37 (stage direction)] om. Qq; *Exit Gent.* (Ff); *Ex. Ros. and* Guild. (Rowe).
40 So haply slander (Capell)] om. Qq Ff; For, haply, Slander (Theobald).
41–44 Whose . . . air] om. Ff.

Scene 2, 2 *Gentlemen. . . . Lord Hamlet!*] om. Qq.
3 But soft] but soft (Q₂); but softly (Q₃ Q₄ Q₅); om. Ff.
6 Compounded (Q₃ Q₄ Q₅ Ff)] Compound (Q₂).
18 like an ape] like an apple (Qq); like an Ape (Ff); as an Ape doth nuttes (Q₁).
31 Hide . . . after] om. Qq.

Scene 3 (stage direction)] As in Ff; *Enter King, and two or three.* (Q₂).
11 (stage direction)] *Enter Rosencraus and all the rest.* (Q₂); *Enter Rosincrane* (F₁); *Enter Rosincros.* (F₂ F₃); *Enter* Rosincros. (F₄).
16 Guildenstern!] om. Qq; *Guildensterne?* (F₁); *Guildenstar?* (F₂ F₃); *Guildenstare?* (F₄).
16 my (Ff)] the (Qq).
16 (stage direction)] *They enter.* (Q₂ Q₅); *They Enter.* (Q₃ Q₄); *Enter Hamlet and Guildensterne.* (F₁).
20 he is (Q₄ Q₅ Ff)] a is (Q₂ Q₃).

28–30 *King.* Alas . . . worm.] om. Ff.
38 indeed, if (Ff)] if indeed (Q₂ Q₃ Q₄); indeed if (Q₅).
40 (stage direction)] om. Qq Ff; *to some Attendants* (Capell).
41 He (Ff)] A (Qq).
41 (stage direction) (Capell)] om. Qq Ff.
45 With fiery quickness] om. Qq.
54 and so (Ff Q₅)] And so (Q₁); so (Q₂ Q₃ Q₄).
59 (stage direction) (Theobald)] om. Qq Ff.
66 congruing (Qq)] coniuring (F₁).
70 were ne'er begun] will nere begin (Q₂); were ne're begun (**Ff**).

Scene 4, 8 *Exeunt all but the Captain*] om. Qq; *Exit.* (Ff).
8–66 *Enter Hamlet. . . . Ham.* Good . . . worth!] om. Ff.
8 (stage direction)] *Enter Hamlet, Rosencraus, &c.* (Qq).
17 speak] speake (Qq); speak it (Pope); speak, sir (Capell).
30 *Exit.* (Dyce)] om. Qq; *Exit* Captain. (Capell).
31 (stage direction)] *Exe. Manet* Hamlet. (Rowe); om. Qq.

Scene 5 (stage direction)] *Enter Horatio, Gertrard, and a Gentleman.* (Qq); *Enter Queene and Horatio.* (F₁).
2, 4 *Gent.*] *Gent.* or *Gen.* (Qq); *Hor.* (Ff).
9 aim (F₃ F₄)] yawne (Qq); ayme (F₁ F₂).
16–20 'Let her come in' is given to Horatio in Qq. In Ff ''Twere . . . spilt' is all given to the Queen. Corrected by Hanmer and Blackstone.
20 (stage direction)] *Enter Ophelia* after 'come in' (Qq); *Enter Ophelia distracted* (F₁ after 'spilt'). Before l. 23 Q₁ has *Enter Ofelia playing on a Lute, and her haire downe singing.*
33 O, ho!] O ho (Qq); om. Ff.
37 all with (Qq)] with (Q₁ Ff).
38 grave (F₂ F₃ F₄)] ground (Qq); graue (F₁).
38 not (Q₁ Qq Ff)] om. Pope.
41 God (Ff)] good (Qq).
57 la (Ff)] om. Qq.
64 He answers (Qq)] om. Ff.
72 *Exit.* (Ff)] om. Qq.
75 *Exit Horatio.* (Theobald)] om. Qq Ff.
77 death. (Ff)] death, [death: (Q₅)] and now behold, (Qq).
82 their thoughts (Ff)] thoughts (Qq).
89 Feeds on his (Johnson)] Feeds on this (Qq); Keepes [Keeps (F₂ F₄)] on his (Ff).
96 *Queen.* Alack . . . this?] om. Qq.
97 Where are (Ff)] Attend, where is [are (Q₃ Q₄ Q₅)] (Qq).
97 *Enter a Messenger*] Qq Ff put this stage direction immediately after *A noise within* (l. 96).
100 impetuous (Q₃ Q₄ Q₅ F₂ F₃ F₄)] impitious (Q₂); impittious (F₁).
106 They (Ff Q₅)] The (Q₂ Q₃ Q₄).

108 *A noise within.*] Qq put this stage direction after 'cry' (l. 109); Ff put *Noise within.* after 'dogs' (l. 110).

111 (stage direction)] *Enter Laertes with others.* (Qq after 'dogs'); *Enter Laertes.* (F₁ after *Noise within.*).

119 brows (Q 1676)] browe (Q₂ Q₃); brow (Ff Q₄ Q₅).

137 world (F₁)] worlds (Qq).

141 father's death] Father (Q₂); Fathers death (F₁).

142 swoopstake (Dyce₁)] soopstake (Q₂); Soop-stake (Ff). Q₁ reads 'Swoop-stake-like, draw at friend, and foe, and all?'

146 pelican] Pelican (Qq F₂ F₃ F₄); Politician (F₁).

151 pierce (Ff)] peare (Qq).

152, 153 eye. . . . *Enter Ophelia.*] eye. *A noyse within. Enter Ophelia. Laer.* Let her come in. How . . . that? (Q₂); eye. *A noise within. Let her come in. Enter Ophelia. Laer.* How . . . that? (F₁).

156 by (Ff)] with (Qq).

160 old (Ff)] poore (Qq).

161–163 Nature . . . loves.] om. Qq.

165 Hey . . . nony] om. Qq.

167 Fare . . . dove] Part of the song in Qq Ff. Adjusted by Capell.

181, 182 O, you must] you must (Q₁); you may (Qq); Oh [O (F₄)] you must (Ff).

185 he (Ff)] a (Qq).

188 affliction] afflictions (Q₁ Qq); Affliction (Ff).

190, 191 he (Ff)] a (Qq).

196 All (Q₁ Ff)] om. Qq.

200 Christian (Ff Q₅)] Christians (Q₂ Q₃ Q₄).

200 I pray God] om. Qq.

200 *Exit*] om. Qq.

Scene 6 (stage direction)] *with an Attendant* (Ff); *and others* (Qq).

2 *Servant.* Seafaring men, sir] *Gent.* (or *Gen.*) Sea-faring men sir (Qq); *Ser.* Saylors sir (F₁).

8 an't (Q₅ F₄)] and (Q₂ Q₃ Q₄); and't (F₁ F₂ F₃).

9 comes (Ff)] came (Qq).

24 good (Ff)] om. Qq.

28 bore (Ff)] bord (Qq).

31 He that (Ff)] So that (Qq).

32 give (F₂ F₃ F₄)] om. Q₂; make (Q₃ Q₄ Q₅); giue (F₁).

Scene 7, 6 proceeded (Ff)] proceede (Q₂ Q₃); proceed (Q₄ Q₅).

7 crimeful] criminall (Qq); crimefull (F₁).

8 Q₂ Q₃ insert 'greatnes' (Q₄ Q₅ 'greatnesse') after 'safetie.' Om. Ff.

11 they are (Ff)] tha'r (Q₂ Q₃ Q₄); tha're (Q₅).

14 She's (F₁ F₃ F₄)] She is (Qq); Shes (F₂).

14 conjunctive (F₂ F₃ F₄)] concliue (Q₂); coniunctiue (F₁).

20 Would (Ff)] Worke (Qq).

22 so loud a wind] so loued Arm'd (Q₂); so loued armes (Q₃ Q₄);
so loved armes (Q₅); so loud a Winde [Wind (F₂ F₃); wind (F₄)] (Ff).
24 And (Ff)] But (Qq).
24 had aim'd (F₃ F₄)] haue aym'd (Q₂); had arm'd (F₁); had
aym'd (F₂).
36 How . . . news?] om. Qq.
36 Letters . . . Hamlet] om. Qq.
37 This to (Ff)] These to (Qq).
41 Of him . . . them (Qq)] om. Ff.
42 (stage direction)] om. Qq.
47 your pardon (F₁ F₂ F₃)] you pardon (Qq F₄).
48 and more strange (Ff)] om. Qq.
49 HAMLET (Ff)] om. Qq.
54 advise (F₂ F₃ F₄)] deuise (Q₂); aduise (F₁).
57 shall live (F₂ F₃ F₄)] liue (Q₂); shall liue (F₁).
58 didest] didst (Qq); diddest (Ff).
63 As checking at (Ff)] As the King at (Q₂ Q₃); as liking not (Q₄ Q₅).
69–82 *Laer.* My lord . . . graveness] om. Ff.
89 topp'd my thought] topt me thought (Q₂ Q₃ Q₄); topt my thought
(Q₅); past my thought (Ff).
93 Lamound] *Lamord* (Qq); *Lamound* (Ff).
99 especially (Ff)] especiall (Qq).
101–103 The scrimers . . . them] om. Ff.
115–124 There . . . ulcer] om. Ff.
123 spendthrift] spend thirfts (Q₂); spend-thrifts (Q₃ Q₄); spend-thrift
(Q₅).
126 your father's son in deed] indeede your fathers sonne (Q₂); your
Fathers [Father's (F₃ F₄)] sonne [son (F₂); Son (F₄)] indeed [in deed
(F₄)] (Ff).
135 on (Ff)] ore (Qq).
139 pass (F₃ F₄)] pace (Qq); passe (F₁ F₂).
141 for that (Ff)] for (Q₂); for the (Q₃ Q₄ Q₅).
160 prepar'd (Ff)] prefard (Q₂); preferd (Q₃ Q₄); prefer'd (Q₅).
163 But . . . noise?] om. Ff.
164 How now, sweet queen?] om. Qq.
164 How now] how now (F₂ F₃ F₄); how (F₁).
168 aslant a (Ff)] ascaunt the (Qq).
169 hoar (F₃ F₄)] horry (Q₂); hoary (Q₃); hoarie (Q₄ Q₅); hore (F₁ F₂)
170 There . . . come] Therewith [There with (Q₃ Q₄)] fantastique
[fantastick (Q₄); fantasticke (Q₅)] garlands did she make (Qq); There
with fantasticke Garlands did she come (F₁).
173 cold (Ff)] cull-cold (Q₂ Q₃); culcold (Q₄ Q₅).
174 coronet (Q₃)] cronet (Q₂); Coronet (Ff Q₄ Q₅).
179 tunes (Q₁ F₁)] laudes (Q₂ Q₃); lauds (Q₄ Q₅).
185 she is drown'd?] she is drownd. (Q₂); is she drownd. (Q₃); is she
drown'd. (Q₄); is she drown'd? (Ff Q₅).

192 speech of fire (Ff)] speech a fire (Q₂ Q₄); speecha fire (Q₃); speech afire (Q₅).

193 douts (Knight)] drownes (Qq F₂); doubts (F₁); drowns (F₃ F₄).

ACT v, Scene 1 (stage direction) with . . . pickaxes] om. Qq Ff; *with Spades and Mattocks* (Q 1676).

9 *se offendendo*] so offended (Qq); *Se offendendo* (Ff).

12, 13 and to perform; argal, she] to performe, or all; she [shee (Q₅)] (Qq). Corrected in Ff.

38–41 *Other*. Why . . . arms?] om. Qq.

49 that frame] that (Qq); that Frame (Ff).

62 (stage direction)] om. Qq.

67 to Yaughan; fetch] in, and fetch (Q₂ Q₅); in and fetch (Q₃ Q₄); to *Yaughan, fetch* (Ff).

67 stoup (F₄)] soope (Qq); stoupe (F₁); stoape (F₂); stoap (F₃).

72 Q₂ Q₃ Q₅ put *Enter Hamlet and Horatio* after 'meet.'

74, 75 that he sings at (Ff)] a sings in (Qq).

81 intil] into (Qq); intill (Ff).

87 now o'erreaches] now ore-reaches (Qq); o're Offices (F₁).

91 good (Ff)] sweet (Qq).

93 he meant (Ff)] a went (Q₂); a ment (Q₃); a meant (Q₄ Q₅).

97 mazzard] massene (Q₂); mazer (Q₃ Q₄ Q₅); Mazard (F₁).

100 with 'em (Ff)] with them (Qq).

105 (stage direction) (Capell)] om. Qq Ff. After l. 104 Q₁ has *he throwes vp a shouel.*

107 quiddits] quiddities (Qq); Quiddits (Ff).

107 quillets (Q₁)] quillites (Q₂); quillities (Q₃ Q₄ Q₅); Quillets (Ff).

108 rude (Ff)] madde (Q₂); mad (Q₃ Q₄ Q₅).

112, 113 Is this . . . recoveries] om. Qq.

114 his vouchers] Qq om. 'his.'

115 double ones too (Ff)] doubles (Qq).

129 O (Ff)] or (Qq).

130 For . . . meet.] om. Qq.

150 taken (Ff)] tooke (Q₂).

155 a (Q₃ Q₄ Q₅ Ff)] om. Q₂.

156 Of all the (Ff)] Of the (Qq).

161 the very (Ff)] that very (Qq).

177 thirty (Qq Ff)] twenty (Halliwell).

181 now-a-days] om. Qq.

190, 191 This skull hath lien you] hath lyen you (Qq); this Scul, has laine (F₁).

191 three-and-twenty] 23. (Q₂ Q₃ Q₅); twenty three (Q₄); three & twenty (F₁); this dozen (Q₁); a dozen (Halliwell).

199 Yorick's] sir *Yoricks* (Q₂); *Yoricks* (F₁).

202 Let me see] om. Qq.

204 borne (F₁ F₂ F₃)] bore (Qq); born (F₄).

214 chamber (Q₁)] table (Qq); Chamber (Ff).

225 he (Ff)] a (Qq).

231 as thus (Q₁ Ff)] om. Qq.

232 into dust (Ff)] to dust (Qq).

239 winter's] waters (Qq); winters (F₁).

240 aside (Ff)] awhile (Q₂); a while (Q₃ Q₄ Q₅).

240 (stage direction)] *Enter K. Q. Laertes and the corse.* (Q₂); *Enter King, Queene, Laertes, and a Coffin, with Lords attendant.* (F₁).

245 (stage direction)] om. Qq Ff; *retiring with* Horatio (Capell).

249, 258 *Priest* (Ff)] *Doct.* (Qq).

252 have (F₂ F₃ F₄)] been (Q₂); haue (F₁).

254 Shards (F₃ F₄)] om. Qq; Shardes (F₁ F₂).

255 crants] Crants (Q₂ Q₃ Q₄); Rites (Ff); rites (Q₅).

260 a requiem] a Requiem (Q₂); sage *Requiem* (Ff); such requiem (Dyce conj.; Grant White); sad Requiem (Collier MS.).

270 treble (F₃ F₄)] double (Qq); trebble (F₁ F₂).

273 (stage direction)] om. Qq.

281 *Leaps . . . Laertes*] om. Qq Ff. After 'Pelion' (l. 276) *Q₁ has Hamlet leapes in after Leartes.*

284 and rash (Ff Q₅)] rash (Q₂ Q₃ Q₄).

286 wisdom] wisedome (Q₁ Qq); wisenesse (F₁).

288 *All.* Gentlemen!] om. Ff.

298 woo't fast] om. Ff.

299 esill] Esill (Qq); *Esile* (Ff); vessels (Q₁).

300 thou come (Ff Q₅)] come (Q₂ Q₃ Q₄).

307 *Queen*] *Quee.* (Qq); *Kin.* (F₁); *King* (F₂ F₃ F₄).

308 thus (Q₅ Ff)] this (Q₂ Q₃ Q₄).

321 shortly (Ff)] thirtie (Q₂); thereby (Q 1605 Q₃ Q₄ Q₅).

Scene 2, 5 Methought] my thought (Q₂); me thought (Ff Q₃ Q₄ Q₅).

6 bilboes] bilbo (Q₂); bilbo's (Q₃ Q₄); Bilbo's (Q₅); Bilboes (Ff).

9 pall (Q₂ F₄)] fall (Q 1605 Q₃ Q₅); fal (Q₄); paule (F₁ F₂ F₃); fail (Q 1695).

17 unseal (F₃ F₄)] vnfold (Q₂); vnseale (F₁); unseale (F₂).

19 O] A (Qq); Oh (Ff).

22 hoo (Ff)] hoe (Qq).

27 hear me how] heare now how (Qq); heare me how (F₁); heare how (F₂); hear how (F₃ F₄).

29 villanies (Capell)] villaines. (Qq); Villaines (F₁); villainy (Theobald).

40 might (Qq)] should (Ff).

43 such-like as's] such like, as sir (Qq); such like Assis (Ff).

46 the bearers (Ff)] those bearers (Qq).

52 Subscrib'd (Q₃ Q₄ Q₅ Ff)] Subscribe (Q₂).

57 Why . . . employment] om. Qq.

63 thinks't thee (Walker conj.; Dyce)] thinke thee (Q₂ Q₃); think thee (Q₄); think you (Q₅); thinkst thee (F₁); think'st thee (F₂ F₃ F₄).

68–80 To quit . . . comes here?] om. Qq.

73 interim is] *interim's* (F₁); *interim* is (Hanmer).

78 court (Rowe)] count (Ff).

80 (stage direction)] *Enter a Courtier* (Qq after l. 67); *Enter young Osricke.* (F₁); *Enter Osricke* (F₂); *Enter Osrick* (F₃ F₄). Osric's speeches in this scene are marked *Cour.* in Qq, *Osr.* in Ff.

83–86 (stage directions)] om. Qq Ff; indicated by Capell.

95, 96 Put your] your (Qq); put your (Ff).

101 But yet (Qq)] om. Ff.

101 sultry] sully (Q₂); soultry (Ff Q₃ Q₄ Q₅).

101 for my (Ff Q₅)] or my (Q₂ Q₃ Q₄).

104 But] but (Ff); om. Qq.

105 he has (F₂ F₃ F₄)] a has (Qq); he ha's (F₁).

109, 110 Nay . . . faith] Nay good my Lord [Lord, (Q₅)] for my ease in good faith (Qq); Nay, [Nay (F₄)] in good faith, for mine ease in good faith (Ff).

110–142 here is . . . Well, sir] om. Ff.

111 gentleman] gentlemen (Q₂); gentlemā (Q₃); Gentleman (Q₄ Q₅).

114 feelingly (Q₃ Q₄ Q₅)] sellingly (Q₂; Wilson); fellingly (Q 1605).

118 dozy] dosie (Q₂); dazzie (Q 1605); dizzie (Q₃ Q₄ Q₅).

132 do't] too't (Q₂); doo't (Q 1605 Q₃ Q₄); doe't (Q₅).

143 is (Qq)] is at his weapon (Ff).

144–150 I dare . . . unfellowed.] om. Ff.

149 for his weapon (Q₅)] for this weapon (Q₂ Q₃ Q₄).

155, 156 he has impon'd] hee has impaund (Q₂ Q₃ Q₄); he has impawn'd (Q₅); he impon'd (Ff).

156 hangers] hanger (Qq); Hangers (Ff).

162, 163 *Hor.* I . . . done.] om. Ff.

166 cannon] a cannon (Q₂); Cannon (Ff).

166 it might be (Q₃ Q₅ Ff)] it be (Q₂); it be might (Q 1605); it might bee (Q₄).

169, 170 is this all . . . it?] why is this all you call it? (Qq); why [why, (F₄)] is this impon'd as you call it? (Ff).

173 hath laid (Ff)] hath layd sir (Q₂).

174, 175 hath . . . nine] hee hath layd on twelue for nine (Q₂); He hath one twelue for mine (F₁).

184 if I (Ff)] and I (Qq).

186 redeliver you e'en so] deliuer you so (Q₂); redeliuer you e'en so (F₁).

191 Yours, yours. He does] Yours doo's [does (Q₅)] (Qq); Yours, yours; hee does (F₁).

194 He did comply with] A did sir with (Q₂); A did so sir with (Q 1605 Q₃ Q₄ Q₅); He did Complie with (F₁).

194 before he] before a (Qq); before hee (F₁).

195 bevy (Caldecott)] breede (Q₂); Beauy (F₁).

199 outward (Ff)] out of an (Qq).

200 yesty (Ff)] histy (Q₂); misty (Q₃ Q₅); mistie (Q₄).

201 fann'd and winnowed (Hanmer; Warburton)] prophane and trennowed (Q₂); prophane and trennowned (Q₃); profane and trennowned (Q₄ Q₅); fond and winnowed (Ff); profound and winnowed (Tschischwitz; Wilson).

203–218 Enter a *Lord . . .* instructs me] om. Ff.

219 this wager] om. Qq.

221 But thou] thou (Qq).

225 gaingiving] gamgiuing (Q₂); game-giuing (Q₃ Q₄); game-giving (Q₅); gain-giuing (F₁).

230 there's a (F₁)] there is (Q₂ Q₃ Q₄); there is a (Q₅).

231 now] om. Qq.

233, 234 it will come (Q₃ Q₄ Q₅ Ff)] it well come (Q₂).

234, 235 all. Since . . . Let be.] all, since no man of ought he [hee (Q₃)] leaues, [leaues (Q₅)] knowes what ist [is't (Q₅)] to leaue [leave (Q₅)] betimes, let be [bee (Q₃)]. (Qq); all, since no man ha's [has (F₃ F₄)] ought of what he leaues [leaves (F₂ F₃ F₄)]. What is't to leaue [leave (F₂ F₃ F₄)] betimes? (Ff).

235 (stage direction)] *A table prepard, Trumpets, Drums and officers with Cushion, King, Queene, and all the state, Foiles, daggers, and Laertes.* (Q₂); *Enter King, Queene, Laertes and Lords, with other Attendants with Foyles, and Gauntlets, a Table and Flagons of Wine on it.* (F₁).

236 (stage direction)] substantially Johnson's; om. Qq Ff.

241 sore (Ff)] a sore (Qq).

251 Sir, in this audience] om. Qq.

255 brother (Q₁ Qq)] Mother (Ff).

261 keep] om. Qq.

261 till (F₁)] all (Qq).

265 Come on] om. Qq.

274 better'd (Ff)] better (Qq).

276 (stage direction)] om. Qq.

283 union (F₂)] Vnice (Q₂); Onixe (Q 1605 Q₃); Onix (Q₄); Onyx (Q₅); vnion (F₁); Union (F₃ F₄).

289, 290 Qq have *Trumpets the while* in the margin; om. Ff.

291 *They play.* (Ff)] om. Qq.

294 After 'palpable hit' Q₂ has *Drum, trumpets and shot. Florish, a peece goes off.* After 'cup' Ff have *Trumpets [Trumpet (F₂ F₃ F₄)] sound, and* [om. F₂ F₃ F₄] *shot goes off.*

296 *They play.*] *They play againe* (Q₁ after l. 292); om. Qq Ff.

297 A touch, a touch (Ff)] om. Qq.

297 confess't] confest (Qq); confesse (F₁).

302 *Drinks.*] om. Qq Ff. Q₁ has *Shee drinkes,* after 'thy mother drinkes to thee': cf. l. 300.

308 You but] you doe but (Qq); you but (Ff).

310 afeard (F₃ F₄)] sure (Qq); affear'd (F₁); affeard (F₂).

311 *Play.* (Ff)] om. Qq.

313 (stage direction)] om. Qq; *In scuffling they change Rapiers.* (Ff). After 'Ham. Come on sir' (which follows 'my conscience,' l. 307) Q₁ has *They catch one anothers Rapiers, and both are wounded, Leartes falles downe, the Queene falles downe and dies.*

319 sounds (Q₂ Q₃ Q₄ F₁ F₂)] swounes (Q₅); swounds (F₃ F₄).

321 *Dies.*] om. Qq Ff; *Queen dies.* (Rowe).

323 *Laertes falls* (Capell)] om. Qq Ff.

324 Qq omit the second 'Hamlet.'

326 hour of (F₃ F₄)] houres (Qq); houre of (F₁ F₂).

327 thy (Ff Q₅)] my (Q₂ Q₃ Q₄).

333 *Hurts the King.* (Ff)] om. Qq.

336 incestuous (Ff Q₅)] incestious (Q₂ Q₃ Q₄).

336 murd'rous] om. Qq.

337 off (Ff Q₅)] of (Q₂ Q₃ Q₄).

337 thy union] the Onixe [Onyx (Q₅)] (Qq); thy Vnion (F₁).

338 (stage direction)] om. Qq; *King Dyes.* (F₁).

342 *Dies.*] om. Qq; *Dyes.* (F₁).

355 good (Ff)] god (Q₂); God (Q₃ Q₄ Q₅).

356 shall live (F₂ F₃ F₄)] shall I leaue (Q₂); shall liue (F₁).

360 *March . . . shot within.* (Steevens)] *A march a farre off.* (Qq); *March afarre off, and shout within.* (F₁).

369 silence. (Qq)] silence. O, o, o, o. *Dyes.* (F₁); silence. O, o, o, o. *Dies.* (F₂); silence. O, o, o. *Dies.* (F₃ F₄).

371 *March within.*] om. Qq Ff. Supplied by Capell after 'hither.'

372 (stage direction)] *Enter Voltemar and the Ambassadors from England, enter Fortenbrasse with his traine.* (Q₁); **Enter Fortenbrasse, with the** *Embassadors.* (Q₂); *Enter Fortinbras and English Ambassador, with Drumme, Colours, and Attendants.* (F₁).

390 to th' yet (Q₃ Q₄ Ff)] to yet (Q₂); to'th yet (Q₅).

394 forc'd cause (Ff)] for no cause (Qq).

403 on (Ff)] no (Qq).

409 royally (Ff)] royall (Qq).

410 rites (Ff)] right (Qq).

414 (stage direction)] as in F₁; *Exeunt.* (Q₂).

GLOSSARIAL INDEX

eye, royal presence, i, 2, 116; iv, 4, 6
eyrie, nest, brood, ii, 2, 354

faction, party, v, 2, 249
fadom, fathom, i, 4, 77
fair, in legible script, v, 2, 32
fair hour, i, 2, 62
fall, to happen, iv, 7, 71; (out), to quarrel ii, 1, 59; (to), to begin, v, 2, 217
false fire, iii, 2, 277
fame, reputation, iv, 4, 61
fang'd, adj., with fangs, iii, 4, 203
fann'd, winnowed, v, 2, 201
fantasy, imagination, i, 1, 23, 54; a whim, iv, 4, 61
fardel, a burden, iii, 1, 76
farm, to take on lease, iv, 4, 20
fat, not in perfect training, v, 2, 298
fatness, pursiness, iii, 4, 153
favour, appearance of the face, v, 1, 215; beauty, iv, 5, 189. See leave and favour
fay, faith, ii, 2, 272
fear, an object of fear, iii, 3, 25
fear, to worry about, i, 3, 51
fear-surprised, seized upon by fear, i, 2, 203
feat, deed, act, iv, 7, 6
fee, value, i, 4, 65; ii, 2, 73; (in), outright, iv, 4, 22
feelingly, v, 2, 112
fell, cruel, fierce, ii, 2, 495; v, 2, 61, 347
fellies, the rim of a wheel, ii, 2, 517
fellowship, partnership, iii, 2, 289
fennel (for flattery), iv, 5, 180
fetch, a device, ii, 1, 38
few. See in few
find, to find out, iii, 1, 193
fine, refined, subtilized, iv, 5, 161; subtle, v, 1, 117
fine and recovery, v, 1, 116
finger, to lay hold on, v, 2, 15
fishmonger, ii, 2, 174
fitness, convenience, v, 2, 210
flats, low country, iv, 5, 100
flattering, adj., soothing, iii, 4, 145
flaw, a gust of wind, v, 1, 239
flush, full of vigour, iii, 3, 81
flushing, redness, i, 2, 155
foil, a set-off, v, 2, 266
foil, a rapier, ii, 2, 334; iv, 7, 137; v, 2, 182, 265, 270, 276
fond, foolish, i, 5, 99
fool, a jester, iii, 2, 49
fool me, iii, 2, 401
fools of nature, i, 4, 54
foot (at), at one's heels, iv, 3, 56
for, as for, i, 2, 112; i, 3, 123; iii, 4, 172; v, 2, 399; instead of, v, 1, 253
for and, and, v, 1, 103
forbear, to let alone, v, 1, 296
forc'd, p.p., exaggerated, v, 2, 394
fordo, to destroy, ii, 1, 103; v, 1, 244

forest of feathers, iii, 2, 286
forgery, an invention, ii, 1, 20; imagination, iv, 7, 90
forgo, to give up, abandon, ii, 2, 307
form, an appearance, ii, 2, 583; an idea, i, 5, 100; courtly behaviour, iii, 1, 161
formal, in proper form, iv, 5, 215
for's, for his, iii, 2, 272; v, 2, 192
Fortune, ii, 2, 240 (note), 515
forward, early, i, 3, 8
foul play, i, 2, 256
four, an indefinite number, ii, 2, 160
frame, structure, i, 2, 20; ii, 2, 308; v, 1, 49; coherent form, iii, 2, 320
frankly, freely, iii, 1, 34; v, 2, 264
free, guiltless, innocent, ii, 2, 590; iii, 2, 252; v, 2, 343
free awe, iv, 3, 63
French falconers, ii, 2, 448
fret, v., iii, 2, 388
fretted, adorned with fretwork, ii, 2, 311
from, away from, contrary to, iii, 2, 21
front, forehead, iii, 4, 56
fruit, dessert, ii, 2, 52
fruitful, teeming, abundant, i, 2, 80
fruits, ii, 2, 145
function, bodily powers, ii, 2, 582
fust, to grow musty, iv, 4, 39

gage, to pledge, stake, i, 1, 91
gaingiving, misgiving, v, 2, 225
'gainst, against, just before, i, 1, 158
gait, procedure, i, 2, 31
gall, capacity for resentment, ii, 2, 604
gall, to gnaw, i, 3, 39; to wound slightly, scratch, iv, 7, 148
galled, inflamed, i, 2, 155; excoriated, iii, 2, 252
gambol from, iii, 4, 144
garb, fashion, ii, 2, 389
gender (general), common people, iv, 7, 18
general, universal, ii, 1, 35; iii, 3, 23
general (the), the common herd, ii, 2, 456
general gender, common people, iv, 7, 18
generous, noble-minded, iv, 7, 136
gentry, courtesy, ii, 2, 22; courtly manners, v, 2, 115
gib, a tomcat, iii, 4, 190
gilded, lined with gold, iii, 3, 58
gin, to begin, i, 5, 90
Gis, Jesus, iv, 5, 58
give, God give, i, 1, 16
give me leave, ii, 2, 170; iv, 5, 113
give o'er, to cease, iii, 2, 279
giving out, utterance, i, 5, 178
glass, mirror, iii, 1, 161; iii, 4, 19
go about, to undertake, iii, 2, 361
go to, interj., i, 3, 112; v, 1, 45
go with, to agree, i, 3, 28
go thy ways, go along, iii, 1, 133
God-a-mercy, gramercy, thank you, ii, 2, 172

impart, to express one's self, i, 2, 112

impartment, communication, i, 4, 59

imperious, imperial, v, 1, 236

impone, to stake, wager, v, 2, 156

import, to signify, iii, 2, 148; iv, 7, 82; v, 2, 21

important, momentous, iii, 4, 108

impórtune, i, 3, 110

imposthume, internal abscess or ulcer, iv, 4, 27

impotence, feeble health, ii, 2, 66

impotent, feeble, i, 2, 29

impress, conscription, i, 1, 75

imputation, reputation, v, 2, 149

in, into, v, 2, 70; in accordance with, iv, 3, 5; (few), in short, i, 3, 126; (yourself), on your own part, ii, 1, 71

incapable, insensible, iv, 7, 180

incontinency, immoderate indulgence, ii, 1, 30

incorporal, bodiless, iii, 4, 118

incorps'd, incorporated, iv, 7, 88

incorrect to, i, 2, 95

indeed, in very truth, i, 4, 20; iv, 3, 37

indenture, a contract, v, 1, 119

index, iii, 4, 52

indifferent, *adj.*, ordinary, ii, 2, 231

indifferent, *adv.*, rather, v, 2, 100; tolerably, iii, 1, 123

indifferently, tolerably, pretty well, iii, 2, 40

indirections, indirect means, ii, 1, 66

indued, adapted by nature, iv, 7, 181

inform against, to denounce, iv, 4, 32

infusion, v, 2, 121

inheritance, possession, i, 1, 92

inheritor, possessor, v, 1, 121

inhibition, ii, 2, 346

innovation (the late), ii, 2, 347

inoculate, to graft, iii, 1, 119

in's, in his, ii, 2, 543

insinuation, v, 2, 59

instance, a sample, proof, iv, 5, 162; a cause or motive, iii, 2, 192

instrumental, serviceable, i, 2, 48

intil, in to, v, 1, 81

into, into the form of, ii, 2, 28

investments, vesture, i, 3, 128

it, its, i, 2, 216; v, 1, 244

jade, a nag, iii, 2, 253

jangled, jarring, discordant, iii, 1, 166

jealousy, suspicion, iv, 5, 19; suspicious nature, ii, 1, 113

Jephtha, ii, 2, 421

jig, a comic dialogue in song, ii, 2, 522

jig, *v.*, to walk with a dancing gait, iii, 1, 150

jig-maker, iii, 2, 132

John-a-dreams, a dreamy fellow, ii, 2, 595

jointress, i, 2, 9

jowl, to dash, v, 1, 84

jump, *adv.*, exactly, precisely, i, 1, 65; v, 2, 386

just, well-balanced, iii, 2, 59

justly, honestly, ii, 2, 284

keen, satirical, witty, iii, 2, 258

keep, to guard, iv, 5, 115; resort, ii, 1, 8

kettle, a kettledrum, v, 2, 286

kibe, a chilblain, v, 1, 155

kind, i, 2, 65

kindless, unnatural, ii, 2, 608

laps'd, *p.p.*, having slipped, failed, iii, 4, 107

lapwing, v, 2, 193

lard, to bedeck, garnish, iv, 5, 37; v, 2, 20

lauds, hymns of praise, iv, 7, 179 (note)

law (of writ), ii, 2, 419

lawless, outlawed, i, 1, 98 (note)

lay, to wager, v, 2, 173

lay to, to assail, iii, 4, 1

lazar-like, like a leper, i, 5, 72

lean on, to appertain to, iv, 3, 59

leave, to cease, iii, 2, 184; iii, 4, 66; give up, iii, 4, 91

leave and favour, gracious permission, i, 2, 51

lecture, a lesson, ii, 1, 67

lenten, poor, scanty, ii, 2, 329

leperous, leprous, i, 5, 64

let, to hinder, i, 4, 85

let be, let it go, v, 2, 235

Lethe, i, 5, 33

letters, a letter, iv, 3, 66

level, with sure aim, iv, 1, 42; iv, 5, 151

liberal, elegant, v, 2, 160; licentious in talk, iv, 7, 172

libertine, a free-liver, i, 3, 49

liberty (the), ii, 2, 419

lie (i'th' throat), ii, 2, 601

liege, liege lord, sovereign, ii, 2, 43, 86

lies, is legally brought, iii, 3, 61

life (of so long), so long-lived, iii, 1, 69

like, likely, ii, 2, 152

like, to please, ii, 2, 80; v, 2, 276

limed, *p.p.*, iii, 3, 68

lisp, to speak affectedly, iii, 1, 150

list, boundary, limit, iv, 5, 99

lists, levies (of troops), i, 2, 32

live, lief, iii, 2, 3

livery, i, 4, 32

living monument, v, 1, 320

lofty, high-pitched, i, 1, 151

loggets, v, 1, 100

luxury, lasciviousness, i, 5, 83

machine, mechanism of the body, ii, 2, 123

main, the main thing, ii, 2, 56; the whole country, iv, 4, 15

main, mighty, powerful, i, 3, 28

star, i, 4, 32; (out of), out of one's sphere, ii, 2, 141

state, government, administration, i, 1, 101; i, 2, 20; i, 4, 90; government of the world, ii, 2, 534; condition, v, 2, 86

station, posture in standing, iii, 4, 58

statist, statesman, v, 2, 33

statutes, v, 1, 111

stay upon, to await, iii, 2, 112

stealers, iii, 2, 349

stick, to scruple, iv, 5, 93; (off), stand out in contrast, v, 2, 268

still, ever, always, i, 1, 122; i, 2, 104; i, 5, 188; ii, 2, 42, 187, 428; iii, 1, 182; iv, 7, 117; constantly, iii, 2, 222

stithy, a forge, smithy, iii, 2, 89

stomach, i, 1, 100

stop, *n.*, iii, 2, 76, 376

stoup, a large cup or goblet, v, 1, 68; v, 2, 278

straight, *adv.*, straightway, iii, 4, 1; v, 1, 4

straw, a trifle, iv, 4, 26; iv, 5, 6

strewments, v, 1, 256

strike (*of a planet*), *v.*, i, 1, 162

strucken, *p.p.*, wounded, iii, 2, 282

stuck, a thrust, iv, 7, 162

subject, subjects (of a king), i, 1, 72; i, 2, 33

succession, ii, 2, 368

sudden, instant, v, 2, 46

suddenly, immediately, ii, 2, 214

suffer, to submit to, iii, 2, 141

sullied, i, 2, 129 (note)

sum, sum total, iv, 7, 74

sun (i' th'), i, 2, 67; ii, 2, 185

supervise (on the), v, 2, 23

suppliance, pastime, i, 3, 9

supply, fulfilment, ii, 2, 24

surprise, to seize upon, arrest, i, 2, 203

suspiration, i, 2, 79

sweet, dear, iii, 2, 58

swinish phrase, i, 4, 19

Switzers, Swiss guards, iv, 5, 97

swoopstake, *adv.*, iv, 5, 142

sword (*swearing on*), i, 5, 147

'Swounds, God's wounds (an oath), zounds, ii, 2, 603; v, 1, 297

table, a tablet, i, 5, 98, 107

table book, tablets, memorandum book, ii, 2, 136

take, to bewitch, enchant, i, 1, 163

tardy, *adv.*, too slowly, iii, 2, 31

target, a shield, ii, 2, 334

tarre, to egg on, incite, ii, 2, 370

tax, to take to task, blame, i, 4, 18; iii, 3, 29

tell, to count, i, 2, 238

Tellus, the earth, iii, 2, 166

temper, to mix, compound, v, 2, 339

temperance, moderation, iii, 2, 7

temple (*of the body*), i, 3, 12

tempt, to coax, iv, 3, 56

tenable, i, 2, 248

tend, to be waiting, i, 3, 83; to await one's convenience, iv, 3, 47

tender, an offer, i, 3, 99

tender, to offer, i, 3, 109; hold, rate, regard, i, 3, 107; iv, 3, 43

tent, to probe, ii, 2, 625

tenures, holdings (of real estate), v, 1, 108

Termagant, iii, 2, 15

terms, a condition, iv, 7, 26

that, what, i, 2, 17; ii, 2, 7; iv, 7, 119

that, so that, i, 3, 67; though, i, 2, 2; if, iv, 7, 63, 152; when, iv, 7, 160

theft, the thing stolen, iii, 2, 94

thereon, on that account, ii, 2, 165

thews, sinews, i, 3, 12

thing of nothing, iv, 2, 30, 31

thinks't thee, seems it to thee, v, 2, 63

thou *and* you, i, 2, 118; v, 1, 131 ff.

thought, melancholy, sorrow, iii, 1, 85; iv, 5, 188

thought-sick, sick at heart, iii, 4, 51

thou't, thou wilt, v, 1, 297

thrall, to enslave, iii, 4, 74

thrift, economy, i, 2, 180; prosperity, iii, 2, 67, 193

throughly, thoroughly, iv, 5, 136

tickle o' th' sere, ii, 2, 338

time (the), the times, the world, iii, 1, 70, 115

tinct, hue, iii, 4, 91

tithe, the tenth part, iii, 4, 97

to, as to, v, 2, 17; against, i, 3, 44; enough to, iii, 4, 76; in comparison with, iii, 1, 52, 53

to blame, blameworthy, culpable, iii, 1, 46

to do, ado, hubbub, ii, 2, 369

too-much, excess, iv, 7, 119

too too, i, 2, 129

top, to surpass, iv, 7, 89

top of (in the), in a louder voice than, ii, 2, 458; (on the), above, ii, 2, 355

to't, go at it, ii, 2, 447

toward, in preparation, i, 1, 77; v, 2, 376

town crier, iii, 2, 3

toy, a trifle, iv, 5, 18; a fancy, i, 4, 75; a caprice, i, 3, 6

trace, to keep pace with, v, 2, 124

trade, business (in general), iii, 2, 346

translate, to transform, iii, 1, 113

trick, a trifle, iv, 4, 61; knack, v, 1, 99; trait, iv, 7, 189

trick, to adorn, ii, 2, 479

trippingly, easily, iii, 2, 2

tristful, sad, gloomy, iii, 4, 50

triumph, a splendid feat, i, 4, 12

trophy, a mark of honour, iv, 5, 214